Patrick White
Fiction and the Unconscious

Patrick White

Fiction and the Unconscious

David J Tacey

Melbourne
OXFORD UNIVERSITY PRESS
Auckland Oxford New York

Published with the assistance of the
La Trobe University Publications Committee

OXFORD UNIVERSITY PRESS AUSTRALIA
Oxford New York Toronto
Delhi Bombay Calcutta Madras Karachi
Petaling Jaya Singapore Hong Kong
Tokyo Nairobi Dar es Salaam
Cape Town Melbourne Auckland
and associated companies in
Beirut Berlin Ibadan Nicosia

OXFORD is a trade mark of
Oxford University Press

National Library of Australia
Cataloguing-in-Publication data:

Tacey, David J. (David John), 1953–

    Patrick White, fiction and the unconscious.

    Bibliography.
    Includes index.

    ISBN 0 19 554867 1.

    1. White, Patrick, 1912–   —Criticism and
    interpretation.   2. White, Patrick, 1912–
    —Knowledge—Psychology.   3. Authors, Australian—
    20th century.   4. English literature—Australia—
    Psychological aspects.   I. Title.

A828'.309

Edited by Sarah Brenan
Designed by Pauline McClenahan
Typeset by Best-set Typesetter Ltd (HK)
Printed by Hing Yip Printing Co Ltd (HK)
Published by Oxford University Press Australia,
253 Normanby Road, South Melbourne, Australia

CONTENTS

Foreword   *vii*
Acknowledgements   *ix*
Introduction   *xiii*

1 The Incestuous Return   *1*
2 The Undying Mother   *18*
3 In the Lap of the Land   *48*
4 The Tree of Unborn Souls   *91*
5 The Tightening Knot   *121*
6 The Mother in Search of Herself   *149*
7 The Delight of Decadence   *184*
8 Conclusion: Problems of Unconscious Genius   *210*

Glossary of Psychological Terms   *236*
Notes and References   *239*
Select Bibliography   *258*
Index   *264*

To Brian Elliott

FOREWORD

The nations of Australia and the United States have much in common. Each nation was born thousands of miles from European culture, and each interpreted the meaning of that event as an improvement over European life. A hundred years ago the literature of each nation contained assurances that the citizens felt fine without the stodgy conventions and corrupt institutions that no one wanted. Old habits would 'melt down like wax in the sun's rays'. We can see now that those assurances implied a large 'if': if the men and women were able to live every particle of their lives consciously, bring each hidden motive and hidden force up into the light, the new nation would go well; the alertness, fresh intelligence and clarity brought about by a new start would create by itself the amazing community that Walt Whitman envisioned.

But something else happened. We in the United States blundered into rape of the countryside, and into those addictions and vulgarizations we all know about, and into a massive disruption of the civilizing instructions, particularly those instructions that pass from the older generation to the younger. Australians would have to delineate their particular disappointments themselves, but I gather from the literature that these have been severe and that Australian culture and life have not met the standards that the earlier writers felt to be assured.

David Tacey's work suggests that if we read Australian literature well we will see that there are parts of the psyche where one can live next to a hostile ghost for years without being aware of it. Taking Patrick White's novels as texts, he speculates on the current state of the battle that Freud brought into visibility by calling up the name of Oedipus. American, and I gather, Australian, men go forward to meet the ghosts of the matriarchy confidently, because the power of naiveté is their shield. The difficulty of separating from boyhood, the belief that merging with nature or the mother is a good thing, infantile longings at the seashore: D. H. Lawrence noticed all that in his *Studies in Classic American Literature.* The naïve man, freed of the melancholic and suspicious tone of mind Europe produces, may mistake his regression for religious transcendence, as divers sometimes mistake oxygen deprivation for religious ecstasy.

David Tacey's work will be important to those longing for literary criticism that avoids narrow limits of deconstruction or biography and valuable to those studying the mysteries of psychological life; and I'm delighted to welcome his book.

Robert Bly
Moose Lake, Minnesota
July 1987

ACKNOWLEDGEMENTS

This book evolved over ten years of research, which included several false starts and a bushfire which destroyed the first four years' work. The present study is only distantly related to its academic predecessor, a doctoral thesis carried out under the supervision of John Colmer and Robert Sellick at the University of Adelaide and submitted in 1981. During the course of writing I have incurred many intellectual obligations which are indicated in the text and footnotes. I wish to acknowledge both a Harkness Fellowship, which gave me two wonderful years (1982–4) to explore the field of depth psychology in the United States, and a special grant from the University of Adelaide (1980–1) which enabled me to reconstruct my library and work after the Ash Wednesday bushfire. I would like to thank the members of the English Department at the University of Adelaide, who made generous contributions, material and otherwise, after the fire.

I wish also gratefully to record the assistance of many colleagues and friends. My major debt is to Brian Elliott, a pioneer in the field of Australian Studies, who fostered this work from its early, murky beginnings, and who provided inspiration and practical advice throughout its various stages. I could not have begun the work without the initial guidance of Molly Scrymgour, who introduced me to the psychology of Jung, and whose insight and psychological integrity provided a model for me as I attempted to enter the at first bewildering field of archetypal psychology and myth studies. Others who made significant contributions to my grasp of depth psychology include Peter Bishop, Margaret Cain, Kevin Moriarty, Ian Fraser, Patrick Jansen, and Janice Daw-Koh.

In the United States my debts are too numerous to record. Valuable contributions were made by James Hillman, Patricia Berry, Tom Moore, and Robert Sardello, my teachers at the Dallas

Institute of Humanities and Culture. Although my own approach to depth psychology and to its application differs essentially from theirs, these scholars of post-Jungian thought provided stimulus, challenge and growth to my own use of Jung and psychological ideas. At the University of Colorado I received support in applying psychology and myth to literary studies from Harold Schechter and Martin Bickman. Other North American scholars who provided assistance and clarification include John Boe (Berkeley), Ralph Maud (Vancouver), and Robert Wilson (Edmonton). The American poet Robert Bly contributed stimulating thoughts and insights about Australian culture, myth, and the psychology of the *puer*-type male. Robert A. Johnson provided warm and personal support, as well as much-needed guidance in relation to the study of the mother-complex in contemporary culture and society. I would like to thank Nancy and Lore Zeller of the C. G. Jung Institute of Los Angeles for their help in rebuilding my library after the fire, and Spring Publications, Dallas, who kindly supplied complimentary copies of books destroyed in the fire. Thanks are also due to Mrs Doris Albrecht, librarian of the C. G. Jung Foundation of New York, for helpful suggestions and guidance in relation to psychological literature.

John Barnes has demonstrated continued interest in and support for the project, and Manfred Mackenzie has kindly read and offered comments on numerous segments of the final draft. I would also like to record my debt to David Malouf for valuable talks on Australian cultural experience during his term as writer-in-residence at Macquarie University in 1984. I am grateful to Patrick White for reading and commenting on some of my published materials, and for his letters from the year 1975 to the present.

The La Trobe University Reprography Department provided assistance with photographic materials, and Mrs Anne Crittenden kindly helped with proof-reading. Finally, I would like to thank my wife, Sharon L. Gregory, for putting up with me during late-night writing attacks and workaholic week-ends.

A section of the Introduction was first published as 'Patrick White: Misconceptions About Jung's Influence', *Australian Literary Studies* (Brisbane), October 1979.

A version of chapter 3 part I was first published under the title 'In the Lap of the Land: Misogyny and Earth-Mother Worship in *The Tree of Man*', in F. H. Mares and P. R. Eaden (eds), *Mapped But Not Known: The Australian Landscape of the Imagination*, Wakefield Press, Adelaide, 1986.

A slightly different version of chapter 3 part II was first published as 'Patrick White's *Voss*: The Teller and the Tale', in *Southern Review* (Sydney, Adelaide), November 1985.

Some of the material incorporated in chapter 5 first appeared in an article, 'Patrick White: The Great Mother and Her Son', *Journal of Analytical Psychology* (London), April 1983.

Some of the material in chapter 7 part II first appeared in an article, 'Patrick White: The End of Genius', *Meridian, The La Trobe University English Review* (Melbourne), May 1986.

D.J.T.
La Trobe University, March 1987

He was still too exhausted by what had turned out to be, not a game of his own imagination, but a wrestling match with someone stronger.

Patrick White[1]

In classical mythology this special entanglement of spirit and maternal world is depicted by the Great Goddess and her young male consort, her son, her lover, her priest. Attis, Adonis, Hippolytus, Phaethon, Tammuz, Endymion, Oedipus are examples of this erotic bind. Each figure in each tale shows its own variation; the Oedipus complex is but one pattern of son and mother which produces those fateful entanglements of spirit with matter which in the twentieth century we have learned to call neurotic. The very desperation of neurosis shows how strong are their mutual needs and that the attempts to untie this primary knot are truly in the ancient sense agonizing and tragic.

James Hillman[2]

INTRODUCTION

The sense of entrapment

> After he retired, Dad would sometimes recall,
> in the spasmodic phrasing which came with the
> asthma, his escape by way of Intellectual
> Enlightenment, and the voyage to Australia,
> from what had threatened to become a
> permanence in black and brown, but in the
> telling, he would grow darker rather than
> enlightened, his breathing thicker, clogged with
> the recurring suspicion that he might be chained
> still.
>
> *The Solid Mandala*, p. 145[1]

Australia has often been imagined in literature and life as an escape from European tradition and restriction, as a movement into space and light from 'what had threatened to become a permanence in black and brown'. Australia is the New Beginning, the place of freedom and the future. If the physical facts of the country thwarted much of this earlier optimism and refused to co-operate with the man-made dream, it was at least felt that Australia might prove to be a country where spiritual and intellectual freedoms could be enjoyed. George Brown, the 'Dad' in the above quotation from *The Solid Mandala*, is a liberal positivist with a belief in intellectual enlightenment and human progress. He believes, as do many Australians, that tradition is disposable, that the religions and superstitions of the past are so much cultural baggage that we can do without, and when he journeys to Australia he expects to find sun, space, and freedom. However, 'in the telling' of this tale he grows 'darker rather than enlightened', 'clogged with the recurring suspicion that he might be chained still'.

What Dad fails to take into account is the psyche and the ever-present danger of being imprisoned by internal forces. Freedom has little, if anything, to do with a change of climate, a change of country, or a change of political system. In Australian experience a literal, visible set of European cultural restrictions is often exchanged for an invisible, psychological set of restrictions. This is Henry Handel Richardson's theme in *The Fortunes of Richard Mahony*, and it is a constant preoccupation in our art and literature. The enemy, as it were, shifts from Britain to ourselves; from the old, repressive political order to psychological forces within the self.

When the Australian ego sloughs off the old British super-ego it wins a certain freedom and liberty, but it also exposes itself to the dangers of the deep unconscious. The super-ego, or more generally, tradition, holds the ego in a fixed position and limits its range and potential, but it also serves as a protective context which shields the ego against the forces of the unconscious. Xavier Herbert's *Capricornia* shows what happens to the Australian ego when it loses contact with tradition and convention: it sinks into the unconscious, becomes savage, animalistic. Herbert sketches in a side of Australian experience which is often missing from the 'official', more humane, popularized image of Australianness. The popular image is that we are a relaxed, easy-going people, disinclined to hard work and certainly not subordinate to authority or to the voice of the super-ego. The popular image emphasizes the positive effects of casting off tradition and the past, our sense of freedom and our good-natured acceptance of things unsophisticated, uncultured and raw. Our literature reflects this image in part but also qualifies it by emphasizing the negative effects of a society which has slipped from its parental frame and has made sudden, dramatic contact with the forces of the psyche.

It is sometimes felt that Patrick White's fiction is un-Australian, but this view betrays a superficial sense of what is Australian. While it is true that White is unconcerned with the Australian persona, with our happy-go-lucky, egalitarian mask, he is concerned (if unconsciously) with what is happening to us on the inside, with processes at work in the depths of our psyche. If we find White un-Australian it is because we are as yet unacquainted with what lies beyond our social persona, that affable mask that even Lawson, one of the 'creators' of the mask, was able to see through.[2] Although Voss, Theodora, and Parker are 'outcasts', they are only outcasts in relation to the more obvious, external side of the national character. The psychic territory they inhabit, the 'country of the mind' they explore, is Australian territory, and is as surely relevant to the cultural history of Australia as are the goings-on in the social and political world. Any worthwhile analysis of the Australian experience must be able to range freely between the depths and the surface of our culture, and to incorporate psychological elements that have hitherto been regarded as eccentric or remote.

White's characters turn away from social structure and convention toward the inner world of archetypes and elemental forces. They go the way that the explorers of any new culture must go, into the unknown. The past cannot be relied upon to provide order or meaning, and so individuals have to undertake hazardous and epic journeys into the unconscious, to ground the culture in new depths and in new psychological soil. However, White's culture–heroes embark on tragic, one-way journeys into the unconscious. They take leave of society and never return to it with the boon that the hero traditionally brings back to his world. They enter a world so pristine, unmarked, weirdly enchanting, that they lose their way and become completely cut off from ordinary human consciousness.

The most insidious aspect of their situation is that White's characters rarely recognize that they are imprisoned in the unconscious. George Brown and his sons Waldo and Arthur are at times acutely aware of their entrapment, but the majority of White's 'mystical' travellers are so intoxicated by the strange world of the unconscious that they remain oblivious to its imprisoning and dehumanizing effect. For the most part the characters congratulate themselves on their escape from the upper world and their new existence in the realm of shadow and dream. Theodora Goodman imagines that she has attained pureness of being; Stan Parker that he is at one with the cosmos; Voss that he has achieved spiritual transcendence. In fact, they have attained nothing grand or remarkable, but have simply been deceived into a sense of their higher status. (I will develop this argument later, in discussing the relevant novels.) In a word, they are psychologically inflated, and are unable to grasp their situation objectively. Nor is White able to prompt them to self-realization, since he is himself duped by the unconscious and unable to recognize its dangers. White idealizes the unconscious as a maternal well-spring and source. Although this 'source' consumes him and his characters, he is not able to see what is taking place, and so a vast array of external forces and figures are blamed for the disintegration. White's fiction is full of 'devouring mothers', scapegoat—women who appear demonic in their desire to destroy, imprison and enfeeble the mystical characters. Society, material objects, fate, women—all are invested with psychic energy and made to appear responsible for internal entrapment and disintegration.

White's fiction reflects a young, unstable society which has yet to develop a right relation to the unconscious. The culture sits precariously upon the aboriginal earth, uncertain of itself, and unable to send down taproots into the native soil. In his first novel *Happy Valley* (1939) White observed that Australian society and Nature are completely at odds, that 'the country existed in spite of the town. It was not aware of it. There was no connecting link'. And White goes on to compare white Australian society with 'an ugly scab on the body of the earth'. 'It was so ephemeral. Some day it would drop off, leaving a pink, clean place underneath'.[3] The new society is spurious and inauthentic; it has yet to forge a creative link with the spirit of place. In *Voss* (1957) White imagines Australian society split between 'huddlers' and 'explorers'. The huddlers cling to the coastal plain and the surface of life; the explorers plunge recklessly and, as I read it, destructively into the desert interior. Both groups maintain unproductive relationships with the land. Huddlers destroy themselves by their sterility and denial of the psychological interior. The so-called explorers are possessed by a death–romanticism, a desire to shatter the human element in the infinite expanse of the mythical world. In either mode there is no connecting link between ego and unconscious, human and non-human, society and Nature. As *Voss* progresses the split becomes more pronounced, until the huddlers seem farcical in their tight, enclosed world, and the explorers ludicrous in their non-reflective, narcissistic romanticism.

What inhibits the creation of a link between consciousness and Nature? Have the original inhabitants of the land placed a curse on the foreign, white invaders?[4] It is possible that the land is simply too old, too alien, too far removed from modern Western consciousness, so that those who attempt to penetrate the Australian psyche get stuck in a 'dreaming' world from which there is no way out. Certainly the Australian landscape could never give birth to an English Romanticism, does not foster 'green thoughts in a green shade', but inspires an almost otherworldly, desert–mysticism, a mysticism of rocks and bones. Deserts need not be life-negating, but they *are* destructive to the over-civilized, British consciousness that first arrived here. Connecting consciousness with the land takes time and effort; it is a work of culture and—in the broadest possible sense—of religion as well. Religion ought to facilitate the connection between a people and the spirit of place, but in white Australian society our (imported) religion has not been able to develop this connection. It may be that in the poetry of Les A. Murray and other recent Australian authors we are beginning to get a sense of what a genuinely Australian religion would look like, and, with this religious sense, an inkling of a possible bridge between white con-sciousness and the aboriginal substratum.

Patrick White is part of the old school, and is perhaps the last of our colonial writers. For him the disjunction between society and Nature is experienced as an acute psychological dissociation. The split between ego and unconscious is not merely his 'theme', his moral concern, but also his personal suffering and emotional burden. White's own psyche contains both the 'huddler' and the 'explorer', the rigidly defensive, even paranoid British persona, and the destructively anarchic Australian ego which falls down into primitive depths and makes no effort to return. In a sense White's 'life sentence' in the unconscious is self-imposed; it is what he himself chooses. His own creative genius tries to lead him out of this subjection at a crucial stage in his career, but even the promptings of his inner development are refused. There is a morbid, dark streak in White's character, a preference for entrap-ment in the unconscious above creative dialogue between upper and lower worlds. White is a pioneer who, like Theseus in Greek mythology, journeyed into the lower realm and grew fast to the rocks. He escaped the bondage of the super-ego and social con-vention only to fall into a new, stranger, less tangible form of psychological imprisonment.

White and Jung

> I have studied practically nothing beyond my
> own intuition—oh, and by fits and starts . . .
> dear old Father Jung who, I am told, I
> misinterpret.
>> Alex Gray (*Memoirs of Many in One*, p. 54)[5]

Since the present work is a Jungian study of White's novels, a few words need to be said about the supposed 'influence' of Jung's ideas on White's fiction. From the 1950s to the present, critics have claimed that White makes use of Jung's psychological discoveries and that he is 'a student of Jung'.[6] A. P. Riemer has boldly supported this view. He argues that both *The Tree of Man* (1956) and *Riders in the Chariot* (1961) rely heavily upon Jungian material and that the recognition of this is important for the comprehension of White's intentions. He even goes so far as to add that 'a novelist's use of such arcane material will inevitably involve questions of propriety: but I prefer to leave this problem of artistic licence to be fought out elsewhere, as I have no doubt it will be'.[7] This line of thought is misdirected. White's novels seem Jungian because the author has in his own way drawn upon the deep unconscious and its archetypes. It is precisely this fact that makes the novels so powerful and accounts for their genuine visionary quality. They are not products of his rational mind, but spring up, as it were, from the creative unconscious. What critics must remember is that if Jung is right, if the archetypes are *a priori* factors, then a creative writer does not have to read him to formulate archetypal configurations—he has rather to turn within and enter into dialogue with his own imagination.

Far from basing his work on Jung, White claims not even to have read him before the mid-1960s, after all his so-called 'Jungian' novels had been written. In a letter to the writer of 14 February 1976, he says: 'I did not read Jung until about the time of *The Solid Mandala*, when somebody gave me *Psychology and Alchemy*.' And again in a letter dated 28 September 1975, he writes: 'I did not know of Jung's work at the time of writing *The Aunt's Story*. I don't think I had even heard of him, though I may have as I had read some Freud.'

Jungian influence is evident in *The Solid Mandala* (1966). The title itself betrays some knowledge of Jung, and the text reproduces passages from his work. Yet even here it is wrong to be deterministic about the relationship, to argue that the psychologist provided source materials. White's vision of the circular form (which becomes 'the mandala' in this work) was in evidence long before his reading of Jung. It appears in every work from *The Living and the Dead* (1941) to *Riders in the Chariot* (1961). It seems to me that White's reading of Jung had little impact upon his literary vision. All it did was to allow him to name, or rather to misname, the image which had been central to his work. I say 'misname' because in reality White's symbol was never a true mandala, a symbol of the integration of personality, but rather a representation of the uroboros, the womb-like image of complete unconsciousness (see Glossary and Figure 1). The crucial distinction between these two kinds of circle images will become clearer in subsequent chapters, but the difference is not grasped by the novelist, for whom every circle image is indiscriminately regarded as a 'mandala'. White's characters merge into the oceanic oneness of the uroboros and, by a systematic misapplication of the individuation paradigm, the novelist translates this movement toward disintegration into terms of self-realization and wholeness. The end result is that White, and his critics, talk about psychological and spiritual triumphs which bear no relation to the actual regressions which take place in the fiction. Thus I do not believe that White's contact with Jung's work was profitable; instead, it engendered confusion and presented a false lead to the critics. If anything it suggested that the novelist did not understand his own work, that the literary vision was autonomous and independent of his conscious intentions.[8]

Archetypal depth criticism

Conventional literary criticism often concerns itself with the author's mind and point of view. It attempts to establish and define the author's intellectual position, assuming that his work is a product of his thought. Archetypal depth criticism is more interested in the underlying, often unconscious, psychic and mythic structures. It assumes that the work is greater than the author, since in the process of writing the unconscious is activated and the author's conscious intentions are sometimes even contradicted by the unconscious. This concern with deep structure is particularly relevant in White's case, because the author's intellectual conception of his work and the archetypal structure of his imagination are completely at odds.

The author's relation to his imagination is analogous to that between ego and unconscious in psychoanalytic dream–work. The ego is often amazed at what the unconscious produces, frequently misunderstands what it is saying, and often forces the imaginal[9] material into an incongruous intellectual frame. In White's fiction the superimposed frame—usually Christianity, but also the Jungian mandala—is itself a kind of defence against the bleak, negative images which arise from his unconscious. If we follow the imaginal material we most certainly end up with a pathological reading of the novels; if we follow the authorial commentary and the imposed interpretation (as many critics to date have done) we invariably read every novel as an heroic quest novel, as a tale of triumphant individuation.

In order to get at the deep structure the archetypal critic must become acutely sensitive to the content and direction of the author's imagination, and be able to distinguish that which is organic from that which is contrived and imposed. The first stage of archetypal criticism is one of complete receptivity to the imaginative material. The second stage—known as the process of amplification—is to relate the material to an appropriate mythological context. Here the critic must proceed with utmost caution, allowing the material to suggest its own interpretive frame by amplifying the mythic resonances already inherent in it. The importance of this technique is to establish the archetypal frame within which the psychic product is operating. By seeking wider parallels one gains more comprehension of the material, is able to relate it to historical paradigms, to connect specific images with universal patterns. The critic must not be led astray by the author's interpretations and suggestions, which may be wide of the mark. The major drawback of the archetypal method (one which makes it almost impossible to conduct at the undergraduate level) is that the critic must have an extensive knowledge of the unconscious and its manifestations in myth, fairytale and legend before archetypal criticism can be attempted. One cannot begin this kind of enquiry with a mere acquaintance with Christianity and one or two Greek myths. In order for the amplification technique to work at all one must be familiar with a wide range of myths and fairytales, be alert to recurring motifs and subtle differences between archetypal patterns, and possess a willingness to look up new references and check materials not yet known.

In White's fiction the superimposed layer consists not only of intellectual constructs and interpretive materials, but also of artificial patterns of symbolism. White's work is a mixture of natural and 'algebraic' symbols.[10] Natural symbols are spontaneous products of the imagination, whereas algebraic symbols are imposed by the author to support his own point of view and moral philosophy. *The Aunt's Story* is one of White's better works because there the concentration of natural symbolism is at its greatest: the rose, the hawk, the garden, the nautilus shell, the crocodile—these 'work' because they emerge naturally from the fictional ground. In *Voss* and *Riders in the Chariot*, however, the presence of algebraic symbols obscures the narrative structures and overlays much that is genuine in these novels. The imported Christian symbols, the use of Kabbalah, Judaism and Hermetic philosophy all point to contexts of meaning which are inappropriate to their fictional settings. The authorial commentary in these works is Christian in outlook, but the imaginal material itself is pagan in character, pointing not to redemptive mysteries but to the triumph of the Great Earth Mother and her defeat of the spirit. The symbol of the Chariot of Redemption is possibly the most deliberately contrived representation in White's fiction. The author foists this symbol upon the narrative, grafts it into the lives of the characters, but it does not work because the story itself will not support the dream of transcendence. The gestures toward redemption and the laboured symbolism represent White's own particular standpoint, but the natural symbols and textual structures point to a decidedly pre-Christian and matriarchal universe. Once the critic has penetrated to the core of White's fiction, and has become familiar with its mythic ground, he is able to differentiate readily between natural and artificial contents, and to ascertain whether a particular symbol is authentic or not.

In the current intensity of interest in French post-structuralist theory few people seem to be aware that archetypal theory and criticism is undergoing a small but significant revival. This revival is headed by James Hillman, a radical, stimulating force in contemporary psychology, and possibly the most outstanding archetypal theorist since Jung. Hillman's works, including *Re-Visioning Psychology* (1975), *Puer Papers* (1979), and *Healing Fiction* (1983), open up new ways of thinking about the psyche, creativity and the nature of the imagination. His works cannot help but provide a creative stimulus to literary theory and criticism—and the extent of his influence in this area is unlikely to be known for some time, until scholars catch up with his work and begin to digest it. Hillman has opened up an imaginal route to Freud and Jung, allowing us to re-read the great psychologists with a post-modern eye.

Other figures in the revival of archetypal theory include Marie-Louise von Franz, Edward Edinger, Robertson Davies and Naomi Goldenberg. Von Franz's work on Apuleius and fairytale, Edinger's on Melville and Blake, Goldenberg's on the archetypal bases of feminism—these works constitute a significant body of materials and suggest that Jungian theory, sometimes thought to be passé and out of touch, continues to make a lively contribution in the present era.

Archetypal criticism made an awkward debut in the work of Maud Bodkin in the 1930s, and it fizzled out soon afterwards. Northrop Frye's 'archetypal' myth criticism, significant and influential in its own right, is non-Jungian and non-psychological, and therefore cannot be claimed as part of the movement I am tracing here. Between the 1930s and the late 70s Jungian criticism moved in fits and starts, often applied ineptly by Jungian analysts (Barbara Hannah, James Kirsch, et al.) who had a reasonable grasp of psychology but little understanding or appreciation of literature. On the basis of these early studies, it is easy to see why Jungian criticism acquired a bad name, and why many felt that it was an amateurish and mechanical enterprise. But with Hillman, von Franz and others Jungian archetypal methodology may well have achieved a level of sophistication which will allow it to become a genuine force in literary studies. Certainly it would be unfair to suggest that Jungian theory has been tried and found wanting. All the signs would lead me to conclude that we have still to experience the mature burgeoning of Jungian criticism.

The intellectual community encounters fundamental problems in coming to terms with Jung, which is why he has been relegated to the margins and sometimes held there by force. Most difficult of all is to accept a scholar who talks seriously of 'other worlds' and 'mythic realms' in an age noted for its determined materialism and scepticism. In order to secure credibility in his own time, Jung claimed for himself the status of scientist, and held that his findings were empirically based. Although I am doubtful of his claim (like so many others), I am certainly unwilling to dismiss his work as 'mere' mysticism. Jung was an intuitive scholar: intuition, not the rational intellect, was his province and his strength. Because our prevailing intellectual paradigm has little room for intuition, it conveniently labels it 'mystical', not to be touched, not to be taken seriously. Intuitive thinking is not otherworldly; it concerns itself with 'other' aspects of *this* world. The problem is that our culture has yet to explore the inner side of human experience with the same gusto with which it has explored its extraverted faculties. To appreciate and understand Jung involves not merely an adjustment of thought but a change of paradigm, a shift in our very mode of knowing.

I have employed a Jungian archetypal methodology because it is an ideal way of encouraging the nocturnal creatures of White's imaginal world to make themselves known to us. Rational investigations of White's fiction have elucidated the merely superficial content of his work, leaving the mythic and imaginal depths unexplored. Intuitive methods are needed to make White's 'other' world accessible.

A note on the works discussed

This book traces the development of an archetypal pattern, the mother/son complex, as it develops in White's novels from its earliest beginnings in personal family relations, through mythologization of the Mother and her archetypal field, to the final stage where the son is absorbed into the mother–personality. I felt that the best way to achieve this overview was to examine each of the novels from *The Living and the Dead* (1941) to *Memoirs of Many in One* (1986). White's first novel, *Happy Valley*, has been omitted because it is no longer available to the general reader (White refused to allow it to be reprinted), and because *The Living and the Dead* affords a more interesting and appropriate starting point for our present purposes. For various reasons, I have not examined White's plays and short stories. Basically, the discussion of the ongoing psychic state, or complex, is best served by confining the analysis to the novels, where a powerful sweep of psychological process is discernible. Several of the short stories are very fine pieces of writing, but analysis of these would have forced me to repeat ideas and concepts already elucidated in the discussion of the novels. The plays vary enormously in quality, from the important and pioneering early pieces, to the inept and vulgar recent works. I feel that what can be said about the better plays has already been said in White criticism, especially in the work of J. R. Dyce and John Colmer. White's self-portrait, *Flaws in the Glass*, is self-explanatory and does not require interpretation. Since it is written from the author's conscious standpoint, and concerns itself largely with personal issues, it is not sufficiently revealing of the mythical unconscious to require archetypal analysis. The self-portrait is referred to at appropriate points, but it is not itself the subject of close examination.

1   The Incestuous Return

*She bore him, loved him, kept him, and his love
turned back into her, so that he could not be free
to go forward with his own life . . .*

D. H. Lawrence[1]

The journey into unconscious regions of the psyche is a crucial
though sometimes perilous undertaking in the life of the
individual. When it occurs, psychic energy is withdrawn from the
social arena and sinks down into the inner world, activating
primordial instinctual forces. This can lead to a pattern of
renewal, where the individual is revitalized by the unconscious,
or it can lead to catastrophe, the individual overwhelmed by what
he encounters in the lower realm. The result often depends upon
the integrity of the personality, its ability to contact powerful
archetypal contents without being absorbed into them. But
whatever the outcome the descent itself is imaged by the psyche
as an erotic incestuous ritual: a penetration (at least for male
consciousness)[2] of the maternal womb, regression to early childhood, immersion into the matrix[3] of Nature. The metaphor of
incest is not merely a Freudian or Jungian invention, but is the
way the imagination itself (in dreams, fantasies, works of art)
speaks of the individual's return to his 'source' and 'origin'. Incest
fantasies are especially common in the life of the creative artist,
for his very creativeness is dependent upon his intimate relation
to the unconscious.[4]

The individual is inclined to deal with the fantasies literally, to
feel that an actual return to the personal mother is what is being
demanded.[5] White's career is deeply involved in this literal
incestuous pattern, and in his second novel, *The Living and the
Dead* (1941) the confusion between symbolic and carnal desires is
strongly pronounced. Elyot Standish is impelled toward the

maternal matrix, and at the same time a profoundly erotic fascination for the personal mother blocks his psychological development. However, it must be emphasized that the protagonist's problem is not his alone, but that it is shared by White himself. White is not 'writing about' incest with psychological sophistication, but is simply writing about his own inner life, which happens to be preoccupied with incestuous fantasies. The fantasies are never brought before conscious scrutiny, nor are they intellectualized or formulated as such, but remain part of the *unconscious structure* of the narrative.

I

Elyot, are you working? his mother called, exasperating him to the point where he ground his ears with his hands, because she knew from the experience of years that he closed his door after breakfast for one purpose. But this was part of the scheme of his mother's morning, to stand on the first floor landing and call to the top of the house. Often he refused to hear. He left the voice to ramble, a voice without purpose on the stairs. Once he had seen her standing vaguely, hand to chin, the sleeves drooping downward from an arm, as if she were listening for a lost voice, or wondering, trying to trace her own purpose on the stairs. (pp. 13–14)[6]

This sequence between mother and son can be viewed as a symbolic portrayal of Elyot's psychic situation. The conscious personality sits above, in his study, trying to pursue intellectual goals and follow his chosen course, while the unconscious matrix, personified by the mother, interrupts his activity from below, with frequent calls and demands. The fact that this is a recurring sequence, 'part of the scheme of his mother's morning', suggests that the maternal matrix has become desperate and insistent in its attempt to draw the ego toward itself. Elyot puts up a violent resistance, and retreats into isolation. The ego has an innate and quite legitimate horror of the maternal depths. It fears that its present structure will be shattered, that it will be drawn into an archaic world and overwhelmed by elemental forces. The personal mother carries this mythic image of the 'devouring maw', and thus becomes a foreboding and fearsome figure.[7] Yet Elyot's resistance is also conditioned by the incest problem: a fear that he is being urged to make an incestuous return to the personal mother. The language of the imagination is frozen in its concrete form, and the inward quest is held up as a result. Elyot cannot act, but remains a victim of his own literalism, caught up in the material or carnal aspect of a psychological idea.

Here the Mother,[8] the archetype that would bring renewal, is herself showing signs of stagnation and inertia. She is 'listening for a lost voice', or 'trying to trace her own purpose on the stairs'. If the ego's attitude is one of constant hostility and rejection, this has an adverse effect upon the archetypal figure. The Mother, the imaginal source, actually weakens and loses direction. This is reflected not only in the quality of Elyot's life, which becomes increasingly dull and sterile, but also in the quality of the story itself. The tale wanders aimlessly at certain points, almost as if the imagination had forgotten what it was trying to achieve. The novel is perhaps White's least accomplished work because the inner life is not being attended, but stagnates as a result of the ego's attitude. The story takes up momentum toward the end, when Elyot allows the transformative process to take place and makes his return to the source. It is this breakthrough that makes possible the extraordinary novels that follow—*The Aunt's Story, The Tree of Man, Voss*—all of which gain their power and visionary strength from the protagonist's desire to return to Nature and to penetrate deeply into the Mother realm. The fiction takes on a dynamic and living character when White gives in to the deeper impulse and allows the imagination to go where it wants to.

But it is important to realize that Elyot does not make his return until after the death of his mother. It is this fact, the removal of the personal figure, that allows the symbolic incest to take place and enables him to move into the archetypal realm. The problem of incest in White is never resolved—and this, in part, accounts for its reappearance later in his career[9]—but is merely side-stepped by the convenient death of the human mother. There is no coming to terms with the incest issue, but an escape from it through circumstantial factors.

II

In early childhood Elyot's relationship with his mother is intensely focused and complicated. There is a deep and binding attraction to her, yet there is also a kind of turning away from the mother due to her apparently destructive pattern of behaviour. At one moment she draws the youth toward herself, lavishing him with love and affection, and at the next she turns away from him, becoming scathing and brutal. It is difficult to determine whether Mrs Standish actually behaves in this manner, or whether the boy's fantasies 'convert' her into a destructive figure. For a child's perceptions of parents are always influenced by psychic factors, and when the son is unusually close to the mother the negative aspect of the Mother archetype often appears with frightening force. In psychological terms, this is because his emerging ego is caught up in the maternal realm, and is unable to develop a separate existence, so that 'mother' seems overwhelming, a force which negates and destroys life. Paradoxically, the child can experience a more positive aspect of the archetype when he surrenders his individuality and sinks back into the maternal source. Then the Mother appears as a vast ocean of ecstasy and support, an inviting womb in which the son is contained and nurtured. She is still the same disintegrating figure as before, but now the process of being overpowered assumes a seductive, pleasurable character. There are indications that Elyot experiences his mother in both contexts, as devouring maw and as inviting matrix, but as the story unfolds the negative image begins to eclipse her other attributes. The seductive aspect is gradually transferred to Nature and to elemental symbols of the Mother, in the presence of which Elyot feels liberated from his selfhood and blissfully dissolved into unconsciousness. This is to become a characteristic split in White's fiction: the human mother as devourer, and Mother Nature as a source of erotic delight and mystical reverie. However in this novel the division is incomplete, and this accounts for the son's ambivalent response, his partial resistance to and desire for the personal mother.

At the time of adolescence Elyot's connection with the mother is intensified by the disappearance of the father, who defects from the family and is never seen again. Elyot assumes the role of the Son–Lover, and looks forward to a period of increased closeness and intimacy. But in this 'marriage' he feels a victim of the mother's instinctual demands, a kind of plaything which she exploits to satisfy her desires. On the night of the father's defection the boy feels 'seized' by her in a coldly impersonal way. She appears to be 'speaking as much to darkness, and still thinking' (p. 71), as she draws him into her bed. Elyot feels eaten up by her, stripped of his integrity and his humanity.

During his mother's involvement in the war in France, Elyot is sent to a country house near the Bristol Channel. It is here that he experiences a more pleasurable and mystical relation to the maternal archetype. As I have suggested, when the son loses himself in the deep unconscious he is no longer in conflict with the Mother but ecstatically united with her. This incestuous return takes place at Ard's Bay through a symbolic union with Nature and the maternal earth.

It was an almost enclosed, almost a circular bay. He spent many hours looking into pools ... He took up the smooth stones in his hand, the red and the mauve stones, that shone when you took them out of the water. And standing on the rim of the bay, holding the rounded stones in his hand, everything felt secure and solid, the gentle, enclosed basin of water, the sturdy trees that sprouted from the sides, his own legs planted in the moist sand. (pp. 101–2)

This is an image of at-one-ment with the elemental sources of life, with the earth mother in her primordial aspect. The 'gentle, enclosed basin of water' is a true symbol of the source, in which the youth feels 'secure and solid', like an embryo nestled within the womb.[10] Here all the powerful mother-symbols are present: circular bay, rounded stones, trees, earth, water.[11] Earth and water are ancient symbols of the Great Mother, earth representing the foundation and water the origin of all life. Trees have long possessed a maternal significance, representing the creative aspect of Nature. The fact that Elyot is depicted as tree-like, his legs sunk deep into the moist earth, emphasizes his psychological fusion with the mother realm. It further suggests that he only feels alive when he has dissolved himself in the maternal embrace. It should be pointed out that it is the absence of the personal mother that allows this symbolic incest to take place. In ordinary conditions the maternal archetype is identified wholly with the parent, and unity with her is rendered impossible by the incest taboo. But in relationship to Nature the son's longing to return to the matrix can be freely enacted.

In the above passage the image of the circle is suggested in the circular bay and is further evident in the rounded stones which Elyot holds in his hand. This is a characteristic symbol of the Mother, representing the all-embracing unity of the unconscious and the Great Round of Nature. The circle as maternal source is known in depth psychology as the uroboros (see Figure 1) in order to distinguish it from its counterpart, the mandala, which points to an entirely different psychic constellation.[12] The uroboros symbolizes an undifferentiated state of wholeness, and is considered otherworldly in that it precedes the development of consciousness and the separation of the opposites. The pursuit of this symbol can lead one out of reality altogether in search of a timeless, inchoate void. The mandala, on the other hand, points to a higher unity which is discovered in time and through a conscious integration of the opposites. Here the desire is not to obliterate the self but to strengthen and develop it so that it can maintain the tension between itself and the archetypal realm. The uroboric path leads backward to a kind of nihilistic source

Figure 1   The tail-biting uroboros (alchemical drawing, eleventh century)
Source: C.G. Jung (ed.), *Man and his Symbols*, Doubleday, New York, 1964, p. 38

The uroboros is the most basic and primordial of all archetypal symbols. It is often discovered in the dreams of psychotics, or of individuals who have regressed to the deepest levels of the psyche. The uroboros symbolizes the all-containing (self-fecundating, self-devouring) nature of the unconscious prior to the advent of human consciousness. Although the uroboros is a symbol of unity, it is to be sharply differentiated from the mandala, with which it is often confused. The mandala represents, as it were, 'unity regained' after the development of consciousness and the emergence of the ego from the matrix. The mandala symbolizes the unity of human and divine, time and eternity, whereas the uroboros points to an otherworldly, pre-human unity outside time.

mysticism,[13] whereas the mandalic vision looks ahead toward possibilities of spiritual development. It is important that we distinguish between these images and their phenomenologies because readers and critics of White have frequently confused the uroboric image with the mandala. The result is that the fiction has been distorted and its significance exaggerated.[14] White's circular forms are not mandalas pointing to high levels of integration, but symbols of an original unity where the personality is as yet undifferentiated from the matrix.

Elyot's longing for the maternal depths is further expressed in his discovery of the cave at Ard's Bay, a place where he feels completely contained by the earth and its mysteries:

> Later he found the cave, going inward through the wall of rock ... He gathered the coloured stones. And on the wall of the cave he scratched with a crumbling finger of stone, no particular design, but he liked to draw, he liked to sing to himself as the line became more and more intricate on the surface of the rock. It gave him great pleasure to feel he was doing this, secretly, unknown to the Macarthys, or Julia, or Eden. He very much needed this secret life. (p. 102)

The cave is of course an ancient symbol of the womb of the Earth Mother, the place where primitive man returned for the sake of renewal and rebirth. Here it is as if Elyot were returning to the cavern of the womb, and, once inside the belly of the Earth, is inspired to sing and draw like a primitive artist in matriarchal times.

Here we have an important reference to the division between Elyot's inner life and his existence in the real world. The inward reality is governed by this image of blissful union with the mother archetype, whereas his day world is ruled by the negative personal mother and her 'devouring' associates (here mentioned are her colleagues, housekeeper and daughter). These opposing experiences are actually the two sides of the one psychological condition, or how the mother–complex is experienced in reality and in fantasy. When the son is in the world as a separate identity, the mother–complex overpowers him and threatens his ego structure. But when he merges into the unconscious, the archetype assumes a cosmic, oceanic quality and he feels nurtured by it.

The split in his universe is dramatically portrayed when he returns home after his excursion beside the sea. He is confronted by the formidable Mrs Macarthy, who wants to know where he has been. The youth refuses to expose his secret life: 'Nowhere, he said. Nowhere much. Because Mrs Macarthy and Ard's Bay were quite separate. They had to stay like that' (p. 102). The relationship between the positive and the negative maternal image is never realized. The unconscious nature of the problem is demonstrated by the fact that the negative aspect is projected outside the psyche and experienced as a quality of an external figure. It is not realized that the desirable experience—the dissolution into the matrix—is itself a defeat for the ego; a defeat which is evident only when he returns from the archetypal depths. The blissful oneness of the uroboros lasts only while the personality is in a dissolved, unconscious state.

Now that he is back in reality, the mother–image proceeds to devalue his symbols of harmony: 'I don't see why you should bring home stones, Mrs Macarthy said. You might start making a collection of stamps. Stamps are educational, she said' (p. 102). Her undermining remark is invested with a certain magical power, for when he contemplates the stones he finds that they have lost their lustre and effectiveness:

He did not answer this. When she had gone, he looked at the stones. He wondered a little himself. They were dull and colourless, unlike the glistening stones he had picked up out of pools. These belonged to the bay. Soon it was dusk, and he picked up the stones one by one, slowly threw them out of the window, heard their heavy landing in the undergrowth. (pp. 102–3)

The beatific vision exists outside time and will not stand the test of reality. It disintegrates as soon as it is brought up into the world of form; its lustre will not shine forth in the ego's realm. In a sense it is not Mrs Macarthy but the Great Mother of Ard's Bay who takes the colour away from the stones. She draws their life back into herself, so that Elyot is left with mere relics of a former splendour. He is forced to admit that the stones 'belonged to the bay', and taken from this context they have no effect or reality.

At this stage Mrs Standish returns from France and the negative maternal image is restored to its central place. The youth anticipates love and intimacy from the parent: 'it was exciting enough, when you ran outside to be kissed, to kiss, the rain getting in between your faces, and the scent that came back; you had almost forgotten so many warm moments between sheets' (p. 109). The mother then reveals her innately destructive aspect, denying him the fulfilment he seeks:

Run along, Elyot. It's cold.
She sounded tired. She was the same, and at the same time different ... Mother had a habit of talking to you as if you were hardly there, it was this now, it was this and more, she looked from side to side in the garden, as if she had forgotten. (p. 109)

The sense of betrayal is reinforced by the presence of her lover, an army officer from France. The son becomes resentful toward the man who has captured his mother's affection. This Oedipal fantasy is developed later in the story, where Elyot assumes a strongly negative attitude toward his mother's affairs, projecting his own frustrated longing upon her sexual life, and regarding it as depraved and reprehensible.

Elyot is now in a critical position, cut off from the personal mother and separated as well from the archetypal source. For an ego wholly dependent upon the maternal realm this is felt as a traumatic separation from life itself. Elyot is overcome by a sense of alienation and despair: 'He had no part in anything. It frightened him a little. He could feel himself tremble ... It began to occupy him more and more, his not being part of anything' (pp. 110–11). The force of life drains away from the face of the world, and people and things acquire an atmosphere of unreality:

the water jug that Julia left you might or might not have seen in sleep or waking, it was not quite real, the sort of daylight real ... And Mother belonged in a way to sleep. Everything she did was not quite real, like sleep, only there was no waking. He stood a long way off and watched. He began to develop a perpetual frown. (p. 111)

Without nourishment from the maternal image the world is benumbed and everything seems as a nightmare, 'only there was no waking'. This disappearance of life-energy is an expression of the same process that led to the devitalization of the sacred stones. As Jung writes, 'The *puer aeternus* [eternal youth][15] only lives on and through the Mother', and once separated from the maternal body his psychical life is destroyed.[16] If he continues to exist at all, it is as a substanceless ego, one of the 'living dead'. From this moment until the end of the novel, when Elyot makes his return to the source, his life is one of stagnation and meaninglessness. Yet there is always within him the memory of the paradise of the Mother, and the youth continues to hover about her image, longing for that at-one-ment which reality has denied him: 'She was so beautiful that he would have liked to touch her. But he did not know what to do, or say. He stood kicking at the frosted ground' (p. 111).

III

The feeling of being isolated is a central fact of adolescence. The ego is cast out of the pleasurable matrix and is forced to develop in the realm of consciousness. In the mythological cycle of the developing ego the Father is meant to become the dominant archetype at this point, guiding the son into the world and facilitating his adaptation to life. In White's fiction, however, the Father is absent, either quite literally, as in the present story, or else spiritually and psychologically, as in all the later works. What this means is that ego development is retarded at adolescence, there is no internal direction into adulthood and maturity, but a perpetual hankering after the psychic past. Yet even the *puer aeternus* is subject to the developmental process to some extent, if not enough to place him firmly in life, then at least to alienate him partially from the maternal source. He is forced to inhabit a twilight zone between the world and the unconscious, ejected from the womb yet not completely in reality. Elyot's response is to feign maturity, to act as if he were adjusted to society even while unable to feel the authenticity of this position.

Out of his bewilderment he had taken refuge behind what people told him was a scholarly mind. (p. 176)

Adopted as a defence, this becomes a habit. Like the intellectual puzzle as a substitute for living, which you chose deliberately. (p. 174)

The *puer* makes an artificial adaptation to reality and imitates a particular lifestyle, in Elyot's case, that of the English intellectual. At Cambridge Elyot lives amidst the educated classes and acts out his part accordingly. He acquires the gestures and habits of what is foreign to him, having not really emerged into life but still largely oriented around the mother–realm. It is to be expected, then, that Elyot finds human society empty and meaningless. It is for him 'an unpleasant dream', 'an elaborate charade that meant something once ... When the figures, the gestures were related to enthusiasms' (p. 214). Critics of White's novels are inclined to read these and other statements literally, as sociological criticisms and appraisals of modern life. Yet they are conditioned by the standpoint of the *puer aeternus*, for whom reality is always inadequate because he is improperly related to it.[17] What Elyot, and White, criticize is primarily a psychological 'place', a mythic state, and not a geographical London or Sydney.

Despite Elyot's awareness of the limitations of his adopted persona, he maintains the scholarly role for about a decade. It is easy enough to emulate, and provides at least a semblance of social identity. More to the point is that he can do nothing else at this stage, for the way back to the source is blocked not only by the developmental process but by the incest taboo as well. The personal mother continues to hold or 'subsume' the archetypal image, so that in her presence the matrix is unapproachable. The mechanism of projection binds him to her, thus inhibiting the realization of his symbolic desire.

During this phase there is only one occasion where Elyot's *puer* longing is revealed. This occurs in his mother's absence, through a brief affair with Hildegard Fiesel. Hildegard, a tall, beautiful, dignified German, several years his senior, seems to possess the appropriate characteristics for his image of the Great Goddess.

Elyot's reaction is to fall immediately into a state of swooning adoration and to abandon his ego–identity. His desire is not to relate to her as an individual, but to allow himself to become absorbed into an archetypal image:

Drawing him into a world of her own, making him acknowledge this, he began to doubt the reality of trees, the stones their feet touched in fording a stream, all these were unreal, undergoing some form of reconstruction in Hildegard's voice ... All that late afternoon, wandering, sitting, in the forest Hildegard made with her voice ... he knew that he was not himself. He was a strange person, subscribing to arguments in which, soberly, he could not believe. But he watched, he listened to her, he was obsessed himself, with the form of Hildegard. He was becoming what she wanted him to become. (pp. 124–5)

The individual enters another world, is bathed in a kind of fluid state and nurtured by the maternal figure. There is also a loss of integrity and will—his ego is annulled and he is made to play the fool, an idiot without an orientation. The beloved Goddess is not only the bestower of ecstasy but also the devourer of personality. The negative aspect, however, is never experienced at the time of the descent, but only afterward, when the *puer* resumes his egoic structure and the ecstatic character is lost.

Immediately after their love-making in the forest Elyot feels resentful toward Hildegard. Her presence 'suffocates' him (p. 127), her smile seems 'bitter' (p. 131), and she appears hostile and undermining. As we found earlier, the negative side of the psychic experience is projected entirely upon the woman, who is suddenly invested with destructive qualities. Hildegard attempts to communicate with Elyot, but each time he cuts away brutally: 'he resented even her appearance now, the face that would blur in a gust of hysteria' (p. 132). The image of the destroying matrix is the only thing he sees in her now. Actually he has never seen Hildegard at all, but merely the faces of his own inner archetype, the Seductive and then the Destroying Goddess. In this way the psychic reality distorts the *puer*'s experience of women, keeping him bound to a relentless mythological drama.[18]

As a result of this abortive engagement Elyot becomes more regimented in his behaviour.[19] When the mask slips he is completely at the mercy of archetypal forces, and so he attempts to reinforce his rational position, eschewing relationship, personal involvement, and anything which might threaten his insular existence:

On the whole people bothered him, the effort, the having to commit yourself, and most of all emotionally. He sometimes shuddered now over the episode of Hildegard. Because this was something over which he had no control. His relationship with Hildegard presented a picture of himself jigging wildly on the end of an invisible rope. (p. 149)

The problem is not this or any human relationship but his own relation to the archetypal feminine.

IV

Elyot maintains his reactionary stand for several years, during which time he completes his education and returns to his mother's house in London. It is here that his rational will is eventually eclipsed by the darker psychic impulse. It is as if his repression leads to or even initiates a reactivation of the complex. Gradually he finds his position undermined, his attitudes contradicted, his values reversed. Because this process is unconscious, taking place outside the ego's realm, it is experienced in terms of external events and situations. People, noises, happenings in the street, all acquire a threatening tone and seem to draw him into an irrational sphere: 'Contact with the living moment, that you watched in your shirtsleeves from an upper window, the vague, formless moments in the street, made you recoil inside your shirt, too conscious of your own confused flesh' (p. 174). The world becomes alive with psyche, the place where threatening forces are encountered. The sense of impending doom is emphasized by the fact that all of Europe is besieged by disruptive forces which culminate in the outbreak of war. There is an interpenetration of psyche and world, which makes Elyot's own situation seem particularly critical: 'You could feel the waiting. For a cataclysm perhaps' (p. 303).

At this stage all aspects of the environment become animated by psyche and point toward change. His sister Eden assumes tremendous significance as a carrier of his own emotional life. Elyot fears his sister's sexual passion, her volatile nature, but there is also a 'half-craving' for what she represents: 'an intenser form of living' (p. 354). Witnessing the intensity of Eden's love for Joe Barnett, Elyot begins to wish for a similar passion in his own life: 'In his fury he wanted to possess something, make it answerable, because he was so far distant from the other, the faces of Eden and Joe Barnett discovering a reality, finding a substance for which the symbols stood' (p. 214). He becomes increasingly self-critical, discontented with his insularity and anxious to break free from his emotional prison: 'he wanted to press with his hands, rouse an element of fear or surprise, some sign of the spontaneous' (p. 293).

Still, for all this, Elyot does not act: 'He shut himself in his room and worked. Outside were the house sounds, the flap of the duster, the rumble of a cistern … All round you there was pointed evidence of your own anachronistic activity' (p. 303). He senses the necessity of change, and the futility of his present pattern, but there is no movement. The scene with which we began this chapter, depicting Elyot's resistance to the 'call' from the mother, suggests why this is so. The return to the source is still associated with a literal incestuous regression. The attachment to the personal mother continues to block the way into psyche.

V

The incestuous attraction for the mother, repressed since early adulthood, has merely fallen into the unconscious, where it now leads a dark, malignant life of its own. It is projected outside the ego and perceived through the mother, who appears to be obsessed by sexuality and lust. His own incestuous longing confronts him in the guise of a morally decadent, lust-ridden mother. It appears that there are more than Elyot's projections at work here, for White seems as determined as Elyot to convert Mrs Standish into a living emblem of degenerate desire. There is a two-way conspiracy, where author and protagonist combine to create a demonized image of the mother. It must be appreciated, here and elsewhere, that White is not analysing the mother–complex but is writing as it were from within it, so that his own psychology is manifest in the narrative. The stories are reflections of psychic life, and his own conflicts are often completely identical with those of the central character.

Upon his return from Cambridge Elyot sees his mother as a loathsome figure:

She listened to men, and gave them the impression she enjoyed it, the yawn caught somewhere in her handsome throat. It was a technique taught her by economic necessity. She could be very gracious at a supper table. And afterwards. She would accept a cheque, after protest, in which she never went too far. (pp. 137–8)

His mother seems to have descended to the level of a harlot, albeit a sophisticated one, the Whore of Ebury Street who receives money from her suitors after a formalized protest. Even here his desire for the mother is evident beneath the loathing and the disgust. He feels isolated and forlorn, watching Catherine Standish satisfy herself while he stands in the background with his unfulfilled longing:

Elyot was a shadow that fell across the substance of her friends, the men who brought her presents, who filled her drawing-room with conversation and cigar smoke. Elyot standing sideways. His manner was perpetually sideways. Smoothing his hair, she could sense withdrawal. Or they sat in untidy silences. She could feel his disapproval of mentioned names. (pp. 138–9)

As Elyot's unconscious desire becomes more intense there is a corresponding intensification of the mother's lustful sexuality. She now sinks 'into the easy, satisfying coma of the flesh, for which ... her whole temporal being craved' (p. 242). Her affair with Wally Collins, the night-club saxophonist, marks the beginning of her total disintegration. She becomes known as Wally's moll, his 'Old Girl' (p. 325). Wally Collins, who is the same age as Elyot, is spellbound by his Old Girl and wonders how a 'dame of her class' (p. 281) could have fallen fo him:

Looking at her in the restaurant his mouth drooped open. All the things he'd never had, and wanted, seemed to put themselves in reach in the body of Catherine Standish. He could not possess her too quickly, in case they removed themselves again. (p. 282)

Wally's desire is expressed in terms which are peculiarly reminiscent of Elyot's childhood feeling toward his mother. He finds in Mrs Standish 'all the things he'd never had, and wanted', which reminds us of Elyot's childhood, his constant desire to get close to his mother, whom he felt contained all he needed. There is even a suggestion here of the mother's dark aspect—her tendency to withdraw her love and support—and so we find Wally clinging desperately to her, 'in case [she] removed [herself] again'. It appears that White has modelled his character along the lines of the son's infantile desires. Collins, in fact, personifies Elyot's unconscious longing.

During her involvement with Collins Mrs Standish suffers a complete breakdown, seemingly consumed by a demonic instinctual force. She never recovers from this episode, but dies in a state of exhaustion. Elyot's last glimpse of her is as a completely wretched creature brought home by Collins after a wild party at Soho:

You remembered how the head lolled, she just wasn't well, he said ... He remembered how ... the eyes opened, watched the trailing of a red skirt, the arm brushing the carpet, as if it had no connexion, or at least sawdust-filled. (p. 328)

The degenerate impulse within her, or rather that projected upon her by Elyot and White, has run its course, resulting in her tragic yet timely disintegration.

VI

The death of Mrs Standish brings Elyot considerable relief. His resistance to the matrix is modified, and he allows the processes of change to take place:

> beyond the rotting and the death there was some suggestion of growth. He waited for this in a state of expectation. He waited for something that would happen to him, that would happen in time ...
> In the morning there would be the funeral. (pp. 344–5)

That this relaxation of defences could take place only after the mother's death indicates to what extent he was bound to her image. Elyot lacked the determination or courage to return to the source while his mother was still alive. The personal fixation is never seen through for its symbolic possibilities, for the metaphorical aspects hidden within the literal attachment.

Even now another form of the same problem inhibits psychic movement. After the funeral there is a transference of the mother image upon his sister Eden.[20] This leads to an archetypal attraction for the sister, countered by resistances and resentment. But again the psychological drama is broken by circumstances. Eden decides to go off to Europe to take part in the war, in service with the medical corps. By so doing she reflects her mother's actions some twenty-five years earlier.

With the mother and sister gone, Elyot is now free to enter the archetypal realm. As he stands at the railway station farewelling Eden, the symbols of the maternal source, lying dormant in his psyche since childhood, are immediately re-constellated and point the way to the return:

> Outside the sighing of an anxious piston, there was still the bay, smooth, almost circular, the glistening of red and periwinkle stones. You went down alone. This was a secret expedition. To lie on the back, the sun glistened on the teeth, a hot sinking of the bones. (p. 356)

Once more he is connected to the matrix, imaged here as an highly erotic absorption into the landscape of Ard's Bay. It is surprising how rapidly the process takes place, how soon after Eden's departure the maternal world opens before him and he becomes at one with it.

The novel ends with Elyot embracing the lost world of his childhood. We are not shown how this upheaval will express itself in his mode of being, but one thing is certain: his former life is over. We feel relieved that he has at last broken free from his ego-bound state; but we are forced to concede that there is no real development suggested here. He is simply back in the original situation, having exchanged a set of defences for his original *puer* longing. He faces the same problems now as he did in childhood: the disintegrative forces of the unconscious, the absorptive character of the matrix, his own secret delight in dissolution. These problems were precisely why he had to adopt a rigidly controlled position in the first place. The strength of the complex is such that a balanced relation to the maternal depths is not possible. When a return is made there is a complete going over to the other side; return in effect means 'devouring'.

The disintegrative aspects are indicated in the above-quoted passage: 'This was a secret expedition. To lie on the back, the sun glistened on the teeth, a hot sinking of the bones'. The emphasis on teeth, bones, and sinking suggests an almost deathly eternality, an experience of the matrix which is overwhelming in its intensity. In this sense it is identical with his childhood descent: 'he lay on the shore, and the sound of the water lapped across his chest, a blaze of sun shone between the bones' (p. 112). The human element dissolves and he becomes the eternal man, drowned in the source. It is a return to the deathly matrix, yet the negative aspect, as we have seen in earlier instances, is not felt or acknowledged at the time of dissolution.

White himself appears unaware of the regressive aspect, and asks the reader to view the close of the story wholly in terms of regeneration and rebirth. In the final section there is a tone of completion, references to 'the end of a journey', and even a choir of anonymous voices which sings, 'Then we are here, we have slept, but we have really got here at last' (p. 358). If we are still unconvinced, there are the closing lines: 'He yawned. He felt like someone who had been asleep, and had only just woken'. These statements do not allay the sense that he is caught in the same fatal complex. Still, from the *puer*'s point of view, the sinking into the matrix is an awakening, the end of mere egohood, and the realization of an ultimate desire. White speaks from within this archetypal perspective, where the return to thè uroboros is regarded as the ecstatic overcoming of human limitation.

The unacknowledged negative aspect continues to be projected outside the uroboric paradise in the later novels and experienced through a succession of demonic maternal figures. As White becomes more convinced that the dissolved state is ideal the 'mothers' become more devouring, until we meet the most terrible of all, the twin-headed succubus of Mrs Flack and Mrs Jolley. Mrs Standish has conveniently been put to rest, Mrs Macarthy and Hildegard dispensed with through time and circumstance, yet the procession of negative mothers cannot be stopped. The psyche continues to put forth demons while the *puer* is obsessed by an ultimately self-destructive fantasy.

2   *The Undying Mother*

> *Theodora took up the thin knife, very thin and*
> *impervious, from where it lay in the zinc light . . .*
> *But this, she trembled, does not cut the knot . . .*
> *She went on to her own room, away from the*
> *act she had not committed, while her mother*
> *continued to sleep.*
>
> The Aunt's Story, p. 123[1]

'But old Mrs Goodman did die at last'. The opening line of *The Aunt's Story* (1948) affirms by negation, as it were, the central role of the mother in the novel. It announces, too confidently in light of subsequent events, the end of her tyrannous reign. Her death is felt to mark an end to enslavement for Theodora, the daughter who has endured years of subservience to this destructive figure. Theodora imagines herself free to explore other parts of the world, leaving Australia to live in England, France and the United States. Yet everywhere she is plagued by negative maternal images, feels imprisoned and under attack. Her bond is not terminated merely by the disappearance of the parental figure. It is her own longing to dissolve in the source which keeps her in a state of matriarchal entrapment long after the death of old Mrs Goodman.

In the previous novel we noted the splitting apart of the mother archetype into positive and negative aspects. The ecstatic element was given to Nature, while the negative side was attributed to the personal mother and the female sex. The split was not complete, however. Mrs Standish attracted Elyot's incestuous libido to the very end, thus maintaining her ambivalence and her central place. In *The Aunt's Story* the mother is dramatically reduced in power. There is a significant transference of sexuality to the father/daughter relationship.

It is not to be supposed that this was a deliberate move on

White's part. The imagination will always strive to transform instinctual impulses, and will take advantage of various devices to shift the personal drama to a symbolic plane. The father–daughter bond is adopted as a way out of the primary situation. Never again will White represent the father as the object of desire. After this novel the incestuous libido is returned to the maternal context, but henceforward as wholly absorbed into an impersonal Mother Goddess. *The Tree of Man* and *Voss* bear witness to the fact that the transformation—at least of the positive maternal aspect—is thereafter complete. But the negative aspect of the archetype never undergoes symbolic elaboration, remaining literal, personal and unimagined throughout the canon.

The relationship between Theodora and George Goodman functions as a masked re-enactment of the Oedipal pattern. There is a matriarchal resonance below and behind the central action. Theodora, despite her sex, has the psychology and even the physical characteristics of a boy. 'Theo should have been a boy, they said, the more obliging ones, hoping to make the best' (p. 32). In later life she has a moustache, wears boots and trousers, and even in women's clothes is said to resemble 'a bloke in skirts' (p. 67). George Goodman has the nurturing character of a mother. For Theodora he represents an idealized maternal figure.[2] He is supportive whereas Mrs Goodman is scathing, he is receptive whereas she is uncompromising and fixed. The association between father and daughter is passionate and warm. They share stories at night, and by day go for long walks across the Meroë plains in order to escape the stifling atmosphere of Mrs Goodman. George Goodman is as much subject to the witch–mother as his daughter. He too makes constant, if also futile, attempts to escape from her murderous control.

Goodman is not equal to the Mother, but, like every male figure in White, is a *puer aeternus* under the dominance of the female image. Mythologically, he is an offshoot of the body of Mater Natura. In ancient myths the spirit of Nature was often portrayed by a male figure, a phallic, life-generating deity in the form of Attis, Adonis or John Barley-Corn.[3] Such boy–gods are slain annually by the Mother Goddess because, according to the myth, she must withdraw her spirit each winter, descending to the dark underworld. The youthful spirit is 'sad by nature'[4] since he does not achieve a separate life, but exists only to serve the Mother Goddess. Like his mythological counterparts, Goodman is co-ordinated with Nature, and when the autumnal decline sets in he can merely look out across the darkening landscape 'with a plaid across his shoulders for the cold that had not yet arrived' (p. 84), and await his early death. Like the boy–gods of antiquity he dies young, but the Great Mother lives on. Throughout this sequence Mrs Goodman functions as the death-dealing mother who maintains supreme power. Goodman projects upon her his dark fate, and she is made to bear a tremendous mythic burden. Still, on the surface she is treated as if she were merely human, a malefic farmer's wife, intent on bringing about ruination and disaster. Too often in White the life-devouring ritual of Nature appears as a wife consuming or hen-pecking a husband to death. The negative force of Nature is not given a fictional frame large enough to contain it.

I

Early in the story Theodora is imaged as an ego–germ nestled inside a totality ruled over by the father:

Altogether this was an epoch of roselight. Morning was bigger than the afternoon, and round, and veined like the skin inside an unhatched egg, in which she curled safe still, but smiling for them to wake her, to touch her cheek with a finger and say: I believe Theodora is asleep. Then she would scream: I am not, I am not, and throw open her eyes to see who. Usually it was Father. (p. 22)

Theodora slumbers in the perfect round and awakens. The father is the guardian of sleep and also the attendant of her awakening. All through this period he stands over Theodora's childhood as a loving, nurturing character. Surprisingly, at this time, little mention is made of the mother, a background figure in these early days. Theodora writes a brief essay about Meroë, the family property in New South Wales, and it is evident that it consists for her exclusively of herself and her father:

At Our Place ... there is an old apricot tree which does not have fruit, and here the cows stand when it is hot, before they are milked, or underneath the pear trees in the old orchard where the cottage has tumbled down. I see all these things when I ride about Our Place, with my Father. Our Place is a decent size, not so big as Parrotts' or Trevelyans', but my Father says big enough for peace of mind. (p. 24)

Everything, for a while, is an idyllic paradise.

But soon she is forced to recognize that her father is not the secure figure she imagines him to be. During one of their walks Goodman takes her by the hand, 'about to lead you somewhere', but Theodora could sense, 'inside the hand, that you were leading Father' (p. 22). She also notices that he 'sighed a lot', and that amid the pines beside his window there was 'a stirring and murmuring and brooding and vague discontent' (p. 21). All is not well with Father. He has an ineffectual quality which belies Theodora's idealized image. It becomes more apparent when she comes into contact with the objective observer:

'Meroë?' said Mr Parrott. 'Rack-an'-Ruin Hollow.'
Which Theodora heard. She was waiting for Father, in town, under the long balcony of the Imperial Hotel. She hung around, waiting, and there were men there ...
'All this gadding off to foreign places,' said Mr Parrott. 'Sellin' off a paddock here and a paddock there. George Goodman has no sense of responsibility to his own land.'
This was awful. It made your stomach sick, to hear of Father, this, that you could not quite understand, but it was bad enough. (p. 25)

And on the way home she felt

oppressed by a weight of sadness, that nobody would lift, because nobody would ever know that she was shouldering it. Least of all Father, who was thick and mysterious as a tree, but also hollow, by judgement of the men beneath the balcony. (pp. 25–6)

She is made to realize that her father is a failure as a farmer and as a practical man. But these are merely the outer signs of a central inner weakness. Goodman is held fast by the unconscious, and unable to wrest an independent identity from the maternal realm.

As Theodora travels home with her father she asks herself why he would want to sell off bits of Meroë and so undermine his reputation and diminish the size of his own estate. And here we discover, in a sequence which unfolds in Theodora's memory, the role of the mother in his psychological and material decline.

'I refuse to vegetate,' said Mrs Goodman. 'Let us go somewhere. Before we die.'
Her voice struck the dining-room door ...
'It's reckless, Julia,' Father said.
'Then let us be reckless,' she said. 'And die. We can sell a paddock. Let us go to the Indies.'
Mother's voice burned the quiet air. It was stifling as an afternoon of fire.
Father laughed. 'I suppose we can sell Long Acre,' he said. 'Old Trevelyan's willing to buy.'
Then they were both silent, as if consumed by Mother's fire.
'The Indies,' Mother breathed. (p. 26)

Mrs Goodman is the agent behind the husband's disintegration. She exerts a kind of numbing, castrating influence upon Meroë and the father–world, which actually decreases in size as a result of her demands. The father's protestations are in vain; they are countered by the mother's supreme wit and a conniving attitude. We must realize that this passage is a memory–sequence in the daughter's mind, and that much is therefore being projected upon the mother as a figure of Theodora's imagination. Her voice 'burned' the quiet air, like 'an afternoon of fire'; at the end they are 'consumed by Mother's fire'. This mother is no mere mortal, but a fire-breathing monster, a creature of the underworld. Her power is elemental and unrestrained. She functions as the primal dragon which is now beginning to take the earth–spirit back into itself.

The mother's voice feels 'stifling'—the ego which is embedded in the matrix is made to feel that it is suffocating, in an airless container. (George Goodman is asthmatic, and many of White's male characters suffer from this condition, wheezing and coughing in story after story.)[5] In another passage we read: 'Then you knew that Mother had won, in spite of Father breathing hard. It was terrible, the strength of Mother. All your own weakness came flowing back' (p. 42). The mother absorbs life into herself, leaving the ego exhausted, weak, breathless. On the other hand, the mother herself appears to gain in breath and life: ' "The Indies," Mother breathed'. Her movement is toward expansion and freedom, whereas the *puer* contracts and is overwhelmed.[6]

About this time, with his strength rapidly declining, George Goodman tells Theodora about a second Meroë and of the ancient world which has him in thrall. ' "There is another Meroë," said Father, "a dead place, in the black country of Ethiopia" ' (p. 23). 'In this dead place that Father had described the roses were as brown as paper bags, the curtains were ashy on their rings, the eyes of the house had closed.' 'Abyssinia', as it is subsequently called, is a realm of fire, death and disintegration. Goodman is understandably obsessed and fearful of the second Meroë, since as Nature–spirit he must eventually succumb to its deathly power. He relates an evocative Ethiopian tale of the trochilus and the crocodile:

He told you something funny. It was the bird that sat in the crocodile's throat. Fanning his larynx, Father said. Herodotus wrote this in a book. It was both funny and strange. And the crocodile lay in a river called the Nile, which flowed not far from Meroë. (p. 23)

The frail, beautiful trochilus inside the jaws of the crocodile is a fascinating image. The winged spirit is caught up in the lower realm, of darkness and reptilian nature, and lives only until the moment when the dragon–jaws shut tight around it. It is drawn to the dragon–mouth in the same way that Attis or Adonis is drawn to the wild boar of Aphrodite, which will ravage and destroy him. The spirit offers itself as a sacrifice to the eternal cycle of Nature. In psychological terms it also suggests the course of the infantile ego which returns to the source in search of an eternal paradise. It enters the maw seeking nourishment (the trochilus actually picks at the teeth for bits of food) yet does not see that it is trapped inside a hellish abyss that must eventually devour it. The bird caught in the crocodile's throat is a crucial image, a vignette which reflects even the author's situation in his innocent hovering around the source and refusal to recognize the devouring maw in which he is held.

The tale of the trochilus is told only once in the novel, but its resonance pervades the story. George Goodman is fascinated by it, but not, we feel, able to penetrate its meaning. Often in White we find characters contemplating in visual or anecdotal form the very essence of their psychic lives, looking on with a kind of uncomprehending fascination. This constitutes a mode of pathos throughout the fiction, in that characters possess the key to their imprisoning myths but are unable to make use of it. The novels as a series do not suggest a pattern of progressive individuation, of the individual entering into dialogue with the mythic realm, but simply of his becoming enthralled and petrified by what he encounters there.

Theodora is more preoccupied with the stark revelation of a second Meroë. It is as if the tragic background of their shared myth had become apparent for the first time: 'she wanted to escape from this dead place with the suffocating cinder breath' (p. 24). Again, suffocation is presented as an attribute of the primal world. There is an anticipation of a negative fate about to overshadow her:

She looked with caution at the yellow face of the house, at the white shells in its placid, pocked stone. Even in sunlight the hills surrounding Meroë were black. Her own shadow was rather a suspicious rag. So that from what she saw and sensed, the legendary landscape became a fact, and she could not break loose from an expanding terror. (p. 24)

The negative polarity rises into view, filling the landscape with darkness and suspicious shadows. No longer is 'Our Place' a blissful world of herself and her father. It now becomes mother's world: Mrs Goodman increases in power and strength as surely as the dark landscape of Abyssinia is now looming into view.[7]

At this point Theodora's life is undermined by the Mother in countless ways.

Figure 2   The demonic paradise (from an Italian manuscript, fifteenth century)
Source: E. Neumann, *The Great Mother*, Princeton University Press, Princeton, 1972, plate 169

When the ego regresses to the source-situation it discovers a realm of unearthly delight and horror. Often, as in this drawing, the personality is so preoccupied by the pleasurable, paradisal aspect that it fails to see the dark maw that must soon engulf it. To 'return to the source' is an infantile dream which invariably meets with tragedy and disaster, for it can only be achieved at the cost of egoic annihilation, madness (Theodora), or death (Parker, Voss, Himmelfarb). Thus whenever White's mystics attempt to realize their goal, images of teeth, jaws, or devouring mothers automatically appear before them, as representations of internal threat and disaster.

'No, no, Theodora,' crackled Mother. 'Not that way. Where is your feeling?' she said. 'This horrible up and down. Can't you feel it flow? Here, give it to me.'
    ... Mother sat down. She played the music as it should have been played. She took possession of the piano, she possessed Chopin, they were hers while she wanted them, until she was ready to put them down. (p. 28)

No matter what she does, or where she turns, the Mother is there to interfere with her activities and to draw everything toward herself. The maternal unconscious invades the field of the personality, robs it of its direction, and renders it ineffectual.

For the most part the mother's lethal attack is still focused upon the father, as we see in this fantasy sequence:

And if Julia Goodman took a knife and turned it in her husband's side to watch the expression on his face and scent the warm blood that flowed, George Goodman stirred in his sleep and changed positions to another dream, of mortgages perhaps, or drought, or fire. (p. 66)

Lamia-like, the mother sucks away his life-blood. As she turns the knife George Goodman is sleeping, or dreaming, which is to say that he is completely unaware of what is taking place. The mother attacks him from his unconscious side, where he is unable to offer any resistance. Moreover, she does this as a kind of sport, and feels delighted at 'the warm blood that flowed'. In ancient festivals of Attis and Adonis the Mother Goddess was gratified at the sight of blood, since this was an offering in her honour, which would sink into and regenerate her ground.[8] She would sometimes cause Attis to open his own veins, pouring his blood into the dry and thirsty earth.

Now Meroë itself is in the throes of autumnal decline. It appears as a dried-out hollow where the spirit of life is absent:

The hills were burnt yellow. Thin yellow scurf lay on the black skin of the hills, which had worn into black pockmarks where the eruptions had taken place. And now the trees were more than ever like white bones. (p. 84)

In this charred, dying landscape sits the ailing George Goodman, who senses his own imminent death. He tells Theodora of his failings in life, and 'mother', of course, is foremost in his imagining: ' "Theodora," he said, "in the end I never saw Greece, because your mother would not come. She said it was a primitive country, full of bugs and damp sheets and dysentery" ' (p. 84). The mother is felt to be responsible for cutting short his journey, for preventing him from reaching his mythological Ithaca. Theodora is terrified at the prospect of her father's death, not only because of her personal connection with him, but because he reflects her own life-generating spirit.

She streamed out beside him on the carpet, kneeling, touching his knees ... 'No,' she said. 'Not yet, Father. No.'
His voice was as pale as the grey light that now sucked and whispered at the pines.
'But there is no reason, my dear Theodora, why I should go on living. I have finished.' ...
'In the end,' his voice said, out of the pines, 'I did not see it.' (p. 85)

The Nature–spirit cannot question his fate; he must surrender to death, obeying the seasonal imperative to return to the body of mother earth. At his death Theodora suffers an acute emotional crisis, drawn spiritually into the same abyss of darkness that has overwhelmed her father:

> She walked out through the passages, through the sleep of other people. She was thin as grey light, as if she had just died. She would not wake the others. It was still too terrible to tell, too private an experience. As if she were to go into the room and say: Mother, I am dead, I am dead, Meroë has crumbled. So she went outside where the grey light was as thin as water and Meroë had in fact, dissolved. Cocks were crowing the legend of day, but only the legend. Meroë was grey water, grey ash. Then Theodora Goodman cried. (p. 85)

Adonis is dead. '[W]ith him is beauty slain, / And, beauty dead, black chaos comes again.'[9] The vital energies of the earth have been withdrawn, and everything turns to darkness and grey ash. Or, in terms of the geographical fantasy of the novel, Meroë has been consumed by Abyssinia,[10] and reduced to a counterpart of that ancient, charred, black land.

II

Whereas George Goodman's relation to the Mother is essentially mythological, he being a Nature–spirit destined to be overcome, Theodora's is psychological: if she suffers a similar fate it is because she chooses the same extinction. We have seen that the mother has been experienced as destructive, undermining her every activity and situation. But there is another side to this process of destruction. Theodora actually longs to be devoured by the maternal image. Not only does she reject social reality in the forms of Spofforths' school, city life, career and marriage, but she wishes to destroy the very structure of her identity. Her selfhood is felt as a burden which she would like to shrug off in order to return to a 'natural' state. There is a gradual identification with things chaotic and elemental, with the black volcanic hills of Meroë (p. 28), with winds (p. 38), fire (p. 53), bones (p. 60), and night (p. 56). Her nihilistic longing is evident in her shooting of the little hawk, with which she had been associated: 'She took aim, and it was like aiming at her own red eye' (p. 71). As the hawk tumbled to the ground she 'felt exhausted, but there was no longer any pain. She was as negative as air'.

Theodora's passion for dissolution is dramatically portrayed in her relationship with Moraitis, the Greek cellist. And here the sexual nature of her longing is made apparent. The ego's movement toward self-extinction is invariably revealed as an erotic process. Its ruling metaphor is incest; its goal, the ecstasy of the womb-like state. Because of Theodora's feminine identity the incestuous attraction undergoes a specific reversal. But this coincides with the author's own sexual predisposition. We observed in the previous chapter White's aversion to hetero-sexuality. Elyot's love-making with Hildegard had evoked the devouring image of incest, the womb as castrating maw. When sexuality is experienced through the incest metaphor the *puer* is made to feel overwhelmed by intercourse, every penetration of the womb a terrible disintegration. According to Marie-Louise von Franz, the *puer* frequently resorts to a homosexual mode, placing the devouring image upon woman, and experiencing the ecstatic dissolution through the homosexual partner.[11] This is by no means put forward as a general theory of homosexuality, but it seems to be how it functions in White's fiction. So the choice of a female protagonist has the additional advantage of catering to the author's own 'ambivalence',[12] as he refers to his homosexual nature. But one does not need the autobiographical confessions to see the homosexuality: it is there from the beginning, in the way the novels reflect the erotic factor. Moreover, sexuality needs to be emphasized here in order to counterbalance previous critical attention upon Theodora's 'saintliness', her devotion to 'purity' and 'God', as if what motivated her were an ideal of righteous-ness.[13] Every one of White's 'saints' is possessed by a dark eros, an incestuous dynamic; if they seem saintly it is because the eros is not—at least not until the novels of the 1970s—expressed literally, but enacted through an essentially symbolic rite or drama.

Moraitis, a sensitive, effeminate artist, awakens in Theodora a fierce longing for extinction in the matrix. In her imagination he is connected with her characteristic symbolism of the source: with Abyssinia, 'the country of the bones' (p. 108), with oceans, death and drowning. All of this, though, is reflected in a positive light, the ecstasy of death–in–incest. And Moraitis himself appears to celebrate death as a welcome and natural comfort: '"Greeks are happiest dying," smiled Moraitis. "Their memorials do not reflect this fatality ... But the Greeks are born to die"' (p. 108). At Moraitis' concerto Theodora undergoes an intensely erotic process of disintegration. This is achieved through a heightened identification with the music: 'Now she was closer. It was no longer a matter of intervening heads or chairs. She was herself the first few harsh notes that he struck out of his instrument' (p. 111). The concerto has an almost magical effect, driving Theodora toward a frenzy of excitement and culminating in a final moment of dissolution. Since the object of incestuous sexuality it to destroy the self, its expression generally contains a sado-masochistic element, and this is apparent in the following sequence:

And Theodora, inside her, was torn by ... all she knew there was to come. She watched him take the 'cello between his knees and wring from its body a ... thwarted, a passionate music ... She was close. He could breathe into her mouth. He filled her mouth with long aching silences, between the deeper notes that reached down deep into her body. She felt the heavy eyelids on her eyes ... There were moments of laceration, which made you dig your nails in your hands. The 'cello's voice was one long barely subjugated cry under the savage lashes of the violins. But Moraitis walked slowly into the open. He wore the expression of sleep and solitary mirrors. The sun was in his eyes, the sky had passed between his bones. (p. 111)

Moraitis dissolves in a high-romantic ritual of ecstasy and pain, and emerges as the eternal man, with the sun in his eyes and the sky between his bones. What occurs to 'Moraitis' here is a description of Theodora's own psychic process. Through a mystical participation with the cellist and his artistry she has achieved an eternal dimension.

When Theodora returns to Mrs Goodman, the mother discovers that she cannot upset or brutalize her daughter in her usual manner:

Mrs Goodman would have said something hard and destructive, only she saw that Theodora was now strong, and for this reason she did not dare. Theodora was removed. She had the strength of absence, Mrs Goodman saw. (p. 112)

Theodora has been psychologically destroyed by her experience, and is now beyond the grasp of the negative mother. Or in other words: the archetypal matrix cannot devour what has already returned to it. Theodora is no longer an ego, and no longer torturable. And so she enjoys once again the perfection and paradisal contentment of the uroboric state:

the absence of Theodora persisted, and in the morning. Many mornings trumpeted across the bay their strong hibiscus notes. The mornings smelled of nasturtium, crushed by the bodies of lovers on a piece of wasteland at night ... And the music which Moraitis had played was more tactile than the hot words of lovers ... the violins had arms. This thing which had happened between Moraitis and herself she held close, like a woman holding her belly ... [H]er contentment filled the morning, the heavy, round, golden morning, sounding its red hibiscus note. She had waited sometimes for something to happen. Now existence justified itself. (p. 112)

More vividly: now existence obliterates itself. In White the incestuous experience is always regarded as the consummation of self, instead of its extinction. What is consummated is the nihilistic desire, which is confused, especially at the end of the novel, with the mandalic experience of wholeness. Here too we find the characteristic circular images: of sun, and flower, and earth. The uroboros resembles the mandala in many ways. But it is the primal circle, the empty void prior to creation, which requires the disintegration of life for its recovery.

Theodora's state of 'absence' does not persist. In time she assumes her egoic state and returns to human existence. And at once she is possessed by a self-destructive longing. At the Agricultural Show in Sydney we find her quite beside herself at a shooting gallery, intent on destroying the bobbing clay ducks with the same demonic enthusiasm which had impelled her to destroy the little hawk at Meroë:

> Theodora took the rifle, closing her eyes to the glare. She stood already in the canvas landscape against which the ducks jerked, her canvas arms animated by some emotion that was scarcely hers. Because the canvas moments will come to life of their own accord, whether it is watching the water flow beneath a bridge, or listening to hands strike music out of wood ... She took aim, and the dead, white, discarded moment fell shattered, the duck bobbed headless.
> [S]he remembered ... the swift moment of the hawk, when her eye had not quivered. It is curious, she felt, and now, that my flesh does not flap. (pp. 119–20)

The desire for disintegration is 'scarcely hers' and emerges 'of [its] own accord', which is to say that it arises from the unconscious and forces her to enact its will. We are concerned with a fully autonomous complex which has the capacity to direct her behaviour. In executing its demands Theodora feels only exaltation and a surge of power. She is habitually blind to the destructive aspect, although her friends watching her activity are disturbed. '[E]ach time Theodora fired, ... a secret life was shattered. It was something mysterious, shameful, and grotesque. What can we say now? they felt' (p. 119).

When she encounters her mother, however, the full force of her destructive pattern is made manifest. As ever, the mother reflects and highlights the pathology of her own complex.

> 'Did you enjoy yourself?' asked Mrs Goodman, half in fear.
> 'Yes,' said Theodora. 'I had a mild success at a shooting range.'
> Mrs Goodman turned her face, as if she were hiding a scar, and her breath some quick stab. She hated her daughter painfully. She hated her feet, which

had always seemed to move over the earth without touching ...

'In front of all those people?' Mrs Goodman said.

'Why ever not? They applauded me,' said Theodora dryly. 'I won a kewpie in a feather skirt.' ...

'You must have looked a sight,' said Mrs Goodman, 'carrying a vulgar doll through the crowd.'

In her hate she would have hewn down this great wooden idol with the grotesque doll in its arms. (pp. 120–1)

The nihilistic ego views its activity as a 'mild success', a further movement toward the eternal realm; but in another sense it is an obscene display of anti-social, inhuman and self-destructive behaviour. Mrs Goodman provides the missing perspective, forcing the central character to see what is overlooked in her craving for dissolution. Theodora is moved to protest against her mother's response, and in the ensuing dialogue arrives at what is perhaps one of the most crucial moments of self-reflection in White's fiction:

'Mother, must you destroy?'

'Destroy?' asked Mrs Goodman.

'Yes,' said Theodora. 'I believe you were born with an axe in your hand.'

'I do not understand what you mean. Axes? I have sat here all the afternoon. I am suffering from heartburn.'

At night Theodora Goodman would bring her mother cups of hot milk, which she drank with little soft complaining noises, and the milk skin hung from her lower lip. She was old and soft. Then it is I, said Theodora, I have a core of evil in me that is altogether hateful. But she could not overcome her repugnance for the skin that swung from her mother's lip, giving her the appearance of an old white goat. (p. 121)

Here the highly-charged image is simply not fitting to the reality of the old, ailing woman with dyspepsia. The projection 'bounces back', as it were, so that Theodora is forced to admit the possibility of a 'core of evil' within herself. Although this is an important reflection, the knowledge is not properly integrated. If it did represent a psychological breakthrough she would not have to keep fighting her demonic impulse in external projections. Even here her 'repugnance' is the same as before, and the mother is still imagined as 'an old white goat', i.e. an image of the devil.

That Theodora should subsequently envisage murdering her mother is itself alarming evidence of the persistence of the projection. In the grey light of early morning Theodora gazes upon the sleeping figure of Mrs Goodman and is filled with an overwhelming nausea and resentment. As she stoops above the mother's bed 'her own breath was choking and knotting inside her' (p. 122), which points once more to the suffocation experienced by the ego in the archetypal mother–bond. As she takes up the little silver paper-knife she wonders whether slaying the mother might 'cut the knot' (p. 123) that binds her. After carefully weighing up the pros and cons, Theodora decides against actual matricide:

> She threw back the thin knife, which fell and clattered on the zinc . . . It has been close, felt Theodora, I have put out my hand and almost touched death. She could see its eyelashes, pale as a goat's, and the tongue clapping like a bell . . . She went on to her own room, away from the act she had not committed, while her mother continued to sleep. (p. 123)

Theodora has confused mythic with literal levels of reality. It is right that she should want to destroy the dragon–mother, to free herself from its repulsive embrace, yet the dragon to be slain is within herself, in her own longing for disintegration. She cannot kill it for that would mean conquering what she values most, the backward-striving movement of her own psyche.

The internal link between her inmost longing and the image of the devouring mother is discovered in certain crucial juxtapositions within the structure of the narrative:

> Sometimes, and tonight, Theodora went and sat beneath the apricot tree. She took a book that she would not read. She marked her page with a dock and sat. And as she sat, there seemed to be no beginning or end. Meroë was eternity, and she was the keeper of it.
>
> Before Mother broke in, 'Theodora, Theodora, where is my little silver paper-knife?'
>
> Mother's voice made the hot air quiver. (p. 79)

> At this point, Theodora sometimes said, I should begin to read Gibbon, or find religion, instead of speaking to myself in my own room. But words, whether written or spoken, were at most frail slat bridges over chasms, and Mrs Goodman had never encouraged religion, as she herself was God. So it will not be by these means, Theodora said, that the great monster Self will be destroyed, and that desirable state achieved, which resembles, one would imagine, nothing more than air or water. She did not doubt that the years would contribute, rubbing and extracting, but never enough. Her body still clanged and rang when the voice struck.
>
> 'Theo–*dor*–a!'
>
> I have not the humility, Theodora said. (p. 128)

In both sections the demanding and abrasive voice of the mother follows hard upon Theodora's longing for self-dissolution. In the first, we find Theodora preparing to merge into an uroboric eternity, with 'no beginning or end', when suddenly the mother's voice shatters the vision of paradise. Then we find her musing about how best she might annihilate her personality, the 'great monster Self', when once again the voice interrupts her pursuit of ecstasy and forces her to attend to its demands. Although she feels she is surrendering herself to the matrix, she is actually being 'seized' by the mother–image and devoured by a hostile force. The regressive longing for dissolution is—in the symbolic language of the inner world—a submission to the witch-like power of the unconscious, a giving in to its demands.

When Theodora discovers one morning that her mother has died she can barely contain her excitement: 'She did not cry. On the contrary, she ran downstairs, so fast that she was afraid her body might hurtle ahead' (p. 129). However, the continuing power of the mother archetype is suggested in a remarkable detail as Theodora views the mother's corpse. Mrs Goodman 'had died without her teeth', and these sit grinning ironically at the daughter 'in a glass beside the bed'. They are suspended there 'in an endless china smile' (p. 129). The teeth of the Mother Goddess have long symbolized the devouring, ravaging aspect of the archetype. In some recent studies this figure is designated the Teeth Mother because she is characterized by enormous fangs, with which she dismembers those who stray within her realm. Often the teeth are imaged inside the vaginal cavity, where, as *vagina dentata*, they suggest the potentially castrating aspect of the maternal source.[14] Thus we find, in the survival of old Mrs Goodman's teeth, a stark image of the mother's destroying aspect which lives on after the mother herself has perished. In fact we could say that her death has merely refined her nature, revealing her devouring quality in its chilling, impersonal aspect. Moreover the teeth are caught in an 'endless smile', as if the figure were mocking her, and saying: you have not got rid of me yet. The image is eternal because she lives, trochilus-like, inside the jaws of the dragon.

III

Theodora is inspired by her apparent release and believes that she can now embark upon her own spiritual journey. But the freedom before her is of dubious value. What little identity she formerly had was tied up in her relation to Mrs Goodman, and without that relationship she can no longer recognize herself: 'Since her mother's death she could not say with conviction: I am I' (p. 13). Her actions appear automatic, and as an onlooker she watches her own deeds:

Theodora went into the room where the coffin lay. She moved one hairbrush three inches to the left, and smoothed the anti-macassar on a little Empire prie-dieu that her mother had brought from Europe. She did all this with some surprise, as if divorced from her own hands, as if they were related to the objects beneath them only in the way that two flies, blowing and blundering in space, are related to a china and mahogany world. (p. 11)

The world outside her too is alien and unreal: 'She was part of a surprising world in which hands, for reasons no longer obvious, had put tables and chairs' (p. 132). Chronic alienation has set in.

Depth psychology warns of the consequences of this *abaissement du niveau mental*.[15] The libido, lost to consciousness, inevitably sinks into the lower realm, activating the imaginal world. In the next phase of Theodora's career there is a tremendous welling-up of spontaneous and unconscious fantasy. Her experiences in the French Riviera suggest that her world is now more psychic than real, that the unconscious has seized control and forces her to live in a perpetual nightmare. Wherever she turns in the Hôtel du Midi she finds evidence of the Teeth Mother, her own activated archetype: in the yawning mouths of roses (p. 139), in the spiky cactus which pricks her flesh and draws blood (p. 140), in the snapping jaws of the hotel guests sucking the last shreds from a chicken bone (p. 137). The world is full of crushing and devouring shapes, all reflecting her own near-extinction in the matrix. This is most apparent in connection with the *jardin exotique*, which appears as a monstrous force bent on destruction:

Somewhere at the back, unsuspected ... fantastic forms were aping the gestures of tree and flower. Theodora listened to the silence, to hear it sawn at by the teeth of the *jardin exotique*. (p. 136)

Now she saw it was, in fact, the garden that prevailed, its forms had swelled and multiplied, its dry, paper hands were pressed against the windows of the *salle à manger*, perhaps it had already started to digest the body of the somnolent hotel. (p. 161)

Theodora had selected this hotel above any other because she had hoped that the *jardin*, portrayed as an alluring paradise in the tourist brochure, would be 'the goal of a journey' (p. 139). She was expecting to find the mythic Garden, the image of satiety and rest. It is not surprising that she should find instead this inhospitable place: every attempt to recover the First Paradise results in misfortune, because that dream is not in the province of humanity but belongs to an archaic past. In Blakean terms it is a regressive way which leads merely to demons at the Gates of Eden. The true spiritual path, according to Blake and other writers of the visionary tradition, must accept consciousness and creation, and work toward a Second Paradise discovered in and through human existence. The way back, if pursued as a release from life and as mere abandonment, leads to the whirlpool, or the devouring serpent.[16] And here the *jardin* is an absorptive, gulping force which 'digests' what has returned to it (cf. Figure 2).

Theodora's activated unconscious reaches into the perceived world and converts everything into an archetypal drama. The people she encounters are dream-like, acting more as fantasy figures than as real persons. This fact has not always been understood or appreciated. We have heard often enough that Theodora 'enters imaginatively into the lives of the Hôtel residents', and critics have commonly applauded her capacity to do so. But from a psychological standpoint it would seem less praiseworthy than inevitable. The reality is that Theodora cannot know the world in any other than a mythological way, because unconscious images control her experience. The critics appear unable to differentiate between a life of enriched imagination, and an involuntary inundation of fantasy. As a result there has been a denial of her pathological condition, and Theodora's actions have been viewed in a purely spiritual or poetic context.

One of the more compelling of Theodora's *jardin exotique* fantasies involves her experience of an earthquake with Katina Pavlou. Theodora's imagination is excited when the Greek girl runs into the garden and announces that she must 'get away ... from all this', and 'go home' (p. 141). Life in the world, and her own emergence into adolescence, is 'suffocating' her (p. 144), and she longs 'to recover the lost reality of childhood' (p. 251). This paradise-seeking girl is hotly pursued into the garden by a 'teeth-sucking' (p. 141) square woman, Miss Grigg, her surrogate mother. Grigg complains that the girl is ungrateful, and insists that she would be happier if she followed her own example and ate heartier meals. '"There's nothing like food"' Grigg chants, and we are never certain that this munching, insatiable Venus does not intend to make a meal out of the delicate Katina. But the situation is a reflection of Theodora's inner world and this initiates an imaginative participation: 'she had become a mirror held to the girl's experience. [They] were like two distant, unrelated lives mingling for a moment in sleep' (p. 142). As Katina asks her guardian if she recalls 'a black island that shook' during their experience of an earthquake in the Greek Islands, Theodora enters another world:

Theodora trembled for the black island. She looked across at the opposite shore, which was just there, in the sea glaze. The earth was a capsule waiting for some gigantic event to swallow it down. Theodora looked at the island and waited for it to move. (p. 142)

The earthquake has been transformed into a metaphor of her own psychic upheaval. The island appears as an image of her personality, tiny and vulnerable, surrounded on every side by threatening waters. The earth makes itself ready for 'some gigantic event to swallow it down', just as Theodora and the girl 'held hands, waiting for a cataclysm of earth and sea' (p. 143). There is a strong sense of anticipation throughout, and also an erotic delight in what is about to take place. There is mention of their own 'nakedness', and of 'their hearts beating openly and together' upon the body of the earth. A sexual element is always present as the personality is drawn back into the engulfing matrix. The sequence concludes with an excited account of the devastation:

The morning light saw the drawers fly out of the chest. Its tongues lolled. The whole cardboard house rejected reason. Then there was a running. They were calling on the stairs ...
'Come,' they called. 'Run. It is the will of God. The earth is going to split open and swallow the houses of the poor.' ...
They were thrown out, all of them, out of the functionless houses on to the little strip of sand. Their bodies lay on the live earth. They could feel its heart move against their own. (p. 144)

The subterranean force readily destroys the human world, which appears frail and insubstantial. Its structures are 'cardboard' and 'functionless' in the wake of the disaster. But the ego enjoys its disintegration, is excited by the primal force which wrenches it out of context and deposits it, exhausted and helpless, upon the reeling earth. At the end of the fantasy Theodora feels strangely satisfied, in a way which is reminiscent of the contentment experienced after the Moraitis concerto. And just as the mother could not harm her after that earlier dissolution, so here the *jardin exotique* has lost its destructive character: 'To Theodora, who continued to sit in the garden, ... the air was no longer altogether dry and hostile. It stroked her' (p. 145). The jaws of the *jardin* no longer threaten her, for she has already been dissolved. It is only while the ego maintains a semblance of identity that the devouring aspect of the matrix is present and actual.

At this point the *jardin* acquires a personified tone and a dream–voice: '[the garden] stroked her. It said: See, we offer this dispensation, endless, more seductive than aspirin, to give an illusion of fleshy nearness and comfort, in what should be apart, armed, twisted' (p. 145). This is a remarkable statement, which summarizes what I have been trying to elucidate about the paradoxical nature of the entry into the matrix. This movement 'gives an illusion of fleshy nearness and comfort' in 'what should be ... [an] armed, twisted' nightmare of disintegration. The *jardin* has emerged in its seductive autonomy during this interlude.[17] It is the 'illusion of comfort' which entices the personality again and again into the womb-like state. This passage is an enigmatic self-revelation of unconscious processes, but yet again there is no reflecting ego which might benefit from what is revealed. As with the image of the trochilus and the crocodile, it is as if the complex is putting itself on display, willing to yield its secrets and expose its hidden life, but the fantasy material is not received or integrated by the individual consciousness.[18] Everything remains in its original state, the ego in its bewitchment, the complex in its superior position. Hence, 'The garden gave up no secrets, if it had secrets to give' (p. 231).

There is a long fantasy sequence, relating to the image of the nautilus shell, which appears to have a similarly heuristic intent. The nautilus, which is reflected as an object of perfection and which is said to contain a wondrous, seductive music, is clearly an image suggestive of the uroboros (see Figure 3). Katina immediately responds to the shell as a symbol of her own ideal state:

'It is lovely, it is lovely, may I look?' asked the girl, rejecting the square woman and the remains of her lunch ...
The girl took in her hands the frail shell. She listened to its sound. She listened to the thick-throated pines fill the room, their clear blue-green water, rising and falling. The music of the nautilus was in her face ... (p. 155)

This is a mana-charged object which sings of blue-green seas and an enchanting beyond. A central question at the Hôtel du Midi is: to whom does the nautilus rightly belong? Does it belong to the devastating Mrs Rapallo, American adventuress, who has purchased the shell from a nearby antique store and who now parades it proudly through the *salle à manger*? Or does it belong to the fatherly Sokolnikov, who has sentimental claims upon it, arguing that he has studied the nautilus for years through the store window and has a more subtle right to ownership? This is a controversy in which Theodora becomes involved, and the fantasy content of the situation is immediately apparent. Since childhood Theodora has believed that her ultimate goal related to Father's world, that Meroë, the soughing pines, the image of eternity were all 'His'. We have seen, however, that although the positive image of Nature bore a masculine aspect it was nevertheless under the Mother's sway. This attention upon what is felt to be 'Father's' is a delusory system which prevents her from seeing the appalling truth: that what she seeks is part of the

Figure 3   The nautilus shell (modern pencil drawing; one-fifth of actual size)
Source: R. Bly, *This Body is Made of Camphor and Gopherwood*, Harper & Row, New York, 1977, frontispiece

In *The Aunt's Story* the nautilus shell is an important symbol of otherworldly perfection and childlike unconsciousness. It is the prized possession of Mrs Rapallo, the bizarre, fearsome maternal figure in the *Jardin Exotique*. Theodora tries to steal this symbolic treasure from its dream-like abode, only to find that it does not stand the test of human reality. One can see here how the spiralic chambers of the nautilus suggest the form of the tail-biting uroboros represented in Figure 1.

Mother's realm and cannot be separated from her destructive character. The psyche attempts to show the dark and matriarchal context of her desired state. The nautilus, that is to say, which sings of other realms and has such enchanting appeal, is a Siren-like call to disintegration.

Mrs Rapallo's entrance into Theodora's vision is fittingly bizarre, for we have to do with a mythological figure of her imagination:

Mrs Rapallo, whom time and history had failed to trip ... continued to advance. Her pomp was the pomp of cathedrals and of circuses. She was put together painfully, rashly, ritually, crimson over purple. Her eye glittered, but her breath was grey. Under her great hat, on which a bird had settled years before, spreading its meteoric tail in a landscape of pansies, mignonette, butterflies, and shells, her face shrieked with the inspired clowns, peered through the branches of mascara at objects she could not see, and sniffed through thin nostrils at many original smells ... Her stiff magenta picked contemptuously at the fluff on the *salle à manger* carpet ... But most marvellous was the nautilus that she half carried in her left hand, half supported on her encrusted bosom. Moored, the shell floated, you might say, in its own opalescent right. (pp. 154–5)

She is a true denizen of the underworld, a fabulous creature 'put together painfully, rashly, ritually'. She is reminiscent of a mythical dragon, weirdly colourful, formidably powerful, displaying its prized possession as it parades before the bewildered onlookers. In periods of psychosis imaginal figures often possess this astonishing demeanour, since libido has sunk down into and vivified the contents of the unconscious. Whereas Theodora is pallid and frail, the imaginal beast, as it were, is possessed of strength. It is fascinating that as soon as she enters the room General Sokolnikov begins to cough and splutter, his lungs so constrained that the walls of the hotel appear to 'swell ... and flap back' with the wheezing. We have a repeat performance of the childhood conflict between mother and father images, only here everything appears in a surrealistic light because of the activated condition of the unconscious.

The perfect round is carried by the mother, and its situation upon her 'encrusted bosom' distinguishes its intimate and erotic connection to her being. The outraged General announces that the shell is rightfully his ('"it is mine from staring at, for many years"' p. 156), and accuses her of being 'a cheeky thief' and 'a murderess': '"A tender, a subtle relationship has existed, which now in an instant you destroy"'. The father–image believes it has suddenly been deposed, but it never had the treasure in the first place. Or rather, as the General's situation aptly suggests, it had nostalgic claims upon it, but never actual dominion. The General concocts a scheme whereby he imagines he will win back the nautilus, only Theodora herself has to perform the dirty deed. She must steal into Mrs Rapallo's room while she is sleeping and liberate the nautilus from her possession.

When Theodora first enters Mrs Rapallo's *boudoir* she discovers that the nautilus is surrounded by a thick tangle of ferns, and watched over by the inevitable grinning teeth: 'Old teeth in an empty jam-jar grinned at her helplessness. She heard the snigger of the tremulous fern' (p. 191). It is clear what Freudians would think of the tangle of ferns and the snapping teeth which guard the object of desire. The fearful moment in regression, they argue, is the encounter with the mother's genitals, often imaged in dreams as a castrating maw. But while admitting to the sexual aspect we are better advised to regard it as part of a larger pattern of symbolism. The sniggering fern and chattering teeth are as much Blakean demons at the Gates, mocking the ego's attempt to recover the First Paradise. A further demon encountered on the way is the pet monkey, Mignon, asleep at the head of Mrs

Rapallo's bed (and mistaken at first for her tangled hair) until it is awakened by the intruder and stirred to life. It alights upon Theodora's head, blocking her vision and clinging with a 'furred, clammy' grip (p. 212). As she enters the matrix, all manner of primitive forces are released to ensnare her. At the last moment these forces manifest as sudden lethargy, and Theodora can barely manage to make her way to the shell.

> I have come here, she said, for the nautilus.
> Though now she had begun to doubt whether she could reach. Whether the pampas of the darkness would allow, and its great clouds of grass, heavy as breath, that she parted with her ineffectual hands. She also doubted whether the nautilus was substance enough, or whether it would blow. (p. 211)

Again there is the sexual element, with the clouds of grass, heavy as breath, which she parts in order to reach the ecstatic image. Theodora rightly suspects that once taken into her hands the uroboric symbol might 'blow', disintegrate. It has a pristine beauty that cannot be connected with reality in the easy way that the ego would like. Elyot discovered this at Ard's Bay, when the circular pebbles picked up out of pools lost their splendour once brought into the world. The way toward integration is a tedious process that involves a life-long relationship between human and eternal worlds. When this occurs the beatific vision itself passes through a course of development, from the preworldly uroboros to the greater unity of the mandala, which encompasses eternal and temporal realms. But this can never take place while the individual is bound to childhood and the mother–complex, for then there is no ego to integrate the divine, but merely a longing to be obliterated by it.

As the General gloats over the stolen shell, Mrs Rapallo appears to reclaim the object. She stands before them in a frightful guise, 'hairless', without cosmetics, and adorned in 'solemn rags' (p. 214). She is a veritable witch from the underworld, determined to spoil what has been taken from her. A battle ensues between the General and the 'swashbuckling' Mrs Rapallo, during which the nautilus is smashed. Although both figures lose possession of the shell it is the General who is most ruined by its loss. '"A murder has been committed"' screams the hysterical Sokolnikov, whose rage later turns to self-pity and despair. After this point there is no further claim made upon the uroboric symbol by the father–figure. His part in Theodora's psychic world has been played out, and more and more the mother is revealed as the central object and focus of her life.

IV

Toward the end of the *Jardin Exotique* section, Theodora's longing for disintegration becomes extreme. The movement in which she is caught cannot be interrupted, but will lead her right into the abysmal depths of the maternal source. The quickened pace of the regression is evident in the rapid succession of fugues and fantasies, the collapsing of one episode into another, the hallucinated atmosphere in which her every activity takes place. As she is drawn into chaos there is the usual compliance with what has seized control: 'she knew she did not really control her bones, and that the curtain of her flesh must blow, like walls which are no longer walls' (p. 196). There is an excited anticipation of 'some act still to be performed' (p. 231). At the same time, however, the destructive force is resisted in its various projected forms. Lieselotte, for instance, is despised because of her delight in devastation, her cruel antics toward Wetherby, her reckless smashing of a glass pagoda. Yet Lieselotte's credo reflects Theodora's own nihilistic passion:

> 'Oh, but I am right,' said Lieselotte. 'We have destroyed so much, but we have not destroyed enough. We must destroy everything, everything, even ourselves. Then at last when there is nothing, perhaps we shall live.' (p. 168)

The complex is never recognized in its naked form, and as the psyche continues to create further externalizations Theodora continues to react against them, thus defeating their heuristic function. In fantasy she meets Anna Stepanovna, a formidable figure who murders a relative to secure a fortune, the notorious Varvara, 'whose first blow would leave the imprint of true suffering' (p. 170), and Muriel Leese-Leese, a *femme fatale* with an insatiable lust for violence and power. All of these are reflections of her ruling complex, yet they are withdrawn from as external atrocities.

That she is about to be absorbed into the matrix is emphasized by the 'devouring roses' which are constellated at this point. The roses in the *jardin*, plastic flowers in the hallway, wallpaper roses in the bedroom, all become aggressively activated and appear to 'wet their lips' (p. 196), make fierce sucking noises, and open and close like demonic vaginas. 'She could not escape too soon from the closed room, retreating from the jaws of roses, ... the teeth bristled to consume the last shreds of personality' (pp. 138–9). The toothed rose is an almost perfect image of the uroboric matrix, more appropriate perhaps than the yawning jaws of the crocodile, which reflected only its destructive aspect. The uroboros is a paradoxical reality, a fragrant rose and a gnashing

maw, where delight and pain are felt together. The rose connects
with old Mrs Goodman, who was associated with roses and
whose first act of sovereignty at Meroë was to establish a rose
garden: 'She said from her sofa, let there be roses, and there
were ...' (p. 21). In early childhood Theodora was imaged as an
embryo at the centre of a rose, or would feel herself bathed in
roselight, so that 'the roses drowsed and drifted under her skin'
(p. 21). She is returning to that former splendour, but the way
back is necessarily through the jaws of paradise.

In this heightened emotional state Theodora hears the crash of
glass the other side of the wall, as Lieselotte throws a lantern at
Wetherby, and within minutes the hotel is ablaze. The holocaust
represents a final eruption of destructive forces, and links us
symbolically with Abyssinia, the black land which 'had once run
with fire' (p. 26), and with Mother's devastating power, her
'consuming fire' (p. 26). As the fire rages through the hotel, its
'fierce mouths' yawning into chaos, Theodora is not frightened
but rather is transfixed by the blaze, drawn into its beauty. As
Lieselotte stands before her, already injured by the fire and at the
brink of death, Theodora can only admire the aesthetics of her
disintegration: 'How beautiful she is now, Theodora saw. As if
some terror has melted wax. Fear flowed in Lieselotte's transparent face. Her gestures and her hair streamed' (p. 246).

There is a grotesque delight in violence, for in this state forms
'flow', bodies 'melt', in a kind of ecstatic incestuous frenzy.
Significantly, Theodora's only desire at this moment is to recover
her mother's garnet ring, rescue it from the burning dresser, and
place it upon her finger.

> She watched the revival of roses, how they glowed, glowing and blowing like
> great clusters of garnets on the live hedge... She was filled with a solid
> purpose. Her handkerchief sachet must be reached ...
> 'There is a garnet ring,' she said, 'that was left me by my mother.'
> She took in her hand the smooth cool stone. ...
> Theodora Goodman put the garnet ring on its usual finger, below the joint
> which showed signs of stiffening with arthritis. It was rather an ugly little
> ring, but part of the flesh. In the presence of the secret, leaping emotions of
> the fire she was glad to have her garnet. (pp. 246–7)

This is the climactic scene of the novel, where Theodora, at the
centre of the consuming blaze and its 'secret, leaping emotions',
takes the mother's ring and effectively becomes one with her in a
ritual marriage. The ring celebrating this union is 'ugly', for as a
symbol of incest it must be ugly, violating as it does psychological taboos and signifying union with a demonic archetypal
figure. In terms of White's intra-psychic reality, an abomination

has been committed, an ugly marriage with the mythical dragon. The ring is now 'part of the flesh', which emphasizes the binding character of this *coniunctio*.[19] Theodora becomes a replica of her mother, a kind of Abyssinian Queen surrounded by the characteristic symbols of fire, garnet, and burning roses. Even the signs of arthritis in the finger reflect her mother, indicating that the archetype has indeed become 'part of the flesh' and incorporated into her character.

It is fascinating that as soon as Theodora assumes this archetypal stature the externalized forms of the negative mother are abolished. Not merely Lieselotte but Mrs Rapallo too is consumed in a burst of Abyssinian fire:

> The window had become quite encrusted with fire. It had a considerable, stiff jewelled splendour of its own, that ignored the elaborate ritual of the flames. Everything else, the whole night, was subsidiary to this ritual of fire ...
>
> But it was obvious that Mrs Rapallo was gratified by such magnificence. From the window she contemplated, only vaguely, the vague evidence of faces. Fire is fiercer. Fire is more triumphant. Then, she turned and withdrew, and there was the windowful of smoke, and Mignon pressing her hands on hot glass. (pp. 248–9)

Mrs Rapallo's fantasy life is over, for Theodora has herself become the incarnation of the maternal image. When the ego is annihilated, and the archetype seizes control, the mother can disappear in a blaze of glory for her destructive mission is complete. Her longevity is assured in Theodora herself, hence she turns 'gratified' into her Abyssinian flames. The simultaneous deaths of Lieselotte and Mrs Rapallo indicate that a long era of suffering has come to an end. It is as if Theodora has moved through and beyond the snapping jaws, through the flaming sword that surrounds the First Paradise (Genesis 3:24), and now inhabits an eternal dream–state outside human boundaries. In this condition there is no longer a human personality as such to be hounded or maligned. If, then, the demonic mother is absent in Part Three this is not, as critics have claimed, because Theodora 'has at last come to terms with her mother' and achieved a fully individuated selfhood.[20] The reverse is true: she fails so utterly in individuation that the archetype replaces personality and she is drawn into a prenatal condition inside the maternal source. The demonism disappears because she is so far regressed.[21]

As the fire dies down Theodora is filled with an 'immeasurable longing' (p. 252) for her native Australian landscape and the scenes of childhood. But when Katina enquires of her plans she simply says she will 'return to Abyssinia'. It is clear that the uroboric world has completely eclipsed Father's Meroë as her place of origin and belonging. But she hardly has to long any more for this other world; she is already there. All that remains is for her to leave civilized France and move to a country where she can celebrate more fully her at-one-ment with primal Nature.

V

Her return to Australia, the 'country of the bones', is made via the Atlantic and the United States. As she travels by train through mid-west America Theodora is intoxicated by the towering corn-fields and the forces of Nature sensed all around her:

> All through the middle of America there was a trumpeting of corn. Its full, yellow, tremendous notes pressed close to the swelling sky. There were whole acres of time in which the yellow corn blared as if for a judgement. It had taken up and swallowed all other themes, whether belting iron, or subtler, insinuating steel, or the frail human reed. (p. 255)

The earth blasts its powerful corn–song across the sky, just as, after the Moraitis concerto, Theodora had enjoyed the 'trumpeting of red hibiscus notes . . . across the bay' (p. 112). It hardly matters whether she is in Kansas or New South Wales, for Nature is the same archetypal force wherever she happens to be. In both situations Nature is enlivened by her psychological disintegration, or, in other words, it is vivified by the life which sinks into its matrix. Theodora, too, continues to experience her own defeat as fulfilment. The food-loving Earth Mother is happy to make a meal out of her, and she is equally happy to be consumed. The savagery of the maternal source is no longer felt or recognized, even though it digests 'belting iron' and 'insinuating steel', in addition to 'the frail human reed'.

At an unnamed station in the south-west of America Theodora abandons her train, and her plans to return to Australia, and walks off into the beckoning landscape of Mother Nature. She has found her Abyssinia. Her assimilation to the earth is experienced as a pleasurable fullness, since through disintegration of boundaries she has 'become' the cosmos:

> The emptiness of this landscape was a fullness, of pink earth, and chalk-blue for sky. And the rim of the world was white. It burned. . . .
> Theodora could smell the dust. She could smell the expanding odour of her own body, which was no longer the sour, mean smell of the human body in enclosed spaces, but the unashamed flesh on which dust and sun have lain. She walked. She smiled for this discovery of freedom.
> In her hand she still held, she realized, the practical handbag . . . There

were also, she saw, the strips and sheaves of tickets, railroad and steamship, which Theodora Goodman had bought in New York for the purpose of prolonging herself through many fresh phases of what was accepted as Theodora Goodman. Now she took these and tore them into small pieces which fell frivolously at the side of the road. (pp. 262–3)

In discussing the kinds of conditions that arise when the ego dissolves in the unconscious, Jung says that one of the most common is 'psychic inflation': an expansion of personality into the cosmos, a swelling to superhuman proportions, a 'feeling of godlikeness'.[22] Having abandoned the human frame, Theodora now looks to the eternal realm for her identity. She feels at one with the pastel skies and painted deserts, and things human seem small and mean. Later in the Johnsons' house, she is nauseated by the solid and static objects in the room, the marble clock, the framed photographs, the furniture (p. 271f). Her 'flowing corn song' (p. 259) is preworldly and cannot include the realities of time and form. The uroboric 'unity' is bogus, for it sharply divides human and archetypal worlds.

Theodora lacks the necessary perspective to see the pathology of her situation, and the pretentiousness of her cosmic role. She feels only the intoxication of the inflated state. Nor can the author coax her into self-knowledge, since he too is identified with the matrix and intent on idealizing it as the ultimate goal. As Theodora moves toward greater dissolution, White comments: 'This way perhaps she came a little closer to humility, to anonymity, to pureness of being' (p. 269). This is characteristic of White's philosophical outlook which expresses the standpoint of the mother–complex. As Hillman has written, 'metaphysical ideas are hardly independent of their complex roots; [they] can be foci of sickness, part of an archetypal syndrome'.[23] Of course the complex finds greatest fulfilment once its destructive pattern is established as a religious truth, its anarchic code adopted as a religious necessity. Inflation leads not only to a distorted understanding of self but to an 'inflated' view of the regression. The reading which sees self-annihilation as nirvana is itself part of the syndrome, and not, as I had felt originally, White's deliberate falsification.[24] Just as the *jardin exotique* offered an 'illusion of comfort' to mask the reality of disintegration, so the complex provides an 'illusion of enlightenment' to obscure the final psychosis and make egoic death seem triumphant.

The bringer of glad tidings is Holstius, himself an illusion of Theodora's imagination. Since reality has been obliterated, his substancelessness is not in itself an issue. All that matters is his

ability to smooth away doubts and make Theodora feel comfortable in her madness. Holstius is an instrument of the Earth
Mother, and his connection to her is immediately apparent.
He arrives triumphantly in the spring, as do all the matriarchal
gods and deities of Western antiquity. And like Attis or Adonis he
appears as a personification of the vegetative life of Nature.[25]
Theodora discovers him in a forest setting, when, looking into the
distance, she notices what at first seems like a 'walking tree'
(p. 279). This in time becomes Holstius, whose very name
(German: *holz*) suggests wood or tree. Holstius is an earth–spirit
whose task is to lead Theodora into complete identification with
maternal Nature. She fittingly regards this figure as a messiah,
and as she kneels down before him his healing hands appear to
'soothe the wounds' (p. 278). And in a sense he does soothe the
wounds, making her once and for all a creature of the elements,
no longer balanced agonizingly between human and archetypal
realms.

Perhaps most ecstatic is the feeling of oneness that arises as he
draws her into the matrix, where all forms are dissolved into an
oceanic unity:

In the peace that Holstius spread throughout her body and the speckled shade
of surrounding trees, there was no end to the lives of Theodora Goodman.
These met and parted, met and parted, movingly. They entered into each
other, so that the impulse for music in Katina Pavlou's hands, and the steamy
exasperation of Sokolnikov, and Mrs Rapallo's baroque and narcoticized
despair were the same and understandable. And in the same way that the
created lives of Theodora Goodman were interchangeable, the lives into
which she had entered, making them momently dependent for love or hate
... whether George or Julia Goodman, only apparently deceased, or Huntly
Clarkson, or Moraitis, or Lou, or Zack, these were the lives of Theodora
Goodman, these too. (p. 284)

Critics have referred to this passage as evidence of Theodora's
achievement of integration. This is the reading that the complex
itself would invite, the Mother's source as mandala, dissolution
as enlightenment. But as I see her, rather than a mystic at the
peak of self-realization, Theodora is more a disintegrated fragment in the primal realm of Nature. The regressed and the
advanced stages of consciousness are similar in their focus upon
unity; but the differences must be emphasized. In the infantile
state things are in chaotic flux, a 'unity' merely because forms
have merged into a collective sea. Sokolnikov, Mrs Rapallo,
Katina appear as so much froth and bubble, their lives 'interchangeable' in this amorphous eternity. In the mandalic state

forms are united but not obliterated; they maintain integrity in the face of the divine, which is why mandala images possess such complex and sensuous design. The difference is that between a unity which is affirmative, permitting an interpenetration of eternity and time, and one which is subversive, drawing everything into the void. The early state lacks a conscious self which is capable of differentiation, hence its unity is characteristically narcissistic ('these were the lives of Theodora Goodman, these too'). To move toward greater wholeness Theodora would first have to come out of her childhood world and realize that there is an objective reality outside the self and the projection-making psyche. What she requires is not increased fluidity, which she has always had in abundance, but an increased respect for the created world and for the uniqueness of people and things. Holstius provides nothing new, but merely sanctifies her solipsism by allowing it to pass as cosmic consciousness.

Holstius uses words and phrases that make us believe that she is within reach of a higher unity. He speaks in a quasi-Jungian way about 'the two irreconcilable halves' ('joy and sorrow', 'flesh and marble', 'illusion and reality'), and urges Theodora to 'accept' both 'halves'. He is a trickster who constructs in language a model of wholeness which has nothing to do with Theodora's actual situation. He communicates a few esoteric truths about the nature of reality (p. 284), and imagines that through these utterances she has become enlightened. '"So you understand?"' asks Holstius, the master of illusion. '"Yes," said Theodora Goodman. "I understand"'. 'She had worked it out, mathematically, in stones, spread on the ground at the toes of her long shoes' (p. 284). Holstius warns that society will regard her present state as madness, but she is 'not to be taken in by this'. Society itself, he indicates, is fundamentally insane, and her own condition genuine lucidity. He firmly advises that she adopt a social persona to hide her wisdom from the uninitiated. '"If we know better," Holstius said, "we must keep it under our hats"'. In this way her psychosis is protected by a feeling of superiority, making a future breakthrough virtually impossible.

Upon the hat which shelters her greater wisdom is a large black rose, which is meant to symbolize her newly won wholeness. The gauze rose is first brought to our attention by the mystical youth Zack, who had 'sensed [its] significance' (p. 283), and is dramatically highlighted in the concluding sentence: 'The hat sat straight, but the doubtful rose trembled and glittered, leading a life of its own'. After Zack a large number of commentators have guessed at its meaning, and there has been general agreement upon its mandalic aspect, leading inevitably to a comic view of the story.[26] The 'illusion of enlightenment' has exerted tremendous power, both within and outside the fictional frame. If we consider the actual context of the rose, its long association with Mrs Goodman, and its blackness in this case, which evokes archaism and death, it becomes less a mandala and more a representation of the uroboric world into which she has fallen. She wears an Abyssinian rose, for in that burnt-out, mythic landscape the 'roses were as brown as paper bags' (p. 23). The dark rose is an appropriate symbol for a life which has sought, and now finally attained, self-extinction in the matrix.

3   *In the Lap of the Land*

*There is also the anti-hero, or hero-in-reverse
who is another form of the great mother's
son ... He just goes along with what is going, a
stream slipping through the great body of mother
nature, ending ultimately in ... oceanic bliss.*

James Hillman[1]

When White returned to Australia from Europe in 1948 it was
associated in his imagination with a return to the maternal realm.
He had found England after the War 'an actual and spiritual
graveyard' and experienced a 'terrible nostalgia' for the landscape
of Australia. 'All through the War in the Middle East there
persisted a longing to return to the scenes of childhood, which is,
after all, the purest well from which the creative artist draws'.[2]
Australia was viewed not only as a source of artistic nourishment, but also of physical sustenance:

Quite honestly, the thought of a full belly influenced me as well, after toying
with the soft, sweet awfulness of horsemeat stew in the London restaurants
that I could afford. So I came home. I bought a farm at Castle Hill, and with a
Greek friend and partner, Manoly Lascaris, started to grow flowers and
vegetables .... Nothing seemed important beyond living and eating, with a
roof of one's own over one's head.[3]

We are concerned with these reflections not as biographical facts,
but as archetypal fantasies, images that provide background to
White's 'Australian' novels of the 1950s. Australia appears as
the mother country, not merely as the place of personal origin,[4]
but as the mythic realm of nourishment and shelter. It is the
place to which the conscious ego, exhausted by the events of the
century, returns for satiety and rest. It is a vast island continent
beyond time and the exigencies of the world. White emphasizes
that he is not attracted to the people, but to the landscape itself,
that it is the earth which exerts a tremendous fascination. He

refers to Australia as 'the country of my fate', meaning, in psychological terms, that he feels destined to live in the *locus* of the maternal image.

Life in the maternal source is never as the *puer* would have it. Instead of sustenance and bliss, White encounters emptiness and despair:

In all directions stretched the Great Australian Emptiness, in which the mind is the least of possessions, in which the rich man is the important man, in which the schoolmaster and the journalist rule what intellectual roost there is, in which beautiful youths and girls stare at life through blind blue eyes, in which human teeth fall like autumn leaves, the buttocks of cars grow hourly glassier, food means cake and steak, muscles prevail, and the march of material ugliness does not raise a quiver from the average nerves.[5]

The *puer*'s return to Nature meets with the inevitable experience of the devouring matrix: the sickening void, nullifying expanses, dissolution and decay. The realm of the unconscious has its own perils and dangers, equal in every respect to the terrors of the world. It is fascinating that in White's Australia the mind is 'the least of possessions', for the archetypal descent has a disintegrating effect upon consciousness. The terrors of this internal process are discovered entirely in human society, in its brutalities and materialism, but White is simply projecting a demonism which he refuses to acknowledge within himself.

It is significant that the demon in paradise is materialism. The *magna mater* and *matter* share not only linguistic but crucial etymological and mythological connections.[6] The Great Mother governs the elemental and instinctual realm, and the primal substance, matter. In myth she is the ever-hungry maw; the Goddess of fertility, blood mysteries, bodily life, and grain. Her body, her matter, is frequently contrasted with the spirit of the Father. To return to the Mother is to return to the elements, to become, as Theodora put it, 'nothing more than air or water'. The consuming aspect of the source may be experienced as the devouring, aggressive qualities of matter, or as a terrible materialism which assaults the intellect and destroys the inner life. Australian society, with its traditionally lowbrow, down-to-earth character, offers some actual basis for this archetypal image, but the malign nature of its materialism is added by White himself, or by the reality-transforming activity of his own imagination.

Not only matter but, as we have seen, the female sex is demonized by this same process. Woman is felt to be stifling and consuming. In *The Tree of Man* (1956) Amy Parker is represented as constantly thwarting her husband, preventing him from achieving his spiritual goal. Mrs O'Dowd, the fearsome, buck-teethed mistress, is the perpetual foil of her husband's dream of a 'static world of peace' (p. 145).[7] Mrs Gage reigns over her artist husband in life, and after his suicide, in which she has played a part, makes a small fortune by selling off his visionary productions. The Mother reduces spirit to matter, converting works of imagination into material reality. White's maternal figures are invariably sadistic, satisfying themselves by destroying the life and dreams of the *puer aeternus*.

When White fell on his back in the mud at Castle Hill and 'started cursing a God [he] had convinced [himself] didn't exist',[8] he arrived at the conclusion that his archetypal opponent was a Father God, and that his psychic drama could be understood within the context of Western patriarchal religion. At this point in his career Christianity enters his fiction, and becomes the central paradigm used to explain and give meaning to the experiences of his characters. White is an authentic explorer of the deep unconscious, but he does not possess any map, code or reliable intuition which could illuminate what he encounters in his journey. He moves forward in the semi-dark, and resorts to ready-made formulae (Christianity, and the mandala) which offer basic explanations and prevent him from having to rigorously examine his strange and disquieting inner world. But the intellectual framework is inherently alien to the imaginal material it is meant to explain, so in *The Tree of Man*, *Voss* and *Riders in the Chariot* Christianity sits heavily and awkwardly upon the fictional ground. The imported edifice crumbles in *The Solid Mandala* (1966), after White's realization that it can no longer accommodate his vision. '"All this Christ stuff . . . doesn't seem to work"' announces Arthur Brown in that novel; and in an interview of 1969 White is forced to conclude: 'I wouldn't say I am a Christian; I can't aspire so high'.[9] But throughout the 1950s and early 1960s, Christianity serves in White's fiction as a legitimizing and aggrandizing framework. The *puer* is elevated to the status of Christ; his longing for self-dissolution is paralleled with Christ's search for spiritual transcendence. Of course the mother–complex benefits from the religious misreading. If the mother's toothed matrix is viewed as God, and if the ego's disappearance into her maw is read as Christian self-sacrifice, then so much the better. This disguises the pathology of the complex, and also forces society to accept the *puer* as a religious hero. In *The Aunt's Story*, where Theodora's madness was transformed into enlightenment, the 'reward' was had at the cost of social alienation. In the succeeding novels society is obliged to take the anarchistic *puer* back into its fold, since he is apparently a saint or mystic. Serving the complex now brings higher rewards, and a greater sense of rightness and self-importance.

1 A Life Sentence

Stan Parker enjoys an ecstatic communion with the Earth Mother, even though he is virtually obliterated in the course of his worship. Whenever the Mother appears to him it is always in tyrannical outbursts of flood, fire or storm. The elemental landscape has a disruptive influence upon his life, yet its anarchic power fulfils a dark need, a longing to be overwhelmed by an archetypal force. It is clear that Parker is 'married' to Nature, and that Amy is merely his house-mate and child-bearer. She hardly ever engages or arouses his deep emotional self, but remains strangely external to his true erotic life. His courtship with Amy does not involve romance, only a 'decision to marry the Fibbens girl', and a simple marriage ceremony conducted in a 'cockeyed little church at Yuruga' (p. 24). The courtship and marriage are ordinary events conducted in an atmosphere robbed of spiritual meaning. The real mystical union takes place between Parker and the Earth Mother; she is his true lover and bride.

Early in the story there is a sense of conflict between Amy and the Earth Mother. By marrying Parker she unwittingly puts herself in opposition to Her. But there is little doubt as to which party will win. Beside the majesty of Nature, Amy Fibbens is made to appear frail and insignificant:

'Does it always blow in these parts?' [Amy] laughed.
He made a motion with his mouth. It was not one of the things to answer. Besides, he recognized and accepted the omnipotence of distance.
But this was something she did not, and perhaps never would. She had begun to hate the wind, and the distance, and the road, because her importance tended to dwindle.
Just then, too, the wind took the elbow of a bough and broke it off, and tossed it, dry and black and writhing, so that its bark harrowed the girl's cheek, slapped terror for a moment into the horse, and crumbled, used and negative, in what was already their travelled road.
Achhh, cried the girl's hot breath, her hands touching the livid moment of fright that was more than wound ... (p. 27)

An effective rebuke from the Mother! A branch of a tree gashes Amy's face and returns to the ground, 'used and negative'. Amy feels acutely overshadowed by elemental Nature, whereas Stan is fully resigned to its apparent 'omnipotence'. For him the Earth Mother's supremacy is a fact of existence. As Amy tends her bloody wound Stan looks at her and sees a confused, frightened girl, 'whom apparently he had married' (p. 27). We find this pattern throughout the novel. Every time the Earth Mother intervenes in events Amy is cut down to size, and Stan is made to look at her with alien, detached eyes. He can hardly believe that the woman at his side, struggling pathetically against the elements, is also his wife.

At the time of the great storm, where Stan's erotic delight in Nature is fully revealed, Amy is further reduced by the tremendous energy of the Earth Mother:

> All this time the big clouds, moving and swelling, pushed and shouldered each other ... The woman in the house got up and closed a door, in an attempt to secure for herself an illusion of safety ... Because the black clouds were bursting on her head. And the grey wool of torn clouds that the wind dragged across the sky raced quicker than her blood and began to rouse the terror in her ...
>
> But the man laughed. He felt a kind of pleasure in the mounting storm. He held his face up flat to the racing clouds. His teeth were smiling in a taut, uncertain humour at the sky ...
>
> Presently the man saw his wife running, her limbs fighting the wind and the stuff of her own dress. Seeing her tortured into these shapes ... he felt that this was not the girl he had married in the church at Yuruga, ... but he forced himself to stumble on towards her. To touch. (pp. 46–7)

This entire episode is underscored with a fierce eroticism. The storm is 'swelling' and 'mounting', Stan is drenched and intoxicated ('Rain filled his mouth'), and the wind uproots trees and knocks over buildings in orgiastic frenzy. Stan and the Earth are engaged in ecstatic intercourse, and Amy is definitely the third, excluded party in this elemental ritual. In fact, Stan can barely contain his revulsion, and has to 'force himself' to move toward her during the storm. Her presence merely frustrates his immediate desire.

It is apparent that the Parkers' sexual life is unfulfilling. In order to feel any passion for his wife, Stan must imagine her to be an image of the Goddess, and make love to her as if she were an impersonal, archetypal figure. In the darkness of night a different relationship takes place: 'Flesh is heroic by moonlight. The man took the body of the woman and taught it fearlessness' (p. 29). No longer Stan and Amy, but the man and the woman, transformed under the light of the moon, itself an ancient symbol of the Goddess. But whenever the ecstasy of orgasm subsides, Amy shrinks back to human proportions and Stan feels remote from her. This pattern forces Amy to resort to sexual fantasies about other men (Mick O'Dowd, Tom Armstrong) and finally to adultery itself. Her own husband cannot break out of his primary incestuous attachment. The love he communicates by day is largely a facade, at best affection, or tender concern: 'Habit comforted them, like warm drinks and slippers, and even went disguised as love' (p. 333).

As well as failing to match up to Stan's Goddess, Amy is also burdened with the negative side of this figure. As Stan strives to find release through Nature his intentions are thwarted as he meets the devouring character of the matrix. This aggressive element is not attributed to Nature but is found in his antagonist–wife, who is associated with materialism, with hard, abrasive objects, with fixity and death. Her symbol throughout is the little silver nutmeg grater, a cherished present from her wedding day, which is subsequently 'stolen' by the pedlar in an attempt to free Parker from the oppressive materiality of his wife (p. 41 f). Amy's womb and house become images of stifling containment. She is continuously pregnant in the early years of marriage, yet does not bring forth offspring. Stan is disturbed by her apparent withholding of life, and begins to suspect that she is committed to his own downfall. He is unaware that he is experiencing an archetypal factor, the destroying power of the Goddess, in whose matrix he is helplessly caught (see Figures 4a and 4b).

During the Wullunya floods, Parker's longing for dissolution is pitted against the ensnaring, containing activity of his wife:

> In the contenting smell of sheets and her warm kitchen, the woman once more possessed her husband; why, she would not have held her children with firmer hand, if they had lived. So she was pleased.
> But the man was looking out of the house into the rain. He had escaped from his wife, if she had but known it. He was standing on a small promontory of land above what had been the river at Wullunya, which he had not visited but knew ... And the shiny horns of cattle swam and sank in the great yellow waters of what was no longer river. It was no longer possible to distinguish the cries of men from the lowing or bleating of animals ... But the arms of men ... were almost not protesting, as they were carried sinking away in the yellow flood that had taken the lives from out of their hands.
> 'Why', said Amy Parker, who had brought the nice plate of pickled pork and put it on the kitchen table, 'aren't you going to come and eat? ...'
> 'Yes,' he said.
> The man sat down at his table to eat what his wife had brought. (p. 71)

Stan expects to find release through the teeming waters, yet even as he dreams of dissolution he is held fast in Amy's house, and

Figure 4a   In the belly of the dragon (ninth-century drawing of Jonah in the whale)
Source: E. Neumann, *The Origins and History of Consciousness*, Princeton University Press, Princeton, 1970, plate 22

In ancient myth and fable the hero is sometimes devoured by a dragon, whale or monster, and lives in its belly for a certain period of time. In psychological language we would say that the ego disappears into the unconscious and is returned to the primordial source. In myths of the development of consciousness the hero becomes aware of his plight and attempts to cut, hack, or trick his way out of the monster. However, in White's anti-heroic world, the ego decides that the matrix is home and makes no attempt to break free.

Figure 4b   Woman as imprisoning matrix (cartoon by Thurber)
Source: C. G. Jung (ed.), *Man and His Symbols*, Doubleday, New York, 1964, p. 78

While the ego languishes in its fake paradise, pretending it is enlightened, the negative side of its containment is projected upon women, wives, and mothers. The female sex is invested with strange, demonic powers, and the ego feels helpless and under attack in the presence of women. The negative influence, however, actually arises from the male's own unconscious, and results from his stifling imprisonment in the matrix.

subject to her domestic power. There is a poetic justice here which is indicative of the *puer*'s situation. To dissolve into Nature is to find oneself in a matriarchal prison. There may be an illusion of freedom, but in fact the personality is devoured and taken into the primal container. The possessive wife, her imprisoning house and her deathly womb, are images of the dark matrix in which the *puer* has been contained.

I

The petrifying aspect of the movement into Nature is made starkly evident when Stan discovers, while rowing across a flooded watercourse, the body of an old man suspended in a tree:

In one place Stan Parker saw, stuck in the fork of a tree, the body of an old, bearded man. But he did not mention this. He rowed ... And soon the old man, whose expression had not expected much, dying upside down in a tree, was obliterated by motion and rain. (p. 74)

This is perhaps the key mythological image in *The Tree of Man*, just as the trochilus caught inside the dragon's mouth proved to be the central motif of the previous story. Both images reflect spirit in the fatal grip of Nature. In ancient mythology dissolution into Mother Nature was often imaged as a return to the maternal tree.[10] The *puer*–god was sometimes called 'he in the tree', since he was born of the tree and buried inside it at his death.[11] In the Attis/Cybele myth the boy–god castrates himself under the sacred pine, and in another version he hangs himself on the tree.[12] In the present story, Mr Gage, the artist, commits suicide by hanging himself upon the tree in his back yard (p. 79). The *puer* is fixed upon the maternal image, which absorbs his ephemeral life back into itself. He is unable to wrest from this primal background an individual life of his own. In this regard it is interesting that the old man in the flood dies upside down in the tree. In a sense, the *puer* lives life in an inverted way. Instead of growing toward maturity and independence he sinks back into darkness, infantilism, and the unconscious. His head points down toward the earth, held in thrall by the great mother.[13]

The inverted corpse disturbs Stan Parker when he first encounters it, especially since at the time he is drifting ecstatically into a 'dissolved world of flowing water' (p. 73). In other words, at precisely the point where the *puer* enters the matrix, the annihilating power of Nature is thrust into view. Parker does not tell the authorities at Wullunya of the dead man, somehow it is too personal, too private an experience. He reflects upon the image for many years, but fails to grasp why it exerts such a powerful fascination. Later he is moved to tell his wife about it, but all he is able to articulate is his guilt about not reporting the incident at the time. As with the trochilus image in *The Aunt's Story*, the symbol disturbs and fascinates consciousness, but the individual is unable to realize its crucial meaning for his own life. The imagination and its productions are always in advance of the protagonist's capacity for self-understanding.

When Parker returns home from the Wullunya floods he brings with him a bath-tub, an item which had been washed up by the torrential stream. At a literal level the taking of the bath is just a bit of socially accepted thievery, but as symbolic action it is quite significant. The bath has long symbolized, in alchemic tradition, the containing soul or anima in which the work of realization can take place.[14] Other variations of the symbol are the vase, the chalice and the retort.[15] If the great mother is a vast ocean, or flood, of limitless proportion, the anima is an enclosed vessel in which the waters of the unconscious become contained and humanly relatable. The personality is extinguished in a flood; it is drowned in it or carried willy-nilly by it. A bath is a different matter: there the unconscious is localized and, as it were, humanized. Parker, however unconsciously, feels prompted to establish a new relationship to the archetypal realm.

Still, nothing happens with the bath, or with the anima-potential within his own life. 'He put the bath in a shed, where it remained quietly. Parkers were always uneasy about that bath' (p. 93). There is a sense of unease, partly because, as a stolen object, the bath does not belong to them, but also because it does not 'belong' to Parker's psychic world, insofar as it is ruled over by the Mother. And, as we might expect in White's symbolic universe, the mother–woman is not in favour of the intrusive symbol:

'What is that?' the woman asked suspiciously.
'That's a bath,' said her husband, banging it awkwardly against the side of the dray, before he heaved it out.
'Whatever for?' she asked. Her voice thickened, as if this second problem was too much ...
'It was there,' said her husband, kicking the hollow object with his toe, not by design, though it sounded like it. 'It was there,' he said. 'Nobody seemed to want it. So I took it. It will come in useful.'
'Oh,' she said doubtfully. (p. 92)

As the voice of his own complex, Amy must necessarily be opposed to the anima–symbol. Mythologically, the Mother is everywhere and at all times antagonistic to the anima and its alternative realm of symbols.[16] If the *puer* wins for himself a vessel of transformation he becomes creatively independent of the Mother's teeming source. Yet Amy cannot be blamed for his own inertia and inability to act. If his enthusiasm about the bath dwindles, it is only because the complex proves stronger than the impulse toward change and transformation.

So, without the containing vessel or anima, everything very quickly returns to its former state: 'the waters subsided soon after . . . and by degrees they forgot to mention the subject' (p. 98). The conscious pattern of life has not been transformed. The waters of the great mother well up, flood, and then disappear from view. Stan returns to his cows and to his dry, mundane life of maternal enslavement. It was the same after the experience of the first great storm. The day after that event there was 'very little evidence that the lightning had struck' (p. 50). When the Mother rules the interior life there are destructive outbursts of psychic energy, but no facility to creatively channel this energy into life. The mother–realm is dynamic, elemental and savage, and the conscious personality remains static, flat and untransformed.

II

About this time, Amy Parker finally gives birth to children, Ray and then Thelma, and it is clear that she exerts a formidable power over them. The mother/child relationship is as darkly ambivalent in the lives of the Parker children as it is in Stan's symbolic life. Ray is the first, and Amy virtually consumes him with her passion. 'She could not love him enough, not even by slow, devouring kisses. Sometimes her moist eyes longed almost to have him safe inside her again' (p. 115). Again we discover the image of the possessive womb, the matrix that will not discharge its offspring into life. Significantly, the father is hostile to the mother's possessive character: '"I'd put it down," said the father. "It can't be healthy to maul it like that"' (p. 115). But as soon as Thelma is born, Ray is virtually abandoned altogether. It is apparent that Amy has merely used her son as an object for her own instinctual energy. And so while Thelma is being cuddled and smothered ('She drew the shawl tighter on the baby, as if to protect it out of existence', p. 123), Ray is left to his own devices. Like Elyot Standish, the first-born of the Standish children, he grows up with a rejection complex and feels isolated and devoid of love. In his confusion Ray takes several new-born puppies that are still sucking on the teats of the mother and drowns them in a nearby stream. If he cannot draw nourishment from the maternal source, his behaviour suggests, neither will they. Stan senses the agony and guilt of the son after this event, but is too inarticulate to help him. Thelma, over-protected and stifled by the mother, becomes 'thin' and 'pasty' (p. 122), and develops a breathing problem, which subsequently leads to asthma (p. 127). Asthma and domineering mother go together in White's world, as in some theories of psychoanalysis. The mother or background of consciousness is overbearing; it stifles the ego and takes away its life–breath.

These primal disturbances govern the psychology of the Parker children in later life, and determine their relationship with society and the outer world. Ray develops anti-socially; his life is structured in opposition to the mother–society–world continuum. Thelma, on the other hand, becomes excessively embedded in and identified with social structures. She secures a comfortable place in society, mindlessly adopts its mores and conventions, and does nothing that would require the assertion of an independent character. Her embeddedness in the maternal image manifests as a kind of social anonymity and amorphousness. In society, as in early childhood, she has no 'space' to breathe as a separate individual. Ray, adopting the myth of the abandoned child, quickly becomes a gangster, an outlaw. He goes it alone and finds support from nowhere. Yet his life of free will and action proves too much to cope with. He becomes frustrated, unfulfilled, and unable to sustain himself financially. Late in the story he returns to his mother for comfort and support, but she rejects him, and his little son, with a vehemence that surprises even herself (p. 420 f). This rejection is experienced by Ray as a final, fatal blow. In fact, the day after he is mortally wounded in a gunfight in a Sydney bar. The outer facts of his death are merely circumstantial, and the portrayal of his inward state at this moment allows us to glimpse his symbolic crisis: 'Ray Parker was shot. He was looking into that blouse ... of a white or oyster satin, that was her colour, it was her colour in the morning ... He could not lower his face to suck the brown waters of the dam' (p. 436). Images arise spontaneously of the unattainable maternal breast, and of the life-giving waters, from which he has been withheld. White has Amy Parker admit that she is 'to blame' (p. 409) for Ray's tragic fate. Again it must be emphasized that this is true only if we see Amy as a psychic or mythological figure, as the maternal source which withdraws its support. Whether faced with the mother who consumes by her presence

(Thelma), or by her absence (Ray), we have to do with a mythological figure, and not a merely human character who must be held responsible for these psychological crimes.

III

Stan's archetypal deity, usually felt to be an abstract force called 'God', and experienced as the earth–spirit, attains personified form at one point in the story. This occurs at the time of the bushfire, when Madeleine becomes a personification of the ecstatic aspect of the mother–world. Madeleine is an aloof, dreamy figure; to the earth-bound Amy she seems 'god-like and remote' (p. 131). Madeleine is seductive, anarchistic, and intent on erotically-toned violence. She is the only one at Glastonbury who is not disturbed by the fire, or by the prospect of death and devastation. In fact, she welcomes it, as is apparent by her languid attitude on the day of the fire, and, in the evening, by her passive acceptance of death as the Glastonbury mansion burns to the ground.

Stan rushes into the burning house, not so much to save Madeleine, as the onlookers believe, as to unite with her. White has carefully set the stage for the climax of Stan's erotic life, for him to break into the mansion and, in an ecstasy of fire, engage in mystical communion with the divine woman.

All that he had never done, all that he had never seen, appeared to be contained in this house, and it was opening to him. Till his head began to reel with fiery splendours of its own, and he was prepared to accept the invitation, and follow the passages of the house, or fire, to any possible conclusion ...

Lamplight made him bigger than he was ... All things in the house were eternal on that night ... Time was becalmed in the passages ... He found the staircase, stumbled, mounted, paying the banister out through his burning hand, feeling his swift shirt sail against his ribs as he mounted on a mission of some mystery into the pure air of upper rooms. (pp. 176–8)

If entering Amy's house is associated with fears of claustrophobia and castration (Figure 4b), entering Glastonbury, the flaming mansion, is like moving into a chasm, or womb, of releasing fire. The erotic tone is emphasized by the swift motion as he plunges into passages of flame, and by the repetition of the word 'mounted' as he moves toward Madeleine. Significantly, these passages 'open' to him and 'invite' him to enter. The 'worshipping man' (p. 176) enters the realm of his Goddess and is released from his egoic structure. He becomes 'bigger' than usual, linked with eternity, and soon carries the sacred fire–woman in his arms:

Approaching some climax, the breath of the saviour or sacrifice, it was not clear which, came quicker ...

Madeleine was wearing some kind of loose gown that shone in the firelight ... He had never seen anything glowing and flowing like this woman ... And suddenly he wished he could sink his face in her flesh, to smell it, that he could part her breasts and put his face between.

She saw this. They were burning together at the head of the smoking staircase. She had now to admit ... that the sweat of his body was drugging her, and that she would have entered his eyes, if she could have, and not returned. (pp. 178–80)[17]

At this point there is a sudden shift and a falling-away of Stan's desire:

Then they came out on to the half-landing and felt the first tongue of fire. The breath left them. Now Madeleine's beauty had shrunk right away, and any desire Stan Parker might have had was shrivelled up. He was small and alone in his body, dragging the sallow woman.

Finally, as they leave the house and arrive at the grounds outside,

she fell on her knees and began a kind of dry retching, holding her head, and falling even to all fours. Most people were silent, from surprise and pity, but one or two let out loud explosions of laughter.

'Madeleine, darling,' said young Tom Armstrong, overcoming his disgust, and putting out his hand, in front of everyone.

'Please,' she said. 'Leave me. Not now.'

And got to her feet and staggered farther into the darkness. Her hair had been burned off. (p. 181)

We observed this same reversal in the Elyot/Hildegard affair, and in Stan and Amy's sexual life. Whenever the *puer* unites erotically with a woman the dark side of the Mother is immediately constellated. His entry into the archetypal feminine is ultimately a movement into terror and darkness, and here are the familiar images of the stifling matrix: sudden breathlessness, the destructive 'tongue' of fire, the woman turned loathsome hag. The otherworldly splendour that originally enticed him evaporates in an instant. Any 'marriage' with the maternal image leads not to erotic fulfilment but to desolation and negativity.

There is a further aspect here. We could say that the Mother, in order to protect her sovereignty, causes Madeleine to be savagely reduced at the end. If the moment at the head of the stairs had been carried through into life Stan would have won for himself a human embodiment of his erotic desire. The Mother will only allow him to love Madeleine in the fire, for that is equivalent to loving Her in Her own realm. Only when she transforms the woman—Amy in moonlight, Hildegard in the forest—is the *puer* permitted a temporary incestuous fulfilment. As soon as they embrace, the beatific vision is destroyed, else she might herself be deposed. The price paid for acting the divine role is enormous: Madeleine's hair is burned off, and she falls to the ground an ugly, retching animal. Stan Parker does not want her, nor does her fiancé Tom Armstrong who attempts to 'overcome his disgust' as he holds out an unwilling hand. We recall that Stan Parker had to 'force himself' to stumble on towards Amy after the storm had ruined her integrity and beauty.[18] The Great Mother is a jealous deity; she will have no other gods—or humans—before her.

After the fire there is a period of psychological desolation, for all richness and life remains buried in the maternal depths. The ego still has no source of energy that would make it independent of the maternal matrix. But the period that ensues is unusually long and exhausting. There are many years, perhaps decades of sterility. A war passes, Ray and Thelma grow up and leave home, but there is nothing forthcoming from the psyche, no flood or storm or fire. It is the period of drought, when the Earth Mother has deserted the world, leaving her devotee dry, thirsting, barren. Stan's Christian world-view cannot accommodate this negative aspect of his deity's character, although we have already seen how he has experienced it in projection upon Amy; and this is precisely what happens here.

IV

As Stan Parker drives home from Durilgai one day and finds the salesman's blue car in the driveway of his house, he is more disturbed by Amy's apparent unfaithfulness than we might expect. After all, his marriage with Amy is by now unimportant, for the only real thing in his life is his relationship with the Mother. Moreover, Stan had already noticed the salesman's car leaving the house on a previous occasion. Yet his reaction is extreme. He drives the car back into town in a desperate state, gets drunk, almost strangles an old hag on the beach, and contemplates suicide. White makes it seem that his Beloved has deceived him, so that life is no longer worth living. We are told that the only things dear to him were 'his wife's form and those glimpses he had had of her soul, and those experiences in which he and she had been interchangeable' (p. 323). But we know that the central figure in his life is not Amy but the Earth Mother. It would seem appropriate to read this scene in a different way—not merely as Amy's unfaithfulness, but as the turning away of the

Mother herself. The archetypal nature of the crisis is immediately apparent:

> There was a paper sky, quite flat, and white, and Godless. He spat at the absent God then, mumbling till it ran down his chin. He spat and farted, because he was full to bursting; he pissed in the street until he was empty, quite empty. Then the paper sky was tearing, he saw. He was tearing the last sacredness, before he fell down amongst some empty crates, mercifully reduced to his body for a time. (p. 324)

We can hardly believe that Amy, the housewife who stifles him, has caused this reaction. This is the rage of a man against his 'absent God', a man deceived and rejected by his highest value. If Stan were on better terms with his Goddess he might have welcomed the idea of Amy's affair. It would have released some of the tension between them and allowed Stan to get on with his Mother–worship. But since his world is 'Godless' he projects this archetypal situation upon his wife and feels harshly treated by her. He cannot imagine that the deity itself has a brutal aspect, that it could abandon him to a mental and spiritual wilderness.

Not only is Amy blamed for his existential isolation, but she is also made a moral scapegoat. Her unfaithfulness provides Stan with an opportunity to exorcize his guilt-feelings about his own unfaithfulness to her. For has he not entertained a long and lasting 'extra-marital' affair with the Goddess? His shame at this bizarre incestuous experience is turned around and placed upon Amy herself. Her relationship with the salesman is a direct parallel to Stan's with the Goddess, only it is the shadow side of Stan's affair, and as such it is acted out in the flesh, as literal sexuality. Witness the description of the adulterous act: 'Buried in the flesh of the woman, he had returned to boyhood, from which poetry had escaped, and would again ultimately' (p. 302). As he enters Amy's womb the salesman feels returned to 'boyhood', and to a lost world of 'poetry', which is precisely what Stan Parker seeks when he enters the matrix of Nature. As Leo enters Amy's house he feels the place drawing him onward, '. . . everywhere the dimness of the inhabited house was opening to him . . . He had never penetrated deeper into any house' (p. 301), just as Parker had felt the corridors of Glastonbury beckoning to him.

And the adulterous wife, like Stan's own wildly erotic Goddess, is said to have a 'passion [which] overflowed the bounds he knew':

'Steady on now,' breathed the man's hot breath into her burning ear . . .
'Take a hold of yourself,' he laughed, touching her with heavy superior hands.
'I'm not gonna run off and leave yer.'
  If he was her inferior in passion, he was her superior in quickly appeased
lust. So he could afford to laugh, and light another cigarette, and watch the
soul writhe mysteriously in her body. (p. 303)

Leo feels as inadequate before Amy as Stan does before the
elemental outbursts of the Earth Mother. The Goddess's passion
comes in torrents and the son–lover feels swamped by it. The
salesman has won his quick release, but now he has to watch the
'soul writhe mysteriously in her body'. His laughter masks his
fear of her feminine power. Very soon he puts on his clothes and
makes a polite dash for the door. Even the house suddenly feels
'stuffy' and claustrophobic (p. 304). The son–lover, caught up in
the agonies of incestuous sexuality, once more attempts to flee
from the grasp of the mother–woman.
  From this we can see how similar Stan's situation is to Leo's.
Yet the author, unconscious of the parallel, converts the adultery
episode into a gigantic moral argument, an attack upon Amy's
integrity. The Mother Goddess supports him in this: she strives
to turn women into whores, while maintaining for herself an
illusion of sanctity and purity. We have noted White's dislike for
Amy, but when he contrives three successive adulterous episodes
with Leo, in which she becomes 'brazen' and 'one of the flash
women' (p. 313), the reader feels that the author has lost his
control.[19] By converting Amy into a moral scapegoat, White's
fictional ego Stan Parker feels itself cleansed of moral darkness
and enjoys a sense of spiritual elevation:

When she had done her duty she watched him go. He was staring up at the
sky, as if to read its intentions, then starting the car, which he always did
rather badly, looking closely at the panel. And as she watched this erect and
honourable man she realized with blinding clarity that she had never been
worthy of him. This illumination of her soul left her weary, but indifferent.
After all, she had done her material duty in many ways. Putting a clean
handkerchief in his breast pocket, for instance. (p. 317)

White has contrived to present an image of the 'erect and
honourable' Stan Parker in company with his wretched wife, but
readers are not so quick to judge her. They have seen her life from
the inside, experienced her isolation and Stan's remoteness from
her. In fact, Amy's brief and unsatisfactory affair is nothing in
comparison with Stan's long-standing passionate engagement
with the Great Mother; he has been unfaithful to her for most of

their married life. In the last analysis one feels inclined to side with Amy against Stan, although the author asks us to damn her and celebrate him. The moral structure of the book falls back on itself.

The adultery sequence also serves to highlight the dubious notion of spirituality that is put forward and supported by the novel. Parker is given a 'spiritual' life because he maintains his incestuous affair at an abstract and otherworldly level; Amy is denied any transcendence merely because she acts out her erotic life in the flesh. As she makes love to Leo we read: 'It was as if she had spat into the face of her husband, or still further, into the mystery of her husband's God' (p. 303). Parker's erotic affair is set up on a religious pedestal, while Amy's is an abomination which leaves her soulless and despairing. After revealing her moral unworthiness, White proceeds to outline her equally dire spiritual situation.

She was standing there, as she had stood many times in church, with people around her who had apparently realized their spiritual aspirations, whereas she could not rise, could not discover to what she should aspire ... She accepted her squat body, looking out from it, through the words of canticles, in dry acceptance of her isolation. (pp. 317–18)

As her husband sings rousing hymns of praise, assured in his belief of a 'God which obviously did exist' (p. 295), Amy is unable to affirm any reality beyond that of her own 'squat body'. If the truth be known, Parker is just as alienated from the Christian mystery as she is herself, but that does not matter since the *puer*/Mother connection gives him the sense of being one of the elect, one of the Chosen Few. It is the mother–complex which provides the sense of the spiritual in White. Those who succumb to it are granted a higher status, those who do not are considered spiritually impoverished.

V

The widening rift between husband and wife allows Stan to retreat further into interior reality and to intensify his bond with the Mother, and he very quickly begins his downward slide into the matrix of the earth. It is important to get a correct perspective on his final phase, because there has been much critical appraisal of his spiritual 'triumph', his supposed ascension to wholeness and integration.[20] Certainly White would have us believe that Parker is about to scale the heights of religious elevation, but a close reading of the text enables us to see that what happens here is a regressive dissolution into the void. To be sure, as the *puer* slips into the matrix he glimpses the unitary nature of all things, but this is not to be confused with the mystic's achievement of wholeness. The *puer* is destroyed by his glimpse of oneness, whereas the mystic strives to maintain his integrity in the face of it, to bring his consciousness and the archetypal world into some affirmative relationship.[21] The difference is between mental disintegration and spiritual health.

After he suffers a stroke, which occurs as he is digging a rock out of the earth, Parker contracts a sickness in a storm. At first it is a slight fever, and then it turns into pleurisy (p. 393). These illnesses relate to his close contact with the elements and the earth. We could say that his bond with Nature is finally taking its toll in physical terms. But the dissolution of consciousness which results from the sickness is not without its positive aspect:

> The night of the storm or shower, when he had got wet, Stan Parker had never seen more clearly ... In his fever he could not have been cleaner swept. All that he had lived, all that he had seen, had the extreme simplicity of goodness ... [He] was surprised at the newness of what he saw. (pp. 391–3)

The deep unconscious invades the field of experience and everything is revealed in its essential nature, as part of a greater whole. And, as Parker moves deeper into the source, Nature appears to be gathering him into itself, or drawing him toward its bosom:

> After she had gone Stan Parker walked about his property, slowly ... while all the time this communion of soul and scene was taking place, the landscape moving in on him with increased passion and intensity, trees surrounding him, clouds flocking above him with tenderness such as he had never experienced. (p. 397)

This is a vision of perfect bliss, the *puer* caressed and nurtured by Mother Nature. But it is a false paradise, because in the wake of this grand embrace his own individuality will be extinguished. The arms of the earth mother not only cherish, they also crush and consume. And we do not have to look far to see the destructive aspect. For at the same time as the landscape is moving in on him so too are the brick-boxes of suburbia, the 'brick tombs' (p. 461). The 'march of material ugliness'[22] keeps pace with the 'increased passion and intensity' of the landscape. Inside every brick box (or so White imagines it) is a teeth-sucking suburban housewife. 'The brick homes were in possession all right. Deep purple, clinker blue, ox blood, and public lavatory' (p. 394). The brick homes of the mothers are taking bites out of the peaceable landscape, and Parker is forced to sell off parts of his property in order to accommodate the suburban sprawl (p. 397). It is apparent that this image has autobiographical significance for White's own life, for at the time of writing he was living at Castle Hill and worried by the 'spread of urban villas ... pressing hard on the boundaries of his six acres'.[23] The invasion of the brick boxes is compelling as a mythic symbol precisely because it is so natural and uncontrived—and of course because the negative *mater* image is carried by society and technology, Nature herself remains undefiled. The *pueri* need never suspect that their own deity wears this same demonically destructive face.

As Parker is drawn toward death his experience of unity becomes overwhelming. He sees his 'God' reflected in every minute object, in every blade of grass, ant, or crack in the concrete path (p. 477). He even sees the divine at the centre of his gob of spittle, which 'lay glittering intensely and personally on the ground' (p. 476). The point is not, as Leonie Kramer has said, that he has 'spat out God',[24] but that the archetypal realm has invaded his being to such an extent that every aspect of existence becomes charged with the numinous. Less sceptical critics have found in this episode a kind of modern apotheosis, equal in every respect to the visions of the great Christian mystics.[25] Others find in it the Jungian panacea: the bestowal of the mandalic vision.[26] I can no more agree with these claims than I can with the agnostic position of Professor Kramer. Stan is neither saint, nor seer, nor sceptic. He is an eternal youth caught up in an uprising of the unconscious which is more pathological than mystical. The oneness is not his 'achievement', but happens to him, a tidal wave over which he has no control. Once again it is Amy Parker who carries the unacknowledged negative side of his psychic situation. She stalks through the boundless garden with her gammy leg and destructive manner, interrupting Stan's quietude and communion with Nature:

the old man continued to stare at the jewel of spittle. A great tenderness of understanding rose in his chest. Even the most obscure, most sickening incidents of his life were clear. In that light. How long will they leave me like this, he wondered, in peace and understanding?

But his wife had to come presently.

'Stan,' she said, approaching, he knew it was she, crunching over the grass with her bad leg, 'you will not believe when I tell you,' she said, 'I was scratching round the shack, in the weed, where the rosebush was that we moved to the house, the old white rose, and what did I find, Stan, but the little silver nutmeg grater that Mrs Erbey gave me on our wedding day. Look.'

'Ah,' he said.

What was this irrelevant thing? He had forgotten.

Branches of shadow were drifting across his face, interfering with his sight. (p. 476)

Stan imagines himself at the height of understanding, yet because he is actually in the maw of the Mother he must necessarily be laid low by the destructive maternal figure. Amy brings him down to earth with a jolt, crunching over the sacred grass as surely as she cuts across his sublime thoughts with her trivializing, rambling commentary. Yet the subject of her talk is significant: the recovery of the little silver nutmeg grater. Amy has found the treasured object which the pedlar had buried in the garden years earlier in the hope that this would defeat her materialism and allow Stan's spirit to soar. The recovery of the object symbolically suggests the triumph of materialism, of the destructive *mater* image. Surrounded by an army of brick tombs, a devouring wife, and the recovered symbol of matter, Parker returns to the deathly womb of the *magna mater*.

Critics have celebrated Parker as the 'Australian anonymous hero',[27] but there is nothing heroic in his character at all. He has made no effort to achieve independence, self-knowledge, or human relationship. He is the classic anti-hero, unable to act, unwilling to challenge the fact of his imprisonment: 'But he knew also there was nothing to be done. He knew that where his cart had stopped, he would stop. There was nothing to be done. He would make the best of this cell in which he had been locked' (p. 13). The *puer aeternus* chooses to lose;[28] he does not struggle against the mother–bond, but merely 'makes the best' of it.

It is fascinating to note that White had originally intended the book to be called *A Life Sentence on Earth*, and later altered it to *The Tree of Man*.[29] Perhaps the earlier title seemed too depressing and White wanted to emphasize the positive side of his mother–myth, appealing to our romantic notions of man's pact with the natural world. But as we have seen, the tree symbol itself is decidedly ambivalent. It becomes a tree of death and fixation for the old man in the floods, as for the artist Mr Gage who hangs himself upon it. And while Stan Parker may well be rooted in the natural world like a tree, he also fixated by the earth, immobile, bound to the spot. The tree of man ensnares him too (see Figure 5). The eventual title has its inherent ambivalence, and should not be read solely in terms of its romantic connotations.

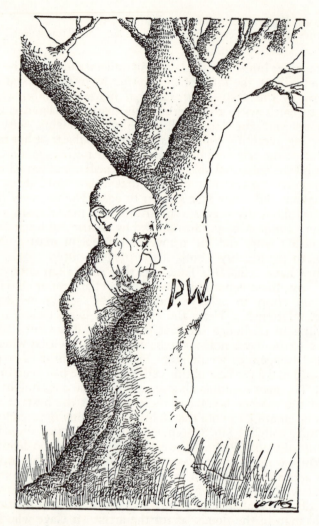

Figure 5   Patrick White's Tree of Man (recent newspaper cartoon, by Coopes)
Source: Sydney Morning Herald, 23 July 1983, p. 33

There is something psychologically correct about this cartoon. The assimilation
of White to the bulging, ancient tree, the static connection to the earth, the fixed
gaze and sullen face, all point to the agony of the incestuous state, the suffering
that results when man weds the maternal image. Even the spiralic twist of his
body around the tree is mythically precise. The son/Mother relation was imaged
in classical mythology as a knot or entanglement, represented most clearly in the
theriomorphic union of Zeus and Demeter as knotted, copulating serpents. [These
associations are not necessarily those of the cartoonist.]

2   *The Dark Inspiratrice*

> *I thought of those two, guarding the door of*
> *Darkness, knitting black wool as for a warm*
> *pall, one introducing, introducing continuously*
> *to the unknown, the other scrutinizing the*
> *cheery and foolish faces with unconcerned old*
> *eyes.*
>
> Joseph Conrad[30]

If Stan Parker leads a static existence governed by 'the nostalgia of permanence', Voss is 'the fiend of motion',[31] a man of compulsive activity and movement. Yet while much can be made of their contrasting patterns of behaviour,[32] mythologically they are identical. Each is held in thrall by the Mother Goddess and seeks to obliterate himself in her embrace. It is simply that one dissolves quietly and uneventfully into the matrix, whereas the other finds his fatal union after much restlessness and impassioned striving. The incestuous impulse of the *puer aeternus* can lead to a life of eternal wandering, a perpetual search for a lost paradise.[33] Parker found his deity reflected in the natural world around him, but for Voss the ideal image is always somewhere else, somewhere mysterious, remote, out of reach. For him the Goddess is a seductive presence at the borders of consciousness, a figure who inspires activity by beckoning him into continental interiors and secret places. His bondage is not to the maternal earth beneath his feet, but to the dark inspiratrice who leads him to his ruin.

Voss identifies with the destructive matriarchal force within his psyche, and it is this which gives him his god-like or demonic character. It is absurd to idealize him in terms of the Nietzschean *Übermensch*[34] because he is the helpless victim of archetypal possession, an ego which has become morbidly assimilated to the deep unconscious. In his youth Voss had a penchant for dangerous sports, and a passion for near-death experiences, which 'through some perversity, inspired him with fresh life' (p. 18).[35] We are even told that, prior to his obsession for the deserts of Australia, he had a certain fascination for an insect-devouring species of flower:

He did study inordinately, and was fascinated in particular by a species of lily which swallows flies. With such instinctive neatness and cleanliness to dispose of those detestable pests. Amongst the few friends he had, his obsession became a joke. He was annoyed at first, but decided to take it in good part ... (pp. 13–14)

This is an evocative image. Theodora Goodman shared a similar fascination for the devouring tendencies of the natural world, imaged in the gaping jaws of the Meroëan crocodile. But we will observe that the aesthetic values are now reversed. Whereas in *The Aunt's Story* an ugly maw destroyed a delicately beautiful trochilus, here the matrix itself is sublimely beautiful and the thing that it destroys 'detestable'. This points to a significant shift in White's symbolic world. By the time of *Voss* (1957), the negative side of the mother–image has become better disguised, harder to detect, and almost impossible to resist. Instead of feeling pursued by a hostile figure the ego now yields to the unearthly beauty of the maternal realm and is snuffed out by a sublime force.

At one point in the story Voss is depicted as a sleepwalker who is the passive instrument of an archetypal power:

> There he was, striped by moonlight and darkness, the stale air moving round him, very softly. Voss himself did not move. Rather was he moved by a dream, Palfreyman sensed. Through some trick of moonlight or uncertainty of behaviour, the head became detached for a second and appeared to have been fixed upon a beam of the wooden wall ...
> The moonlight returned Voss to the room. As he was moved back, his bones were creaking, and his skin had erupted in a greenish verdigris ...
> Next morning [Palfreyman] remarked:
> 'Mr Voss, do you know you were sleep-walking last night?' ...
> 'I have never been known to, before. Never,' he replied, but most irritably, as if refusing a crime with which he had been unjustly charged. (p. 177)

It is interesting that Voss's actions appear to Palfreyman to be involuntary—'Voss himself did not move. Rather was he moved ...'. It is not Voss's will which is in control,[36] but an unconscious force which drives him from within. Significantly, Voss refuses to acknowledge this. According to von Franz,[37] the *puer* is quick to deny that he is the instrument of an archetypal power; he believes that he acts from himself and that his life-course is unique. Yet to the extent that he is identified with an archetypal power his life is not individual at all, but highly predictable, a re-enactment of myth. The reference to moonlight is important here: Voss's sleepwalking takes place 'under the indicator of that magnetic moon' (p. 176). He is held under a Luna spell, or bewitched by the Moon Goddess. In relation to this, it is fascinating that Palfreyman imagines that Voss's head has been removed from his body as he walks out into the night. In a sense, this is a prefiguration of his decapitation at the hands of the Aborigines in the Australian desert. But in psychological terms Voss has already 'lost his head', he has lost his reason and mind to the destructive lunar forces of the inner world.

I

In relation to his fellow explorers, Voss acts as the hypnotized hypnotist[38] who draws other men into the nightmare in which he is himself ensnared. His colleagues must already have something of the *puer* nature in them to be involved in Voss's enterprise, but the German leader acts as the satanic figure who brings to life their latent desires for self-annihilation. One such follower is Frank Le Mesurier, who, like Elyot Standish, is 'in' the world, seems adjusted and normal, but inwardly is completely tied to the fantasies of early childhood. When Voss arrives on the scene, he appeals to Le Mesurier's cravings for the maternal depths, and invites him to join the inland expedition:

'in this disturbing country, so far as I have become acquainted with it already, it is possible more easily to discard the inessential and to attempt the infinite. You will be burnt up most likely, you will have the flesh torn from your bones, you will be tortured probably in many horrible and primitive ways, but you will realize that genius of which you sometimes suspect you are possessed, and of which you will not tell me you are afraid.'
Tempted, the young man was ... afraid—but ... he was also flattered.
'All right then,' said Le Mesurier .... 'What have I got to lose?'
[He] was now thrilled by the immensity of darkness, and resented the approach of those lights which would reveal human substance, his own in particular. (pp. 35–6)

This is a good example of how the German leader, surely a spiritual relation of the fascist Hitler,[39] seduces another *puer*-type male into joining him in an orgy of disintegration. He teaches Le Mesurier to resent the human, the realm of limitation and mortality, and to 'attempt the infinite', which, as Voss describes it, is a savagely masochistic plunge into the primal void. Voss's recruiting works by contagion, by drawing others into the spell of his obsessive myth, and by their eventual succumbing to his powerful vision. His death-romanticism stirs their blood in an irrational way, and hence is all the more effective in producing the desired result—their unquestioning support and subordination.

Harry Robarts is a young recruit who reminds us of the innocent fool Bub Quigley in *The Tree of Man*. He is simple and good 'but superfluous' (p. 21); 'an easy shadow to wear' (p. 31). Harry is helpless before the German's tyrannical power. He devotes himself to Voss, calls him his 'Lord', and is subservient to him throughout the expedition, until he meets his ghastly but inevitable death in the Australian wilderness. Turner is a drunkard and a 'derelict soul' (p. 42), whose longing for annihilation has already expressed itself in his alcoholism and self-destructive lifestyle. For Turner the expedition is a chance to self-destruct in grand style, rather than dissolve anonymously in the gutters of Sydney. It is Turner who readily admits the morbid, perverse side of the expedition, and who announces that Voss's followers have '"Contracted with a practisin' madman ... for a journey to hell an' back"' (p. 43).

A follower of a slightly higher order is Palfreyman. Palfreyman's life story revolves around the image of his hunchback sister, whom he feels he has betrayed, and to whom he will offer himself as a willing sacrifice. During the expedition we discover that Palfreyman had developed an impossible mother/son bond with his sister, who is several years older than himself, and who appears in his dreams and fantasies as a devouring earth-mother.[40] Palfreyman found his sister overbearing in her love, and was agonized by his own incestuous longing, and so he escaped to another hemisphere,[41] leaving his sister to her own fate. Of course his passion was merely aggravated and intensified by a sense of guilt and betrayal: 'It was ... this same sister from whom he had run, at least, from her passionate, consuming nature, with the result that he was never finished wondering how he might atone for his degrading attitude' (p. 287). This is Palfreyman's state as Voss encounters him. He views the expedition as a means of atonement, whereby he offers himself to the mother–world and dissolves into the landscape as into her own image. By serving the Earth Mother as the natural scientist of the party, and by journeying toward her secret depths, he relieves himself of his guilt and satisfies his unrequited longing at the same time. For Palfreyman Voss is a kind of deliverer, a figure who enables him to live out his incestuous fantasies.

Apart from Voss himself, whose maternal image is carried throughout by Laura Trevelyan, Palfreyman is the only member of the party whose inner complex is personified by a female figure who coaxes him into the Australian interior. At several points in the story his sister appears before him as an apparition, and as his death approaches she takes him by the hand and leads him into the Beyond. The others, Le Mesurier, Turner, Robarts, merely experience the maternal realm as an imageless void; an impersonal abyss into which they fling themselves and by which they are consumed.

II

It has become almost a cliché in Australian literary criticism to speak of the Voss/Laura relationship as an animus/anima involvement. But it is clear that the central relationship is based upon the *puer*/Mother myth, a vastly different category of archetypal experience.[42] James McAuley was the first to announce that Laura Trevelyan is 'the Jungian anima', and since then Barry Argyle, Peter Beatson and Judith Wright, among others, have made the same erroneous analysis.[43] The problem is that a kind of half-knowledge of Jung exists among literary circles, and the psychological terms are rarely employed with the precision that they demand. 'Anima' and 'animus' are used far too loosely, and to read the novel in these terms is to inflate the meaning of the central relationship and to lose sight of its darker side. In anima/animus involvements the transformative aspect of the unconscious is brought to the fore, enhancing the personalities and furthering the conscious development of both parties. But in the *puer*/Mother relationship the erotic connection is destructive. From the woman's side, the *puer* figure is not so much the positive animus as he is the 'Ghostly Lover' of ancient folklore, who leads the woman into madness and disintegration.[44] To be drawn into the realm of these archaic figures is to be swallowed up in the depths of the collective unconscious. Laura may seem like the anima, in that she is young and maidenly, but she functions as the enchantress who drowns her lover in a sea of eros. Her mythological counterparts are not Dante's Beatrice, or Petrarch's Laura, as has been suggested, but Circe, the Sirens, the Lorelei, and all those ancient beauties whose task it was to captivate men and draw them toward an ecstatic death.

It is fascinating to observe the transformation in Laura's personality as the Ghostly Lover invades her character from within and converts a conservative English gentlewoman into a dissolution-striving mystic. At first Laura is resistant to Voss. She finds him disturbing and 'repulsive' (p. 72), and clings to her identity as the sheltered niece of Edmund and Mrs Bonner. Gradually Voss acquires a certain fascination for her. Her family dismiss him as a 'madman' (p. 27), or more simply as a 'foreigner' (p. 7), but, much to their surprise, Laura begins to admire his grandiose designs. She argues that Voss is 'not afraid' of this country, whereas 'everyone [else] is still afraid, or most of us, . . . and will not say it' (p. 28). And she remarks: '"We are not yet possessed of understanding"', assuming, of course, that Voss is. The fact that he is a foreigner merely adds to his attractiveness, because the contrasexual figure of the unconscious is a 'foreign' element in a woman's psyche, and is often experienced through strange or exotic men.

At her second meeting with Voss, Laura is decidedly inspired and moved by the foreigner's presence:

She did not raise her head for [the words] the German spoke, but heard them fall, and loved their shape. So far departed from that rational level to which she had determined to adhere, her own thoughts were grown obscure, even natural. She did not care. It was lovely. (p. 63)

Here we find that a deeper, more 'natural' level of her being is being evoked. An archetypal process has begun and she allows it to take full possession. Laura's assimilation to the infantile *puer*–animus is emphasized by her sudden association with the idiot youth Willie Pringle. Willie, 'a boy, or youth ... with a rather loose, wet, though obviously good-natured mouth' (p. 63) is a classic *puer* figure, a counterpart of Bub Quigley and Harry Robarts. There can be little doubt that Laura would have given this boy short shrift prior to her descent into the unconscious, but now she is inspired by his child-like wonder, his clumsiness and irrational nature. Poor Willie takes Laura's interest personally and imagines himself as her consort, but it is apparent that the fascination is purely archetypal. He is a fleeting image of her *puer*–animus, an image which is more completely carried by Voss himself.

The awakening of the contrasexual masculine side is evident in Laura's sudden penchant for witticisms and great thoughts, and in her philosophical outbursts in public and social situations (p. 82 f). Shy and introverted before her meeting with Voss, she now becomes forthright in her behaviour. She succeeds in outwitting all the men in her social circle, and makes fools of Tom Radclyffe and Mr Pringle. She becomes an intellectual monster, feared by men and hated by women. The masculine side manifests as an intellectual force, but its effect is negative because the archetype is not controlled or humanized by the conscious mind. Laura's spiritual pronouncements never quite hit the mark, her assessment of Voss's progress seems inflated, and her so-called revelations ('"Dear Christ, now at last I understand your suffering"') appear stilted and forced. Her personality progressively disintegrates as the *puer*–animus, represented throughout by Voss, seizes full control, leading her finally to emotional and mental collapse.

Up until the time of the departure of the expedition, Voss has thought little of Miss Trevelyan. There have been momentary feelings of warmth, but he is more preoccupied with his inner, mythic lover, and he shows little interest. Even at their wharfside farewell Voss dismisses Laura in a blunt manner, causing her to recoil and become defensive. She is not yet his companion, but a mere human woman who can never compete with the Mother Goddess. It is only later, when he is riding through the wilderness, that he falls in love with Laura—or, we should say, that his internal figure begins to take on her form, her guise. Distance is not an obstacle to their love, it is the essential precondition for it. It is only from afar that their forms begin to acquire mythic dimension and to merge with the inward figures.[45] The entire affair takes place in imagination and has no personal basis. If, somehow, the lovers were to be physically reunited, the relationship would dissolve immediately, because Voss's or White's Goddess will never allow a mortal woman to wear the divine mantle. Still further, the sexual complication would ensure its final collapse. The negative, devouring-womb image would inevitably be projected upon the woman, making intercourse virtually impossible. Their relationship can take place at the level of divine love, or *agape*, but would not stand the test of sexual contact. Their minds and fantasies mingle, and the product of this *coniunctio* is Rose Portion's child Mercy. Conveniently, the entire sexual issue is parcelled out to Laura's maid, whose profane coupling with Jack Slipper leads to the timely birth of the unwanted child. Even more conveniently, the mother dies soon after the birth, leaving Laura to cherish her very own spiritual child. The whole episode involving Mercy is an ugly and unnecessary literalization of the 'fruit' of the Voss/Laura marriage, but more to the point it serves to highlight the tremendous gulf between sexuality and love in White's world. The *puer*/Mother marriage is a marriage of the spirit only, an invisible tie that does not permit a full, bodily, human interaction.[46] When Voss later realizes that he and Laura 'had been married an eternity' (p. 269) he is simply acknowledging the complete integration of his internal psychic image with the fantasy of Laura, and is not making any statement about the real woman back in the Bonners' drawing-room.

III

As she appears at the wharfside, seated 'sculpturally upon her mastered horse' (p. 109), Laura begins to emerge as a truly mythic figure. All the men at the docks are immediately drawn to this singular woman. Like Stan Parker's Madeleine, who was also frequently astride a gallant steed, she is an object of desire, yet aloof, remote and strangely untouchable. Tom Palfreyman engages in brief conversation with Miss Trevelyan, but as he turns away from her to board the *Osprey* he is overwhelmed by a sensation of drowning and dissolution:

She looked towards Palfreyman. As he withdrew through the already considerable crowd, he received the impression of a drowning that he was unable to avert, in a dream through which he was sucked inevitably back.

Ah, Laura was crying out, bending down through that same dream, extending her hand in its black glove; you are my only friend, and I cannot reach you. (p. 109)

This is the first indication that Laura is to function as a destructive Siren figure. Palfreyman feels that he is being drawn into the disorienting vortex of nightmare, that he is being 'sucked inevitably back'. As the ego enters the mother–world, it loses its centredness and feels that it is dissolving in the unconscious. Laura's operatic gesture and gloved hands link her all the more clearly with the image of the beckoning enchantress. She is the angel of death who invites Palfreyman, as her 'only friend' to unite with her. It is evident that Palfreyman has unconsciously associated Laura with his goddess-like sister, the primary carrier in his life of the seductive feminine image. This suggests how fluid, impersonal and collective are his images of the Goddess. 'She' appears now as his sister, now as Laura, now as the Australian landscape into which he dissolves. The incident also shows that the experience of Laura is not limited to Voss alone. Laura is a powerful archetypal image, and in a sense every member of the expedition is held under her sway.

As the party moves westward, toward the centre of the continent, it is the pleasurable side of egoic dissolution which predominates at the outset. Voss feels as if he is entering a 'gentle, healing landscape' (p. 124), and Le Mesurier and Palfreyman begin to sense the relief and joyousness which is a characteristic feature of matriarchal incest. Like Stan Parker, Voss imagines that he is being upborne and caressed by the landscape itself: 'At once the hills were enfolding him ... and he was touching [them] and was not surprised at their suave flesh' (p. 139). As the men approach Rhine Towers, the joyous aspect of their 'homecoming' to the mother is reflected in the manner of the little children who run out to meet them: 'the children would run along the track in the wake of the riders, jumping the mounds of yellow dung, shouting and sniffing, as if they had know the horsemen all along' (p. 125). Always, in White, children represent the positive, vital side of the mother's world, and wherever they get together in song and celebration it is as if a pagan or natural rite were being enacted.

The approach to Rhine Towers sets the scene for the unearthly entry into the mother–world:

[I]t was the valley itself which drew Voss. Its mineral splendours were increased in that light. As bronze retreated, veins of silver loomed in the gullies, knobs of amethyst and sapphire glowed on the hills, until the horsemen rounded that bastion which fortified from sight the ultimate stronghold of beauty. (p. 128)

This is no mere entry into an outback Australian settlement. It is a mythical homecoming to the Eternal City, a place full of marvellous light and jewelled splendour. The rocky entrances are like the portals of another world, the opening to childhood paradise.

The splendid vision soon disappears as the *pueri* penetrate the maternal realm: 'Now the beauty of their approach to Rhine Towers appeared to have been a tragic one, of which the last fragments were crumbling in the dusk' (p. 129). Significantly, the first person they meet as they enter the disintegrative source is Mrs Sanderson, a powerful, materialistic mother–figure. Voss's immediate response is to feel trapped and ensnared by her materialism. He rejects her offer to sleep inside her house (cf. Figure 4b), much to the amazement of Mr Sanderson, their kindly host. Le Mesurier sees the woman as an evil force: 'the serpent has slid even into this paradise, Frank Le Mesurier realized, and sighed'. As soon as Mrs Sanderson insists that the men must sleep inside her house ('"But all the beds are aired," ventured the be-wildered Mrs Sanderson') Palfreyman collapses in his saddle, and falls to the ground. The *puer* has been overcome by the Mother's power. Palfreyman is carried unconscious into the house, and Voss and his party sleep in the imprisoning matrix after all. Their external protest is pointless, because they are bound, psychologically and mythically, to the destructive power of the maternal realm.

It is at Rhine Towers that Judd, the emancipist convict who will become leader of the mutinous party, joins the expedition. Ralph Angus also enlists at this point, and he and Judd are strong, muscular men who represent a threat to Voss's visionary nature. Judd tends to override Voss's leadership at crucial moments, and proves more capable than Voss of handling the practical realities of the expedition. At Rhine Towers the *puer*–spirit is not only laid low by the devouring Mrs Sanderson, but it is challenged within its own ranks by the inclusion of an earthly, material element. In mythology, the *puer* is always reduced by a shadowy, material force, for it is his encounter with the dark side of the *magna mater* which eventually destroys him.

IV

The mythologization of Laura progresses steadily as the party moves further into the interior. The landscape which had earlier seemed to surround and embrace Voss is further enlivened by its imaginative identification with Laura: 'He continued to think about the young woman, there on the banks of the river, where the points of her wooden elbows glimmered in the dusk' (p. 152). The earth has become a living presence, a realm of feminine contours and forms, a landscape imbued with the image of the Great Mother:

All the immediate world was soon swimming in the same liquid green. She was clothed in it. Green shadows almost disguised her face, where she walked amongst the men, to whom, it appeared, she was known, as others were always known to one another, from childhood, or by instinct. (p. 198)

A dark, ambivalent aspect begins to invade this wonderful apparition: 'Then he noticed how her greenish flesh was spotted with blood . . ., and that she would laugh at, and understand the jokes shared with others, while he continued to express himself in foreign words, in whichever language he used' (p. 199). This Green Goddess, then, is decidedly pagan and chthonic.[47] She is spotted with blood. As she cavorts with the ordinary men and enjoys their jokes, Voss begins to suspect that his mystical bride is not his at all: 'Only he was the passing acquaintance, at whom she did glance once, since it was unavoidable'. Laura does not belong to Voss, any more than the spirit of the land belongs to him. He cannot truly wed the Great Mother, for she is too vast, amorphous and collective. Like the goddess Aphrodite, Laura is a shared experience, a woman who enjoys the company of many and who can never be tied down to one man. Only the anima–bride respects the single alliance, for the anima symbolizes a more differentiated, humanized aspect of the feminine realm. And so Laura assumes an ambivalent character that Voss had not anticipated. Gradually her Kali-like nature begins to surface.

Voss has a dream which highlights this demonic aspect. He dreams that he enters a pond of lilies with his beloved, only to find that he is being drawn toward his death. 'Now they were swimming so close they were joined together at the waist, and were the same flesh of lilies, their mouths, together, were drowning in the same love-stream' (p. 187). This is a classic representation of the Siren-like character of the mother–world, and of the sickly death–romanticism that is at the background of every *puer*/Mother alliance. The reappearance of the death-lily at this late stage is significant. It shows that the image is still alive in Voss's psyche as a symbol of the seductive matrix. Now *he* is the doomed insect–man who flies unwarily into the gaping maw. The dream goes on to connect Laura with the death-lily. Holding the womb-shaped flower in her hands, she informs Voss that she maintains the superior position in their relationship, and that it is 'the woman who unmakes men, to make saints' (p. 188). This is a bold, explicit statement of Voss's inner situation. The dream reverses the attitude of his conscious mind, showing him in his truly helpless position, at the mercy of a figure who 'unmakes men' and leads them to their doom. The dream also points to the consolation prize that is offered to the destroyed *puer*: the illusion of sainthood. We have seen throughout how the mother archetype provides all manner of illusions and enticements to keep the *puer* bound to its service. In Elyot's story it was the illusion of spiritual awakening, in Theodora's it was cosmic consciousness, and with Parker and Voss it is Christian transcendence. The disintegration of the mind is made to appear as Christian self-sacrifice; the dissolution of the will is disguised as the realignment of the will with the divine. The religious misinterpretation is primarily conveyed to us through the utterances of Laura Trevelyan,[48] so that her voice becomes the vehicle through which the Mother puts forward her distorted reading of Voss's suffering. If we read the story through Laura's eyes, we end up espousing the same inflated standpoint that the complex itself provides.[49]

At this point the cavalcade is plagued by drought, heat, famine and disease. Even the ground becomes rocky, treacherous, and covered with crawling insects and reptiles. Voss's horse is attacked by a snake, and as it bucks up in terror the rider's forehead is gashed by a tree. Then he is kicked in the stomach by a staked mule, and has to spend several days recovering from the blow. In the presence of these painful events, Voss notices that his ever-present Goddess is radiant and smiling:

When they had remounted and were riding on, Voss wondered how much of himself he had given into her hands. For he had become aware that the mouth of the young woman was smiling. It was unusually full and compassionate. Approbation must have gone to his head, for he continued unashamedly to contemplate her pleasure, and to extract from it pleasure of his own. They were basking in the same radiance, which had begun to emanate from the hitherto lustreless earth. (pp. 208–9)

The negative attacks of the brute landscape give way to the ghostly smile of his demonic inspiratrice. And because the earth mother delights in his ritual disintegration, the *puer* is able to glean 'pleasure of his own', for his greatest fulfilment is to serve and placate his goddess. In spite of the appalling physical conditions he is able to 'bask in the radiance' which emanates from the smiling head. Hereafter there is frequent juxtapositioning of horrifying physical events with consoling apparitions and erotic fantasies associated with Laura. The seductive fantasies act as a drug, dulling the nightmare of the *puer*'s self-disintegration.

Palfreyman's fate reveals most dramatically the horror of this kind of archetypal entrancement. On the eve of his death at the hands of a tribe of natives, Palfreyman reviews his relation to his goddess-like sister in the following sequence.

He . . . was a small, weak, ineffectual man that his sister had flung upon a bed of violets. There, upon those suffocating small flowers, he had failed her kisses, but would offer himself, as another sacrifice, to other spears. The close cave intensified his personal longing. One side of him Voss, the other his lady sister, in her cloak that was the colour of ashes. Towards morning her hand, with its unnaturally pronounced finger-joints, took his hand, and they walked into the distant embers, which hurt horribly, but which he must continue to endure, as he was unfitted for anything else. (pp. 281–2)

This is a vivid example of the workings of the demonic mother in the psyche of the *puer aeternus*. She comes to him in the night, a creature of the unconscious, and lures him away to a fantasy world of 'distant embers'. The approach to the nether world 'hurt horribly' because the fantasy voyage is nothing less than a journey into disintegration. The fantasy is a prefiguration of Palfreyman's death, which occurs soon after. The passage informs us that 'he had failed her kisses, but would offer himself . . . to other spears'. Clearly, he invites the Aborigines to subdue him. It is no mere external attack, but a bizarre fulfilment of his own compulsive death-romanticism.

At the scene of his death, Palfreyman walks out unarmed amongst a horde of desert natives. He announces that he will 'trust to his faith' (p. 341), and even Voss has to admit that his claim 'sounded terribly weak'. As he moves out in long, confident strides, he invokes the image of his sister, recalls 'the love he had denied [her]', and now feels ecstatically reunited with her. Palfreyman becomes 'clearer' and 'more transparent' with each step, until, when the fatal spear strikes his chest, he bursts into a fit of laughter, the hysterical laugher of a *puer* who has finally returned to the matrix. We can hardly blame the Aborigines for his death; on the contrary, they have merely facilitated a dream, or have helped bring a mythic process to its final consummation.

V

In complete contrast to these scenes of frenzied self-mutilation are the scenes of the conservative, fearful 'huddlers' back in Sydney. The chapters which keep returning us to the life of the Bonners and their circle during the course of the expedition have not only a narrative function, but a psychological function as well. They provide a necessary opposite pole to the nihilistic *pueri* in the desert, anxious to destroy themselves in pursuit of a childhood dream of paradise. Whenever the desire for dissolution reaches the intensity reflected in Voss's party, the psyche is impelled to constellate an opposite position, a kind of survival instinct which resists the movement toward death. It is not appropriate to speak of a life–instinct in this case, because the huddlers represent a nullifying, conventional resistance to everything psychic and interior.

'I would not like to ride very far into [this country],' admitted Belle, 'and meet a lot of blacks, and deserts, and rocks, and skeletons, they say, of men that have died.' (p. 28)

'There may, in fact, be a veritable paradise adorning the interior. Nobody can say. But I am inclined to believe, Mr Voss, that you will discover a few blackfellers, and a few flies, and something resembling the bottom of the sea.' (p. 62)

They have a negative attitude toward the unconscious, and skate around on the surface of life, clinging to what is known and rationally acceptable. The point is that no matter how much White despises the Bonner group, he is bound to portray them as being rigidly defensive, because they represent the corollary of the anarchic sensibility that has been established in the explorers. The instinctual fear of incest and the matrix is not apparent in the inland story, and so must be pursued outside the central focus, in emotional tones which equal the tenacity and fanaticism of the explorers. Because of the psychological nature of the Sydney/ outback duality, we must not view the huddlers as an accurate portrayal of Australian society in the 1840s. White is primarily concerned with his own internal conflict, and is dealing with historical issues only insofar as these provide a context for his psychological drama.

But the novel suffers from the intra-psychic débâcle. The endless to and fro movement between opposite societies becomes tedious, the two worlds seem irreconcilable. In photographic terms, the Sydney scenes are over-exposed, there is too much brute light and everyday reality. The huddlers are referred to as 'the children of light, who march in, and throw the shutters right back' (p. 16). The inland scenes are dark and mystical in comparison. There we have to focus more circumspectly, upon a nightscape full of grotesque happenings and ghostly fantasies of the mind. The alternating contrasts become more pronounced and disturbing as the novel progresses. As the story moves toward its climax, the tensions in White's psyche become extreme, the resistance to disintegration keeping pace with the fanatic desire for it.

We found these conflicting elements in the character of Elyot Standish. There was a desperate longing for the maternal depths matched by an almost hysterical resistance to anything dark, mysterious, irrational. Thus the tensions which were originally contained in Elyot's psyche have split apart and now confront each other as separate societies or worlds. The problem, at its very essence, is that mind and imagination are dissociated in White's fiction. The dissolution-striving *puer* figure continues unthinkingly, and unconsciously, upon his course. Time and again we sense in White an acute absence of the intellect, a lack of reflection in relation to his symbolic material, and a blind faith entrusted to the imagination. When Elyot made his return to the landscape of childhood, he did not reflect upon the process, but merely plunged into the psychic world. This appears to be White's own pattern: his civilized mind and educated Cantabrigian self is thrown out of the way, tossed off as excess baggage, when it comes to following the impulses of his inner life. The conscious self, upon which the huddlers appear to be based, remains dull and boorish, heavy with its educated superfluities and conventional manners, while the untutored inner self remains trapped in its archetypal entrancement and nihilism.

Within the inland group the survival instinct does make a partial appearance. As the party moves further toward extinction, a second 'huddler' society emerges within the cavalcade itself. It is Turner who strives to create the split-off group, and who suddenly urges Judd and Angus to support him in a bid for safety and refuge. After the horrifying spectacle of Palfreyman's ritual death and Le Mesurier's madness, it becomes obvious to the others that they are not involved in an exploration of a continent,[50] but in a cult of the dead. Turner tells Angus, who has partly to be won over, that Voss and his inner circle are intent on 'mad things' and strive to 'blow the world up'. '"People of that kind will destroy what you and I know"'' says the voice of conscience, or the now-converted 'huddler' personality: '"It is a form of madness with them"'' (p. 255). Finally Judd is forced to recognize the cult-like, dangerous nature of the enterprise, and decides to flee from 'the deserts of mysticism' to 'his own fat paddocks' (p. 345).

But the mutinous party does not survive. Turner and Angus die agonizing deaths on their attempted return, and Judd survives only in the flesh, for his mind is tortured and insane by the time he reaches civilization. Even as he arrives at this property Judd finds that his wife and children have died, and that his fat paddocks are ruined. This is only to be expected in White's fiction, for once the personality has set foot in the mother–world, it tends to be shattered by the psychological experience. The mutinous *pueri* disintegrate like the others, only their deaths are without ecstasy because they have turned their backs on the prospect of matriarchal incest.

VI

After this disruption, 'the division led by Voss seemed to move with greater ease' (p. 358). This is understandable because the unconscious resistance to the expedition has been exorcized by the mutinous party. Now the *pueri* can move all the more readily into incestuous annihilation. Finally Voss's party reaches a circular plain of stones, which is the mythic *locus*, the goal of the journey, where their horrific deaths and suicides are to be enacted. As they approach the sacred site the desert Aborigines line up on either side of them, as if to provide an 'escort' (p. 363) for their mythic homecoming. Just as the bush children greeted them at the gates of Rhine Towers, so here the ancient 'children' of the earth facilitate their entry into the mother–world. But as they move to the centre of the quartz field, the Aborigines close in behind them, and at once they feel imprisoned in this archaic place: 'It was seen that the two columns of natives had come upon their rear, and were standing ranged behind them in an arc of concentrated silence' (p. 364). This is a wonderful expression of the sudden shift from positive to negative experiences of the matrix, a pattern noted throughout White's fiction. At first the matrix appears inviting, but once it is penetrated it becomes a place of ruin and imprisonment. The natives who had so playfully guided them into this realm suddenly become aggressive gaolers, barring their escape. At this point Jackie, Voss's Aboriginal guide, turns hostile toward the explorers. He joins forces with the enemy tribe, and acts as an associate of two native women, one young with 'nubile breasts' (p. 377), the other old and haggard. These are the young-old mothers who arrange for the dismemberment of Voss and the disposal of the white corpses. The devouring activity in White is always conceived in a symbolically matriarchal context. When Jackie finally hacks off the head of Voss he is not acting from his own initiative, but is merely 'obeying orders' (p. 377) which are handed down from the mothers of the tribe.

The movement into this matrix is accompanied by a series of hallucinations of Laura Trevelyan. The Goddess stands in the wings, as it were, whispering all kinds of comforting remarks and assurances as Voss enters the final stage of his self-torture. Chief among these is the characteristic religious rhetoric about his achievement of transcendence and near-divinity. '"Do you see now?" she asked. "Man is God decapitated. That is why you are bleeding"' (p. 364). This kind of grotesque, over-blown rhetoric can be found throughout this last phase, distorting Voss's but also the reader's understanding of what is taking place. It is not entirely White's own conscious contrivance, but derives in part from the mother–complex itself. The Mother delights in consuming the *puer*, drinking his life-blood and essence, while telling him that it is all for his own good.

As Voss is dissolved in the maternal image the terrible numbing and loss of willpower that results is misinterpreted by Laura, and by White, as his achievement of humility. '"Now that he is humble"' Laura announces, '"[and] has learnt that he is not God ... he is nearest to becoming so"' (pp. 386–7). Laura's interpretation has governed most critical responses to the novel. The thumbnail sketch that is usually provided is that *Voss* is about a proud man who is 'truly humbled'. This is what the mother archetype would like us to believe. But there is a tremendous difference between psychological castration, or the loss of self in the matrix, and humility, an affirmative condition in which the self recognizes its true position in relation to higher powers. *Humilitas* is not a pathological dissolution but an active and carefully considered attunement of the personality to the divine. In every case, White's 'religious' figures are not genuine illuminates but castrated *pueri*. Voss has been 'unmade' by the Mother, deprived of masculine power, and set up as a mock saint.

When Le Mesurier asks his 'deliverer' for his plan, Voss simply replies: '"I have no plan, but will trust to God"' (p. 379). At this Le Mesurier stumbles away toward a dead tree and cuts his throat with a pocket knife. This is a classic image of the self-mutilating *puer aeternus*. One is reminded of the *puer* god Attis, who castrated himself beneath a pine tree and bled to death. Attis destroyed his manhood in a state of frenzy, crying 'For thee, Cybele!', as he flung the severed phallus to the ground.[51] Attis's blood was said to rejuvenate the earth, to please the Goddess Cybele, and to cause her to 'make the world green' and bring on the spring.[52] In his Rimbaud-like prose poem, Le Mesurier writes, '"Flesh is for hacking ... My blood will water the earth and make it green"' (pp. 296–7).[53] He ends the savage poem with an incantatory hymn to the earth-spirit, expressing his desire for total anonymity, to become one with the elements and to be 'everywhere and nowhere' at the same time. A mythic process has taken control, he identifies with the pagan sacrificial god, and in his self-mutilation beneath the tree he carries out to the letter the archaic celebration of the Earth Goddess.

As Voss dies he is watched over by an Aboriginal elder, a shaman who has come to defeat his 'white man's magic'. In a state of total delirium, Voss imagines that this shamanic figure gradually changes into an image of his beloved Goddess:

[I]n the grey light it transpired that the figure was that of a woman, whose breasts hung like bags of empty skin above the white man's face . . . . While the woman sat looking down at her knees, the greyish skin was slowly revived, until her full, white, immaculate body became the shining source of all light. By its radiance, he did finally recognize her face ... (p. 383)

It is fascinating that Laura appears as an Aboriginal woman before she assumes the form of a 'full, white, immaculate body'. It is, as we have noted, the Aboriginal mothers who arrange Voss's death, and the most powerful figure, the old, ugly woman, is said to have sagging, empty bags of breasts (p. 383). This sequence of images suggests that Laura is at bottom a dark, destroying figure who shares a psychological affinity with his primitive captors. It is here that Voss has a sudden vision of Laura's head with leeches, wounds and running blood upon it; an image having associations with the death-dealing Gorgon.[54] But these spontaneous representations do not cause Voss—or White—to reflect upon the nature of the figure who guides him. And by now, of course, it is too late. As he is slain by order of the Aboriginal mothers, Voss dreams that Laura hands him the death-lily which has haunted him since his early youth.

VII

Laura's journey into 'the country of the mind' (p. 446) is as darkly ambivalent as that of her fantasy lover. Up until Voss's death she is lured, by her own *puer*–animus, into disintegrative regions of the unconscious, by which time her ego is all but obliterated. The Sydney doctors are bewildered by her condition, and appear unable to effect a cure. Eventually Dr Kilwinning, never at a loss to provide a remedy for a paying client, orders Laura's hair to be shaved and applies leeches to her head so that they might draw out the badness and cure her of her 'brain fever' (p. 353). Such mediaeval treatment seems to please the Bonners, and on the eve of Voss's death the leeches are applied to what then becomes the 'medusa-head' (p. 386). When Voss's head is hacked off, her own inner tie to the Ghostly Lover is severed, and she is released from the destructive grip of the unconscious. The Bonners interpret her change according to their own frame ('"Oh, dear . . . the fever has broken!"'), and Laura sinks into a post-psychotic state of exhaustion. Laura's personality has not been transformed by her involvement with the Ghostly Lover. When she recovers from the psychological adventure she returns to her earlier state of being before she met Voss. She emerges from the chaos as if nothing ever happened, as if she were surfacing from a bad dream only to reawaken to her former self. The whole experience has taken place in the inner depths, and has occurred without conscious awareness, so that the reinstated ego is unaffected by it.

In some ways Laura's personality seems more rigidly rational than before. In her role as headmistress of Misses Linsleys' Academy for Young Ladies she is described as 'regimented', 'stilted' (p. 411), and 'stern' (p. 430). The ego has not assimilated anything of the inner journey, but has simply erected a defensive barricade in order to protect itself against further inundation. In her new regime there is no room for an inner life, and no place for the *puer*–animus:

The vows were rigorous that she imposed upon herself, to the exclusion of all personal life, certainly of introspection, however great her longing for those delights of hell. The gaunt man, her husband, would not tempt her in. (p. 404)

When Colonel Hebden tries to prod her for information about Voss, she takes fright and even denies her intense involvement with the explorer: '"It is all done with. I knew the person in question very slightly. He dined once at my uncle's house"' (p. 406). The emotional interaction sinks into the unconscious, and she remembers only the insignificant factual aspects of their meeting. Voss and all he represents is now taboo, because she has no way of coping with the disintegrative forces that this figure unleashes in her life.

In White's fiction the ego either abandons itself completely to the unconscious (Voss, Parker, Laura during the expedition), or it lives in absolute denial of anything interior (Laura at the beginning and end, Elyot Standish, the Bonners). It can strike no balance between rigidity and dissolution, between sterile order and anarchical chaos. The archetypal background is too powerful and explosive, causing the ego to adopt either one of these extreme positions. *Voss* ends on this divisive note: explorers disintegrate and huddlers, with the addition of Miss Trevelyan, continue to huddle. The novel leaves off with an intra-psychic war between ego and unconscious, and a disastrous rift between social and interior worlds.

VIII

White criticism tends to go astray by focusing upon the author's stated intentions and claims, instead of paying careful attention to the novels themselves. It is disturbing to see how often commentators suspend critical judgement in order to make way for the author's views. For example, in relation to *The Tree of Man* White tells us that he wanted to write a book about 'an ordinary man and woman', about life in the Australian bush, and immediately critics begin to extol the 'ordinariness' of Stan and Amy Parker.[55] They have commented approvingly on how unlike Theodora Goodman Stan Parker is, and how his attitudes are 'positive', 'affirmative', and 'social'.[56] But this is sheer nonsense. White may strive to present an image of the ordinary man, but this is not what he achieves. Beneath his farmer's disguise, Stan Parker is Bub Quigley, or Mr Gage, or the man suspended in the tree. He is a *puer aeternus* who shares all the traits which were characteristic of Theodora: he is dissolution-striving, other-worldly, estranged. It is simply that Parker is outwardly less eccentric than Theodora. Inwardly he is no less committed to the same mystic longing.

We find the same anomaly in the characterization of Voss, who is presented by the author within the classic heroic context, and who is celebrated across the country—in academic journals, newspapers and school textbooks—as a national hero.[57] But Voss is not the hero that White, Laura or Australia wants him to be.

Voss is an obsessed madman whose primary motivation is to annihilate himself and a few others in the maternal source. The noble concerns of scientific exploration, heroic achievement, national identity, do not impinge even slightly upon his consciousness, yet these are the concerns which are said to inspire the undertaking.[58] The great expedition—the preparations, the patronage, the talk—is so much stage machinery, an excess of social obligation which actually runs counter to the real need of the *puer*: mystic dissolution. James McAuley realized this when he wrote, 'The whole journey is unreal to Voss as a practical enterprise'.[59] Perhaps it would have been better if, as he once suggested to Laura, he had set off into the desert barefoot and alone. That would have been a truer act, more appropriate to his actual longing.

In the final analysis Voss is no more convincing as an explorer than Stan Parker was as a pioneer farmer. Somehow neither character fulfils the prescribed role, for the roles are heavy with social responsibility and that is what the *puer* shuns at every turn. White is more honest with characters like Theodora Goodman and Hurtle Duffield, who are allowed to live out their anti-social impulses in a naked way. When he tries to create national heroes he is actually working against himself, against his own mythic force. For White's mode is both anti-heroic and anti-national. The *puer aeternus* is not concerned with achievement and social identity. He strives to escape from his individual existence in time and place.

This brings me to my next point: the Australianness of White's contribution. In the past critics have been anxious to identify and celebrate the Great Australian Novel, and *The Tree of Man* and *Voss* have been obvious candidates for this title. Yet so anxious were we as a nation to fill the cultural void, that we praised White's books on superficial appearances alone, and did not bother to penetrate their meaning. We thought—or wanted to believe—that they affirmed the Australia that we knew, that they gave expression to the country's values and sensibility.[60] But Parker and Voss are both alienated mystics. They are not interested in society, mateship, family, the quality of life; they inhabit a kind of dream-world where such external realities are irrelevant. Stan Parker finds his self-definition in relation to the land, but his experience of Nature is archetypal and universal. We feel that he might as well be Theodora Goodman, wandering obliviously through the landscape of south-west America. With Voss, too, the vision of the Goddess and her mythic world outweighs or even annihilates specific categories of time and space. For White the country of the mind is the primary reality, and the impassioned plunge into maternal depths is for him more important than questions of national identity.

There may be another, deeper sense in which Voss and Parker are Australian. They could be seen to represent the unconscious life of this country, the heavily repressed but at the same time ever-present longing for extinction, oblivion, anonymity. This has been a constant element in Australian literature from colonial times, and it is exemplified in the work of such diverse writers as Henry Lawson, Christopher Brennan, David Malouf and Kenneth Slessor. It would require another study to fully establish and clarify this nihilistic preoccupation, as well as to explore its political and social ramifications. But there can be no doubt that beneath the busy, achieving Australian consciousness is a completely opposite and alien factor, a tendency toward self-abnegation and dissolution. The pull toward Nature is particularly strong here, and I do not simply mean Nature 'out there', the literal outback, but Nature within ourselves, the 'natural' layers of the psyche. When the early settlers and convicts left familiar shores and moved to the underside of the globe, they were making as well a psychological descent into the unconscious. At first the Western ego saw its mission as colonizing and imperialistic. It came to claim all for England, to impose foreign values, to civilize what was seen as a God-forsaken country. But a few artists and sensitive Australians have concentrated on the reverse process: to what extent is this new-old world claiming or conquering us? What exactly does it mean for a white culture to suddenly plant itself upon aboriginal soil? Is the apparition of Laura as a destroying, Aboriginal woman more than Voss's private vision, but an image of the primitive forces which are drawing the white European consciousness toward its ruin? These questions follow those put forward by Judith Wright twenty-five years ago:

Are all these dead men in our literature, then, a kind of ritual sacrifice? And just what is being sacrificed? Is it perhaps the European consciousness— dominating, puritanical, analytical, that Lawrence saw as negated by this landscape?[61]

It is in this archetypal sense that White's vision is perhaps profoundly, if disturbingly, Australian. His work may be a record of what is happening to us on the inside, the compensatory vision to our national colonizing and imperialism.

If Voss and Stan Parker enact what the nation feels as an

archetypal pressure, yet cannot enact—the desire to dissolve into archaic Nature—they may well be legendary figures, not heroes exactly, but legends who sacrifice themselves to the national longing. They offer themselves as fodder to the dragon in the depths, to the fierce, annihilating power at the centre of the Australian psyche. It is ominous that our 'heroes' are anti-heroes, men who fail abysmally to come to terms with the destructive forces of the mother–world. It is as if we have dispensed with the model of the classical hero, of Odysseus bound to the mast yet hearing the Siren song, and celebrate instead those men who unplug their ears and rush wildly toward their ruin. If Voss and Parker are our cultural models it would point to an essential infantilism in the Australian character, a failure on the part of a young society to develop anything more than boyish, puerile ways of relating to the maternal source.[62]

If White's novels are Australian in this deeper mythic sense it is not because of White's efforts, but in spite of them. He strives to obfuscate the *puer* pathology, to cover over the archetypal complexity by converting everything into a familiar, and comforting, story of Christian salvation. The crucial task in our reading is to differentiate between the artificial religious design and the authentic mythic structure. Most often, the Christian frame is asserted through rhetoric and statement, whereas the *puer*/Mother myth is established internally, and sensually, through narrative patterns and archetypal imagery. It is through the *image*—the death-lily, the Aboriginal bride, the hunchback sister, the Medusa head—that we reach into the living matriarchal structure of the work. We need to gain respect for the relative autonomy of the tale, and to understand that it can lead a life of its own independent of the author who created it.

4   The Tree of Unborn Souls

> *An artist usually intellectualizes on top, and his*
> *dark under-consciousness goes on contradicting*
> *him beneath.*
>
> D. H. Lawrence[1]

In *Riders in the Chariot* (1961) the division between the author's religious frame and the actual life of the tale is carried to a further extreme, creating a serious discontinuity in the structure of the work. In this novel the reader has to dig deeper to uncover the narrative myth, because the author has imposed a heavy layer of Jewish and Christian mysticism upon the story. White is inspired by the mother archetype—here personified by Mrs Godbold—to style the tragic fate of the *puer aeternus* in classical religious terms, and to make his otherworldly career conform to the external appearances of holy life. The result is that many readers view the work as 'an essay in Jewish mysticism'.[2] *Riders in the Chariot*, despite its title, its apparent design and its mystical jargon, owes virtually nothing to religious tradition, and is not organically related to Judaism or to Christianity.

The novel is unconsciously based on the pagan vision of the Great Goddess and her son. Mrs Godbold assumes the role of the *magna mater*, and Himmelfarb, Miss Hare and Dubbo all appear as her children, offshoots from the maternal source. They cling to her life like infants to the breast, or like 'unborn souls' to the symbolic Tree of Life. The image of being attached to the maternal tree is central to the novel, and later we find that Alf Dubbo, the artist among the *pueri*, paints a canvas of 'a most unnatural tree' with several 'foetuses' dangling upon it. All of White's characters are caught upon the maternal tree, are unborn souls who have yet to break free from early childhood and are incestuously attracted to the maternal image. The idea of the *unborn* is a useful concept to bear in mind as we approach the novel, since it provides us with a key to the mythic structure, and is not, like the Chariot or the Messianic quest, an alien image imposed upon the text and leading away from its meaning.

I

'All human beings are decadent,' he said. 'The moment we are born, we start to degenerate. Only the unborn soul is whole, pure.' (p. 36)[3]

Norbert Hare's words to his uncomprehending daughter express White's *puer* philosophy as it has emerged from *The Living and the Dead* to the present. For White, growth and development are degenerate, because growth takes the individual away from the unconscious, innocent wholeness of early childhood. The state of uroboric non-existence, which in *Voss* is synonymous with death but which here is primarily a prenatal paradise, is felt to be desirable because it is connected with the idea of ecstatic absorption into the Mother-of-All. But the happy vision is continually defeated by the presence of a 'teeth mother', who symbolizes the disintegrative aspect of this same process. In a sense this archetypal figure is a guardian of human evolution, for if it were not for the devouring monsters of the deep, humanity would surely have succumbed long ago to the delightful prospect of eternal paradise. These devastating figures keep us in life, in reality, in time and space, and make us think twice about the advantages of regression. We can always detect a flawed mystical vision by the presence of teeth mothers, for this suggests that the personality is hankering after an infantile unity, and is about to be devoured by the mythical figures of early childhood.[4]

Miss Hare is perhaps the best and clearest example of the unborn soul in White's work. She lives close to Nature and the elements, and, as her name implies, is virtually a creature of the animal world. Our image of Miss Hare is of a small, freckled figure scurrying through the undergrowth, or kneeling in silent worship before the mysteries of the earth.

Speckled and dappled, like any wild thing native to the place, she was examining her surroundings for details of interest. Almost all were, because alive, changing, growing, personal, like her own thoughts, which intermingled, flapping and flashing, with the leaves, or lay straight and stiff as sticks, or emerged with the painful stench of any crushed ant. (p. 15)

Often we find Miss Hare associated with circular, uroboric imagery; she is 'curled like a foetus' in the grass (p. 22), or she is nestled inside a 'tunnel' of undergrowth, where she is 'embraced by twigs' (pp. 16–17). Her life takes place in the Great Round and she is a mere extension of maternal Nature, or at least she does not have a self which conflicts with it. Like Theodora Goodman, she is possessed by a longing to merge even more completely with the elements and assume a state of absolute anonymity. She rejects life in this world and longs for 'the ecstasy of complete annihilating liberation' (p. 12).

Little wonder, then, that a teeth mother creeps into her garden and attempts to subdue her (Figure 2). For she has summoned this figure forth from the depths of the archetypal world. This psychological fact is given realistic elaboration in the novel, for it is Miss Hare herself who *invites* Mrs Jolley to share her abode at Xanadu. Moreover, she feels compelled to invite her, even against her better judgement (p. 17). The point is that the infantile mystic is never complete without a devouring mother, and although Miss Hare experiences her presence as an alien imposition, she has as much right to Xanadu as Miss Hare herself. Mrs Jolley belongs at Xanadu, just as Amy belonged in Stan Parker's garden or Mrs Goodman in Theodora's Meroë.

As soon as Mrs Jolley gets off the bus at Sarsaparilla, Miss Hare is aware of the teeth of her housekeeper, and imagines them to be 'growing visibly impatient' (p. 40). It is clear that a Teeth Mother has arrived on the scene, and that Miss Hare invests this figure with the demonic image which assails her from within. I say 'invests' because it is not always clear whether Mrs Jolley is as atrociously evil as her employer feels her to be. The problem is compounded to the extent that the narrator is identified with Miss Hare's position, and fails to present Mrs Jolley in an objective light. For him she is pure, unregenerate evil, a creature from the primordial realm. Every action she makes, every swing of her hips, or puzzled tone in her voice, is given an insinuatingly evil stamp by an author over-hasty to project his own inner darkness upon this maternal figure. It is disturbing to realize that Mrs Jolley is never allowed an opportunity to redeem herself, but is foredoomed from the beginning to the pit of hell. For all the reality she conveys to us, Mrs Jolley could well be Miss Hare's hallucination; she is little more than a lurking presence, an anonymous, imaginal force. 'She would appear in doorways or from behind dividing curtains and cough, but very carefully, at certain times. She carried her eyes downcast' (p. 69). The psychic origination of the destroying mother is even more evident in the case of Mrs Flack, whom Miss Hare has never met but whose presence she 'infers' from her ebullient imagination.

Miss Hare could feel [Mrs Flack's] presence. In certain rather metallic light, behind clumps of ragged, droughty laurels, in corners of rooms where dry rot had encouraged the castors to burst through the boards, on landings where wall-paper hung in drunken brown festoons, or departed from the wall in one long limp sheet, Mrs Flack obtruded worst, until Miss Hare began to fear . . . for the safety of her property. (p. 78)

This hysterical passage emphasizes the fantastic nature of the images that are confronting Miss Hare from her highly activated unconscious. As the narrative unfolds, White becomes less a social realist and more a writer of fairytale and myth. 'Flack' and 'Jolley' become interchangeable names for the one mythic force. At any moment we expect the witches to sit naked around a boiling pot and cast a spell upon the innocent mystics. When Mrs Jolley returns from her visits to *Karma* she appears to her employer as 'a communicant returning from the altar' (p. 78). Eventually the housekeeper assumed 'monumental stance' and Miss Hare is 'almost turned to stone' (p. 71) by Mrs Jolley's lethal gaze, a fact which confirms the latter's fantastic, Gorgon-like nature.

For all her evil power Mrs Jolley has a potentially positive aspect. She is not a mere diabolism of the external world, but a creative experiment of the protagonist's own psychic construction.[5] Her task is to act as a mirror in which Miss Hare might perceive her own self-devouring aspect. The hints are there in the text—'The sound of the two women's breathing would intermingle distressingly at times' (p. 41). Mrs Jolley, the Evil One, presents her employer with a cake, with 'For a Bad Girl' written on it in icing, but Miss Hare does not comprehend her meaning. There are other familiar clues:

'I have been in the bush,' Miss Hare confessed.
Mrs Jolley sucked her perfect teeth.
'And on a Sunday!' (p. 63)

but Miss Hare does not recognize the appropriateness of Mrs Jolley's scarecrow image to her own destructive longing. And this, finally, is what makes their meeting and life together at Xanadu such an abortive and tedious affair. Miss Hare does not deal with her companion at an inner level, but sees her merely as an external, outside annoyance. '"You do not know me"' Mrs Jolley insists, '"any more than you don't know nothing at all"' (p. 54). Her claim is truer than Miss Hare is able to realize. She knows nothing of the witch–power that holds her fast from within.

II

In her childhood relation to her father, Mary Hare carries the demonic role that she will later project upon Mrs Jolley. This is a fascinating reversal of roles, because it shows how flexible and relative the diabolical image is in White's world, how easily it is transferred from one character to another. It also points to what I have been suggesting, that Miss Hare is possessed by a demonic power, and so can act as a carrier of this energy for other characters.

Norbert Hare's situation is similar to that of the ego-bound huddlers in the previous novel. He is an image of White's rational personality, which erects a defensive barricade against the inner world, yet which is constantly plagued by inner disturbances. Norbert's attempt at a barricade is represented by the construction of Xanadu, the European extravagance which is imposed upon the primitive Australian landscape. By daring to erect such a proud and alien structure, Norbert invokes the destructive spirit of the land. Soon after its completion we find that the 'native cynicism' of 'the grey raggedy scrub' (p. 15) begins to undermine his grand designs, and that within a few years the massive Pleasure Dome starts to dissolve into the earth. Here again in White we find that the Australian landscape, the *spirit* of the country, is antagonistic to the structures of consciousness. It does not accommodate or accept the European edifice, but exerts a disintegrative effect upon it. In this country the crucial balance between man and Nature, conscious and unconscious, is disturbed by the archaic character of the continent. We have yet to discover a style of consciousness that can hold its own against the spirit of the place. In White's fiction, the 'elder' generation (the representatives of the old colonialism) fights vainly to impose European standards, while the 'new' generation of Australians is dangerously absorbed into the country's archetypal field: 'The scrub, which had been pushed back, immediately began to tangle with Norbert Hare's wilfully created park, until, years later, there was his daughter, kneeling in a tunnel of twigs which led to Xanadu' (p. 15). In the short space of Australia's history, we have swung from colonizer to colonized. The aboriginal spirit which 'had been pushed back' has returned with a vengeance, claiming all for itself.[6]

Since Miss Hare is virtually an extension of the Australian earth, it is obvious that she should have a destructive effect upon Norbert's life. In his eyes Mary is a sickly, pathetic child—as he confides to his wife, ' "Who would ever have thought I should get a *red* girl! By George, Eleanor, she is ugly, ugly!"' (p. 22). Towards the end of his life the archetypal stature of Mary Hare erupts into full view, when Norbert is forced to exclaim, '"Ugly as a foetus. Ripped out too soon"' (p. 56). Mary functions as the psychologically ageless unborn soul, whose presence aggravates and disturbs the strivings of the ego. On one occasion the mere sight of this foetus–child munching on a stick of celery is enough to drive Norbert to madness and to cause him to shoot at himself with a pistol. It is interesting that Norbert cries '"Munching! Munch–ing!"' (p. 34) as he aims the pistol at his head, for that is the essential activity of the unconscious in White's fiction. It munches and swallows back what the ego has constructed. When Norbert looks at his daughter her 'sees' the devouring image of his own unconscious, just as Miss Hare herself 'sees' this negative aspect in Mrs Jolley. Every character projects the destructive force upon someone else, and no one, except Theodora for a crucial moment, realizes that it is within him- or herself.

Norbert's attempted suicide is followed by a finally disastrous event. He is driven to a bout of frenzy by a further sight of his ageless girl curled up in the grass. He rushes crazily to the back of the house, and soon after the daughter hears his cries from the bottom of the icy cistern. Mary finds a pole with which she intends to fish him out, but for the drowning man it appears that she is using it to push him further in:

Then he appeared more afraid than before, as if she were looking truly monstrous from that height and angle, as she held the pole towards him.
    He was crying now, like a little boy, out of pale, wet mouth.
    'Some-one!' he was crying. 'Mary! Don't! Have some pity!' (p. 57)

Norbert cannot conceive that the pole is intended to save him, and so 'he warded it off with blue hands'. As far as the rational ego is concerned the indwelling child or *puer* self is bent on its destruction, and can only be seen as a demon of darkness. But although Mary does not kill him, his own perception of events is psychologically accurate. He is destroyed, from the inside, by the psychological reality that he has rejected and ignored. His drowning is itself symbolic of an ego which has been 'reclaimed' by Nature and the deep unconscious. As he floats at the bottom of the icy cistern, his eyes and face frozen in a fixed gaze, the daughter notices 'for the first time ... how very similar his expression was to one of her own' (p. 57). He is drawn into his indwelling, *puer* nature in death ('crying now like a little boy'), whereas Mary is locked in a state of eternal childhood in life. The spirit of the place is the same retrogressive, imprisoning force, whether one resists it or voluntarily surrenders to it.

III

When Miss Hare first encounters the Jew Himmelfarb, it is during one of her desperate, entranced excursions into the native bushland. This is an important point because Himmelfarb is equally bound to Nature and held fast by the maternal source. When the two mystics finally share their life experiences it is beneath an enormous flowering plum tree in the forsaken and overgrown orchard at Xanadu. The tree provides a sacred shelter for their meeting and seems to facilitate the communion of souls. Its great flowering branches, which formed a kind of 'canopy' (p. 89), 'hummed with life' above their heads, as they sat together 'on two stones which could have been put there for them at the roots of the tree' (p. 91). This is no ordinary plum tree—it is the all-sheltering Tree of Life, the image of Mother Nature, which gathers the child mystics into its protective embrace. It is significant that this same tree manifests an overwhelming and superior aspect, not only in its sheer size, but also in the energy-field which it seems to transmit. 'It was perfectly still, except that the branches of the plum tree hummed with life, increasing, and increasing, deafening, swallowing them up' (p. 91). During the course of Himmelfarb's life story we read: 'the tent of the tree contracted round them ... The lovely branches sent down sheets of iron, which imprisoned their bodies' (p. 156). This single image of the sheltering yet ensnaring tree anticipates Himmelfarb's inner situation in a fascinating way. It suggests the paradoxical image of the dual Mother which is to dominate his life story and future career at Sarsaparilla.

In discussion with Miss Hare, or so we must imagine it, Himmelfarb recalls his early youth and immediately uncovers the central image of his childhood: his mother Malke Himmelfarb. Malke is strongly imagined in these early passages, and is represented by his memory as a formidable archetypal presence. We soon learn that the mother's influence far outweighed that of the father, the worldly Moshe, who fades into insignificance by comparison:

It was evident from the beginning that the boy was closer to the mother, although it was only much later established that she had given him her character. To casual acquaintances it was surprising that the father, so agreeable, so kind, did not have a greater influence ... But it was out of the mother's silence and solitude of soul that the rather studious, though normal, laughing, sometimes too high-spirited little boy had been created. (p. 99)

White's characters inhabit a fatherless world, a point of far-reaching psychological and archetypal significance. When the father is absent (physically or psychologically), the son's connection to the maternal source is strengthened, and he falls all the more readily under the sway of primordial Nature. The father archetype represents mind, reason and the traditions of *logos*, as opposed to the maternal instincts, eros, and the natural mysteries of the unconscious.[7] In such an environment, it is towards natural, Goddess-centred worship, not patriarchal religion, that the son will inevitably turn.

The critical event of his early memory is that of his mother leading him ceremoniously to the centre of a geometric carpet, where she presents him to a rabbi so that he may receive a sacred blessing:

In the obscure room, talking to the foreign rabbi, for the greater part in a language the boy himself had still to get, his mother had grown quite luminous. He would have liked to continue watching the lamp that had been lit in her, but from some impulse of delicacy, decided instead to lower his eyes. And then he had become, he realized, the object of attention. His mother was drawing him forward, towards the centre of the geometric carpet. And the rabbi was touching him. The rabbi, of almost womanly hands, was searching his forehead for some sign. He was laying his hands on the diffident child's damp hair. Talking all the time with his cousin in the foreign tongue. (p. 97)

Here the mythic image is that of Mordecai as the son—priest of the Mother, who escorts him to a sacred place so that a divine figure may bestow boons upon him and endow him with spiritual power.

It is crucial to realize that the mother, who 'had grown quite luminous', appears to be undergoing some epiphany herself. The son appears to act as a carrier of her own spiritual side, and so she glows with an inner light because her *puer*–animus is being venerated. The rabbi (a close relative) and son are symbolical extensions of herself, so that this ceremony could be seen as a celebration of her capacity to renew herself with her own spiritual source.

This is the image which stands at the back of Himmelfarb's memory and which exerts a profound influence upon his development. We see the beginning of that pattern by which the mother dominates the son by forcing him into the image of her *puer*–animus. Himmelfarb's future spiritual commitment must be seen in this matriarchal context. He remains throughout the son–priest of the Goddess, unconsciously forced to enact the tragic fate of Attis/Adonis.

In his youth Himmelfarb felt the demands of his mother's animus as an imprisoning force which kept him tied to the Jewish faith. At six years of age he was impelled by her to turn toward religion and begin a study of the scriptures, despite protestations from the father, who would have his son turn to more worldly matters: '"Do you want to load the boy already?" [he would ask] "And worst of all, with Hebrew?"' (p. 101). In adolescence Himmelfarb was constantly drawn away from life and forced to remain righteous and pure, so that 'the mere mention of his mother involved him more deeply than ever in the metaphysical thicket from which he was hoping to tear himself free' (p. 112). As a means of reinforcing his own instinctive masculinity, Himmelfarb was impelled to seek refuge at the local brothel where he would indulge himself in the pleasures of the flesh and strive to experience his own manhood. Perhaps as an over-compensation for the castrating influence of the mother, Himmelfarb's exploits at the brothel tended to be exaggerated and over-energetic, so that even the whore has to complain: '"You Jews! ... The little bit they snip off only seems to make you hotter"' (p. 108).

In later life Himmelfarb marries a woman who is psychologically identical with Malke. Reha has a demanding spiritual animus which expects great things of Himmelfarb:

> 'But we—some of us—although we have not spoken—know that you will bring us honour.'
> She took his fingers, and was looking absently, again almost sadly, at their roots. She stroked the veins in the backs of his hands.
> 'You make me ashamed,' he protested.
> Because he was astounded.
> 'You will see,' she said. 'I am convinced.'
> And looked up, smiling confidently now. (pp. 125–6)

These words of inspiration are perhaps better regarded as an animus–curse—she is carrying forward the bewitchment of the mother, forcing her husband into a powerful mythic role. Her expectations inevitably induce a sense of impotence in Himmelfarb, a sense that he will never be able to live up to the image in the way demanded of him.

Reha attempts to mask her demands under an attitude of self-condemnation, by emphasizing her own spiritual inadequacy: '"I am afraid [that] I may fail you"' (p. 125), whereas the unconscious corollary of this—I fear you will fail me—is what comes closer to her real feelings. This becomes evident later in the story, when Reha begins to despair at her husband's ineffectuality: 'And she would hang her head . . . because she sensed the distance between aspiration and the possibility of achievement, and she was unable to do anything to help him' (p. 141).

The mother's demands were similarly disguised under a martyr-like attitude of self-reproach. Malke's final communication with Himmelfarb was by way of a letter in which she expressed her remorse at his father's defection from the faith, and emphasized her fear that he too might turn renegade: 'Oh, Mordecai, I can only think I have failed him in some way and dread that I may also fail my son' (p. 116). Soon after this communication the mother dies of an unspecified illness, but we are left in no doubt that the cause of her death is her husband's defection, which wrought a spiritual affliction too painful to bear (cf. p. 118). This indicates that her love for her husband was conditional on his fulfilling her expectations, and when he failed to do this she was forced to turn away from life itself. In this sense we see that the mother's cry of remorse actually contains a cry of rage: My husband has betrayed me and I dread that my son too will betray me.

Since this is her final plea, it serves to intensify the grip of her animus and to exaggerate Himmelfarb's sense of obligation to his wife, for the debt to the mother has now been transferred to her. Then his guilt is sealed forever by a dreadful sequence of events. Himmelfarb seeks refuge at a friend's house on the night of a Nazi raid, during which his wife is seized by the Gestapo and never seen again. He takes full responsibility for this horrific deed, and sees himself as Reha's betrayer. He is so broken by the guilt that he contemplates suicide, eventually surrenders to the Nazi authorities, is sent to the gas chambers—where he narrowly escapes death—and soon finds himself on a *kibbutz* with distant relatives in the Middle East. Although all through this sequence the narrator tends to emphasize Himmelfarb's guilt in relation to his wife's fate, essentially the guilt arises from a crippling sense of obligation to the *mother–image*; Reha is another mother–figure for Himmelfarb, and her seizure is the final consummation of his life of guilt. Like Palfreyman in *Voss*, he spends the rest of his short career attempting to atone for his 'betrayal' and trying to secure moral retribution. And like his exemplar he finds his fulfilment in Australia, where he is to sacrifice himself, psychologically and physically, to the maternal image.

IV

Himmelfarb's life sentence in Australia is to live out the role of the maternal spirit, to serve the Mother and allow himself to be put to death by her destructive animus. His task is to serve Mrs Godbold by performing the expected and required spiritual role, and to submit to the wicked intrigues of Mrs Flack and be bound to the Tree of Death by her son Blue. To the casual observer it may not be readily apparent that Flack and Godbold share a secret relationship, that they are parts of the one Mother–image. Mrs Godbold is the *inspiratrice* and nourisher, and Mrs Flack the enfeebling agent of destruction. The paradoxical aspects which were originally contained in the figures of Malke and Reha have split apart and now confront the central character as separate personages:

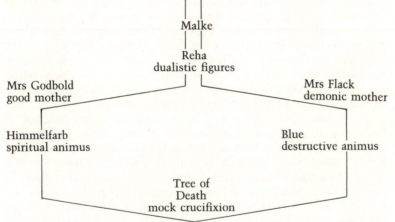

This has been a characteristic feature of White's fiction. Whenever an archetype manifests a certain ambivalence there is always a tendency to split the figure into two distinct entities (e.g. Laura and Rose Portion; Voss and Mr Bonner). This splitting allows the author to emphasize the psychological traits of either 'aspect', yet the effect is often harmful at the fictional level. For instead of having a few intensely realized and complex characters he has a multitude of pseudo-characters, or caricatures. And so instead of Reha or Malke loving and hounding him at the same time, we now find Himmelfarb loved by Mrs Godbold and hounded by Mrs Flack. We have dramatic plurality at the cost of psychological complexity. Yet the tension is still present, for the appearances of loving-kindness emerging from Ruth Godbold are constantly matched by the relentless intrigues and schemes of Mrs Flack. The author is compelled to keep the psychological forces in tension, even if he separates the fictional characters.

Like Malke and Reha, Mrs Godbold has a spiritual animus which longs for transcendence and which strives upward toward ethereal heights. Her notion of spirituality is aptly expressed in her favourite hymn:

I woke, the dungeon flamed with light,
My chains fell off, my heart was free,
I rose, went forth, and followed Thee. (p. 229)

It is a lofty, escapist idealism sung by a woman who is herself the embodiment of all that is dark, heavy, earthy. Her spirituality is a kind of over-compensation for her earth-bound nature. She is the earth itself longing to soar into the ether: 'So the massive girl . . . might have been some species of moth, or guardian spirit, poised on magnolia wings before huge, flapping flight' (p. 242). Despite rare moments of elevation her enormous rump remains on the maternal earth, and in the daily round of existence. When Himmelfarb takes up residence near her tumbledown shack in Sarsaparilla it is a great opportunity for her to displace her unlived spiritual life upon the Jew. The longing for transcendence is forced upon Himmelfarb and serves to accentuate his already animus-burdened (by wife and mother) spirituality. And it is this kind of exaggerated spirituality that Himmelfarb is forced to live out in his religious career. Instead of genuine spirituality there is otherworldly aspiration, a kind of obsessive compulsion for the ethereal and the macabre. Religious discipline becomes an attempt to escape from earthly reality; preoccupation with eternity is distorted into a disregard for time. *Puer* spirituality is a fitful, overblown striving for the infinite, for an ecstatic absorption into the source. Needless to say, Mrs Godbold's religion is not Christianity, any more than Himmelfarb's is Judaism: hers is the pagan worship of the earth–spirit, and his is the animus compulsion of sonship. At best, Himmelfarb's Jewishness is a structural device, which allows him to say with Miss Hare, '"I, too, am different"'. He does not follow the God of the Jews, nor is he spiritually related to the incarnational mysteries of Christianity. Nevertheless, the Great Mother, always prone to make inflated claims for her dependent son, reads his experiences at a high level. For her, he is equivalent to the Messiah himself, a modern-day Charioteer of the heavens.

In the background of Himmelfarb's religious career there lurks the all-destroying Mrs Flack, because the pagan god, or his imitator, is always slain by the dark character of the Goddess. Himmelfarb is pitifully unaware of his situation, and of the dark maternal aspect which is soon to crush him. Hence Mrs Flack remains a subversive figure, a mistress of doom unknown to his waking consciousness and never encountered in daily life. While Himmelfarb enjoys the attentions of the good mother, Mrs Flack is lurking behind the scenes, her presence all the more powerful because she remains unseen:

'Beggar *me!*' shrieked Mrs Flack ...
'There!' she suddenly hissed, and restrained her friend's skirt.
It was as though an experienced huntsman had at last delivered a disbelieving novice into the presence of promised game.
The two ladies stood in the shelter of a blackberry bush to observe the house in which the foreign Jew was living ... Then, if you please, the door opened, and out came, not the Jew, that would have been electric enough, but a woman, a woman ...
'Why,' Mrs Jolley said now, 'what do you know! It is that Mrs Godbold!'
Mrs Flack was stunned ... [Then] the owner himself emerged. The Jew. The two ladies clutched each other by the gloves ... The phlegm had come in Mrs Flack's mouth, causing her to swallow quickly down.
'Who would ever of thought,' Mrs Flack just articulated, 'that Mrs Godbold.'
Mrs Goldbold and the man were standing together on the steps of the veranda, she on the lower, he above, so that she was forced to look up, exposing her face to his and to the evening light.
It was obvious that the woman's flat, and ordinarily uncommunicative face had been opened by some experience of a private nature, or perhaps it was just the light, gilding surfaces, dissolving the film of discouragement and doubt which life leaves behind ... The Jew stood talking, even laughing with his friend, in that envelope or womb of light ... Mrs Jolley and Mrs Flack could only crane and swallow, beside the blackberry bush, beneath their hats, and hope that something disgraceful might occur.
Mrs Flack sucked incredulous teeth. She was quite exhausted by now.
'Tsst!' she added, quick as snakes.
Mrs Godbold had begun to turn.
'See you at church!' hissed Mrs Jolley.
'See you at church!' repeated Mrs Flack. (pp. 213–16)

This passage highlights the intrinsic connection between nourishing and destroying mothers. While Mrs Godbold comes to Himmelfarb to support him, and (as we learn later) to bandage his hand which he has damaged at Rosetree's factory, the spectral figures spy on the innocents from behind thorn bushes and make all kinds of devouring, gulping and attacking gestures. The teeth mothers represent the demonic aspect of the *puer*'s situation, that aspect which is overlooked by author and protagonist, but which is emphasized by the tale itself. Himmelfarb can go on thinking that he is a religious figure while he is constantly being victimized by a matriarchal force. The reference to Mrs Godbold's face glowing with light reminds us of Malke during Himmelfarb's childhood ritual, in which he was first initiated into the pattern of the Great Mother's animus. Mrs Flack's sexual innuendo is not entirely inappropriate, for the *puer*/Mother connection is incestuous in a symbolic sense. Even here we find the ecstatic son nestled in a 'womb of light' and nurtured and entreated by the Mother. Mrs Flack's gossip adds, in a perversely literal form, the missing ingredient to the idyllic picture. As ever, the dialogue between Mrs Flack and Mrs Jolley degenerates into a sharp, monosyllabic exchange, a chant-like ritual between hissing snakes.

V

Behind the scenes of the central drama, Mrs Godbold manifests a certain ambiguity which releases her from the stereotyped role of nourisher and nurse. In relation to her husband Tom, Mrs Godbold functions as the overpowering mother who destroys her companion with an unredeemed maternal instinct. Like Malke Himmelfarb, Ruth appears at one level to be at the service of her worldly and degenerate husband. Yet beneath her selflessness lies a castrating power which has a numbing effect upon her man:

'But I would bear all your sins, Tom, if it was necessary. Oh, I would bear them,' she said, 'and more.'
That made him leave off. He was almost frightened by what he meant to her. (p. 263)

In her efforts to redeem her husband she undermines his individuality and makes him a child and subordinate, in her keeping. Even in their love-making Tom Godbold is reduced to a helpless *puer* who is enveloped by the greater forces of the Goddess: '[Ruth Godbold held] him on her breast. She buoyed him up on that dark sea. He floated in it, a human body, soothed by a mystery which was more than he could attempt to solve (pp. 262–3). His task is to be her phallic attendant, to fecundate the Mother so that she may remain permanently with child and able to assert her primordial dominance. Tom struggles in vain with his formidable companion, often expressing his internal anguish in bouts of physical violence. He is also forced to frequent Mrs

Khalil's brothel in an attempt to assert his instinctive masculinity. The final collapse takes place when Mrs Godbold goes to collect her husband from the brothel. For her this is an act of loving-kindness, but it actually destroys the last remnant of his manhood: '"You done a lot to show me up, Ruth, in our time, but you just about finished me this go"' (p. 286). After this incident, Tom flees from Sarsaparilla, never to return to wife or family. When, years later, we find Mrs Godbold weeping beside the disease-ridden corpse of her husband we can only see her, in mythic terms, as the mourning Cybele or Isis who weeps for the son–lover whom she herself has destroyed.[8] Mrs Godbold is an incarnation of the Great Goddess, and so her life is lived according to the nurturing–devouring pattern of this archaic figure.

In the central drama, however, White restricts Mrs Godbold to the single role of the good mother. He cannot have a death-dealing mother in charge of his child mystics because this would raise serious doubts about the desirability of the unborn situation, which he seeks to celebrate. In the sub-plot he is able to relax his intellectual grip, and allow the imagination to paint the picture of Mrs Godbold that it wants to paint. It presents her as a pagan mother; he strives to portray her as a Christian Madonna. In the sub-plot, too, the dark aspects of the *puer aeternus* are allowed to appear, whereas they are masked or ignored in the central narrative. Tom Godbold manifests, albeit in grossly extreme form, the unrecognized negative traits of Himmelfarb's character: the helplessness of the son–lover, the defeatist style, the ineffectuality and lack of will. Even the brothel-going and excess drinking reflect aspects of Mordecai's character, his forgotten past or repressed present. What is left out of the author's conscious frame, his field of recognition, is made up, in exaggerated and distorted form, by the imagination. Mrs Flack and Mrs Jolley are in the end no more than grotesque parodies of the pagan darkness that White will not allow in his central maternal figure.

VI

It is during her visit to Khalil's brothel that Mrs Godbold encounters the drunken Aboriginal Alf Dubbo, and extends to him such loving-kindness as we have seen her give to Miss Hare and Himmelfarb. Dubbo is a major *puer* figure in the novel, the visionary artist who will record the passion of the mystic community in symbolic images. In many ways Dubbo is the

Aboriginal complement to the European Himmelfarb. They share the same matriarchal background, but whereas Mordecai is born of a 'white' goddess, Dubbo is the child of the black Madonna, the primordial mother. Dubbo too undergoes an education of a sort, supervised by the Reverend Timothy Calderon and his widowed sister Mrs Pask, who hope to make the boy into a spiritual re-deemer. Great things are expected of this young boy–god, who is subsequently coerced into religion and forced to act out in his life a spiritual mission which his elders failed to realize in theirs. But despite the Christian framework which is imposed upon him by Reverend Calderon, and by Patrick White, Dubbo is no Christian or messenger of the spirit. He is a child of pagan mysteries.

The parson told of spiritual love and beauty, how each incident in Our Lord's life had been illuminated with those qualities. Of course the boy had heard it all before, but wondered again how he failed continually to appreciate. It did seem as though he could grasp only what he was able to see. And he had not yet seen Jesus Christ, in spite of his guardian's repeated efforts, and a succession of blurry colour-prints. Now he began to remember a night at the Reserve when his mother had received a quarter-caste called Joe Mullens, who loved her awful bad, and had brought her a bottle of metho to prove it. Soon the boy's memory was lit by the livid jags of the metho love the two had danced together on the squeaky bed. Afterwards his mother had begun to curse, and complain that she was deceived again by love. But for the boy witness, at least, her failure had destroyed the walls. He was alive to the fur of darkness, and a stench of leaves, as he watched the lightning-flicker of receding passion.

'Earthly love is not the faintest reflection of divine compassion,' the rector was explaining. 'But I can tell you are not concentrating, Alf.' (pp. 320–1)

This could stand as a general statement about the position of Christianity in White's fictional world. It is a thin overlay, of good intentions and limp ideas, below which lies the vaster world of pagan mysteries; the image of the aboriginal Mother and her realm of raw energy. The dialogue between the parson and the native boy is a testimony to the perpetual conflict between White's European consciousness and his dark inner life, but the latter always wins out because it has the full force of his imagination behind it. As Dubbo re-lives this event through memory he is transfixed and captivated. He is made to feel alive and expansive (the mother's love-play had 'destroyed the walls'), his perception is heightened ('he was alive to the fur of darkness'), and he is buoyed along by that same erotic passion which inspires his mother. No mere observer, he is emotionally participating in the event. Before the image of incestuous union, the words of the parson hold no authority or conviction. Similarly, White's creativity attends not to the moral instructions of Christianity but only to the primitive longing for incest, the desire to return again to the primal source.

This same conflict between Christian and primitive elements is evident within the parson himself. Much of his enthusiasm for converting the Aboriginal boy to Christianity arises from his crippling sense of failure to uphold and realize the Christian ethic in his colonial outpost. The Reverend's belief in a divine order and his preaching about spiritual love appear inadequate to transform his own sexual passion into the higher realms of devotion. Psychologically, his seduction of Dubbo and the boy's subsequent departure is another expression of the ineffectual father–image in White, and its inability to assimilate or contain the energies of the instinctual world. Culturally, it is further evidence that the imported patriarchal structures fail to fulfil their task in upholding the exalted values of the Christian world. Timothy Calderon's Church of England is as readily undermined by the primitive spirit of Australia as is Norbert Hare's elaborate Xanadu by the native scrub.

Dubbo's first painting, done while he was still a lad in the protection of Reverend Calderon and Mrs Pask, is of tremendous significance for our present study. Not only does it express his own relation to the maternal image, but it also encapsulates the primordial relation of every White mystic to the source. We first learn of his painting through his dialogue with Mrs Pask, who is shocked and horrified by his pagan vision:

'But what,' she asked, still breathing hard, 'whatever in the world, Alf, is this?'
Looking at his paper.
'That is a tree,' he said when he was able.
'A most unnatural tree!' ...
He touched it with vermilion, and it bled afresh.
'What are these peculiar objects, or fruit—are they?—hanging on your tree?'
He did not say. The iron roof was cracking.
'They must mean *some*thing,' Mrs Pask insisted.
'Those,' he said, then, 'are dreams.'
He was ashamed, though.
'Dreams! But there is nothing to indicate that they are any such thing. Just a shape. I should have said mis-shapen kidneys!'
So that he was put to worse shame.
'That is because they have not been dreamt yet,' he uttered slowly.
And all the foetuses were palpitating on the porous paper. (pp. 316–17)

This drawing, which might be called the Tree of Unborn Souls, expresses in graphic form the relation between the *puer aeternus*

Figure 6   The tree of unborn souls (Turkish, eighteenth-century)
Source: C. G. Jung, *Symbols of Transformation*, Princeton University Press, Princeton, 1956, plate xxxix

White's mystics are caught up on the maternal tree and bound to the cyclical pattern of natural life. In this woodcut we discover something of the meaning and symbolic context of Dubbo's painting of the Tree of Unborn Souls. The intimate relation between human fruit and maternal tree expresses both the ecstasy and the horror of the unborn or infantile situation. The unborn soul exists in a state of permanent symbolic incest and matriarchal security, but it can never enter life as an independent being or become fully human, and when the seasonal cycle draws to a close, the *pueri* are returned to the darkness of the maternal source.

and the maternal source. It reminds us of the earlier image of Himmelfarb and Miss Hare sitting beneath the all-containing tree at Xanadu, but here the archetypal situation is more inhuman: the foetus-like forms are actually dangling on the tree, like fruits of the maternal source (Figure 6). White's entire *oeuvre* has pointed toward this single image, and the various meanings it suggests. The unborn state is imagined in terms of ultimate security and shelter; one is protected and nourished by the world-tree. And there is poetry and mystery here. The painting is otherworldly, mysterious; the embryonic figures are dreamlike and opaque. But there is an ambivalent aspect in the conception of the work. Are the dangling foetuses the early forms of 'fruit' which will mature and leave the parent tree, or are they fixated at this embryonic stage, unable to detach themselves from the source? In all probability, the latter is indicated by the context of the novel. Mrs Pask highlights this morbid aspect in her pointed remark: '"I am afraid it is something unhealthy," [she] confided in her brother' (p. 317). Always in White critical objections to the *puer aeternus* and his otherworldly mysticism arise from maternal characters such as Mrs Pask, Mrs Gage (in *The Tree of Man*), and Mrs Macarthy (in *The Living and the Dead*). The imagination puts forward this alternative perspective, but due to White's hostility toward these seemingly 'normal' women, and his personal identification with the *puer* point of view, their negative reports are never considered; the critical objections are never heard. It is fascinating that Dubbo describes his foetuses as 'dreams ... which have not yet been dreamt', since Jung defines the *puer* as 'an anticipation of something desired and hoped for ... a dream of the mother, an ideal which she soon takes back into herself'.[9] The world-tree provides nourishment and shelter but keeps its child victim bound to its image, and entirely subordinate to its crushing embrace.

VII

It is Himmelfarb who is forced to realize most agonizingly the meaning of Dubbo's vision, and the ambivalent aspect of being a 'child of the tree'. For him the world-tree can become equally the blossoming and fruit-bearing tree at Xanadu, or the gnarled and mutilated jacaranda at Rosetree's factory, upon which he is 'crucified' and hoisted above the ground like a dangling corpse. He is bound to the tree at the behest of Mrs Flack, and the act of subjugation is performed by Blue, her servile son and consort. The point is that the Goddess herself does not wield the fatal blow, she arranges for her masculine counterpart to perform the bloody deed, just as the wicked Set acted on orders from Isis, and, in the Attis/Adonis myth, the young god was slain by the animal representative of the Mother Goddess.[10]

It must be emphasized in light of White's imposed religious schema that Himmelfarb's passion is not a Christian drama, but a re-enactment of the pagan sacrifice of the maternal spirit. There are apparent resemblances between his suffering and Christ's, just as there are similarities between the pagan cycle and the Christian story, but the two mythologems are quite distinct and ought not be confused.[11] The pagan god is born, slain, and born again, year after year, his religious festival an annual celebration of the rhythms of the earth and the seasons. He is born of the Mother, slain by the Mother, and returned to her fecund womb at the end. His mission is natural, cyclical, and, being as inevitable as the seasons, somewhat mundane. Christ is not a Mother's son, but a son of the Father God, whose 'business' he fulfils on earth. His passion is not cyclical but lineal and absolute—it is concerned with the incarnation, in historical time, of the divine Word. His task is not merely to perpetuate existence but to transform it, to connect matter with spirit, to elevate creation to a divine transcendental reality. In spiritual terms, the pagan myth appears as a defeat of the masculine spirit by Nature, whereas in the later story spirit appears to triumph, or at least to hold its own against the natural world. Insofar as Himmelfarb is subordinate to Nature and Mother, he is actually Jesus-in-reverse, a figure who achieves not redemption but merely the disintegration of spirit into the world of Nature. Although their archetypal missions are opposed, there are points of formal correspondence between Attis/Adonis and Christ. Especially significant for us is the fact that the Phrygian Attis was crucified upon the tree, and because his passion seemed to anticipate that of Jesus he was subsequently dubbed the 'pagan Christ'.[12] Even his annual festival and mourning took place at Easter, on 23 March in the pagan calendar. The fact, therefore, that Himmelfarb is crucified upon the tree, and at Easter, is entirely in accord with the mythic process of the novel. What makes his story appear pretentious and overblown is the exalted Christian interpretation that is placed upon it. As we found in *Voss*, it is primarily the mother-figure (here Mrs Godbold) who spins the web of illusion, making the career of her son–victim appear miraculous and transcendent.

The events immediately preceding the subjugation of Himmelfarb are of great interest from the mythical point of view. The

Lucky Sevens, a gang of workers from Rosetree's factory, get drunk on the day before the Easter vacation after having won the lottery. On their return to the factory they make their way through the streets of Barranugli in ritual style, clanging dustbin lids, banging drums, and one of the Sevens plays a shrill tune on a fife. Then they encounter a circus which has pitched its tent opposite the factory, and witness several of the clowns perform a 'public hanging' on the platform of a lorry. At first they imagine that the hanged figure is an actual clown, but later realize that it is a life-size dummy, which one of the clowns tosses into a tent. This is a fascinating sequence, not to be dismissed as drunken roguery or as unrelated to the central story. In the festivals of Attis the worshippers of the sacrificial god would become intoxicated by wine and take to the streets in song and merriment; even the instruments used were drums, cymbals, and fifes.[13] The object of the festival was to offer sacrifices to the Goddess, so that she might replenish the earth after winter and bring on the spring. J. G. Frazer[14] reports that a human effigy was hung upon the pine in the likeness of Attis, and that this rite was followed by an actual human sacrifice, usually the death by hanging of a youth, or a eunuch priest who had lived his life in the service of the Mother Goddess. This ancient ritual is in enigmatic agreement with the activities of the Lucky Sevens as they make their way from the incident of the hanging clown to the crucifixion of Himmelfarb. Blue performs the mock crucifixion for the sake of Mrs Flack, who coaxes him to participate in an orgiastic blood ritual for her delight:

someone that we know of must *consort*—to put it blunt. Eh? Blue! Blue! . . . Enjoy, boy, enjoy, then! Bust your skin open, if that is what you want! It is only a game to let the blood run when there is plenty of it. And so red. (p. 397)

This hysterical, barely credible outburst can only be understood in a mythic context: as the command of a voracious Goddess for a blood sacrifice. The maternal earth is craving for blood, for violence, for the return of the *puer aeternus* to the matrix. Blue 'remembers' his 'auntie's' (actually his mother's) call for sacrifice when he returns to Rosetree's factory, and finally leads Himmelfarb out toward the jacaranda:

Towards the present travesty of tree, its mutilated limbs parched with lichens of a dead, stone colour, with nails protruding in places from the trunk, together with a segment of now rusted tin, which somebody had hammered in for reasons unknown, it was agreed by consent of instinct to push the victim. (p. 409)

The lopped jacaranda is no Cross of Calvary, it is an image of Mother Nature in its empty, desolate, denuded aspect—precisely that side of the Mother which thirsts for a living sacrifice. The fact that Himmelfarb is utterly powerless before the field of the chthonic mother indicates that the *puer* is destined to be undermined in this way. His spirit was borrowed from Nature, and is returned to Nature through the agency of Blue. 'The Mother gives and the Mother takes away.'[15]

It is fascinating to look at the role played by Mrs Godbold at the time of Himmelfarb's subjugation. 'At that hour', we read during the passion sequence,

Mrs Godbold took the sheets which she had washed earlier, and ... began to iron [them], and soon had them ready in a pile ... while remembering ... how the women had received the body of their Lord.
And would lay the body in her whitest sheets, with the love of which only she was capable. (p. 411)

How, we may well ask, was she to know that her boy–god was at that moment being destroyed? There is almost a direct link between herself and Mrs Flack; she 'knows' what the other woman has arranged, and has prepared herself for the consequences. If Mrs Flack is the violent, hideous left hand of the Mother, Mrs Godbold is the consoling right hand, which attempts to sweeten the blow the victim has been dealt, to lay his wrecked body in freshly laundered sheets, and to bewail his death. As they are presented by the author, Mrs Flack and Mrs Godbold are completely opposed, but their symbolic connection is sensed by the clockwork-like precision with which each fulfils the appointed task. Notice here that Mrs Godbold acts out her part of the ritual in Christian terms. She is the Virgin Mary at the foot of the Cross, waiting to 'receive the body of [her] Lord'. Not only does this elevate and spiritualize Himmelfarb's suffering, turning him into a modern saint, but it also justifies the Mother's longing for pagan sacrifice in terms that are readily endorsed and honoured by society. The Mother Goddess can carry out her ruthless cycle to the end, and no one need ever suspect that a pagan archetype has ruptured the surface of civilized Australian society.

Appropriately, Himmelfarb is buried by Mrs Godbold, by arrangement with the local authorities, and does not receive a burial befitting a Jew. When Haim Rosenbaum (alias Harry Rosetree) comes to claim the body, Mrs Godbold proudly informs him that she has already performed the necessary functions, and has given him what she calls a 'Christian burial'. But it is clear that this is not a Christian event, but a pagan and earthly ritual.

'I walked to the ground—it is not far—with a couple of my more sensible girls. And was there to receive him. It was that clear. It was that still. You could hear the magpies from all around. The rabbits would not bother themselves to move. There was a heavy dew lying from the night, on grass and bushes. No one would have cried, sir, not at such a peaceful burial ... and afterwards we was glad to dawdle, and feel the sun lovely on our backs.' (p. 446)

The accent here is on earth, plants, the animal kingdom—Nature itself, in an almost ceremonious state, bears witness to the return of spirit to the earth. Mrs Godbold's eagerness to 'receive' the body is suggestive of her sacrifice-demanding aspect. She personifies the hungry earth which swallows down its ritual sacrifice. Himmelfarb does not have a Jewish, or Christian, funeral because his life has never followed the course of the transcendental spirit. Mrs Godbold was right to intervene in this way, claiming for herself what was rightfully part of the matriarchal cycle.

VIII

White has represented Himmelfarb throughout as an heroic, transcendental figure, and now, despite the evidence of the story, which speaks of the defeat of the son by Mother Nature, he goes on to assert that he is a triumphant Christ. In order to communicate this view he has Alf Dubbo undergo a miraculous 'conversion' to the Christian faith as he witnesses the sacrificial figure upon the tree:

As he watched, the colour flowed through the veins of the cold, childhood Christ, at last the nails entered wherever it was acknowledged they should. So he took the cup in his yellow hands, from those of Mr Calderon, and would have offered it to such celebrants as he was now able to recognize in the crowd. (p. 412)

The problem with White's fiction is that ritual action of any kind is immediately drawn into a Christian frame. Instead of being broadened and challenged to the discovery of a new deity, White chooses to view it all as a rediscovery of what parental figures *told* him to believe. This may well be a part of his puerility, an inability to explore outside the mental landscape of early childhood. What Dubbo perceives is genuine archetypal experience, but his religious frame, which is *handed to him* by Mr Calderon, is completely inappropriate.

It is well, then, that we cast a cautious eye on the inflatedly religious passages which describe Dubbo's canvases of the passion sequence (pp. 451–61). If we put aside the imposed Christian schema we do find certain genuinely mythic aspects in Dubbo's paintings. There is, for instance, an evocative image of Mrs Godbold, 'the Mother of God waiting to clothe the dead Christ' (p. 454), with her enormous breasts dribbling and overflowing with the milk of loving kindness. There is even a sense of the overbearing nature of the Great Mother's nourishment, since Dubbo has to 'reject' the 'smell of milk that stole gently over him'. Her loving kindness is too strong, and the energy which flows from the breasts tends to surround the *puer* like a fixating substance. It is interesting to find that the breasts of 'the immemorial woman' were 'running with a milk that had never, in fact, dried' (p. 454). In a sense, none of the child mystics has been weaned from the source. Each is still dependent on her for life; a human fruit clutching to the maternal tree.

Dubbo's portrait of Miss Hare gives further dimension to this theme. She is imaged as an unborn soul inside a vast cosmic womb: 'He painted the Second Mary curled, like a ring-tail possum, in a dreamtime womb of transparent skin, or at the centre of a whorl of faintly perceptible wind' (p. 455). Miss Hare is an embryonic figure within the Great Round of Nature. She is not in human reality, but is outside the dimension of time. The Australian Aboriginal mythology referred to here is more appropriate to her situation than the Christian. The idea of the Dreamtime (or more correctly, the Dreaming) is an Aboriginal equivalent to the ancient Greek notion of the uroboros (Figure 1), the primordial world prior to the creation of man. The Dreamtime, like the uroboros, is imaged as a prehistoric reality, a time before the development of consciousness, but Aboriginal authority insists that this 'time' also exists in the present, and extends into the future as well.[16] White's world re-evokes this archaic cosmos, and although it is felt to relate to the 'past', in the sense of a lost image of childhood (*The Aunt's Story*), or life-in-the-womb (*The Tree of Man*), it remains present in the human imagination, which is why Miss Hare can be sixty or seventy years of age, and yet still remain one of the unborn. She lives psychologically in the source, a child of the depths and of night.

White spoils this delicate image by insisting on the Christian schema. He tells us that this embryonic possum–figure is supposed to represent the Second Mary, or 'the Second Servant of their Lord' (p. 455). How she can be Mary Magdalene and a ring-tail possum at the same time is difficult to conceive; a clear indication of the contrived, wilful nature of the religious frame.

In Dubbo's final canvas White makes an attempt to reunite

the novel with its title, and with the concept of redemption associated with the Chariot. We have seen from our analysis how little the motif of the Chariot actually impinges upon the basic structure of the novel. It occurs here and there, in the hymns of Mrs Godbold, the readings of Himmelfarb and Dubbo, and every fresh appearance is as unconvincing as the last. It is interesting that the Chariot symbol comes to the characters second-hand from books and pictures; it does not arrive with the force of a natural symbol, but seems oddly remote and intellectual. Nevertheless, the author is determined to argue that a Chariot of Redemption flies above the skies of Sarsaparilla, and so he makes Dubbo paint the Chariot before he expires from a tubercular haemorrhage.

White's intuition exerts certain restraints on his intellectual standpoint. Dubbo cannot fully realize *The Chariot-thing*, which remains indistinct and blurred: 'Just as he had not dared completely realize the body of the Christ, here the Chariot was shyly offered' (p. 458). The horses, too, which were supposed to be 'touched with gold' and blazing with heavenly light, according to the original plan, are executed in a darker, more sombre tone. '[They] could have been rough brumbies, of a speckled grey, rather too coarse, *earthbound* might have been a legitimate comment' (p. 458). It seems that Dubbo's Chariot does not want to get off the ground. The tension at this point is great: White's image-making capacity will not lie, even as he tries to manipulate it to his own ends. But the tension is finally obliterated by a typical White assertion: 'So they were carried on, along the oblique trajectory, towards the top left corner' (p. 459). Dubbo's art could not affirm the upward movement, so White steps in and pushes the Chariot off into the heavens. The assertion, with its introductory conjunctive, 'So they . . .', is reminiscent of White's willed affirmation of Dubbo's Christian faith, 'So he took the cup . . .' (p. 412), previously quoted. The crucial 'so' does not follow from what has gone before, but is simply imposed upon the text. The mythic vision will not support the happy dream of transcendence, because the story has long since lost its spiritual force.

IX

The deaths of the *pueri*[17] all point, not to the redemptive vision, but to the dissolution of the human spirit and its subjugation by material forces. Miss Hare literally dissolves into the elements. One report suggests that she drowned in a stream, others that she died in the undergrowth at Xanadu. The earth can no longer bear her up, so she sinks into it, blissfully: 'Her instinct suggested ... that she was being dispersed, but that, in so experiencing, she was entering the final ecstasy' (p. 439). But when White's child mystics disappear ecstatically into the matrix there are always images of the devouring maw which takes them back into itself. These images are displaced upon society, or 'material progress' as it consumes the once-sacred grounds of Xanadu:

Just before the house was completely razed, the bulldozers went into the scrub at Xanadu. The steel caterpillars mounted the rise, to say nothing of any sapling, or shrubby growth that stood in their way, and down went resistance ... Gashes appeared upon what had been the lawns. Gaps were grinning in the shrubberies ... and they were sober individuals indeed, who were able to inhale the smell of destruction without experiencing a secret drunkenness. (p. 477)

Miss Hare's return to the 'dreamtime womb' is experienced as bliss and fulfilment, but at the same time the monster of *mater*ialism has triumphed. It feeds upon the grounds of Xanadu in an attitude of drunken, frenzied delight. The demonic force which subdues Miss Hare's world[18] represents, once again, the missing perspective in White's romantic image of matriarchal incest.

Dubbo is similarly consumed by material forces. While completing his painting of *The Chariot-thing* he suffers a tubercular haemorrhage and dies in a pool of blood: an Attis-like image of the defeated *puer*. After his death the paintings are sold by his teeth-sucking landlady Mrs Noonan, who sends them to an auction where they 'fetched a few shillings, and caused a certain ribaldry' (p. 461). We will recall that the postmistress in *The Tree of Man* sold Mr Gage's visionary works, and that these were laughed at by a tribe of hostile women. The maternal world is always anxious to undermine the products of spirit, reducing these to matter, to material gain, to laughter. The Mother plunders the higher reality and drags it into banality and dirt, just as 'materialism' quickly converted the mystique of Xanadu into half-acre allotments.

At the end of the book there is an astonishing coda in which we find many crude and literal reductions of spirit to matter. It is here that we discover that Mrs Flack and Mrs Jolley were responsible for the deaths of their respective husbands. Will Flack did not 'fall' from a roof, but committed suicide because he could no longer stand the relentless persecutions of his wife. Nor was Mr Jolley's death accidental, as we had been led to believe, but was carefully and subtly calculated by his killer–wife.

Near the very end we witness the gathering in a restaurant of three Sarsaparillan women. Each is a widow who has played the game of life to her advantage, and who survives comfortably on her husband's fortune. The pattern of the predatory wife is announced when the mothers declare, in chant-like ritual, 'the men went first' (p. 482). During the course of the conference the women undermine the entire spiritual drama that has passed. Mrs Wolfson, former wife of Himmelfarb's employer (who committed suicide after the crucifixion), makes derisive remarks about 'the Jew' and 'the abo bloke', and Mrs Colquhoun ridicules 'the madwoman' of Xanadu. We even learn that Rosie Rosetree, a *puella* obsessed by visions of purity and transcendence, has suffered a severe mental breakdown, and is currently resident in the local asylum.

One almost feels that this final chapter is a compulsive over-compensation for all the willed espousals of victory and triumph in the central narrative. It is as if an autonomous literary voice were urging the author to recognize the reality of the defeated spirit, and to direct his attention away from the fantasy of transcendence. The crassly literal, explicit and repetitive nature of these incidents (e.g. mother kills or ridicules son–husband) would point to the unconsciousness of the negative image. It is not received or integrated by the author, and so is forced to appear in crude, physically concrete forms. Of course the central drama itself has enough evidence of the defeat of spirit. But the tale feels impelled to accentuate this fact, particularly in the minor sequences where the author is not moved to impose his Christian and idealistic design upon the narrative.

X

Riders in the Chariot has not been subject to the same degree of critical scrutiny as *The Tree of Man* and *Voss*. Many Australian critics appear to be embarrassed by it; they do not know what to do with its explicitly religious, or at least mythological, design. It is not considered among White's best because it is not 'Australian' to the extent that the previous works, apparently, are. The problem, however, is not that *Riders* is un-Australian, but that critics have a too narrow, too constricted view of what constitutes Australia. It is true that White does not give us the country that we know and easily recognize. We do not, for instance, find a reflection of Furphy's Australia, the free, democratic country which has broken from the past and which is governed by simple political idealism. White's focus is upon the psychic, less visible side of the nation. This side is ruled not by political ideals but by unconscious, archetypal forces. Here we are less free than we imagine, but are still bound by the myths of the past, acting out ageless and universal patterns. White's novels envision us, a colonial culture in a 'barely inhabited country',[19] at the mercy of Mother Nature, in her hands not merely literally and physically, but spiritually and mythologically as well.

Australia, as a very new society, has fallen back into the natural levels of the psyche, a level where pagan instinctual forces operate, and where Christian forces can hardly be said to exist at all. Australia cannot borrow its cultural and spiritual light from Europe. We cannot simply carry on the torch of Western society, try as we might to do so. We have more fundamental, more basic, yet also more challenging tasks. Our culture has to acquire natural depth before it can attain spiritual elevation, and that quest for solidity means going down into aboriginal soil, making connections with the primitive ground of being where Nature holds sway. Australians are subordinate to Nature, to the instinctual impulses of life as well as to the harsh external landscape. We are a basic, practical, non-intellectual people, preferring the ordinary realities of existence to flights of mind or imagination. We value the group more than the individual; the individual being endorsed only insofar as he embodies the general view of the majority. We pride ourselves too, on this lowbrow, purely natural existence, seeing European—especially British—culture as stuffy and restrictive. We enjoy tearing down authority, bucking the system, exposing high culture for its 'pretentiousness', and directing our sardonic humour at anything which attempts to be other than natural. We have the same effect upon established culture as the 'grey', 'raggedy', 'cynical' landscape (p. 15) has upon the elaborate structures of Xanadu. Our national preoccupations are those which support the natural man: sex, which is a continual devotion to the Goddess of Fertility; drink, which dulls the mind and releases instincts; sport, which holds our attention outward and keeps us bound to the body and its condition. There are numerous ways in which Australia can be looked upon as a pagan society held at an instinctual level of civilization. Spirit in this country is kept down, laid low, by Nature: which makes Himmelfarb's bondage to the Tree something of a national symbol. R. F. Brissenden finds the story of Himmelfarb's crucifixion oddly eccentric, rejecting it on the basis that it could not happen in Australia.[20] But the ritual destruction of spirit is absolutely central to our culture, an act of violence which takes place whenever mind or imagination is put down, ridiculed, or reduced to matter. The very fact that White's works of imagination are read literally suggests that spirit is unavailable to us, that it is not part of the national character, and that our perceptions are stuck in the concrete. We are a nation of materialists; there is an element of Blue and the Lucky Sevens in every one of us. We all contribute to the destruction of spirit, thereby serving, however unconsciously, the will of the Great Mother and her longing to keep the world natural, material and elemental.

White may seem at odds with his Australian context, but in reality he is the mythologist of his country, telling tales about the triumph of Nature, our subjection to its laws, our inevitable materiality. If the author stresses his cultural eccentricity it is because he does not properly perceive his role as mythologist of Mater Natura and materialism. White's relentless attack upon Australian materialism strikes me as vain and misplaced hitting out at the material force which annihilates spirit in his world. White is at odds, then, not with Australia, but with himself, unable to comprehend his pagan mythologem or to accept its darker implications.

Now whether we approach *Riders in the Chariot* through the author's intellectual framework, or through the mythic structure established by the tale itself, has considerable bearing upon our assessment of the novel. In the past, critics have tended to focus upon White's commentary, skimming off as it were the philosophical assertions and embellishments as they make their way through the book.[21] They have not touched the living substance, but have merely dug up the superimposed religious frame.[22] Little wonder that their general impression has often been unfavourable, that they have found the work contrived, calculated and systematic. White fails, it seems to me, as an allegorist, a dealer in systematic symbolism. His strength lies not in his superficial religiosity but in the depth of his mythic vision. At this level he speaks not just as one man, dabbling self-consciously with his art, but as the voice of an archetype, reasserting its ancient pattern in modern times.

Mrs Godbold appears quite differently when viewed from a deep structural standpoint rather than from the author's allegorical point of view. As White presents her, Mrs Godbold is an unlikely candidate for spiritual vision, and unconvincing as one of the *illuminati*. As one of the four 'Riders' of Ezekiel's vision she must be regarded as a failure, a character who does not win her seat in the Chariot. This is perhaps the most persistent and damaging criticism made against the novel, repeated by those who seek to expose it as a flawed work. But in the tale itself Mrs Godbold is a convincing embodiment of a pagan Earth Mother, the central figure around which the *pueri* attain their definition. She is the Earth Goddess, and it is not her function, or her task, to ascend to spiritual heights. She inspires the fly-weight mystics heavenward, and then she brings them back to earth, participating with Mrs Flack in the ritual subjugation of the favoured son.

Himmelfarb too is a stilted caricature at the allegorical level, but a living figure in relation to the *puer* myth. The author defeats him by insisting on the Christian symbolism, by making him appear transcendent, whereas his mission has been natural, to return to the earth what sprang forth from it. Dubbo is also maligned by White's designs. The author acts as the unseen Reverend Calderon, manipulating his boy–god into the required role. Nevertheless we remember Dubbo not as the Peter who denied his Lord,[23] but as the Aboriginal artist who bears witness to pagan mysteries.

Despite a brief and abortive appearance as the 'Second Mary' Miss Hare emerges unscathed by White's religious designs. She seems to elude, or reject, the author's allegorical frame, just as she rejects Himmelfarb's suggestion that she is one of the sacred *zaddikim*. At Himmelfarb's statement she blushes in shy embarrassment (p. 155). And that, I would say, is how the imagination reacts to the grand design. It is embarrassed and tries to shrug it off, but White keeps persisting, to the detriment of the created work.

5 The Tightening Knot

'If it would help I would give it to you, Waldo,
to keep,' Arthur said.
Offering the knotted mandala.
While half sensing that Waldo would never
untie the knot.

The Solid Mandala, p. 273[1]

In *The Solid Mandala* (1966) the course of White's fiction takes a dramatic turn. In this novel the imagination itself reacts against the author's religious misinterpretation, and the psychopathology of the mother/son myth is made fully apparent. Here the inner life assumes personified form in the figure of Arthur Brown, the 'retarded' shadow–brother who rejects the Christian frame ('"all this Christ stuff ... doesn't seem to work. But we have each other," Arthur said', p. 200) and who urges his 'intellectual' twin to see exactly what is taking place in the inner world. Arthur strives to show Waldo that he is caught up in a hidden complex— the subtle 'knot' at the centre of the glass marble[2]—and that he must extricate himself from it before any spiritual maturity can be achieved. Arthur suggests a way out of the bondage by means of a careful consideration of inner contents. *The Solid Mandala* is the most significant of all White's novels, because we have an unveiling of the central myth as well as a decisive movement toward a new style of psychological existence. It is at the same time White's most keenly felt book, depicting an individuation crisis in the author's life.

It seems that a masculine part of White's psyche is urging him to move on from where he has been caught ever since *The Living and the Dead*, when Elyot made his fatal descent to the maternal source. White has interpreted this regressive condition as enlightenment and religious ecstasy, and so Arthur has a particularly difficult task before him. He must somehow re-educate the ego to the rhythms of descent-and-return,[3] urging the ego to return to the human world and to develop a separate, individual existence of its own. Arthur repeatedly shows Waldo the marble with the knot inside, which is the image of his (Waldo's) own erotic bind to the source, the primary knot which has long symbolized the agonizing embrace of spirit and maternal world.[4] In ancient mythology the knot was sometimes used as a symbol of incestuous binding, as in the case of Zeus and his mother Demeter, whose erotic entanglement was imaged as a pair of snakes entwined together in sexual embrace (cf. Figure 5). When Theodora Goodman stood over her mother with the paper-knife, her breath 'choking' and 'knotting' inside her, her primary aim was to 'cut the knot' (*The Aunt's Story*, p. 123) that bound her to this regressive figure. Himmelfarb was pinned to the tree by a series of ropes and pulleys, and when the foreman finally arrives to cut him down he has to 'negotiate a knot' and 'saw through a section of rope' (*Riders in the Chariot*, p. 416) to release him. The image of the knot, the tangle, is central in White's fiction, and it occurs in the present novel in more than one context: 'George Brown had to suffer. The threads of his breath tangled in his chest . . . He rarely succeeded in cutting the tangle' (p. 158). In previous works the tangle was tolerated, endured, even enjoyed, but now there is a sense of crisis, a dawning realization that the knot is stifling life and must be released. Arthur does not (and cannot) formulate the task in overtly analytic terms but impresses the issue upon his brother by insinuation, evocation and repetition; by holding the *image* of the knot constantly before Waldo.

However, Arthur is not just the good angel who has dropped from the skies to help the bewildered ego discover its orientation. Arthur too has very specific and very urgent needs, and bringing Waldo to consciousness is really one way of helping himself. He is, so to speak, the unlived, unrealized potential within White himself. The unconscious of a man contains more than the Mother archetype and buried incestuous libido for Her. There is also a higher self, a potential for spiritual realization, maturity and masculine development—none of which can be fulfilled while the ego is fixated obsessively upon the mother–image. Because this inner self is unlived and dormant it invariably emerges at first in a negative form: as ugly or infantile, since it is, as it were, locked up in the unconscious, shut away from the world. Arthur is slightly retarded ('a shingle short', p. 81), fat, lumpy, boyish. He is the image *par excellence* of repressed life, life which throughout the last twenty-five years—or more—of White's career has not been allowed to live. Arthur, then, is no external vision, but White's own masculine shadow, his positive spirit, his capacity for change and transformation.

Arthur implies that if the knot can be unravelled there will be a kind of twofold release for himself and Waldo. He will be allowed to come into being, and Waldo will be freed from his erotic bondage to the source. Arthur in fact offers an uroboros, a confused unity, which could become a mandala if Waldo attempted to make sense of it, to work on the knot, to see where he is bound. The mandala is the same cosmic totality, but only after consciousness has ordered and differentiated the stuff of the psyche.[5] Here the obvious parallel is with folk- and fairytale: an archetypal figure offers the ego something apparently foolish, or ridiculous—in this case a boy's toy—which could become a divine symbol of another order of existence if the ego would accept it as it stands, in its present condition. By giving the knotted symbol attention, concern, understanding, Waldo could change the mythic representation from one form to another, as in the transformation which ensues in fairytale when a simple kiss is bestowed. For the first time in White's fiction the symbol of the round functions potentially as a mandala,[6] although it first has to be worked on, and the primal knot recognized as the central reality that it is. In psychological terms, Waldo would have to accept the gift, recognize the knot, and extricate himself from it by surrendering his desire to dissolve in the source.

As we might anticipate, Waldo does not take the course that is offered. Waldo reveals that characteristic inability to deal with the inner realm that we have come to expect from White's ego or persona types. Elyot Standish, the huddlers in *Voss*, Norbert Hare, are the earlier forms of this type of character, and each one is as desperate to avoid a confrontation with the inner world as the other. White's ego will not risk a *conscious* descent into the interior, which is partly what stands behind his resistance to psychoanalysis and his unwillingness to regard seriously analytic enquiry into his work.[7] The rational self clings to high ground and surfaces, while the nihilistic *puer* self plunges recklessly into the maternal womb. And I think it is apparent why the rational ego persists in its denial: it does not want to face the sordid reality of the incestuous knot, and, perhaps more importantly, it fears that it too will become engulfed in the womb, that it too will be sucked right through into psychological anonymity. This, ultimately, is the homosexual nightmare: the female womb as destroyer and devourer of personality. All that holds White back from psychic disintegration is the no-saying homosexual ego; the ego which will not enter into the maternal matrix. And yet at the same time unless he risks disintegration the knot will remain tied and everything, his life, his vision, his work, will remain held at the *puer* level. Unless he faces the depths, development will not take place, the mandalic vision will be shattered, and Arthur, his own inner self and, I believe, his genius, will not come into being.

This is precisely Waldo's dilemma as the story opens upon the Brothers Brown at the end of their shared career. Waldo must go into the psyche to untie the knot; yet he cannot do so for fear of being annihilated. He projects his own puerile fixation upon Arthur, and views Arthur's offer of the knotted mandala not as an opportunity for freedom, but as an invitation to extinguish himself in the source. The offer of the boy's toy is for him an assault upon his rational, adult integrity, a way of subverting him into regressive infantilism. The fact is that Waldo could be right, for every White character that has entered the matrix has been destroyed by it. They were destroyed because they *willed* their own destruction, choosing to remain in the matrix, and viewing their slow disintegration as a path of ecstasy and enlightenment. The *puer aeternus* destroys himself; his values and 'religious' ideas contributing to his ruin. Whereas before the male figure had as his companion the great mother, who sanctioned his puerility and made him see her matrix as heaven, he now has his own shadow–brother to help him see the reality of his situation, and to help release him from his matriarchal prison. It is a unique moment in White's psychological life, the one time when the ego would not be ruined by the unconscious, but would be lovingly upheld and supported by it. Arthur attempts to assuage Waldo's fears: '[It's] all right, Waldo. Because we'll be together ... And if you should feel yourself falling, I shall hold you up, I'll have you by the hand, and I am the stronger of the two' (p. 210). Instead of the Goddess wickedly urging the ego to self-destruction, here is Arthur offering genuine support for the ego in the inner journey. What Waldo—and White—requires at this point is psychological faith, a belief that if the journey is made, knowingly and responsibly, it will not be completely disintegrative. Still, there can be no guarantee of success in the psychic realm. There are real dangers, and the ego must actually go out and confront them. The shadow–brother can point the way, and give reassurance, but the ego must actually make the journey.

The conflict between Arthur and Waldo may also be conceived in specifically artistic terms, relating to the interaction between White's mind and his unconscious genius.[8] White's mind is several steps behind his imagination, or at least is out of rapport with it. When his imagination presented the *puer*/Mother myth,

White saw it as an entirely positive, Christian mythologem; and now that the imagination presents a truly positive, mandalic vision, the mind, Waldo, views it as puerile and undermining. The controlling intellect misses the mark, with the result that there are manifold confusions and inconsistencies in the novels, as well as a kind of tragic inability on the author's part to grasp the imaginative moment and to draw out and explore its possibilities. In this work, especially, it is unfortunate that White, or the rational White that is Waldo, is unable to perceive what the imagination is doing. Arthur is attempting to bring a new vision, a new art into existence, not an art which is religious or moralistic in the way that *Riders in the Chariot* and *The Tree of Man*, for instance, were, but an art which is wholly modern and profoundly psychological. '"All this Christ stuff"' is put aside, and instead Waldo is urged '"to concentrate on . . . a glass marble. Or a brother, for instance"' (p. 200). Arthur tries to draw White away from his confined Church of England standpoint into a *religio* of internal reality. The final chapter, 'Mrs Poulter and the Zeitgeist', is a testimony to the way in which Arthur has drawn White out of his nineteenth-century frame of reference into the internal complexities of modern life. In this chapter not only Mrs Poulter's 'God' is 'brought crashing down' (p. 311), but White's metaphysical system too is plunged into utter disintegration. Never again will White view his experience through a comforting Christian perspective. The inner, psychological approach that Arthur is offering is not embraced either, for White does not follow the promptings of his own genius. Tragically, Arthur makes White suffer the death of his former God, but is unable to relate him creatively to the inner riches of his psyche.

Arthur, the visionary artist and secret poet of the Brown family, strives to make White see the reality of the mother–bind. '"One day perhaps I'll be able to explain—not explain, because it's difficult for me, isn't it, to put into words—but to make you *see*"' (p. 57). He cannot put the problem in abstract terms. He can only present it in images, and this he does, I believe, in very moving ways. There is first of all the crude but effective cow-tragedy enacted on the mock-classical veranda, a play about a calf which dies in the womb of its bewildered and suffering mother. We will return to this crucial scene later. There is also the 'disgusting blood-poem' (as Waldo calls it) about the maternal womb and its blood-mysteries, and about the 'common pain' of the brothers. Arthur urges Waldo to help him in his art; he wants Waldo to collaborate with him in the cow-tragedy, and to help with the *unfinished* blood-poem. This is not merely a call for technical and formal aid—although he certainly needs that as well—but a call for consciousness, for the rational self to participate in what is being created. The unconscious desires to be made known.[9] It is not merely an impersonal source of images and archetypes that can be exploited by the artist. To be most fruitful, the artistic process should be a two-way process, involving a return of energy and attention back to the imaginal source. The artist himself, through development and awareness, through educating his mind to the mystery of what he sees, may have to prove himself worthy before anything further is revealed. This book records the cry of the imagination for recognition and understanding. The time is up for White's irresponsible dabbling with the unconscious; it now makes tremendous demands upon him. White proves unable to meet those demands, with the result that his intellectual relationship with the imagination is lost altogether, his mandalic vision is ruined, and the unrealized mother–bind proceeds to devour his personality.

I

In the beginning there was the sea of sleep . . . in which they lay together . . . nesting in each other's arms the furry waves of sleep nuzzling at them like animals. (p. 215)

In their early childhood the brothers were psychologically identical, two *pueri* swimming in the fluid depths of the unconscious. Waldo had not yet become Waldo, but was merely an extension of the inner world, or a different version of Arthur. As a growing schoolboy Waldo maintained an integral relation to Arthur, and was 'lost without his twin' (p. 32).

Sometimes Waldo buried his face in the crook of Arthur's neck, just to smell, and then . . . they would start to punch each other, to ward off any shame . . . Sometimes on evenings of sickly light, before Arthur had returned, Waldo approached the looking glass, his face growing bigger and bigger, his mouth flattening on the throbbing glass, swallowing, or swallowed by, his mouth. Until he would hear Arthur, books falling on the kitchen floor . . . And Waldo would drag himself out of the mirror's embrace, and run to meet his brother. (pp. 32–3)

This is one of our clearest expressions of the inward, symbolic role of Arthur Brown in Waldo's life. As the rational twin approaches the looking glass, his mirror–self begins to appear like Arthur: fleshy face, large sensual mouth, even a suggestion of an overbearing aspect. The fact that the mouth appears to be swallowing him indicates that the shadow–brother has begun to take on an ambivalent character, and to be associated with matriarchal devouring imagery. Then, as if this image had materialized before him, Arthur runs into the kitchen and begins to wrestle with his twin. Already the brothers are becoming quite distinct—Arthur appears as the feminine container, and Waldo as the contained masculine ego. Arthur, I have argued, is not merely Waldo's reflection, but White's as well, the other self who 'fluctuated in the watery glass' (*Flaws in the Glass*, p. 1) in his own childhood landscape. We discover more of White's hidden, buried self in *The Solid Mandala* than we do in *Flaws in the Glass*, because in the fictional work the depths of his imaginative life are revealed, whereas in the autobiography we have a more narrowly focused, external perception of the artist's world. *The Solid Mandala* allows us as it were to walk through the glass and experience the mysteries of the imaginal self from the inside, from Arthur's perspective, whereas in the self-portrait we are held on the observer's side, the side of the rational ego, which looks somewhat confusedly and bewilderedly at the shapes in the glass.

As Waldo develops he experiences Arthur as a regressive influence, a handicap to his growth and upward striving. 'Waldo would have liked to go permanently proud and immaculate, but his twin brother dragged him back repeatedly behind the line where knowledge didn't protect' (p. 46). The ego cannot afford to be drawn below the threshold of consciousness because it associates the downward movement with disorientation and absence of identity. It cannot be dirtied by unreason, but wants to remain 'proud and immaculate' in the shadowless light of consciousness. Of course Arthur does not represent the threat to his existence that Waldo imagines. Arthur is not the matriarchal devourer that his twin fears, but the helpful shadow[10] who strives to protect Waldo from the destructive forces of the inner world. Arthur is a tough, sturdy figure, with many masculine attributes that Waldo himself lacks. Still, the insecure male ego gives everything that is alien to it a negative connotation: '"You're a big fat helpless female"' (p. 42), Waldo accuses his twin. 'Waldo could not bear to listen to Arthur breathing the way he breathed ... He could not bear what he had to bear, his responsibility for Arthur' (p. 41).

As Waldo struggles to assert his own independence, the archetypal background becomes darkly threatening and malign. As soon as the ego makes a bid for freedom, the matrix exerts a nullifying, life-threatening inertia, which the ego must learn to recognize and fight against. It is against this psychological background that we can best appreciate Waldo's childhood essay, 'What I see on the Way to School':

'There is the old stone tumbledown house amongst the pear trees where nobody lives any longer, the roof has gone, which looks like a house in which somebody might have committed a few murders ....'
He almost could not bring himself further, in front of all those others. And Mr Hetherington. And Johnny Haynes. Some things were too private, except perhaps in front of Arthur...
'Sometimes when it is early or late,' Waldo's voice came bursting ... 'I have thought I saw the form of a man hurrying off with a basin of blood.'
Here Mr Hetherington grunted in that fat way.
'Of course it is only the imagination. But I think this person, if he had ex- isted, would have murdered the many children he lured in through the black trees.' (p. 43–4)

This has something of 'the catcher in the rye' in it: a malevolent being lives in a ghostly house and attempts to lure children into his murderous domain. Mythologically the figure could be seen as a creature of the underworld, one of the shades who demand blood oblations from the living and who capture unwary travellers who stray too near the nether world. The image of blood is central in White, representing the essence, the libido, the stuff of life. The tale suggests that Waldo is in danger of having his blood, his libidinal direction, stolen from him. His bid for freedom has invited a destructive counter-attack that he must now contend with.

After Waldo reads the essay to his class we find a marvellous conjunction of realism and myth. Johnny Haynes and Norm Croucher, the bullies of the school, decide to act in accordance with Waldo's tale and draw blood from him in the manner indicated in the story:

'Come on, Normie, we'll show Waldo what we got in our bloody basin.'
They walked all three down to the pepper trees. If Waldo accompanied them voluntarily it was because he knew it to be his fate. There he stood, a little apart, on the white, windswept grass. With Johnny saying: 'That bloke hadn't reckoned on one more murder. Amongst the pear trees,' he added. Waldo heard the knife click. (p. 44)

At the mythic level we could say that Waldo's classmates simply act out the role of the inner antagonist. And here there is an ironic twist. Arthur, Waldo's apparent antagonist and *doppel-gänger*, breaks in on the scene and flattens Norm Croucher and Johnny Haynes in a magnificent display of strength; but Waldo is disgraced by his brother's intrusion, it highlights Waldo's vul- nerability and weakness. Although Arthur rises up over them in redemptive glory—'It was as if the flaming angel ... stood above them, or ... flailed and flickered' (p. 45)—Waldo sees his intrusion as belittling and undermining: '"You only want to make a fool of me," Waldo said ... "You've always got to show us up"' (p. 45). Waldo thinks himself superior to Arthur, and refuses to allow Arthur to come to his support. There is a deeper sense in which Waldo does not want to be protected from the destructive forces of the inner world. He accepts the attack because 'he knew it to be his fate'. There is something perversely satisfying in this horrific ritual ('He could not explain a ritual to Arthur', p. 46); something sadistically pleasurable in feeling 'the blood shoot out ... from his wincing flesh ... in little jets of scarlet fountains'. The *puer aeternus* prefers to shed blood, to return his life to the matrix, rather than fight off the hostile pursuer. He yields before the destructive forces of the unconscious, caught up in a fatal bondage to the archetypal source.

Thus while Waldo sets out on an heroic course, an attempt to liberate the ego from the infantile background, he gets stuck by virtue of a fundamental quiescence, an inertia. Waldo makes gestures toward liberation, but these are mainly outward, futile attempts to free himself from Arthur. '"Leave me!" Waldo shouted. "How many times have I told you not to hang on to my hand?"' (p. 45). He adopts a proud, aristocratic, haughty manner, which is not based on real development but is merely a pretence to disguise his psychological fixation. 'His top half' to borrow John Updike's metaphor, 'felt all afloat in a starry firmament of ideals and young voices singing; the rest of his self was heavily sunk in a swamp where it must, eventually, drown'.[11] Ironically, it is Arthur, not Waldo, who is possessed of true heroism and masculine drive. The apparently 'unconscious' brother is the one who fights off the bullies and who carries the heroic spirit that the ego will not carry. The shadow–brother is on the side of life, even if the conscious personality prefers death and dissolution.

About this time Waldo decides to write a play, a 'Greek tragedy', to be enacted under the classical pediment of the Brown house in Terminus Road. Waldo has literary ambitions throughout his career, but he is unable to realize his creativity because it lies bound up in his inner world, caught up in his 'Arthur' personality and unavailable to his conscious mind. When he tells Arthur he will not allow him to act in his play (the hubristic ego excluding the archetypal figure), Arthur decides to write his own 'Greek tragedy', and enacts it then and there upon the stage-like veranda of the house. His play is about a cow ('"A cow's as Greek,

I suppose," said Dad, "as anything else"'), or more particularly about a still-born calf, and the despair of its failed mother.

'This is a big, *yellow* cow,' he told them. 'She's all blown out, see, with her calf. Then she has this calf. It's dead. See?'
There was Arthur pawing at the boards of the veranda. At the shiny parcel of dead calf.
Everyone else was looking at the ground by now, from shame, or, Waldo began to feel, terror.
'You can see she's upset, can't you?' Arthur lowed. 'Couldn't help feeling upset.'
It was suddenly so grotesquely awful in the dwindling light and evening silence.
'Couldn't help it,' Arthur bellowed.
Thundering up and down the veranda he raised his curved, yellow horns, his thick, fleshy, awful muzzle. The whole framework of their stage shook.
'That's enough, I think,' said Dad ...
Dad got up and limped inside. You could hear him lifting the porcelain shade off the big lamp. (p. 40)

This play is the metaphorical equivalent of Dubbo's Tree of Unborn Souls in the previous novel. We have to do with the same psychic elements: the maternal matrix and its tragically-depicted offspring, but here the tree and human fruit metaphor is exchanged for that of cow and calf. This image has its precedent in *The Tree of Man*, where the Parkers' cow, Julia, gave birth to a succession of still-born calves, and where Amy Parker experienced a series of miscarriages and remained childless for a number of years. There the image related to the life-denying character of the mother/son bond in White's world, and here it is the same: the ego–principle is regressively bound to the matrix, and cannot live its own life. Waldo Brown and his father are attached to the source-situation, and unable to be born into the conscious world. George Brown's chronic asthma, his subservience to his wife, show him to be a victim of the maternal image and a direct descendent of George Goodman, White's prototypical ineffectual father. His characteristic limp and club foot link him mythologically with Oedipus (literally 'swollen-footed'). If George Brown gets up and limps away from Arthur's play it is because the drama mirrors his own tragic situation too clearly, and is too painful to bear.[12]

It is interesting that the cow parades around the stage in utter desperation, deeply disturbed by the death of its offspring. In *The Tree of Man* and *Riders in the Chariot* the reverse of this was true: the maternal archetype was a darkly ambivalent power which held fast to the developing offspring and did not want it to leave the matrix. If before we found a regressive mother–image that inhibited life, now we have a defective ego that cannot, or does not want to, live. The obstacle to growth in this novel is not the mother, but the ego itself which blocks its own development. It is apparent that Arthur, who appears in his symbolic role as feminine container, identifies with the cow's despair. In the 'Arthur' section, where the same event is retold through Arthur's eyes, his identification with the animal is more precisely delineated: 'As he stamped up and down, pawing and lowing, for the tragedy of all interminably bleeding breeding cows. By that time his belly was swollen with it. He could feel the head twisting in his guts' (p. 230). The implication is clear: if Arthur is the containing matrix, Waldo is the contained, still-born ego, the 'shiny parcel of dead calf'. The reference to the head 'twisting' in Arthur's guts links this image to that of the knot at the centre of the glass marble. The ego is twisted or knotted up inside the matrix, causing its own death as well as the suffering of the feminine source. The image of Waldo imprisoned inside Arthur's body foreshadows Waldo's actual death, since he dies in Arthur's embrace, as his brother strives desperately to awaken him to life. And Arthur experiences his brother's death as his own doing, just as the dumb animal appears to be taking the responsibility of the calf's death upon itself. But the point is that the ego is inherently flawed; it will not live, but remains bound up in eternity.

Waldo is astounded by Arthur's play, and remains standing under the classical pediment long after the others have departed. 'He could not help wondering how Arthur of all people had thought about that play. Ridiculous, when not frightening' (p. 40). Waldo's response is one of fascinated horror. He is struck by the performance, but does not know why. This is the characteristic response of White's characters to the symbols that rise up before them. They are moved, but in an unknowing way. Whether we consider Theodora's response to the bird in the crocodile's mouth, or Parker's reaction to the man suspended in the tree, the pattern of uncomprehending fascination remains the same. This surely is the greatest tragedy of all in White's fiction—not that the human ego is devoured, but that the imagination throws up guiding or therapeutic imagery which is never recognized by the conscious personality.

Waldo is also shocked by the evident creativity of his shadow–brother. His own play is still a mere fancy, a projected possibility, whereas Arthur's is already conceived and executed before them. The ego–figure is full of dreams and ambitions, yet it is the simpleton brother who is spontaneously creative and able to express his innermost thoughts. Arthur's creative expressions will remain crude and rough until he can mobilize his 'Waldo' personality, his reason and intellect, so that the images of the unconscious can be shaped and given aesthetic form. Until each can constellate the inner counterpart, or until the brothers can work together as a creative unit, Waldo will remain a sterile aesthete, with little creative force, and Arthur will remain a crude, primitive artist, close to the mythic imagination but lacking discipline and intellectual rigour. These are the purely aesthetic consequences of psychic dissociation, but they are important in a novel which addresses itself to the specific problem of creativity, and to the wider conflicts at work within White's own artistic life. It is impossible to avoid the impression that the novel points to a tremendous potential, a magnificent art greater than White has produced so far. If the Waldo and Arthur personalities would work together we would have the art of true genius, which is to say *conscious* genius, an imagination that is self-possessed and intelligently guided. As it is, this level of achievement is merely hinted at, obliquely suggested, but never fully attained.

The conflict between the brothers ceases at certain points in the novel, not because resolution is achieved, but because Waldo simply gives in to his brother out of sheer exhaustion:

> That night Arthur tried to drag him back behind the almost visible line beyond which knowledge could not help...
> Arthur was taking, had taken him in his arms, was overwhelming him with some need...
> [Waldo] ... should have struggled, but couldn't any more. The most he could do was pinch the wick, squeeze out the flickery candle-flame.
> The stench of pinched-out candle was cauterizing Waldo's nostrils. But he did not mind all that much. He was dragged back into what he knew for best and certain. Their flesh was flickering quivering together in that other darkness, which resisted all demands and judgements. (pp. 47–8)

Waldo is depicted as a helpless, exhausted child ego in the embrace of his shadow–brother. This state of surrender is to be sharply differentiated from that of creative co-existence. It simply marks the temporary collapse of the ego, its resignation to 'Arthur', to darkness (Waldo himself snuffs out the candle), and to unconsciousness. 'He was dragged back into what he knew for best and certain', i.e., he returns to where he 'belongs', to his negative at-one-ment with the matrix. But at first light Waldo resumes his rational position far above the threshold of the inner world. Then his brother becomes once more the antagonist and Waldo attempts to defend his rationality, until 'night' takes him back into Arthur's arms. This is the relentless course of the infantile ego: it oscillates between flight and resignation, between rigid resistance and nihilistic surrender.

II

It is to be expected that Waldo, with his fear of the maternal realm, should experience a resistance, even an hostility, toward women, sexuality and the female womb. Many of his forebears in White's fiction, Elyot Standish, Voss, Palfreyman, experienced a fiercely irrational misogyny because the female sex was felt to be the carrier of the devouring maternal image. What assails White's male protagonists from the inside is transferred outside and expressed as a general loathing of the opposite sex. For Waldo woman is a devouring force and the vagina is seen either as an absorptive-seductive maw (pp. 103, 184) or as a disease-ridden organ associated with 'syph' and 'the pox' (pp. 116, 173). When Johnny Haynes and his wife come to visit the elderly Waldo he muses that 'the wife or whore, was going to give [her husband] syph or a stroke' (p. 191). Womankind is seen as the despoiler of man, and sexual intercourse is linked with primal fears of disintegration. It is little wonder that Waldo refrains from heterosexual activity throughout his career. The only surprising thing is that White does not have him engage in homosexual activity, since Waldo has the classic psychological disposition for the homosexual lifestyle. We can only assume that White was reluctant to disclose his homosexual preference at this stage in his work, and was forced to repress his character's libido and have him lead an aridly celibate, passionless life.

Waldo's relationships with women are entirely mythological and predetermined. When he first meets Dulcie Feinstein, his psyche converts her into an image of his own seductive, devouring feminine world. We are told that 'Waldo would have hated to touch her, for fear that she might stick to him, literally, ... in spite of himself' (p. 90). Psychologically this relates to the feminine as an undifferentiated mass, which would 'stick to' and absorb an approaching masculine ego. It reminds us of the fate of Theseus, the Greek hero who journeyed to the underworld, only to grow fast to the rocks when he first made contact with the maternal ground.[13] The masculine ego is unstable and easily devoured, so that the maternal image appears glutinous, absorptive. Waldo cannot relate to the actual woman, only to the negative psychic image which appears before him. The mythological element is accentuated in a later meeting:

He did look back just once at Mrs Saporta, increasing, bulging, the Goddess of a Thousand Breasts, standing at the top of her steps, in a cluster of unborn, ovoid children. This giant incubator hoped she was her own infallible investment. But she would not suck him in. Imagining to hatch him out.
    'I'm past the incubation stage!' he called.
    So much for Dulcie Feinstein Saporta and her lust for possession. He was tempted to look back again, to see whether his scorn had knocked her bleeding to the steps. (pp. 157–8)

Here the gap between reality and mythic projection reveals how completely irrational and paranoid his response to woman is. Waldo 'sees' Dulcie as an awesome mother–goddess who longs to possess and overpower him, whereas in reality Dulcie has just rejected his marriage proposal and has escorted him to the door. Her *rejection* of him has damaged his frail masculine ego, causing a demonic psychic image to erupt into full view. Interestingly, we discover here the process of projection at work, as Dulcie, 'increasing, bulging', transforms into an archaic fertility goddess, reminiscent of the many-breasted Diana of Ephesus. Waldo shouts abuse at this archaic idol as he turns away in fright. Ironically, he defines his own mythic situation by a negation: '"I'm past the incubation stage!" he called'. As Erich Neumann has pointed out, the intellectual *puer* frequently claims to have transcended the thing that continues to hold him fast from within. As he says of the failed Hippolytus of Greek tragedy, 'he remains bound to the Goddess, although he defies and denies her with his conscious mind'.[14] Waldo scorns the mother and her 'cluster of unborn, ovoid children', yet the very fact that this mythic image has forced itself upon him indicates that he is himself one of the 'unborn', at the mercy of the unconscious and its archetypal forces.

Yet while having a great fear of the feminine, Waldo displays a secret yearning for that Other world, since much of his psychic energy is bound up in the complex. This ambivalence is particularly marked in his relationship with Mrs Poulter. When she first moved into Terminus Road Waldo's immediate impression was that she 'had stupid-looking calves, which Waldo thought he would like to slap if he had been following her up a flight of stairs. Slap slap. To make her hop' (p. 140). Here is a sadistic denigration of the feminine which is characteristic of the mother-bound man. Yet at the same time the 'stupid-looking' woman exerts a powerful fascination upon Waldo, as we discover in the scene where he is found spying upon Mrs Poulter through the bathroom window.

It was so dark, it was understandable he should have been drawn to the square of light. He couldn't resist it. And there stood Mrs Poulter, normally so high of colour, turned waxen by the yellow light inside the room. Her breasts two golden puddings, stirred to gentle activity. For Mrs Poulter was washing her armpits at the white porcelain washstand basin ... Waldo saw the draggle of jet in the secret part of her thighs. (p. 61)

Although White does not link this scene directly with his Tiresias theme, it is related to it. At one point in his career Tiresias surprised Athene at her bath and was punished for his importunity by blindness and, later, by being transformed into a woman.[15] Mythologically, the movement into the feminine region is fatal for a masculine ego which is not prepared for the encounter. It is 'blinded' (loses consciousness) and transformed into a woman (overwhelmed by the contrasexual archetype). In the Greek myth, Athene gives Tiresias insight by way of compensation, but in the present context it is Arthur who seems to have the insight of Tiresias and Waldo merely his blindness. Waldo is overtaken by the apparition of the woman at her bath, he loses his rational attitude and becomes obsessed by her form: 'He had never felt guiltier, but ... could not have moved for a shotgun' (p. 61). So too (anticipating Eddie Twyborn) is he transformed into a woman in a later scene in the story, thus fulfilling his mythic destiny as a victim of the Mother Goddess.

The transvestite scene represents a climactic point in Waldo's relation to the internal feminine. For a time he is completely overwhelmed by the maternal archetype, which causes him to abandon his masculine form and to adorn himself in his mother's ballroom dress:

To the great dress. Obsessed by it. Possessed. His breath went with him, through the tunnel along which he might have been running. Whereas he was again standing. Frozen by what he was about to undertake. His heart groaned, but settled back as soon as he began to wrench off his things ... (p. 193)

Waldo is robbed of his free will and is totally at the mercy of the invading archetypal content. And adorned in his mother's dress and clutching the hideous broken fan, Waldo carries out a grotesque ritual in which he is transformed into the goddess Memory, mother of the Muses:

When he was finally and fully arranged, bony, palpitating, plucked, it was no longer Waldo Brown, in spite of the birthmark above his left collarbone ... Memory seated herself in her chair, tilting it as far back as it would go, and tilted, and tilted, in front of the glass. Memory peered through the slats of the squint-eyed fan, between the nacreous refractions. If she herself was momentarily eclipsed, you expected to sacrifice something for such a remarkable increase in vision .... She could afford to breathe indulgently, magnificent down to the last hair in her moustache, and allowing for the spectacles.

When Waldo Brown overheard: 'Scruff! Come here, Runty! Runty? Silly old cunt!'

Arthur's obscene voice laughing over fat words and private jokes with dogs. (p. 193)

It is important that this transvestite ritual takes place in front of the looking glass, for it is truly Waldo's mirror–self or double that rises up before him. This archaic mother–personality is the genuine *flaw* in the glass, the one which White refuses to integrate and which, consequently, failed to be represented in his autobiography. The personality is described in grotesque, theatrical, quean-like terms, but this is because Waldo's inner life *is* grotesque and dark. It has been shut up for so long in the unconscious that it has grown old, bizarre and archaic. Yet the figure is reeling with energy and libido, because the mother–complex devours most of Waldo's energy before his masculine ego can get at it. His consciousness is dry and sterile, but at his depths is this dynamically alive, shimmering, glowing, archetypal self.

At the climax of this transvestite scene, Arthur and his dogs intrude upon the ghastly ritual and force Waldo to return to his former state. It is inevitable that Arthur should intervene, for he is part of the same archetypal field which is currently invading Waldo's personality. Arthur as person lumbers down the sideway of the house, but Arthur as image erupts into Waldo's mind as a result of his mythic descent. In the 'Arthur' section we find that the all-seeing twin identifies himself with Waldo when he catches him 'celebrating something' through the bedroom window. 'Oh he might have cried, if he hadn't laughed ... at himself in Waldo's blue dress. Bursting out of it. His breasts were itching' (p. 291). Here we find a conjunction of fictional roles: Waldo becomes Arthur and Arthur becomes Waldo. The brothers are fused again in the 'sea of sleep', in the fluid depths of the unconscious.

As we might expect, the desperate ritual ends in despair. Waldo tears off the 'wretched dress' and returns to the sterility of his ego. He is humiliated by Arthur's intervention, throws the dress into a corner, and hopes he has not been caught out. This follows the same pattern as before: a sudden descent into the unconscious and then a corresponding leap back to his position above the threshold of the inner world. There is no sign of self-awareness in this schizophrenic ritual, much less any suggestion of his ever achieving an integration of his masculine and feminine selves.

III

Arthur becomes increasingly impatient with his brother's inadequacy. He realizes that if Waldo does not move toward consciousness and freedom, he will not achieve liberation either, but will be condemned to his present state of psychological retardation.[16] The inner self tries to hurry the ego along toward integration. As we have seen, the knot at the centre of the glass marble becomes the symbol for what Arthur senses is Waldo's psychological fixation, his regressive pact with the source. Arthur makes a desperate bid to urge his brother to accept the knotted mandala, so that they might work together on the *opus* of realization:

> Arthur had turned, and was towering, flaming above him, the wick smoking through the glass chimney.
> But his skin, remaining white and porous, attempted to soothe. Arthur put out one of the hands which disgusted Waldo . . .
> Arthur said: 'If it would help I'd give it to you, Waldo, to keep.'
> Holding in his great velvety hand the glass marble with the knot inside.
> 'No!' Waldo shouted. 'Go!'
> 'Where?'
> There was, in fact, nowhere. (p. 169)

This presents Arthur in his prophetic role, as a figure 'towering' and 'flaming' above the ego, reminding us of his appearance as the 'flaming angel' in the schoolyard fight episode. Arthur attempts to lead the ego toward individuation, yet Waldo, habitually suspicious and cynical, appears to view the offer of the glass marble as an assault upon his integrity. Waldo views the mandala as an invitation to dissolve himself in boyhood, infantile fantasies ('"I never cared for marbles. My thumb could never control them"', p. 214). He is unable to see through the outward appearance of the boy's toy to the depth of meaning behind it. Nor does he realize that the knot is presented as something upon which he must work, something which demands an active response. Waldo's response is inadequate and miscalculated, yet Arthur cannot correct him verbally or conceptually, he can only keep on insisting that his brother accept the talisman which has been reserved for him.

As this scene is retold in Part Three, from Arthur's point of

view, we are made aware of the shadow–brother's growing despair
and hopelessness:

> 'If it would help I would give it to you, Waldo, to keep,' Arthur said.
> Offering the knotted mandala.
> While half sensing that Waldo would never untie the knot.
> Even before Waldo gave one of his looks, which, when interpreted, meant:
> By offering me a glass marble you are trying to make me look a fool, I am not,
> and never shall be a fool, though I am your twin brother, so my reply, Arthur,
> is not shit, but shit!
> As he shouted: 'No, Arthur! Go, Arthur!' (p. 273)

Arthur is tired of being dismissed as an idiot, though the language
of symbolism, of the seemingly infantile glass marble, is the only
one he knows. Waldo, unable to appreciate the symbolic dimension, is tired of being treated as a fool, and begs Arthur leave him
in peace. This is the stalemate situation in which the brothers are
caught, a situation which finds its parallel in the Doppelgänger
stories of E. T. A. Hoffman and Edgar Allan Poe, where the ego's
misapprehension of the shadow–figure's intentions invariably
leads to sterility, conflict and death.

It is partly because he fears that Waldo 'would never untie the
knot' that Arthur carries out a desperate, if fitful, search for
knowledge. By way of *The Brothers Karamazov, The Upanishads*,
Japanese Zen, and Jung's *Psychology and Alchemy*, Arthur hopes
'to storm his way, however late, however dark the obscurer
corners of his mind' (p. 280). But he is not at all suited to intellectual pursuits. His lumbering mind cannot deal with abstract
thought: 'As for the Indian lotus, he crushed it just by thinking on
it' (p. 281). The shadow–brother is trying to do the work that
should be done by the irresponsible ego. Arthur makes very little
progress in his mission of self-education beyond discovering the
word 'mandala', and recognizing its shape in Mr Saporta's carpets,
as in his own glass marbles. In a sense it is a foregone conclusion
that he will not succeed. The inner self, or unconscious genius,
cannot reach its goal alone. It can guide, facilitate, even force the
ego into recognition, but it cannot complete the process of
realization itself.

Poor Arthur becomes obsessed by 'the Books' and makes
regular visits to the public library, where he is the cause of
amusement among the library staff. It is here that Waldo, an
officer at the library, catches his brother reading at a desk, and
where he reveals his paranoid stand against Arthur's quest for
understanding.

> 'What will it do for you? To understand?'
> 'I could be able to help people,' Arthur said, beginning to devour the words.

'Mrs Poulter. You. Mrs Allwright. Though Mrs Allwright's Christian Science, and shouldn't be in need of help. But you, Waldo.'

Arthur's face was in such a state of upheaval, Waldo hoped he wasn't going to have a fit, though he had never had one up till now ...

'Everybody's got to concentrate on something. Whether it's a dog. Or,' he babbled, 'or a glass marble. Or a brother, for instance. Or Our Lord, like Mrs Poulter says.'

Waldo was afraid the sweat he could feel on his forehead, the sweat he could see streaming shining round his eyes, was going to attract even more attention than Arthur's hysteria.

'Afraid,' Arthur was swaying in his chair. 'That is why our father was afraid .... He was afraid to worship some thing. Or body.'

Suddenly Arthur burst into tears.

'That's something you and I need never be, Waldo. Afraid. We learned too late about all this Christ stuff. From what we read it doesn't seem to work, anyway. But we have each other.'

He leaned over across the table and appeared about to take Waldo's hands. Waldo removed his property just in time.

'You'd better get out,' he shouted. 'This is a reading room. You can't shout in here' ...

'Please,' he repeated, and added very loudly: 'sir!' (pp. 199–200)

Arthur has sensed the urgency of their situation, and now puts it nakedly before Waldo for the first time. He has arrived at the crucial point: fear. It is Waldo's fear of the depths, of the unknown in himself, which prevents him from embarking on a spiritually mature existence. And it is because Arthur's diagnosis is so accurate that Waldo is forced to order him out. But before he goes Arthur insists that Waldo need not be afraid, because they 'have each other'. In others words—or so I read it—Arthur assures Waldo that he would not fail him if he should decide to turn within, to uncover meaning and spiritual value. Arthur rightly supposes that the orthodox religious way is not for them, that they must seek redemption through the inner, psychological path. Arthur boldly proposes a new *religio* involving a 'concentration' upon the glass marble and upon symbolic realities. Still, Waldo fails to separate the essence of Arthur's discourse from its fragmented presentation: it remains absolute nonsense to him.

IV

The final and almost epic event in the life of the twins is the walk down Barranugli Road, an event which is woven throughout the scenes of the first half of the novel, to provide a thread of continuity as well as to act as an allegory of their life's journey. The walk appears to summarize the agonizing relation between the brothers, for while Waldo sees the walk as his attempt to destroy Arthur, to drive him to a heart attack, Arthur views the walk as his final attempt to get Waldo to turn toward the urgent and pressing psychic realities. The ironic twist is that it is Waldo who dies at the end of the walk, for Arthur's dramatic exposure of the contents of the unconscious proves fatal for Waldo's defective personality. The walk therefore encapsulates the contradictory strivings of the brothers, and its outcome points to the fate of the rational self which continues to resist individuation when it is being demanded by the brother within.

Arthur's first move is to draw Waldo's attention to his irrational misogyny and to the problem of the maternal feminine. He does this by referring to Mrs Poulter, and by goading Waldo into a recognition of his hatred for her:

> 'I wonder why Mrs Poulter is so awful?'
> Arthur, puffing, threatened to topple, but saved himself on Waldo's oilskin.
> 'I don't say she's *awful*!'
> 'If you don't say, it's likely to fester,' said Arthur, and sniggered ...
> 'It's splinters that fester,' Waldo answered facetiously.
> 'Perhaps,' said Arthur, and sniggered again. (p. 28)

Waldo cannot articulate his hatred of the maternal principle because it is an irrational, psychic problem, but Arthur warns that what cannot be expressed is likely to fester. Here Arthur displays his awareness that Waldo is refusing to admit to a crucial inward factor. In this instance Arthur functions in his paradoxical capacity: he is the divine child with a profound awareness of symbolic reality, and he is the infantile shadow who goads his brother and who 'sniggers' at Waldo's inability to face up to the maternal image.

Arthur then turns his attention to the problem of Waldo's writing. He realizes that his brother's creativity is 'festering' in his inner world and tries to urge Waldo to write about simple things. Perhaps in concentrating on simple things his brother will shift his perception to a deeper level of reality. He invites Waldo to write about 'Mr Saporta and the carpets, and all the fennel down the side roads', because, he argues, simple things 'are somehow more transparent ... you can see right into them, right into the part that matters' (pp. 29–30). Waldo is shocked and disgusted by his brother's advice: 'He could have thrown away the fat parcel of his imbecile brother's hand'. Waldo cannot believe that his brother could be anything other than a source of annoyance. He retorts: '"What do *you* know?"', indicating that Arthur, his handicap, his burden, could never help him in his work, much less provide genuine inspiration.

Arthur remains persistent:

'You know when you are ill, really ill, not diphtheria, which we haven't
had, but anything, pneumonia—you can't say we haven't had pneumonia—
you can get, you can get much farther in.'
'Into what?'
It tired Waldo.
'Into anything.'
The wind coming round the corner, out of Plant Street and heading for Ada
Avenue, gave Waldo Brown the staggers. Arthur, on the other hand, seemed
to have been steadied by thoughtfulness.
He said: 'One day perhaps I'll be able to explain—not explain, because it's
difficult for me, isn't it, to put into words—but to make you *see*. Words are
not what make you see.' (p. 57)

Arthur again directs Waldo inward, into the centre of things, the
essence of experience; but the path to the silent matrix is for
Waldo a journey into disintegration and night. His ego could not
cope with the archetypal descent, whether through illness, as
Arthur suggests, or through acceptance of the irrational dimensions of experience. Although he would find poetry enough to fill
his notebooks and fulfil his creative dreams, he is not willing to
risk the journey and be rejuvenated by the source.

At this point in the walk Arthur directs the discussion toward
his own need, his desire to become conscious and achieve self-
awareness:

'I dunno,' Arthur said . . . If he stumbled at that point it was because he had
turned his right toe in.
'Mrs Poulter said,' said Arthur.
'Mrs Poulter!'
Waldo yanked at the oblivious hand. Mrs Poulter was one of the fifty-seven
things and persons Waldo hated.
'She said not to bother and I would understand in my own way. But I don't,
not always, to be honest. Not some things.' (pp. 57–8)

By implication, Arthur links his own quest for understanding
with his urgent beckoning of his brother toward the inner world.
Arthur needs his brother to turn within so that he too might see.
The reference to Mrs Poulter is most intriguing. She tells Arthur
'not to bother' with his work of realization. Here Mrs Poulter acts
as the Great Mother who is antagonistic to knowledge and *logos*,
and Arthur's differentiation from her suggests that he is moving
away from the maternal image.

But again Waldo refuses to become involved, he 'would not
listen any more', though Arthur himself was 'tired of telling'
(p. 58). Both parties are exhausted: Waldo by constant demands,
and Arthur by rejection and disappointment. At this stage Waldo
recalls the purpose of the long walk: to induce a heart attack in

Arthur's big, old-man's body. Waldo increases the pace of the walk, while Arthur, 'trotting like a dog' (p. 63) behind him, tries desperately to keep up. And as they turn a corner at speed Waldo is almost collected by a passing vehicle, which causes them to steady themselves and finally to turn home. This gives further dimension to the *doppelgänger* theme: although Waldo is trying to abuse Arthur he merely endangers himself by his course of action. The truck slams into the flap of his oilskin as he tries to drive Arthur to his death. Denial of the brother is ultimately a denial of self; the desire to kill the shadow–personality is a form of self-murder.

It is to self-destruction that his thoughts now turn:

> But he would arrive, and after they had struggled with that gate, and pushed the grass aside with their chests . . . he would go . . . and collect the box from on top of the wardrobe, that old David Jones dress box in which Mother had kept the little broken fan and some important blue dress . . . now he would make it actually his, all those warm thrilled and still thrilling words falling from their creator's hands into the pit at the bottom of the orchard into ash smouldering brittly palpitating with private thoughts. (p. 118)

If he cannot defeat Arthur, or resist him successfully, he gives in to the unconscious and turns self-destructive. This is apparent in his desire at this point to enter the 'devouring' female womb, to have sex with 'some lovely lousy girl', and 'get the pox and not do anything about it' (p. 116). This shows that the downward drag of the complex is finally defeating his masculinity and his habitual resistance to the lower realm. Also, the image associated with the anticipated destruction of his writing is maternal: he would push aside the grass with his chest and destroy his papers in the pit at the bottom of the orchard. This denotes a sacrificial ritual in the likeness of the *puer*–god: a surrender of himself to Nature and a giving over of his creative essence to the maternal earth. In reality, his masculine spirit has always dwelt in the depths of the matrix—just as his fragmentary writings have been stored in his mother's dress box—but now he contemplates consigning his consciousness literally into the maternal source.

As the twins return to their house in the aptly-named Terminus Road, we find Waldo unable to resist Arthur's demands for love and unity. However the unity achieved here is not the desired mandalic integration, but incestuous and undifferentiated fusion:

> Arthur . . . was waiting to trap him, Waldo suspected, in love-talk. So that he broke down crying on the kitchen step, and Arthur . . . led him in, and opened his arms. At once Waldo was engulfed in the most intolerable longing . . .

Arthur led him in and they lay together in the bed which had been their parents', that is, Waldo lay in Arthur's vastly engulfing arms, which at the same time was the gothic embrace of Anne Quantrell [that is, Anne Brown (*née* Quantrell), his mother] soothing her renegade Baptist. All the bread and milk in the world flowed out of Arthur's mouth onto Waldo's lips ... Arthur was determined Waldo should receive. By this stage their smeary faces were melted together. (p. 208)

Characteristically, Arthur's need to unite with his brother, to bring him support and loving-kindness, is interpreted by Waldo as a negative seduction into incestuous non-existence. When Waldo gives in to Arthur he surrenders to his own mother–complex, *not* to Arthur's mandalic vision. While Arthur works to the benefit of the ego, the ego works to its own demise. It is pitifully unaware of what the shadow–figure requires it to do.

From here Waldo's course is a steady decline into disintegration. Arthur's demands become greater as he makes a last bid for development. He recovers the blue dress, which Waldo had thrown into the laundry after his transvestite ritual, and now holds it up before him, 'so that Waldo might see his reflexion in it' (p. 212). Waldo screams '"Put it away! ... Where it was!"', but this dreadful image of his maternal fixation has already re-awakened his guilt and anxiety. Here Arthur acts, as always, as the psychopomp who digs up the past and thrusts its images before the ego. And now there is the discovery of Arthur's so-called blood poem, which appears in the story as a kind of 'extension' of the dress.

Arthur threw away the dress.
Which turned into the sheet of paper Waldo discovered in a corner ... On smoothing out the electric paper at once he began quivering.
Then Waldo read aloud, not so menacingly as he would have liked, because he was, in fact, menaced:
'my heart is bleeding for the Viviseckshunist
Cordelia is bleeding for her father's life
all Marys in the end bleed
but do not complane because they know
they cannot have it any other way'
This was the lowest, finally. The paper hung from Waldo's hand. (p. 212)

All the contents of the psyche have at last burst forth in a spectacular procession of images. And these images appear to be interchangeable: the dress 'turned into' the blood poem. In the psychic complex everything is intermingled and interrelated, so that its contents sometimes merge into a symbolic continuum. The poem evokes the image of the teeming maternal womb, the cycle of blood in which life is bathed. It is a kind of hymn to the *magna mater* in her various aspects, evoking her destructive aspect (as Vivisectionist), her life-sustaining aspect (the Blessed Virgin Mary), and her perpetually mourning character (Cordelia). Arthur says that the poem was written to 'celebrate their common pain' (p. 294), and we can only assume that he was trying to come to terms with the meaning of the mother archetype, to bring to awareness this potent image from the depths of their shared psyche.

Waldo is enraged by the poem, not merely because it activates his complex, but because it is a literary form—however inadequate—which threatens his own role as the poet of the Brown family. After he turns away from Arthur to examine his writings, Waldo is forced to admit that his poems are 'lustreless' and that 'time had dried ... his papers', whereas 'Arthur's drop of unnatural blood continued to glitter, like suspicion of an incurable disease' (p. 212). At this Waldo is moved to destroy his writings in the manner already elucidated in his waking fantasy. And after he 'scatters his seed' (p. 213) he turns his rage toward Arthur. In desperation Arthur offers the knotted mandala, but by this stage all is lost. Waldo launches an attack upon Arthur, but in so doing he kills himself, dying in a paroxysm.

V

Waldo's death signifies the dissolution of masculine consciousness into the mother–world. Arthur is now alone, and his own rationality and orientation appear to disintegrate with the death of his brother. He too descends into the matrix, not in death, but in madness, a kind of psychological death.

After fleeing from the scene of Waldo's death he embarks on a journey into the underworld. He becomes an idiot child blubbering on street corners. He sleeps in dark alleys, under towering grass, and is urinated on by wandering drunks, one of whom mistakes him for a rotting corpse. He contemplates appealing to Dulcie for help, but realizes that his tragedy is too great for her to bear; he must journey alone through his desolation, and through the desolated streets of a nightmare suburbia. It is during this phase that he loses the glass marble with the knot inside in a clump of weeds, indicating that the mandalic vision is lost forever.

Part of Arthur's burden at this stage is what can only be described as a psychosis of guilt. He imagines that he has killed his brother: 'he, not Waldo, was to blame. Arthur Brown, the getter of pain' (p. 294). In one sense this is true. As the shadow–figure who forced the ego into an encounter with the inner forces, he is partly responsible for Waldo's death. But Arthur was merely attempting to urge his brother to 'see', to realize the contents of his unconscious mind. If Waldo was shattered by the encounter the tragedy was brought on by himself, by his own refusal to come to terms with the inner reality. Arthur's overwhelming guilt is symptomatic of his present disintegration; the psyche engulfs him in a wave of self-pity, sentimentality and infantilism. He is now a helpless *puer*, wrecked by experience.

As Arthur undergoes the agony of disintegration, another process is at work in the fictional psyche. We have seen in previous novels that the defeat of the masculine ego is experienced in a positive light in the realm of the maternal unconscious. Symbolically, the 'mother' as matrix is rejuvenated by the descending libido. The life-blood gushes from the *puer*'s wounds and quickly vivifies the earth and 'makes it green', as we found in *Voss*. The son's failure, his loss, his ruin, is immediately converted into the earth mother's triumph. The Aboriginal mothers shriek in ecstasy as the German explorer begins to dissolve into the Australian soil. In *Riders in the Chariot* Mrs Flack bursts into hysterical, satisfied laughter when she learns that Himmelfarb has been subdued, and Mrs Godbold, the self-styled 'good' mother, is delighted when she receives the ruined body of her *puer* after his crucifixion upon the tree. And so it is here: Mrs Poulter suddenly comes into her own, delighted at the death of Waldo Brown, and exultant that poor, ruined Arthur has become her very own dribbly child, her subdued lover: 'the aged man or crumpled child began to whimper, so she went to him again, because it was necessary to take him in her arms, all the men she had never loved, the children she had never had' (p. 311). Prior to Arthur's mental catastrophe Mrs Poulter was a relatively minor presence in the novel, but suddenly she assumes archetypal proportions and emerges as a formidable, smothering earth mother. This transformation has puzzled many readers. Kiernan, for instance, argues that the change is unconvincing, that Mrs Poulter's transformation is 'stated ... rather than fictionally "argued" and discovered'.[17] I take his point, but the view is largely determined by realistic expectations about character development. Mrs Poulter is not a 'character' in the conventional sense, she is a mythic figure, and she does not have to 'earn' her sudden endowment; she merely has to claim it. Her transformation derives from the sudden rush of energy into the maternal image.

Arthur encounters the ecstatic Mrs Poulter at the end of his horrific journey through the streets of Sarsaparilla. After the personality is dismembered, it experiences the oceanic comfort of the Great Mother: she soothes all wounds and promises never to betray the heart that loves her. Arthur is completely seduced by Mrs Poulter's lavish kindness, but he does maintain his integrity to some extent, especially in regard to the value he places upon Waldo, his 'rational' counterpart:

> 'I don't think, Mrs Poulter, I could live without my brother. He was more than half of me.'
> 'Oh no,' Mrs Poulter said. 'No more than a small quarter.' (p. 310)

Here we witness the subtle undermining of the Great Mother— she denigrates the value and meaning of the masculine ego. To the mother archetype the 'Waldo' personality, the mind, is insignificant. She has encouraged each of White's central characters to abandon consciousness and let go the mind, just as she attempted to persuade Arthur 'not to bother' (p. 58) with his mission of understanding. She would annul individuality, drawing everything back into the fluid matrix of the unconscious.

A crucial moment in the final scene is where Arthur and Mrs Poulter contemplate one of the glass marbles and see their faces reflected upon its shiny surface: 'she saw their two faces becoming one, at the centre of that glass eye, which Arthur sat holding in his hand' (p. 312). This indicates that Arthur's sacred talisman has become an uroboros, reflecting the unity of the maternal world, the conjunction of the Mother and her unborn child. The mandalic aspect of the marble was a mere possibility, something never realized because consciousness would not co-operate in the emergent vision. Much of the success of the central symbol is due to its inherent fluidity at the anagogical level. It can just as easily anticipate the mandalic union of mind and unconscious genius as it can symbolize the uroboric fusion of Mother and son. However, unless the reader can adapt to the challenging alternations of rhythm and meaning, he or she may be easily led astray. Because the text does not make it clear that the marble now appears in a wholly different archetypal context, the reader may be inclined to interpret the conjunction of Arthur and Mrs Poulter in the 'glass eye' as the realization of the novel's mandalic vision. A. P. Riemer asserts that Mrs Poulter becomes 'the custodian of this symbol of perfection'; 'she is the anima', he says, 'capable of mandalic experience'.[18] Similarly, Thelma Herring argues that the novel demonstrates the fulfilment of the quest for totality.[19] These readings fail to grasp the crucial difference between the marble as mandala and the marble as maternal uroboros. As usual, critics tend to inflate the importance of White's symbolic patterns, refusing to recognize the pathological context in which this final union (or fusion) occurs. If the uroboros triumphs it is only because Arthur, Waldo and the mandalic vision have failed.

VI

If critics continue to inflate and distort White's symbolic designs, the author himself refuses to indulge in his characteristic 'big endings'. The processes of decay and degeneration are too obvious to ignore, and too dearly 'felt' to allow the author to gloss over them with a transcendental gesture. At the close of the novel there is no religious inflation of his theme. There is some excitement as the ego dissolves into the maternal round, but Arthur is not presented as an illumined being (as was Theodora Goodman), nor is he equated with Christ (cf. Voss, Himmelfarb) or Anthropos (Stan Parker). Mrs Poulter does suggest that Arthur is her new-found object of worship, but this is acceptable within the context of the *puer*/Mother mythologem:

she slid down painfully to her knees, along his side, until by instinct she was encircling her joy and duty with her arms—ritually, as it were . . . She would [carry] him for ever under her heart, this child too tender to be born. (p. 311)

This is an appropriate ritual as the exhausted ego sinks back into the matrix, becoming again an unborn soul protected by the mother's encircling embrace. The mother naturally wants to celebrate what has returned to her, and what is now consigned to her care. In the past White would have allowed the Mother's intoxication to become his own, mistaking her jubilant excitement for his spiritual triumph. The long-standing misapprehension, or religious illusion, is now over. White no longer confuses his situation with that of the Mother, since the fact of the *puer*'s disintegration is now firmly and tragically established. This enables him to present his theme with a new sense of detachment, a detachment which allows irony and realism to lighten the previously dense texture of his apocalyptic moments:

When Sergeant Foyle came in, there was that Mrs Poulter kneeling beside Arthur Brown . . . . There she was, wiping and coaxing that nut, as a woman will cuddle a baby, provided it is hers, after she has let it mess itself. The sergeant couldn't abide a slut. But this old, at any rate, elderly biddy, was clean. Clean as beeswax. And as she half-turned, rising half-sighing on a probably needle-riddled foot, taking the weight off her numb knees, he was reminded of a boyhood smell of cold, almost deserted churches, and old people rising transparent and hopeful, chafing the blood back into their flesh after the sacrament. (p. 313)

The 'religious' critic will still see in this the familiar symbolism of divine communion and apotheosis, but of course the tone and presentation have changed dramatically. The 'detached eye' provides a distancing, ironic perspective upon the mother/son mystery. Sergeant Foyle's thoughts, the references to Arthur as a nut and helpless infant, and to Mrs Poulter as an old biddy, enable the reader to keep a sense of proportion in relation to this psychologically infantile ritual. The pathological element is finally incorporated as part of the matriarchal pattern. As Arthur goes off to an asylum, muttering aloud that it will not be so bad if Mrs Poulter brings him his favourite lollies every Tuesday, the reader does not feel that Sergeant Foyle or society is doing him an injustice. His insanity is treated gently and sympathetically, but it is insanity nonetheless. White does not attempt to disguise it.

The tone changes from here on in White's work. No claims are made for White's male characters, fewer demands are placed on the reader's credulity, and the elevated religious rhetoric seems to disappear altogether. '"Where has God got to?"' asks Peter Beatson in an essay on the later novels of Patrick White, and he answers that 'He' is still there, only 'His' presence is not so obviously apparent.[20] This is an optimistic reading of what amounts to a complete collapse of White's former metaphysical system. That system was based on the illusion of the *puer's* spiritual elevation, an illusion originally initiated and upheld by the mother archetype, but no longer tenable given the stark facts of Waldo's disintegration and Arthur's insanity. There is something final, if also fatal, about *The Solid Mandala*. The *puer's* illusions are shattered—which we must welcome after all this time—but at the same instant the *puer* himself has been cancelled, annulled, and can no longer attain any integrity in White's fiction. The novel seems to pose a desperate ultimatum: develop, or exit from centre stage. The *puer* collapses along with the religious system, and the life which he could not live is given over to the archaic personality in the deep unconscious.

6   The Mother in Search of Herself

> *Now if the process of individuation is not*
> *realised, it happens all the same in the*
> *unconscious, but in a negative form.*
>
> Marie-Louise von Franz[1]

With the collapse of Arthur and Waldo Brown, development of the masculine personality comes to an end in White's fictional world. The male figures henceforth are buried in the matrix and exist in a state of permanent psychological incest. Hurtle Duffield, Basil Hunter and Eddie Twyborn have an easy access to the maternal womb, yet each is incapacitated by the same ecstatic source. Duffield senses that he has spent his career inside a 'padded dome, or quilted egg, or womb ... He continued dragging round the spiral, always without arriving'.[2] Basil Hunter is 'womb-happy'[3] and lives in a perpetual incestuous fantasy. He is held fast in the mother and unable to develop a separate identity: 'He [saw] himself in the belly of a spiritual whale: unlike Jonah's, his would not spew him out till she died, and perhaps not even then' (p. 501). Eddie Twyborn languishes in an orgy of auto-eroticism and infantilism, but he has no real personality of his own. He takes on the character of the mother archetype and lives as a female figure. Everywhere the masculine ego is swamped by forces over which it has no control; it is assimilated to the maternal world.

While the male figure sinks into oblivion, the mother arche-type pursues a vigorous and extraordinarily productive course of development. Hurtle, Basil and Eddie are hollow men, but their *mothers* are powerful figures, eagerly pursuing their own careers and positively committed to the task of their individuation.

Psychologically, the conscious personality has aborted its own development, but the energy and direction which it could not utilize is taken up and co-ordinated by the mother–complex. The fact is, one cannot destroy the developmental instinct; one can only refuse to take it on, whence it falls into the unconscious and serves the archetypal images. The game of the soul has been played out, and the Mother emerges as the glorious victor, but only because the ego has blindly relinquished its own position.

The mother's central task in the novels of the 1970s is the integration of her dark, pagan aspect into her total personality. In her various guises as Alfreda Courtney, Elizabeth Hunter, Ellen Roxburgh and Eadie Twyborn the goal of her journey is always the same: to reach back and down into the past, into hidden depths, and into the primitive landscape of Australia, and bring up something of her 'lost' instinctual nature. From the beginning of White's career the Mother archetype has been separated into light and dark aspects. When the *puer* was centre stage we had to do with an idealized image of the Mother on the one hand (as 'God', Nature) and a negative, destroying image on the other (teeth-sucking mothers, society, *materia*). The *puer* was constantly jostled between contradictory maternal images, and we could say that his incomprehension of the situation served to push the two sides of the archetype further apart. If the desired source was all-loving, then its destroying aspect had to adopt extreme, diabolically bizarre expressions. There were indications that the mother was trying to move toward wholeness—Laura Trevelyan and Mrs Godbold covertly revealed pagan aspects—but these were overruled by the author, who was intent on idealizing and Christianizing his *imago dei*. With the collapse of the *puer aeternus* and his dualistic frame of reference, the ruling archetype is now in a position to reveal its complete character.

In the final phase of White's fiction we find a new sense of balance, as the archetype strives to draw its paradoxical attributes toward an integrated centre. We no longer find purely diabolical creatures such as Mrs Flack and Mrs Jolley, because the impetus now is to integrate evil with the mother archetype's inherent goodness. Nor do we find rarefied, spiritual goddesses, because the new movement is to direct spirit *toward matter*, to bring the divine animus of the Mother out of gnostic otherworldliness into the world of flesh, body and the senses. The Mother is freed from the *puer*'s (and White's) idealizations and so can recover her *mate*rial nature. The *puer*, dissolved in the source and hence no longer 'threatened' by it, is not compelled to demonize matter or the body in the usual way,[4] allowing these elements to be readily integrated into the mother's character. Moreover, society is no longer the hostile enemy that it was for the *puer*, but becomes the very *locus* in which the Mother achieves her very remarkable integration. There is a significant toning down of White's fiction in mood, temper and aspiration, a rediscovery of the material world previously shunned by the *puer*.

It must be stressed, however, that none of these changes comes about as a result of White's maturing, undergoing a personal development from the angry days of *The Aunt's Story* to a mellower, integrated vision in *A Fringe of Leaves*. Critics have tried to claim this and more for White's later novels. They have wanted to show that his nihilistic, boyish mysticism has finally given way to affirmative, responsible social attitudes. For the last fifteen years we have heard the warming, heartening talk about 'White's Progress',[5] his entering into a new 'humanistic' phase,[6] his final acceptance 'of human life as we know it'.[7] And critics have seen this 'growing up' as sure ground for the awarding of the Nobel Prize in 1973. I would argue that, ironically, the new turn of his fiction results from the dissolution of his conscious artistic position and the taking over of his imaginal world by the Mother. Any maturity revealed by the later work is due to the effort of the autonomous archetype and occurs *in spite of* the author. If the final phase of White's fiction is his best, then this is merely to say that the unconscious personality is the better artist, that the Mother is supreme in running—and ruining—the man. Certainly, 'she' makes a better job of her development, achieving individuation and wholeness where he did not. White does not benefit from the Mother's individuation, but is adversely affected by it, acting merely as the servant to an archetypal mystery which lies beyond his comprehension or control. Her desire for individuation is felt by him merely as an impulse to create fictions that deal with her development.[8] Critics have felt White to be responsible for all these changes, thereby overestimating his intellectual contribution and ignoring the regression which has made the final phase possible. The humanist stance of most critics, their generalized notions of progress and development in art and artist, all tend to obscure the situation. They need to be put to one side before we are able to see what goes on in the half-dark world of White's imagination.

1   Under Moonfire

> '*And they're under no ordinary attack. Can't you*
> *see? The moon is* shitting *on them!*'
>
> Olivia Davenport (*The Vivisector*, p. 336)

Hurtle Duffield's art is not about himself, but about the self-education of the maternal image. His paintings record the incarnation of a dark matriarchal power, and the fitful attempts of the mother–figure to incorporate this power into her total personality. The fact that his works act archetypally and collectively is expressed in the frenzied enthusiasm with which female admirers purchase his canvases and worship them as if they were fragments of divine revelation. The female characters find in Duffield's works an expression of processes going on in the depths of their own being. He holds a mirror up to them, in which they discover their own repressed natures. As Hero Pavloussi says before the savage canvas, 'Lantana Lovers under Moonfire', '"In some senses I am myself obscene and repulsive. Why must I not recognize it? ... This painting [conveys] something of what I have experienced—something of what I am"' (pp. 334–6). In *The Vivisector* (1970) the maternal-feminine image is in process of radical transformation, and Duffield's career is dedicated to this archetypal movement. He experiences his art not merely as an occupation or act of will, but as a burden which is forced upon him. As for White himself,[9] images well up from the unconscious and he is impelled to transform them into works of art. His Muse is the archetypal Mother, thrusting her archaic material up from the depths of the psyche and forcing him to attend to *her* individuation.

I

Duffield begins life as the son of two mothers, and it can be argued that he never escapes the motif of the dual mother during his career. Born as the son of Bessie Duffield, washerwoman and wife of a 'no-hope bottle-o' (p. 235), Hurtle soon becomes the adopted child of Mrs Alfreda Courtney, the wealthy mistress of Sunningdale. Mrs Courtney is an over-refined socialite who is engaged in a private war against evil and social injustice. At the same time, she has an unrecognized instinctual and erotic need, which her husband is unable to fulfil. When the Courtneys adopt Hurtle the innocent youth becomes the target of Alfreda's erotic burden, the carrier of her repressed sexuality. Hurtle becomes the vehicle through which Mrs Courtney ('Maman') is able to meet and contact her estranged personality. He makes possible a complete transformation of her character. So, in a different way, does this radiant boy–god help fulfil the unconscious desires of Mumma Duffield. This massive woman is in many ways similar to Mrs Godbold; she is mundane, earthy, married to a derelict, but with a deep spiritual need to transcend her material existence. From the outset it is clear that Hurtle, of her seven children, is her favourite. His good looks and inquisitive nature make him a logical object for the projection of the mother's spirit, her *puer*–animus: '"You're what I've been trying to tell them about. You're what Pa and me knows we aren't," Mumma mumbled' (p. 22). Hurtle is the one who is given the opportunity to begin an early education, to learn his Latin verbs and French nouns even before he enters primary school. The family has to sacrifice much in order to support this high-flying youth, but everything is sanctioned by Mumma ('"It's the edgercation that counts"', p. 141). Eventually the mother sacrifices him completely, by selling him to the Courtneys for a few hundred pounds. This does not mean that she has become selfless, concerned solely for his future welfare. The *puer* actually serves her best by leaving the fold and achieving status and recognition in the world ('"I pray—every night—for a better life for our boy . . . I would give Hurtle, if the opportunities were there"', p. 54). She has the secret satisfaction of knowing that her boy–animus has left the ordinary realm and found a place in a higher reality.

Thus his removal from the lower working-class slums to the Sunningdale estate fulfils the pattern of the earth-mother's spirit and marks the beginning of his servitude to Mrs Courtney. This is the recurring pattern of his life. He is handed to and fro between maternal figures, and is required to perform vital tasks for each of them.

II

Upon arriving at Sunningdale, Hurtle is given a lecture by Mrs Courtney on avoiding immoral behaviour, sexuality and the appetites. Duffield is amazed at why such an obviously sensuous, even voluptuous woman—always devouring expensive sweets or spilling hot chocolate down her 'creamy bosom' (p. 123)—should be so concerned about moral issues. She is a fierce supporter of humane societies, secretary of the anti-vivisection committee, and defender of the Church and other bastions of civilized morality. It is evident that Mrs Courtney's campaign against evil is a projection of her own inner conflict upon the social arena ('"The city is full of vice, and human nature is weak. But we ... must help others help themselves"', p. 34). She is engaged in a battle against her own instinctual nature, which is threatening to disrupt the idealism of her conscious attitude.

Mrs Courtney is the prototype of White's mothers of the 1970s, those many women who struggle with an erotic burden, attempting ultimately to arrive at a more complete state of being. In her the repressive and puritanical mode of the previous era is still partially intact, yet is being undermined by the sudden eruption of erotic life. Viewed retrospectively, from the position of Elizabeth Hunter or Ellen Roxburgh, Mrs Courtney reflects White's maternal figure at the brink of change, yet fearing the consequences of her imminent transformation.

Mrs Courtney's repressed instinctual nature is personified in her daughter Rhoda, the stunted, dwarfish child who is associated with animality, cats and filth. Rhoda's ugly body, with its humped back and pointed, rat-like face—one side covered with moles, the other with 'a big birthmark the colour of milk chocolate' (p. 62)— is a fitting expression of Maman's own grotesquely misshapen animal self. Maman makes gestures of loving kindness toward Rhoda, and refers to her as the 'cross' she has to bear, but in reality she brutalizes her daughter and attempts every means to help civilize her appearance:

'Did you do your board exercises? Did you? I know it's unpleasant, but it's for your own good. Did Nurse see that you lay on the board?'
Rhoda made some watery sounds. Her head trembled on her frail neck ... [She] started a high crying ...
Mrs Courtney herself had begun to whimper like a little child, her lovely face crumpling into an old rag. She looked as though she was about to creep on all fours, to make herself long and thin like some animal children were tormenting.
It was then that Rhoda spat. It gummed itself to her mother's face. One end of the spit was swinging. (pp. 36–7)

This sequence is an apt description of the inner drama within Maman herself. She demands that her instinctual self submit to the 'civilization' process, and then this same animal force turns against her. In tormenting instinct she brutalizes herself, causing her sophisticated persona to be destroyed by the outburst of animal passion.

Alfreda's repressed nature emerges in bouts of compulsive erotic behaviour. In unguarded moments she coaxes Duffield to sensualism ('"Don't be afraid to touch, darling, if it gives you pleasure"'', p. 88) and lures him into a world of intense erotic excitement (pp. 89 ff). All the while she seems unconscious of her actions, since she continues to lecture him on the importance of correct moral behaviour. The erotic exchange goes on un-acknowledged, culminating in her savage sexual assault (p. 166), which causes Duffield to leave Sunningdale. The assault is not entirely unpleasant, in fact Duffield wishes he could have 'smothered' in her love, and soon after he masturbates while remembering voluptuous dreams 'of being received' (p. 167). The incident illustrates his erotic fantasies and underscores the incestuous and violent aspects of all erotic interchange in White's later fiction. At the end of her drunken assault Maman assumes the posture of her humpbacked daughter, 'hunching up her back' (p. 166) as she runs out of the room. Here the autonomous per-sonality breaks through and she becomes identical with Rhoda, the shadow self or 'humpbacked queen' (p. 98).

III

In addition to Rhoda, the novel presents us with another dark female figure in the whore Nance Lightfoot. Nance is not specifically Maman's *alter ego*, but is, as it were, the shadow of White's idealized mother–image. She is everything that Mrs Godbold and Laura Trevelyan are not; she is a personification of all the repressed sexuality and unacknowledged power and violence of the archetypal mother–image. As has been indicated, the final phase of White's career is devoted to the self-evolution of the mother personality, and this involves dredging up all that has been lost or repressed in the maternal character. Nance is more a fragment of the repressed psyche than a fully rounded character, and readers looking for conventional character development will be disappointed with her. She is one-dimensional, with a single-minded focus upon sexual expression:

> 'Oh God,' she kept gobbling and crying. 'Love me—what's yer bloody—love me—*Hurtle!*' gnashing and biting and sobbing, until he took possession. (pp. 185–6).

Her sexuality is desperate, violent and indiscriminate (she's not even sure of her lover's name). The problem with Nance is that she reflects a level of instinctuality which is inhuman and unmanageable. The mother's shadow throughout this novel is too potent and anarchistic to be incorporated into a meaningful totality. This is basically what makes *The Vivisector* an uneven, distorted novel, whereas *The Eye of the Storm*, where the central character achieves a magnificent integration of her shadow side, is a more integrated and balanced work. In White the state of the ruling archetype determines the condition and balance of the novel as a whole. The archetype is the structural foundation of his imagination, and when it is out of order the literary edifice falters. Nance's eros overwhelms her as surely as it does her ponce. And so we are not completely surprised when Mrs Lightfoot commits suicide by throwing herself into a rocky gully. The mother's eros at this stage is wild and self-destructive. The dark nature has erupted from the depths, but it cannot yet be integrated.

In mid-career Duffield is supported financially by Olivia Davenport, who is another version of Mrs Courtney, an over-refined, sexually frustrated heiress. Mrs Davenport conceals an animal nature which has been injured by repression. Appropriately, we discover that Olivia Davenport is Boo Hollingrake, a childhood friend of Rhoda's, and a girl remembered by Duffield for her 'lashing thighs' (p. 156) as she brought Hurtle to his first orgasm upon the leaf-mould at the back of the Courtneys' house. Here White employs a device which he is to use with greater success in *A Fringe of Leaves:* the refined lady is actually another person, or at least she conceals a dark, coarse nature beneath a civilized persona. The heiress is in search of her lost primitive self, her childhood spontaneity and passion, and she employs Duffield to help her recover this erotic dimension.

Mrs Davenport covets those works of Duffield which deal explicitly with sexual and bodily imagery. She purchases his series 'Animal Rock Forms', depicting a 'configuration of large, soft, passive breasts' (p. 280), and acquires the canvas 'Marriage of Light', which features 'the burnt-out cleft of Nance Lightfoot's formal arse' (p. 187). She also greedily devours 'Pythoness at Tripod', depicting Rhoda standing naked and grotesquely misshapen beside a bidet. Duffield's art beomes the central means through which she contacts her shadow side and the world of eros. She confesses upon her first glimpse of 'Pythoness': '"It's not only as a painting that it haunts me, it's part of my life ... that [I've] lost, Hurtle"' (p. 293). She even adds, '"I wonder whether I don't understand your paintings better than you do yourself"' (p. 281). In a mythic sense she is right. Olivia is in a far better position to understand his paintings, which have to do with fundamental transformations occurring within the feminine self. Duffield himself, like White in this later phase, is a servant to an archetypal mystery taking place beyond his consciousness.

Olivia is so pleased with Duffield's contributions to her development that she arranges for him to meet her friend Hero Pavloussi. Hero most nearly corresponds to White's original idealized image of the mother. She is delicately built, sublimely beautiful and, of course, Greek. In White's fiction, Greece has long acted as the ideal spiritual place, the home of ecstatic characters (Moraitis, Katina, et al.) and is the country most often associated with divine love. Madame Pavloussi's fall from her sublime position into the world of animality further expresses the descent and disorientation of White's ruling archetype.

Hero, who is 'anxious to own a Duffield' (p. 318) purchases two minor works and eventually seizes his masterpiece 'Lantana Lovers under Moonfire'. The conception and execution of this work is the pivotal episode of the story. It begins with his meeting with Mr Cutbush in a city park, with the grocer's conversation punctuated by the cries of lovers from the ravine below. As he walks back toward his Flint Street house Duffield notices Cutbush masturbating into the ravine, 'a gunner-grocer shooting sperm at marked lovers' (p. 269). These are the details upon which the artist constructs his painting, in every respect a testimony to the savage eros which has invaded White's fictional world. The moon has long been associated with the dark mother, and is the central symbol of Hecate and Aphrodite.[10] That this 'big-arsed moon' (p. 269) is 'firing' and 'shitting' upon the lovers indicates the power and intensity with which the mother's dark side has erupted. 'Shitting' also suggests vengeance; as if the repressed lunar force were now able to let fly its malign eros upon the face of the world. The inhuman element is emphasized by the dark depths of the gully, the wild, sex-crazed lovers, and by the attacking spears of moonlight. The reference to the grocer's ejaculation 'scattered in vain on barren ground' (p. 263) indicates that his passion has no human connection; it is directed to an anonymous source. In 'Lantana Lovers under Moonfire' we are confronted with harsh, unrelated instinctuality, an archetypal eros which has yet to be modified by human contact or control.

Although Madame Pavloussi says, '"I know in my insides what [the painting] conveys to me"' (p. 335) she is nonetheless completely helpless before this mythic eros when it awakens in her own life. As her lunar aspect is revealed it proves to be an untamed, brute force which leads her to ruin. Duffield is overwhelmed by the animal passion within this seemingly stately woman: 'She had been so hungry on arrival he had hardly closed the door on the street before she fell on him ravenously, propelling him with her greed . . .' (p. 348). Her sexuality is bestial and undifferentiated, as is evident in her preference for sado-masochism and anal-erotic behaviour. As she admits, her 'daemon' (p. 349) has been let loose, and she becomes a 'monument to lust and depravity' (p. 351). She develops a worn appearance, and falls into alcoholism. Eventually she is put in an asylum, where she dies, we are told, of a cancer of the womb. The disease is itself significant: the place of female sexuality and instinctual life is diseased. She dies of a malign eros which has erupted from the unconscious and which is the burden of every female character in White's later fiction.

IV

Most readings of the novel place Duffield at the centre of power and action, and argue that the female characters disintegrate as a result of his penetrating vision.[11] 'He is the Vivisector', reads the note on the back cover of the Penguin edition, '[and] ... the women who court him are the materials of his art'. Nothing could be further from the truth. Duffield is very much a secondary, servile figure in the novel, since he attends a lunar energy which dwarfs him in every respect. It is this dark matriarchal power which destroys the female characters and 'vivisects' their moral and spiritual lives. Duffield simply provides the women with visual images of their internal world, and if anything initiates in them a gradual process of self-discovery and self-awareness.

The problem is compounded by the fact that White himself consistently identifies Duffield with the destructive archetypal force which is the subject of his art. When an archetype is unconscious it invariably becomes associated with the human personality in which it operates. The result, in this case, is a grotesque distortion of Duffield's capacity for evil. What belongs to the lunar force, to Hecate the Destroyer, is attributed to the artist's personality.[12] The inflation of the artist's evil has had a detrimental effect upon the critical reception and assessment of the novel. In 1970 the Swedish Academy decided it could not award the Nobel Prize to 'an author whose latest work elaborates on the not at all attractive conclusion that the artist steps over dead bodies in order to give free sway to life; that he consumes people as the raw material of his art'.[13] This misrepresents Duffield's actual career, and yet, ironically, the author invites these conclusions by insisting on his inflated role as The Destroyer.

The central character is inflated in still another way. Although Duffield is not involved in a separate spiritual journey, but is merely the acolyte of the Mother's transformation, White attempts to present Duffield as a spiritual genius who is striving for higher levels of being.[14] Nowhere is this grand design more evident than in the final passage, where White has Duffield straining toward the ultimate religious experience:

All his life he had been reaching toward this vertiginous blue ... Now he was again acknowledging with all the strength of his live hand the otherwise unnameable I-N-D-I-G-O ... Too tired too end-less obvi indi-ggoddd. (pp. 616–17)

Not only do the words and syntax fragment at the end, sense and credibility fragment as well as White strives to make Duffield achieve oneness with the sublime 'indi-ggoddd'. One would have hoped that White's regrettable penchant for the 'big ending' had terminated with *The Solid Mandala*, where a new honesty and moderation seemed to come to the fore. Here it is again, 'bigger' than ever, with a pretentiousness so rich as to make it seem like a parody of White's former style.

2   The Dreaming Queen

> *Whether asleep or awake—in fact her life had*
> *become one long waking sleep—Mrs Hunter*
> *slipped back into the dream she had left.*
> *The Eye of the Storm, p. 22*

In *The Eye of the Storm* (1973) the ruling archetype achieves a new kind of integration. Although in *The Vivisector* the mother was imbalanced by the uprush of instinctual energy, here she appears to have integrated this eros into a greater wholeneess. What facilitates the creation of the total personality is the fluid, amorphous nature of Mrs Hunter's character. She rests, as it were, midway between conscious and unconscious, in a liminal state where oppositions are dissolved and where contradictory forces are united. The era of the sharply divided mother, whose personality consists of a rigid persona overlying an unlived world of instinct, has come to an end. Now spirit and instinct interpenetrate, overlap, and even enrich each other.

In this novel, perhaps more than anywhere else, we are made aware that the central character is not a 'real' woman in any external sense, but an archetypal creature of the inner world. Although she creates an illusion of her social reality, Mrs Hunter is a personification of the author's unconscious life. 'She' is now what is best about 'him'; the archetypal feminine self which individuates in response to the ego's abdication of its development. Mrs Hunter is a powerful mythic personage, whose sole aim is to interweave the various events and experiences of her existence and to integrate the disparate aspects of her character. She achieves an authentic unity, whereas the masculine personality falls into chaos and disintegration.

Mrs Hunter's proximity to the unconscious is reflected in her mode of being: always sleeping, dozing, half-waking, almost dying. She is a 'submerged' character, spending more of her life in the night-world than in the conscious state. She is intimately connected with the realm of memory, and is engaged in a reconstruction of time past, and an anticipation of future events. She is possessed of genius; there is something awesome and omniscient about her character. She is all things to all people, and her masks are as incongruous as they are numerous: bed-ridden geriatric, lustful mistress, domineering mother, 'old witch' (p. 83), 'chrysalis' (p. 9), 'barbaric idol' (p. 116), 'ancient queen' (p. 398). She can be experiencing mystical fulfilment at the eye of the storm and sitting on the commode at her Centennial Park residence at the same time. Eternity and time, sacred and profane, all fixed categories are transcended or obliterated as she makes her sublime journey toward integration. Never before in White's fiction have we seen such a complex, multi-dimensional figure. But the complexities inherent in the archetypal mother are such that it would be difficult to conceive how else this personage could have become manifest. Only a vastly inclusive figure such as Mrs Hunter is large enough to allow the Goddess to 'incarnate' into fictional reality.

I

Mrs Hunter is the centre of all that takes place in the novel. The story appears to emanate from her, as though it were a product of her dreaming. All the other characters appear as mere extensions of her being. None has autonomy or free will, but each is subjected to the mother and made to act as a catalyst to her process of growth. The minor characters, described as 'human satellites' (p. 431), 'acolytes' (p. 73) or 'priestesses' (p. 14), embody particular attributes of her nature, and are urged to undergo various ordeals so that she, in the end, can arrive at a greater wholeness. Sisters de Santis and Manhood embody her spiritual and instinctual selves, which are at first opposed, but which, through suffering and realization, achieve a working relationship

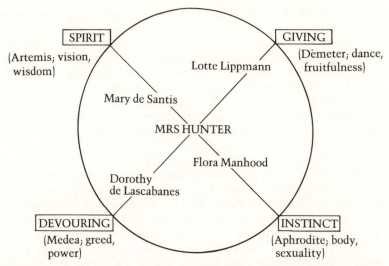

with each other. Dorothy de Lascabanes is the power-seeking daughter who is forced to learn the limitations of power, and the housekeeper Lotte Lippmann is the all-giving, nourishing mother who must attempt to control her undifferentiated personality. The novel traces several minor individuations, none of which amounts to anything truly significant in itself, but which together form part of a cohesive integration inaugurated by the central figure.

The diagram below attempts to represent the complex field of the archetypal mother in the novel. Two structural axes have been established, representing the main lines of tension in the personality of Mrs Hunter. As we might expect after *The Vivisector*, the spirit/instinct polarity is the central focus of attention, and the other axis is of somewhat minor significance in comparison. At the end of each axis an archaic goddess is named in order to personify and mythologize the archetypal qualities discovered in the mother–image. The fact that so many mythic categories have to be enlisted to encompass her character suggests the power and scope of this figure,[15] a situation entirely without precedent in the earlier novels, where figures such as Flack and Godbold could be designated by the simple epithets 'good' or 'bad', 'spiritual' or 'carnal'.

It is interesting to pursue for a moment the relation between the fragmentary part-personalities and the central figure. Although each of the human satellites accepts the unqualified superiority of Elizabeth Hunter, there is an underlying element of fear in their relations to her. This is accentuated by the fact that Mrs Hunter, being the whole, can look down upon and point her finger at the limitations and weaknesses of the partial figures. '"You can't escape me"' (p. 10) she warns her various attendants, who tend to shy away from the brutal truths which she brings forth. Her visionary capacity is ironically juxtaposed against her increasing physical blindness; she sees into others even though her eyes are closed to the world. Her nurses stand in awe of her 'blind yet knowing stare' (p. 108).

In psychological terms Mrs Hunter is the symbolic centre of the personality, that inward core which sees what the partial self is doing, which wrenches it out of its complacency, stirs it to action ('she whipped you on', p. 546), and forces it to see what it does not want to see—its own shadow or undeveloped side. To the shy and over-refined solicitor Arnold Wyburd, Mrs Hunter is a constant source of embarrassment, reflecting for him the baser side of human nature and raising sexual questions at untimely moments. Earlier in her career she had seduced the solicitor as an 'exercise in desire' (p. 37), much to the horror of Wyburd himself. When Lal Wyburd visits Mrs Hunter in later years her 'torturer' informs her that '"Arnold was hairless—so smooth"' (p. 517). Much of the excellent humour in the novel derives from Mrs Hunter's ability to shock the minor figures with her candid remarks. Whether the satellites love or despise the ancient queen is dependent upon their willingness to face the unknown in themselves. For Dorothy, a character resistant to growth and change, the old woman is an atrociously hateful figure, always cutting her down and appearing to defeat her personal interests. Others, like Manhood, adopt a more philosophical view:

'From what you told me' [Col Pardoe says], 'you always hated that old woman.'
'Yes!' she cried. 'No—I didn't *hate*! She understood me better than anybody ever. I only always didn't like what she dug up out of me.'(p. 554)

The point is that the partial self can never experience its relation to the archetypal centre as being completely favourable. It is inherently flawed, one-sided, and will always regard the promptings of the greater self as a personal rebuke, at best a challenge.

It is precisely this ordering, archetypal centre which wanted to become manifest *in consciousness* in *The Solid Mandala*. The same dynamic, transformative power that we see in Mrs Hunter could have belonged to the male personality, to White's personality, had he been able to accept the gift of the knotted mandala. The archetype of the mandala (Jung's Self)[16] is a harmonizing structure, which draws various part-selves and fragments around a kind of magnetic centre, in much the same way as in the above diagram. Since White rejected this archetype it now falls to the deep unconscious, integrating the mother's personality instead of his own. The tragedy of the mandala (chapter 5) is the comedy of the maternal uroboros. The mother wins not only the son's psychic libido, but the treasure, the talisman or vision of unity, which as it were fell out of Arthur's hands only to be greedily devoured by Mrs Poulter and the mothers who followed her. To take on the sacred talisman is to become a royal figure, to be touched by divinity. Thus, we might say, by devouring the treasure the ordinary, suburban Mrs Poulter transforms into the extraordinary and omniscient Mrs Hunter.

II

Mrs Hunter's instinctual side is emphasized throughout the story. At the age of seventy-two she dazzles Edvard Pehl with glimpses of her 'still formidably sensuous body' (p. 391). Her sexuality contrasts strongly with that of Hero Pavloussi or Alfreda Courtney in that it is completely under her control. It is a contained vital force which finds its natural outlet and fulfilment. Her Venusian aspect is mirrored in her favourite nurse, the young and pretty Flora Manhood. As 'Flora' suggests, she is earthy, sensual and appealing. In the story she is associated with the womb, blood, rhythm, colour and instinctive behaviour. She is plagued by men of all ages and classes, who are spontaneously drawn toward her radiant sexuality. It is Flora who is responsible for Mrs Hunter's physical appearance. She is 'guardian of the wigs' (p. 116), sole keeper of the stately jewel case, and supervisor of cosmetics. Mrs Hunter delights in Flora's sensual nature, and enjoys touching her body: 'an animal presence is something the mind craves the farther the body shrivels into skin and bone' (p. 82). Embarrassingly for Manhood, the 'old witch' (p. 83) seems able to plot her sexual career with devastating accuracy. After Flora has had a lustful morning with Col Pardoe Mrs Hunter informs the nurse that she can detect her recent activities: '"after a woman has been with a man you can smell her—like a doe after she's been to the buck"' (p. 84). The relation between Manhood and Mrs Hunter is like that between the sacred whore of

Aphrodite[17] and the great Goddess herself. Flora is the active, human embodiment of her erotic nature.

Mrs Hunter also enjoys a rich and productive spiritual life, which finds its fullest expression in her experiences at the eye of the storm. Her spiritual aspect is personified in Mary de Santis, the nun-like devotee from Smyrna, Greece. De Santis carries forward White's Greek image of spiritual purity, which was evident in Hero Pavloussi before her fall into animality and lust. Mary is the night nurse, and is associated with solitude, meditation and service. In the diagram she is related to Artemis, because she is pure, chaste, forbiddingly independent and mysterious like the virginal goddess of Nature.[18] It may seem incredible that the worldly Mrs Hunter contains any virginal aspect. Yet despite her many involvements, she remains strangely isolated and aloof. She confesses to de Santis that she never really loved her husband (p. 20), and says that her enduring obsession was for solitude. '"Love"', she tells de Santis, '"is not a matter of lovers"' (p. 164). The original concept of 'Virgin', a title sometimes bestowed upon Aphrodite herself,[19] was not used in the narrow, modern sense of a *virgo intacta* but of a pure, whole and independent woman. It was meant to describe not a bodily condition but a psychological state, an uncontaminated soul.[20] In this broader sense, Mrs Hunter shares in Mary's spiritual virginity, her Artemisian grace and inwardness.

Because Mrs Hunter encompasses the opposites of spirit and instinct, she is an enigmatic and awesome figure to both Manhood and de Santis. The nurses intuit in her nature something which is unknown and unfathomable in themselves. Manhood is haunted and disturbed by what she senses as a deeper spiritual dimension. The day nurse had never been bothered by the more abstract, subtle aspects of reality until her appointment at Moreton Drive. For her the old woman comes to represent the totality of being, or her own potential wholeness:·

Momentarily at least this fright of an idol became the goddess hidden inside: of life, which you longed for, but hadn't yet dared embrace; of beauty such as you imagined, but had so far failed to grasp ... and finally, of death, which hadn't concerned you, except as something to be tidied away, till now you were faced with the vision of it. (p. 116)

Increased contact with this complex figure causes Manhood to become restless, to demand more of herself and of life itself. Her sense of incompleteness expresses itself in bouts of irritability, and in a rebelliousness towards society, which she senses has kept her chained to the role of the dumb, pretty woman. She becomes aware that her relationship with Col is empty and superficial, that it gratifies the senses but not her spirit. A period of creative unrest ensues, in which she abandons Col and lives with her cousin Snow Tunks, during which she experiments with lesbianism with the 'dyke' Alix. Throughout much of the novel she is on the move, seeking new experiences and a release from her stereotyped existence. And while Mrs Hunter initiates the process of change she also acts as the pivotal centre of her world, the stable element which enables her to restructure her life without falling into complete chaos.

Mary de Santis is forced to undergo a similar awakening to her limitation and one-sidedness. While Mary experiences spiritual kinship with her patient, Mrs Hunter is a constant reminder of bodily nature, especially with her failing excretory organs and ageing animal body.

> Doubts seldom arose at night ... [but] this morning Sister de Santis was unreasonably pursued by faint faecal whiffs, by the insinuating stench of urine from an aged bladder; while the light itself, or iron thorns, or old transparent fingernails, scratched at her viciously. (p. 16)

Mary is safe at night, in her own world, but by day, the time of *bios* and light, she feels under attack. Her instinctual life is dangerously repressed, so that it appears to be 'pursuing' her in grotesque, hideous forms: faecal whiffs, stenches of urine, iron thorns at the window. The life-force has grown against her, *bios* is foul and putrid, and her spiritual equanimity is threatened.

It is partly through encounters with Manhood that she comes to realize her psychological predicament. She begins to notice, for instance, the wonderful colours of Manhood's clothes, and the general drabness of her own. She secretly envies Flora's vitality and the physicality of her relations with men. Flora, jealous of 'St Mary' (p. 190) and her special affinity with Mrs Hunter, strives to provoke the night nurse at every turn. After rudely torturing her with the question: ' "Have you ever had—have you ever *wanted* a man?" ' she adds, more scathingly: ' "Sorry, darls, for my indecent curiosity. I'll leave you to the pure pleasures of night duty with Mother Hunter" ' (pp. 149–50). Such exchanges leave de Santis devastated, for she senses that Manhood's attack is justified, she is so pure that life has passed her by. After hours of desolate brooding, and of fantasying herself as Col's would-be lover, Mary strips off her drab costume in a bid to release her animal passions.

She began unbuttoning her uniform, tearing at the straitjacket beneath to free her smoothest offerings. Which he [Col Pardoe], or anyone, would have rejected, and rightly. Though dimpled under pressure, and arum white, their snouts pointed upward to accuse the parent sow. (p. 169)

The breasts appear as autonomous bestial forms which point upward to *accuse* her repressive consciousness. Instinct in White's world is still in a state of rebelliousness, claiming its due after long exile in the unconscious. We expect that Sister de Santis will go the way of Madame Pavloussi, the woman ruined by her encounter with unruly instinct. But Mary is not ruined. Instinct makes its assault, but she regains her integrity. This is mainly due to the presence of Mrs Hunter, her stable centre in times of crisis. At the end of this scene Mary scrambles up the staircase, still struggling with her torn and loosened clothing, arriving sobbing and wretched at the foot of Mrs Hunter's bed. Although the royal figure remains sleeping, Mary is soothed and healed by her presence. If Hero was destroyed by a similar situation, it may be because she lacked a symbolic centre and image of wholeness to support her during her crisis.

III

Basil Hunter is an outsider to the positive matriarchal movement of the novel. 'Sir' Basil has suffered a psychological collapse, and returns to Australia to lose himself in infantilism and incestuous, orgiastic sexuality. White provides a long and exhausting account of Basil's situation, showing how his acting career and personal life have led him to ruin, but the facts of his case are merely circumstantial. In the later fiction *every* male character suffers collapse because White's masculine ego is no longer able to sustain itself. The real cause of Basil's predicament lies in the disaster represented in *The Solid Mandala*, from which no male character can arise with integrity. Basil's dissolution into the maternal source is enacted literally in his incestuous coupling with his sister in his mother's bed at 'Kudjeri' (p. 508 f). It is an increasing tendency of White's fiction, as it sinks further into degradation, to enact psychic processes literally and to give a grotesquely concrete formulation to that which belongs to the metaphorical realm. The psychic collapse of which I am speaking manifests *fictionally* as a collapse of symbolism, and a substitution of polymorphous perverse sexuality for the elaborate constructs of White's symbolic world.[21] Sir Basil is a wreck of a man, and he further celebrates his dissolution by munching hot pies and tomato sauce ('symbols of his boyhood', p. 452), by frequent masturbation and auto-erotic behaviour, and by curling up 'in the shape he had been longing to assume: that of a sleeping possum, or a bean before the germinal stage, or a foetus in a jar' (p. 470).[22] This process of masculine degeneration contrasts strongly with the healthy feminine individuation beside which it is placed. Yet the two processes are not contradictory, for the egoic masculine dissolution, by releasing energy to the unconscious, makes the feminine archetypal development possible.

We have seen in previous stories how the mother 'makes use' of the aborted masculine energy. Mrs Poulter utilizes the broken Arthur Brown as a libidinal image and object of worship, and Olivia and Hero exploit the passive Duffield in order to further their internal processes and erotic lives. Similarly, the collapsed Basil Hunter is utilized by Mary de Santis and Flora Manhood to further their individuations. Flora arrives at a plan by which she hopes to win love from Col Pardoe and avail herself of a meaningful lifestyle. She plans to visit Sir Basil to be made pregnant by him, intending to claim Col as the father of the child and establish for herself a family unit in which love will grow. 'At least the actor would go away, and need not know. It was the rightful father who would remain and know' (p. 311). Sir Basil shows himself to be the buffoon he is by fulfilling the plan and even by falling in love with his scheming partner: '"Don't you feel this is real, Flora?"' (p. 312). He fails to see how he is being manipulated by her, just as, at the inner level, he cannot see how completely he is assimilated to the feminine archetype.

After the coupling of her acolyte and son, Mrs Hunter—who apparently has 'smelt out the whole circus' (p. 304)—is shown to be in a highly celebrative mood. It is as if she has been renewed and invigorated by her son's intercourse with her close associate and symbolic extension of herself. She orders Manhood to bring her the case of jewels and asks that she keep for herself the pink sapphire ring. In ancient times, according to Frazer,[23] women worshipping at the temples of Aphrodite were required to prostitute themselves to a stranger prior to marriage. Fulfilment of this ritual was believed to incur the blessing of the goddess and to ensure her support in maternity, childbirth and love. Appropriately, Manhood sees Mrs Hunter's gift as a talisman, and clearly associates it with fertility: '. . . my children are human we hope Mrs Hunter if the blessed sapphire works' (p. 555). Further, Mrs Hunter requests that the ring be used to seal her engagement with Col. A mythic pattern is here consummated between goddess and acolyte, fulfilling the rites of fertility and preparing the way for the devotee's fuller experience of love through marriage.

If Manhood makes use of Sir Basil as a stepping-stone upon which she moves to a higher level, de Santis uses him as a means by which she comes down from her pedestal and approaches bodily reality. Ostensibly, de Santis calls on the actor to protest against the plan to shift Mrs Hunter from her expensive home to the village for geriatrics. But she becomes so preoccupied with her own needs that she forgets all about her mission of good will. There is no suggestion of overt sexual activity—that would be too far removed from her character—but she does draw greedily, if surreptitiously, on Sir Basil's obvious sensuality. Not knowing how to act in the presence of a man the Sister begins to emulate 'the ladies seen at dinner parties' (p. 334), and becomes tipsy from 'unaccustomed drink', launching into raucous fits of laughter. Social propriety and conventional graces are put to one side as de Santis gives full expression to her instinctual side. Walking barefoot with her companion along the beach Mary recovers a 'joy in life' which she finds reflected in the 'launchload of children dangling their hands in the transparent wavelets' (p. 336). At the end of the day she finds herself 'more than a little drunk' and falls to the ground, bursting her stockings and causing her hair to fall around her. She recalls the night when she stripped off her clothes—'there were times when her breasts were still pointed at her'—but here there is less violence and despair, and a sense of joy at the recovery of her lost eros. As Basil attempts to help de Santis to her feet he feels he has 'defiled this pale nun' (p. 344), whereas he has in fact aided in her development. From this point there is a noticeable increase in spontaneity and sensual feeling in her experience. She begins to delight in the early light of morning, in the dew upon roses and the flight of birds. Her purchasing of the great orange hat, which others find uncharacteristic and even 'sacrilegious' (p. 319), is nevertheless a sign of her willingness to admit colour and life into the night-world of her spiritual idealism.

IV

A further structural tension in the novel is that between nurturing and devouring aspects of the mother-image. By comparison with the spirit/instinct axis this polarity is unproductive, in that it is constituted of fragmentary characters who make no real progress toward integration. The nurturing side is personified in Lotte Lippmann, the Jewish cook and housekeeper at Moreton Drive. Her devotion to her employer is unequalled and she extends nourishment and concern to all who enter the sacred precinct of Mrs Hunter's abode. To the ancient queen herself she is less housekeeper than resident dancer and artist, since she regularly performs and sings at the foot of Mrs Hunter's bed. Lotte might be related to the ancient earth-mother Demeter, whose dominant aspect is nourishment and whose central religious activity is dance.[24]

However, Mrs Lippmann is so self-effacing and humble that she appears ineffectual and down-trodden. As Mrs Hunter ironically observes, the Jewess 'had grown accustomed to carrying a cross of proportions such as no Christian could conceive' (p. 525). She seems to lack a central core, to be watery and diffuse, knowing herself only in relation to others. With her ill-defined nature she cannot accept criticism in any form, and so does not benefit from Mrs Hunter's brutal though transformative wisdom. Of all the 'fragments' in the story Lotte is perhaps the most fragmentary. But her nourishing capacity is a vital force in the novel, and her dance is an important ritual element in the 'house become shrine' (p. 146).

It may be difficult to recognize any Demeter aspect in Mrs Hunter's character, but it is there. In her earlier life she enjoyed dancing and spontaneous celebration, and her giving capacity is evident in her gifts of the sapphire ring to Flora, the satin sash and party dress to Mary, the ballroom gown to Lotte Lippmann, and the generous cheques to Basil and Dorothy. Moreover she gives the fragmentary characters the greatest gift of all: the opportunity to discover and develop themselves. Whether they accept or reject is their own doing, but the invitation to join in the mystery of wholeness and to participate in her own greater liminality always stands.

We are perhaps more aware of Mrs Hunter's Medea-like aspect, her brutal, power-seeking character. She tells de Santis that throughout her life she '"longed to possess people who would obey me—and love me of course"' (p. 156). But in spite of its brutalities and excesses it is this same power which enables her to control her inner 'persons', to order the conflicting selves around a central core of personality. It is interesting to note that those characters who find Mrs Hunter most 'devouring'—Dorothy, Basil, Arnold, Lal—are the ones who are least equal to the challenge of her wholeness. When weak personalities approach a royal archetypal figure they are inevitably assimilated to its greater force.

> They accused her of devouring people. Well, you couldn't help if it they practically stuck their heads in your jaws. Though actually she has no taste, or sustained appetite, for human flesh. (p. 87)

This may well stand as a testimonial in support of the mother figure in White's fictional world. She *is* devouring, that cannot be denied, but only because the human figures around her, especially the male figures, are so insubstantial that she cannot help but overwhelm them. In White's fiction the ego enters the maternal source without reinforcement, without heroic strength or spiritual knowledge, and so it is not surprising if it is consumed. The reference to these figures putting 'their heads in [her] jaws' reminds us of the frail trochilus in *The Aunt's Story*, a symbol of Theodora's ego which strayed, recklessly and self-destructively, into the killer jaws of the maternal archetype.[25]

The character who personifies the power element in the mother–image, and who is, ironically, most deeply maligned by the Medea-like aspect of the central figure, is the Princesse de Lascabanes. The power principle in the daughter, 'a horse-faced version of Elizabeth Hunter' (p. 50), is a purely personal, avaricious force which is not put at the service of individuation. It is a travesty of the power principle, or power for its own sake. Dorothy's marriage to Hubert de Lascabanes was for the sole purpose of acquiring the title of 'princess'. Although she wins the desired prestige, Hubert, it appears, had little money, and when resources run dry she is forced to return to Australia to draw funds from her mother. It is Dorothy's scheme to get Mrs Hunter out of her wealthy mansion and into the ugly but economical Thorogood Village. Through careful tactics and subtle wile she manages to win the solicitor, Arnold Wyburd, and her brother Basil to her cause.

Princesse de Lascabanes does not become fully aware of her brutality and selfishness until she meets her childhood friend Cherry Cheeseman at a Sydney party. Cherry, like herself, is intent on power and self-promotion, but she lacks the sophistication which partially disguises Dorothy's baseness. Cherry tells how she has made her own life comfortable by sending her mother to the geriatric village, thereby securing the family fortune for herself. Dorothy is struck by the parallel with her own scheme and is appalled by the attitude of her friend when she announces that the mother died soon after her transfer to the village. Dorothy is so overcome with self-disgust that she is forced to flee the party: 'If there was no running away from herself, she must at least escape from the Cheeseman house, with its implications, and downright accusations' (p. 287). Much self-examination follows as the daughter is forced to recognize the meanness of her character. There are no spectacular changes or reversals, but at least this guiltless, avaricious woman has become morally conscious of her situation. She has acquired a burden of guilt which makes her more human and ensures that she is unable to deceive herself.

Dorothy goes through with the proposed scheme, which prompts her mother's death and results in her securing half of the fortune. However the ancient, dreaming queen, not to be outdone by a mere princess, dies before they are able to move her to the geriatric home. She arranges her own death, just as she arranged her life, to suit herself and to create the best possible situation for the realization of her wholeness.

V

When Basil and Dorothy inform Mrs Hunter of their plans, she accepts the news with apparent resignation and begins to set into operation a complex ritual of integration. During the few days in which the Hunter children are enjoying incestuous delight at 'Kudjeri', Mrs Hunter weaves together the loose threads of her life and dies upon the stately commode like a queen upon her throne. Her first move is to have Lotte Lippmann perform her dance of celebration, for which she has Flora Manhood make up her face and adorn her in her favourite jewels and lilac wig. Mrs Hunter is totally blind at this stage, and so does not see Lotte dancing for her. But it is enough to know that the dance is being performed, and that it is being held for her honour and glorification.

Mrs Hunter then drifts into a waking dream, into the realms of memory, where she re-enters the eye of the storm on Brumby Island and re-experiences the earlier moments of heightened perception. The actual experience on the island ought not to be stressed, because it serves merely as a metaphor for what she always has recourse to: the still centre of her turning world. The 'eye' of the storm exists more in interior space than in literal time, an ideal image of the Self, the integrative centre which seems to transcend the 'ten thousand things' which surround it. Her 'eye' is the true Self, not the bogus paradisal image which occupied White's former protagonists, his *pueri*. The infantile paradise precedes the world and the ego, so that moving into the primal centre destroys the human element. There are always images of devouring—teeth, jaws, knives, crushing shapes— which accompany the *puer*'s 'transcendence' and which point to the destructive nature of his experience. But here there are no jaws and no devourings. Mrs Hunter does not seek an infantile escape route but a way through and beyond the world. Her spiritual goal (identical with Jung's Self, Blake's Second Paradise) is post-conscious and includes the world of human experience. It is a oneness which is constellated after the development of personality and the differentiation of her various part-selves and archetypal attributes. Her triumph is not in self-dissolution but in self-realization, and her desire to preserve the integrity of her ego is apparent to the very end. Unlike the *pueri* she does not abandon self in the face of the divine, but seeks to consolidate and intensify it, so as to experience a conscious transcendence: 'Now the real business in hand was not to withdraw her will, as she had once foreseen, but to will enough strength into her body to put her feet on the ground and walk steadily towards the water' (p. 532). She is said to be 'the equal' of 'the seven swans . . . massed' around her and of the 'endlessness' in which she is 'enfolded', which is to say she is the true partner of eternity, the vehicle through which the divine image becomes manifest. The moment of death is a supremely apocalyptic experience, an affirmation of all that she has been and of everything she has become. In the hauntingly beautiful death sequence there are references to her primitivity and animal nature (the torn dress, the matted hair, the exposed breast), and to her more ethereal aspect (uncanny light, swans, a mythical sea). The polarities of her being are brought into an ideal and almost incomprehensible totality.

And so Mrs Hunter dies while sitting on the commode. One of the greatnesses of her life is the way it brings together the sublime and the banal, the grandly spiritual and the creaturely human. It is a comic finale, not only in the sense that we can laugh about the ironic situation, but also in the sense that hers is a happy ending, a triumph, a divine *commedia*. She is the most successful of all White's characters, the greatest artist of the self and the most able to benefit from the spiritual and material richness of the world. The commode scene also serves to bring us back to the earthly reality of Flora Manhood, who arrives to find that the 'old totem' has 'slipped sideways on her throne' (p. 533). Flora is shocked by her death, but also strangely elevated by it, sensing that her own 'emptiness' might at any moment 'be filled with understanding'.

There is no doubt that Mrs Hunter's triumph of realization has certain positive effects upon her part-selves and human satellites. A healing radiance seems to infuse the closing passages, illuminating the minor characters and filling their lives with humour and well-being.

> The two nurses exchanged remarks, both practical and comforting, in subdued voices. Sister Manhood brought a fresh sheet to cover the body. After they spread it, and smoothed it over the major peaks and ridges, Manhood trimmed the nails. But it was de Santis who laid the handkerchief over the face. As their hands touched during their work or they bumped against each other, or rubbed shoulders in passing, Flora Manhood came closest to expressing the love she might have been too abashed to feel for Elizabeth Hunter. (p. 548)

Here the acolytes are united in lyrical interplay, as if to reflect the new integration of spirit and nature in the maternal image. They both appear transformed, but Manhood in particular seems elevated into the mystery of love and the world of inwardness embodied in Sister de Santis. As we often find in fairytale and myth, the acolytes experience the triumph of the royal figure as a boon to their own personal quests for integration.[26]

VI

A central feature of this novel is that the attainment of unity is not accompanied by any theological abstractions or authorial rhetoric, but is allowed to suggest itself subtly through narrative action and image. The vision of wholeness is never stated or formulated, but wells up spontaneously from the fictional ground. As A. P. Riemer observes: 'there are, merely, possibilities of significance connected with Mrs Hunter's death, no absolute statements'.[27] One could claim that the increased detachment is a matter of artistic maturity and reticence, as Peter Beatson has argued.[28] But in light of the present argument the detachment must surely be due to the relative autonomy of the mother's individuation. The wholeness attained does not have any direct bearing on White himself; the author merely allows a mythic process to reach its goal. The individuating impulse has been taken over by the unconscious personality, and hence we no longer find authorial commentary about its fulfilment or realization. The mother archetype takes the lead in every way, expressing its pattern of development in the imagistic and non-intellectual language which is its natural form of expression.

3   Surviving Australia

> ... *the English characters in* A Fringe of Leaves *get a stronger dosage of Australia than they had bargained for.*
>
> Peter Wolfe[29]

In White, Australia has been imaged as the destroyer of masculine consciousness, a continental matrix which overcomes the personality. Voss is consumed by the archaic landscape, Parker is absorbed by Nature and crushed by Australian materialism, and Himmelfarb and others experience the country as a psychological prison, in which they are condemned to serve and be sacrificed by a mother–figure. 'Australia' for White is simply the unconscious world, in particular *his* unconscious with its negative matriarchal character, but also *the* unconscious of a colonial culture which still experiences the earth beneath it as primitive, hostile and devouring. White's maternal characters experience the country in quite a different way. Mrs Godbold in her wooden shack, Laura Trevelyan in her desert, Mrs Hunter on Brumby Island not only survive but triumph in their respective Australian locations. They are not of White's egoic world, but representatives of the maternal matrix which receives the broken body and spilt blood of the *puer aeternus.* They benefit from the very experiences which destroy the men. (Significantly, White's non-maternal female characters, Miss Hare, Theodora, Rosie Rosetree, disintegrate with the men, because they are part of the same masculine principle which is overcome by the mother–world.) For the mothers Australia is a boon rather than a threat to existence, a world of archaic forces and primitive experience which acts as a powerful stimulus to matriarchal growth.

I

Although *A Fringe of Leaves* (1976) is a so-called historical novel, the processes at work within the maternal archetype dominate any professed or intended authorial concern for Australian history.[30] White's imagination uses the story of Eliza Fraser and her fateful journey to Australia to carry forward, or dream onward, the mother's search for integration and wholeness. The pattern is by now familiar: the over-civilized woman is in search of her primitive nature, which must be brought into closer proximity to her social persona. The imagination transforms the historical facts into a wonderfully simple and lyrical tale of self-discovery, a kind of modern folk-tale with all the fascination and appeal of this genre. The novel steers a brilliant course between the realm of fantasy on the one hand and the world of reality on the other: there is enough identifiable reality to hold the attention and sustain belief (even for readers who prefer only 'factual' novels), and there is enough archetypal resonance and evocation to stimulate the imagination. It is an almost perfect recipe for success, the same kind of admixture that characterizes the best of Henry Lawson's stories.

In accord with its imaginative reconstruction of real events and places, *A Fringe of Leaves* creates an archetypal topography for the dominant personalities of the maternal character. England, associated throughout with Ellen's conscience and her moralistic mother-in-law, is the place of the civilized and refined mother, and Australia, 'a country of thorns, whips, murderers, thieves, shipwreck and adulteresses' (p. 280),[31] is the land of the pagan, earthly mother. England undergoes a further imaginal division into Birdlip estate, Cheltenham, and the little town of Zennor on the moors of Cornwall. Zennor, near Land's End, is itself a sort of modified Australia, a wilderness area beside a wild, unruly sea, stuck out at the end of the known world. Ellen Roxburgh's life is in constant and dynamic movement between these two worlds, the archetypal extremes of refined culture and raw, primitive Nature. Her experience is quite unlike Mrs Hunter's, who rests statically in bed while inhabiting a fluid psychic realm where divisions between spirit and instinct are almost magically transcended. Ellen is perhaps closer to Flora Manhood and Sister de Santis, the internally divided acolytes, than to the dreaming queen herself. Her experience is more human, her dualities more apparent, her suffering more acute. She is also younger and less removed from social and historical limitations.

In some ways Ellen's mythic model is not the Mother Goddess who unites many worlds, but the archetypal daughter and maiden, Kore-Persephone, who moves constantly between upper and lower worlds.[32] Persephone, daughter of Demeter, was rudely abducted by Hades into the Underworld, after which she was forced to lead a life divided between Hades' dark realm and the heavenly world of Demeter and the Olympian gods. Ellen's initiation into the lower world is also violent and involuntary. Her ship, the *Bristol Maid*, founders on a reef off the coast of

Queensland and she is later seized by Aborigines and forced to become their servant, nurse and tribal icon. Like Persephone, however, she learns to live in the realm of darkness and shades, making a remarkable adaptation to primitive customs and ways which allows her to survive the ordeal and to incorporate her experience into a broader sense of her identity. Her wholeness, like Kore's,[33] is not discovered on an abstract plane beyond the conflict of opposites but in and through her lived experience of 'the two incompatible worlds' (p. 335). Her triumph is her ability to sustain the paradoxicality of her existence and to accept that she belongs equally to the world of darkness and to the world of light.

As in previous novels, it is the subsidiary masculine figures who support the female in her personal quest and who make possible her experience of the various aspects of her character. It is through Austin Roxburgh that Ellen Gluyas is able to rise above the dreariness of her workaday world at Land's End and achieve refinement and status as mistress of the Roxburgh estate in Cheltenham. The marriage with Austin is experienced by the uneducated farmer's daughter as her first opportunity for self-development, a complete break with the past and a chance to realize the potential woman inside her. This transformation, aided by the elder Mrs Roxburgh, is achieved with great skill, and as we encounter her at the beginning of the story she appears to have convinced herself as well as others of her legitimate claim to sophistication.

Already in the early scenes there are signs that her civilized life is becoming sterile, that she has lost touch with an essential instinctive vitality. She continues to enjoy the comforts of her Roxburgh existence, but now there is a secret yearning for things passionate and dark. These yearnings are realized through her contact with Garnet Roxburgh, the 'lapsed gentleman' (p. 28) of Van Diemen's Land, and ultimately through her association with Jack Chance, escaped convict and native inhabitant of the Australian bush.

Although the Wordsworthian epigraph establishes Ellen as 'A perfect Woman, nobly planned', who will readily submit to the controlling dictates of men,[34] the reverse is true: she is a keen and inspired exploiter of the male sex. She hardly has to wait for the advent of feminism and the twentieth century to reverse the conventional roles and to demonstrate her personal power. First she marries Austin to fulfil her moral, cultural and developmental needs, then she directs Garnet and Jack Chance to satisfy her erotic and libidinal desires, and at the end she remarries an English gentleman, Mr George Jevons, to regain contact with society and re-establish her moral and financial stability. She is not overtly exploitative in the manner of Alfreda Courtney or Elizabeth Hunter, but manages to hide her manipulation under a conventional mask, to appear helpless and unable to survive without the attentions of men. Of course the men are only too willing to offer support, and experience Ellen's manipulative handling of them as their personal fulfilment.

II

When Mrs Roxburgh first encounters her reprobate brother-in-law in Hobart Town she is at once repelled and attracted by him. Her 'Roxburgh' personality finds him uncouth and disagreeable, but her 'Gluyas' self is immediately drawn to him: 'He had about him something which she, the farmer's daughter and spurious lady, recognized as coarse and sensual' (p. 74). Her real need at this point is to activate her natural sensuality, which has been stifled throughout her married life. Her resistance to Garnet is due to her fear that the recovery of instinct will shatter her Roxburgh persona, and take away the stability and identity that her civilized existence has given her. As the weeks pass at 'Dulcet', the call of the Australian bush and her own Gluyas self becomes stronger. Ellen finds herself responding positively and nostalgically to the antipodean environment (p. 73). During a walk across Garnet's property Ellen discovers a damp, mossy tunnel of undergrowth which leads to a small clearing of decaying leaves. It is here that she has a dream about making love with Garnet, who is a mere shadowy extension of the landscape itself. Upon awaking, Mrs Roxburgh is terrified by her presentiment of a moral crisis soon to overtake her, but she finds herself driven by her instinctual need. After the Christmas Day celebrations Ellen saddles the frisky mare and rides off toward the leafy enclosure. She lashes the horse to a wild gallop and, approaching the remembered site, slides free of the saddle and lands 'spread-eagle on the miraculously soft leaf-mould' (p. 101). As she lies upon the forest floor in a state of expectation Garnet comes to her 'rescue' and her dream of passion is realized. 'She closed her eyes again for an instant, to bask beneath the lashes in an experience of sensuality she must have awaited all her life, however inadmissible the circumstances in which she had encouraged it' (p. 103).[35] The irony is that Garnet considers himself engaged in an act of seduction, and apologizes for taking advantage of her. For Ellen he was 'less her seducer than the instrument she had chosen for measuring depths she was tempted to explore' (p. 104). As with every male figure in the later fiction, Garnet is the unknowing servant of the female protagonist, and a crucial contributor to her process of growth.

The psychological descent which takes place at 'Dulcet' is merely the prelude to the *nekyia*[36] which Ellen is forced to undergo off the coast of the Australian mainland. After the shipwreck the Roxburghs and crew are forced to take to the boats. Here, amid squalor, disease, and starvation, Ellen feels herself 'returning, and not by slow degrees, to nature' (p. 188). It is in the waterlogged long-boat that Ellen is delivered of the child she has carried since the beginning of the journey, but the infant is still-born and is delivered into the ocean. No fruit or new life can come of her union with Austin Roxburgh; all her life–energy must be focused upon herself, to sustain her during her underworld experience. The wretched survivors eventually land upon what is today Fraser Island and are greeted by a tribe of Aborigines who spear the men to death and take Mrs Roxburgh captive.

It is significant that only the woman survives the encounter with these underworld figures. We are not actually surprised to find Austin Roxburgh slain in the attack: he is an empty, priggish Englishman who is unlikely to endure the encounter with primitive Nature. Austin has been the victim of internal, psychic 'attacks' throughout his career, which have pointed to the destructive, revengeful character of his own inner world (pp. 45, 105, 141). 'His mind glided marvellously when not threatened by the ... bedevilled depths of his own nature' (p. 131). His death at the hands of primitives is no mere external crisis, but the expression of his own primitive self turned against him.[37]

The Aboriginal women strip off Ellen's clothes and with this her Roxburgh persona is ritualistically divested. She has, as we know, her childhood Gluyas self to fall back on, a layer of experience which allows her to come to terms with primitive life. Austin had no such psychic background, but merely a top layer of culture which was easily undermined. The male, that is to say, lacks the inner depth and cultivation to turn the fateful encounter into positive transformation. With Ellen there is even a sense of exaltation as the primitive hands hack away at her vestments until 'she was finally liberated' (p. 218). She surrenders completely to the process of de-civilization and soon adapts to the Aboriginal lifestyle.

As a slave to the tribe Ellen is often depicted as a naked creature, foraging for food amongst bushes, or climbing trees in search of honeycomb. Her hair becomes matted, her fingernails broken and her skin blackened under the harsh antipodean sun. Her separation from her civilized life is emphasized by the fantasy dialogues she has with the figure of old Mrs Roxburgh, where the mother-in-law's gentility and refined language are pitted against her recovered Cornish dialect and rough manner (p. 232). In her act of cannibalism Ellen reveals most starkly her descent to primitive levels of reality. In fact it is suggested that she sinks to a level even more primitive than that lived by the Aborigines themselves. The women force Ellen to do the unpleasant things that they do not want to do. She acts as nurse to the disease-ridden children, who suckle greedily at her long and leathery breasts, and is eventually adopted as a kind of demoness by the shaman of the tribe. The Aborigines look with horror and disbelief upon the white totem whose head is covered with beeswax and tufts of down; even the cockatoos shriek in apparent disapproval (p. 249). In White the archetypal feminine personality frequently falls to a level of being which is inferior to that of primitive man. At her lowest she is identical with an inhuman darkness, an abysmal realm of psychic reality.

III

Jack Chance appears to Ellen on the night of the great corroboree to mark the movement of her adoptive tribe from the island to the mainland. During the course of the festivities Ellen realizes that he must be an escaped convict who has become assimilated to the Aboriginal world, and is quick to take full advantage of the situation: '"Bring me to Moreton Bay"', she commands, '"and I promise they'll give you your pardon"' (p. 252). Jack, at first too much of a 'native' to understand her words, recognizes her need and decides to carry out her request.

Jack serves Mrs Roxburgh in a twofold way. He acts as the rescuer, freeing Ellen from her bondage to the Aborigines and facilitating her return to white society. But he also allows her to move closer to her inner darkness, to realize the instinctual depths of her personality. Thus Jack is simultaneously the servant of Mrs Roxburgh *and* of Ellen Gluyas, the figure who makes possible her full experience of sensuality and her ultimate return to civilization. In this way he reminds us of Basil Hunter, who was doubly exploited by the Sisters of Moreton Drive; for 'higher' purposes in the case of Manhood, and for 'lower', instinctual reasons for de Santis. But here, in a remarkable *coup,* we have the one woman using the male to ascend to culture as she furthers her descent into the natural world.

During their trek through the bush Ellen and Jack are involved in a passionate, wildly sexual affair. 'Her body might never have been touched, not even by her husband' (p. 267). The tame embraces of Mr Roxburgh can hardly compare with the brute, animalistic manners of Jack Chance, who handled Mrs Roxburgh 'as though she had been a wheelbarrow, or black woman' (p. 268). Ellen is driven to sexual frenzy by her convict lover: 'She began such a lashing and thrashing, her broken nails must be tearing open the wounds which had healed in his back' (p. 269). In fact, the convicted murderer is himself overwhelmed by the animal passion released in Mrs Roxburgh. He becomes mystified by her lust and is forced to remark: '"When I rescued a lady, I didn't bargain for a *lubra"'* (p. 285).

Ellen also scours the depths of moral darkness when she experiences a psychological identification with Mab, Jack's former mistress. As Mab, a sort of queen of the English underworld, Ellen becomes the associate of pimps, prostitutes, robbers, sword-swallowers and other strange denizens of the lower realm. In later fantasies she trudges with Jack through the sewers of London, looking for 'articles of value' amid rivers of excrement and populations of rats (p. 293). Ellen enters this realm of darkness with the same unrestrained vivacity which characterizes her erotic life at this point, but the goal of her descent is never total indulgence in immorality, nor a Rousseauian identification with the primitive. She is involved in a kind of spiral sweep in the direction of primitivity for the sake of recovering passion and instinct, but not at the cost of her essential humanity.[38] Hers is a classic regression for the sake of advancement, where the world of culture is eclipsed for a time but is not extinguished.

It is significant that at the very point where she is most reduced to the natural, where she is completely naked and has even lost the wedding ring that she had kept hidden in her fringe of leaves, the outskirts of civilization become clearly visible to her. Culture and Nature, conscious and unconscious, are not completely antithetical in her world, but seem to be mutually sustaining. This, to be sure, is the secret knowledge of Kore-Persephone, the figure who is at once Queen of the Underworld and goddess of eternal spring.

As this modern Kore approaches the threshold of the upper

world she becomes acutely aware of the moral complications that will arise as she re-enters 'the rational world of civilized beings' (p. 361). Her own difficulties in adjusting to the new environment will be real enough, but the problems of returning to a penal settlement with a 'convicted murderer' and 'shambling human scarecrow' (p. 297) seem too great to bear. White apparently wants us to believe that Ellen is mentally and physically distraught and is unable to arrive at a real solution. Because of her condition we are asked eventually to forgive her her failing.[39] It is apparent that her archetypal pattern does not include rescuing a mere male from the psychic underworld. Jack has served his purpose and is of no use to her in her next phase. She now regrets having 'rashly promised' so much in the beginning (p. 295). Although Ellen tries to mask her real feelings, Jack rightly senses her change of attitude: '"Your heart isn't in it, Ellen. It's like as if you'd went dead on me"' (p. 292). So when they arrive at the edge of Oakes's farm Jack turns and runs back into the bush. He realizes he can win neither love nor freedom from this woman who has betrayed him. He has fulfilled his fate as servant to her individuation, and now must return to the landscape from whence he came.

IV

As she recovers from her journey, Ellen is at first not certain whether she is Mab, Ellen Gluyas, or Mrs Austin Roxburgh. She experiences a temporary mental crisis in which each of her separate selves jostles for a place in the totality of her being. But it is clear that her Roxburgh personality will triumph, and that she will undergo the same kind of moral and psychological elevation that she experienced when she first left her Cornish farm and moved to Austin Roxburgh's Cheltenham estate. Just as a wealthy gentleman facilitated her upward climb, so here an Englishman of 'substantial means' (p. 355) appears before her on the London-bound ship and offers her his support and the opportunity of marriage.

Some critics claim that Ellen achieves a complete unification of her character, a kind of transcendent wholeness similar to that achieved by Elizabeth Hunter.[40] It is true that she attains a vision of unity in Pilcher's chapel, the rough-hewn stone structure where forces natural and cultural interpenetrate and where a magnificent peace 'encloses her like a beatitude' (p. 353). But it is a momentary vision during the course of her ongoing see-sawing career; a glimpse of an ideal realm which she is unable to realize.

Ellen is not of Mrs Hunter's stature, but is a more limited figure who remains more or less on the side of Nature or of culture. The most she can achieve while in the Persephone mode is a lessening of the distance between the two sides of her archetypal being.

As Ellen makes her speedy return to the Old World her separation from the realm of passion and instinct is evident in her highly sophisticated attitudes and mannerisms. She chastises Miss Scrimshaw for her occasional 'vulgarities' (p. 362), and finds herself engaged in 'spontaneous moralizings' (p. 324) with the young children on the ship. Her alienation from the psychic underworld is suggested in her resistance to the memory of her convict lover: 'she almost dared not sleep lest Jack Chance the convict appear in a dream and offer her his love' (p. 358).

Fate does not let her out from the claims of her lower nature quite so easily. By what is described as 'infernal intervention' (p. 365) Mr Jevons, her suitor, inadvertently spills a cup of tea on her dress. The tea-stain, we are told, began 'widening' and 'darkening' in the folds of her skirt, almost as if her too-white, too-polished persona had required this toning down. Jevons embarrassedly rushes to mop up the mess, when Ellen bursts out in her childhood dialect:

'Dun't! 'Tis nothing ... 'Tisn't mine, and 'tisn't spoiled,' ...
'It is nothing, I do assure you, Mr Jevons,' she repeated in what passed for her normal voice. (p. 365)

The sudden ejaculation of the Cornish idiom suggests that she is not as re-assimilated to the values of culture and high society as she would like. The natural self still rests there, just below the surface, liable to break out at any unguarded moment. The worlds of darkness and light are not as far apart as they were before her Australian *nekyia*.

V

One of the things which strikes the reader of *A Fringe of Leaves* is the sense of fate and determinism which pervades the novel. Chapter One is laden with prophetic forewarnings and antici-patory remarks which seem to suggest that Ellen's *nekyia* is inevitable, or willed by a force outside her control. '"I will tell you one thing"' announces the sybilline Miss Scrimshaw in the opening scene. '"Every woman has secret depths with which even she, perhaps, is unacquainted, and which sooner or later must be troubled"' (p. 17). And the prologue closes with an equally prophetic remark, this time uttered by Mr Merivale: '"I wonder," he said, "how Mrs Roxburgh would react to suffering if faced with it?"' (p. 21). Ellen's course is established from the outset; it is down into 'secret depths' which 'must be troubled'. The process is autonomous, working below the threshold of awareness, and appears as incontestable as fate itself. Nothing can stand in the way of the archetypal female's development, and all members of the 'cast' of which White's interior life is composed are focused upon her psychic experience.[41] Not only are all the male characters at Ellen's disposal, and forced to serve her quest, but even the very minor characters, whom we meet only once or twice, are concerned about Ellen's 'secret depths' and her 'suffering'. What small portion of interiority is allotted to Miss Scrimshaw or Mr Merivale is completely governed by the impending experiences of Mrs Roxburgh.

White's fiction becomes more and more dominated by the theme of the mother's quest, which has become not only central but peculiarly obsessive and compulsive. The psychic economy resembles that of a totalitarian state, where everything is made to serve one goal, one ruler, one quest. The only alternative theme which White is able to explore is the continued disintegration of male consciousness, which is the corollary of matriarchal development, and the preconditon for it. White is bound to these repetitive themes and will probably never escape them, for it seems unlikely at this stage that anything else could restructure his imaginal world.

7 The Delight of Decadence

1 Decomposition

> *Around him the fortified soil, the pampered*
> *plants, the whiffs of manure, the moist-warm air*
> *of Sydney, all were encouraging the vegetable*
> *existence: to loll, and expand, fleshwise only,*
> *and rot, and be carted away, and shovelled back*
> *into the accommodating earth. He closed his*
> *eyes. He loved the theory of it. The palm leaves*
> *were applauding.*
>
> Basil Hunter (*The Eye of the Storm*, p. 264)

White's later fiction records the advanced stages of psychic disintegration, the decay of consciousness and its assimilation by the archetypal world of the feminine. The male's absorption into the depths is partly expressed in *The Twyborn Affair* (1979) in transvestism, the taking on of the contrasexual archetypal character into which the ego has fallen. Transvestism adds nothing essentially new to White's work, but is a logical extension of the ego's increasing subordination to the archetypal realm. It is a short step from the psychological effeminacy of Hurtle Duffield to the demonstrative and ritualistic femininity of Eudoxia/Eddie/Eadith Twyborn. Even Waldo Brown, that drily intellectual *puer*, was moved to shed his masculine persona and adorn himself in his mother's ballroom dress. But if Waldo's demonstration was secretive and guilty, E's[1] is open, flamboyant, and guiltless. Not only did public attitudes change on matters relating to sexuality and lifestyles in the years between *The Solid Mandala* (1966) and *The Twyborn Affair*, but White has developed in his later years a certain boldness in promoting sexual modes of a bizarre or deviant nature. As the male ego disintegrates White appears set to defend its course to the very end, finding delight in its assimilation to the mother, humour in its decay, and baroque splendour in its fragmentation.

What impresses the reader about both Waldo's transvestite scene and Eddie Twyborn's story is that the *puer* is only alive, 'radiant', 'magnificent' (*The Solid Mandala*, p. 193) when assuming the female role, and that when the drag is put aside he becomes empty and uninspired. This is to say that the conscious self is vacuous, and that the unconscious world, alive with libido, fills him with creativity and excitement. The *puer* does not simply become any woman, but *the* woman, archetypal femininity, a royal personage. He soars above human limitation, in the inflated world of the archetypal, whether as the Goddess Memory (Waldo) or as Empress Eudoxia, Queen of Byzantium. The camp display would be humorous, as White intends, if it were not so deeply pathological. It is difficult to laugh about the masculine self in the final stages of ruin.

Many positive readings of the novel represent it as an enquiry into bisexuality, an appropriately modern or post-modern exploration of androgyny, which has recently been hailed as a powerful symbol of wholeness. This response is largely due to White's characteristic manipulation of his reader. In his authorial commentary and in certain moments of dialogue, White makes cryptic remarks about E as self-searcher, a figure who overcomes gender categories in order to discover his 'true self'.[3] E is not an androgyne whose wholeness causes him to transcend his gender, but a psychological cripple whose collapsed masculinity forces him to adopt a quasi-feminine-matriarchal character. The difference between androgyny and matriarchal possession is enormous, but it is one which the author's commentary constantly blurs and diminishes.

Even as White tries to represent E's condition as androgyny, the smell of decomposition pervades the novel. At virtually every point we are made aware of shit, dirt, urine, semen, sewage, rotting weeds, farts, stinking salt-pans or decomposing animals. The novel smells because the ego is in a state of slow putrefaction, decaying in the matrix of the unconscious. The stench of decay overwhelms the glamour of the camp facade, rising up from behind the spangled fan and the pomegranate shawl.

I

As we have seen elsewhere, the rotting corpus of the *puer* acts as fertilizer to the psychic growth of the mother. E's decadence inspires Joanie Golson—Mrs Twyborn's pal and acolyte—with fresh life, fills her with possibilities of renewal.[4] She does not even notice the stinking salt-pans and putrid odours surrounding Crimson Cottage, where E lives in a nest of sensuality and lust with ageing decadent Angelos Vatatzes. Joanie finds the derelict villa 'enchanting', the surrounds 'invigorating'; it is 'Curly' Golson and the chauffeur, Teakle, who notice the foul stench, and who realize that 'the air was far less restorative than she had implied' (p. 12).[5]

There is considerable humour in having this Australian woman of Sewells' Sweat-free Felt Hats and Golsons' Emporium track down the exotic Eudoxia Vatatzes in a remote corner in the south of France. At one level it is a social comedy involving the chance meeting of two Australians abroad, both trying desperately to shrug off their Australianness. Joanie's discovery of E is an archetypal necessity: she is led by force of instinct down the stony, rutted road of St Mayeul, knowing that in that precise location a source of psychic energy vital to her own development is to be discovered. As always, the collapsed male is an embodiment of eros, a concentration of sexual and instinctual libido which the over-refined mother has lost and must regain by her association with the *puer*.

Joan Golson's connection with Eddie/Eudoxia is primarily voyeuristic. For her E is a sublime image worshipped from afar, a divine icon of 'terracotta' skin and 'votive' hands (p. 21), which is conveniently framed by the shuttered window of the remote villa.

As she stood by the wall watching the scene through the open window, the tears were streaming down her cheeks, for joy, from the music she was hearing, and out of frustration, from the life she had led and, it seemed, would always lead, except for the brief unsatisfactory sorties she made into that other life with Eadie Twyborn; probably never again, since Eadie had been aged by her tragedy. (p. 18)

Watching E awakens her 'other life', the life of passion and instinct, of spontaneity and eros. Her experience at the window reminds us of Olivia Davenport's epiphanies before the erotic canvases of Hurtle Duffield. Both the paintings and this 'snapshot'—as Joanie refers to the window scene—reflect the mystery of sexuality for the onlookers, and just as Olivia recognizes in the canvas '"a part of my life ... that I've lost"' (*The Vivisector*, p. 293), so Joanie is forced to deal with her unlived life, with memories of her repressed instinctual nature, once enacted in lesbian sorties with E's mother, Eadie Twyborn.

The fact that E is experienced by Joanie as female only makes the mythic dimension more apparent: the mother is searching for a part of *herself*, her own instinctual side. E's masculinity is irrelevant to the mother—as it is even when he takes on a masculine persona in the middle section of the novel. Throughout the novel the mother–figures look with considerable disdain upon men, viewing them as lesser mortals, or at least as outsiders to their own mysteries.

II

The mother's search for herself is extended later in the story to her search for her lost daughter, where E comes to represent the daughter that Eadie Twyborn 'always wanted' but 'never had' (p. 423). Even at the outset Joanie Golson strives to connect Eadie Twyborn with the apparition of E at Crimson Cottage. 'Write to Eadie ... Eadie would have hugely enjoyed yesterday's "snapshot"' (p. 13). In her undelivered letter she tells Eadie that the appearance and sudden disappearance of Eudoxia 'concerns you more than anyone else' (p. 129). Is Joanie guessing that E is Eadie's child after all? Have 'those extraordinary eyes' (p. 129) betrayed a Twyborn nature? Perhaps so, but there is a mythic dimension at work here. Eadie Twyborn is *the* mother–figure of the novel, and Joanie Golson merely one of her symbolic extensions. By referring her encounter with E back to Eadie, Joan is simply deferring to the central matriarchal authority, just as the acolytes and subordinates in *The Eye of the Storm* always referred their crucial experiences back to Elizabeth Hunter. Any move toward rediscovering the missing part of the feminine self concerns her, because we have to do not with a whole series of minor individual quests, but with one individuation emanating from a central authority.

The mother's search, then, is not merely for a literal daughter, but for a mythic daughter, the *hetaira*, the embodiment of youth, feminine eros, and new life. In the ancient mysteries of Eleusis the mother Demeter is constantly searching for her lost daughter, Kore-Persephone, as the youthful, vital aspect of her own feminine nature.[6] As Neumann notes, 'The essential motif in the Eleusinian mysteries and hence in all matriarchal mysteries is the *heuresis* of the daughter by the mother, the "finding again" of Kore by Demeter, the reunion of mother and daughter'.[7] There are several astonishing parallels between this myth and *The Twyborn Affair*, not, I believe, because White based his novel on the myth, nor even because he had it loosely in mind at the time of writing, but because the structure of the archetype is naturally mythical, and as White is led further into matriarchal territory the contents and stories of which the archetype is composed spontaneously reveal themselves. Precisely because the myth functions unconsciously it operates at a mundane level, as a kind of comedy of errors, or as romance bordering on farce. The losing and finding of the daughter is an almost slapstick cat-and-mouse chase, carried out in both hemispheres and in three countries. The longing for the daughter is entirely sexualized, so that the goal of the *heuresis* becomes lesbian involvement rather than spiritual fulfilment:

On meeting 'Eudoxia' I could have eloped with her, as you too, Eadie, would have wanted, had you been here. We might have made an *à trois*, as they say! I would have been jealous ... To lie with this divine creature, breast to breast, mouth to mouth, on the common coverlet ... (p. 128)

As has been noted, a major consequence of the psychic catastrophe in *The Solid Mandala* is loss of the symbolic world. Mythic patterns continue to dominate White's fiction, but myth operates in an entirely eroticized, non-metaphorical way. Every connection between mythic figures involves erotic interplay or sexually-inspired behaviour; every epiphany is an orgasm. Myth collapses into an orgy of sex, an ever-present danger whenever consciousness loses touch with the inner meaning of the dynamic forces.

A central element of the Persephone myth is the suddenness of the daughter's disappearance and the subsequent grief of the mother figure. Persephone is gathering flowers in the meadows when suddenly Hades emerges from the lower realm and claims her as his wife, to rule at his side as Queen of the Underworld. Demeter is so distraught by the abduction that she wanders the earth in search of Kore, exploring both the natural terrain and the cities of men. Eddie Twyborn is engaged to Marian Dibden, a social alliance which has been engineered by Eadie, until, on the eve of the marriage, E disappears and is not seen again until after the Great War. Eadie is shattered by the disappearance, and experiences years of suffering and anguish. As Joan Golson realizes, her sorties with Eadie are probably over because 'Eadie had been aged by her tragedy' (p. 18). Like Kore, Eddie goes off to live sexually with an 'old Greek' in another realm. Vatatzes not only lives in a remote corner of another hemisphere, but inhabits another mental reality, the landscape of madness and delusion.

He imagines himself 'Emperor of All Byzantium' (p. 32), and sits regally upon his 'throne' with his queen by his side.

When Joanie glimpses E through the window she is moved by the ritual quality of the couple, and senses instinctively that the lover, 'the man in black' (p. 14) is her enemy. Joanie's desire is to free E from the sickly, demanding Greek, and to lead her out of pre-war Europe to sunny, peaceful Australia. But she suspects that the mad lover has a hold on E, and stealing her from him might not be easy. In the myth Hades gives Kore the pomegranate seed, which subsequently binds her to his realm. She will be able to make 'visits' to the upper world, but must return each year to Hades' abode. Vatatzes has given E 'a shawl embroidered with pomegranates' (p. 23), which she is wearing when Joanie first glimpses her.[8] Like Persephone, E is bound to the lower realm and will never be entirely free of it.

The bondage to Hades means that the mother's suffering will be cyclical, that she will undergo repeated tragedy as the daughter appears from the depths, only to be drawn back to them again. E appears suddenly after the war, only to disappear a second time to another hemisphere. Eadie writes to Marcia Lushington: 'What I would like to convey to you is that losing a child in death is so much better than losing a grown—what shall I say? *reasoning* child, to life. As happened to me for the second time' (p. 301).[9] Joan Golson's experience is particularly frustrating: her moment of 'perfect feminine collusion' (p. 54) is shattered when Empress and Emperor flee St Mayeul to an unknown destination. Joanie does not get to see E in Sydney, misses him/her at Bogong, and fails to recognize E during a chance meeting in London, even though Eadie ecstatically reunites with her 'daughter' in the same city. The mythic cycle is of losing, finding, losing again. At Eleusis the disappearance and *heuresis* of Kore was enacted every year as part of the matriarchal festival. The mystery is tragicomic in character because, as in the seasonal cycle, the spirit of life is always lost and always recovered. Persephone was eventually identified with the spirit of the corn, a female version of Attis-Adonis, who was similarly lost to the realm of darkness to be reborn anew in the spring. If the Attis-Adonis/Great Mother mythologem of White's early and major work has given way to the Kore/Demeter myth as ordering principle and ruling archetype, this is only to say that, in the course of his long career, and as a result of the ego's collapse, White has moved out of the sphere of masculine mythology altogether into a world of archaic matriarchal mysteries.

III

Although Joanie's arrival at Crimson Cottage is cause for maternal celebration, for E it is a sign of imminent disaster and ruin. 'A day which should have been idyllic grew increasingly black, ending in storms, after a real Visitation' (p. 22). Seemingly as a result of Joanie's presence the Emperor and Empress lose their appetite and begin to quarrel, E experiences Angelos as 'an aged revenant' (p. 95) from whom she '*must* break away' (p. 77), Angelos falls ill and suffers a seizure during one of Joanie's formal visits, the garden is wrecked by storms, and the housekeeper absconds to Joanie's hotel. E's world is under some kind of mythic attack, requiring incantatory defence: 'Text for every day to come: *I must not dwell on Joan Golson's arrival on the scene*' (p. 23). The diarist attempts to place the disaster in philosophical context: 'Everything, I now see, has been leading up to this act of aggression. Gentle perfection is never allowed to last for long' (p. 22). What the diarist fails to see is that he/she lives in a fake perfection, the perfection of the maternal matrix, and that aggressive maternal forces must overpower him. As with Miss Hare at Xanadu, the splendour of the infantile paradise lasts only until 'a soft, silly woman' (p. 22) appears on the scene to lay waste the cherished abode.

The archetypal background of E's situation is revealed in the dream E has after Joanie's arrival:

the shutter has flown open, the whole cliffside a churning mass of pittosporum and lantana scrub pressing in upon, threatening all man-made shoddiness. The giant emu's head and neck tormented by the wind. As its plumage is ruffled and tossed, its beak descends repeatedly, almost past the useless shutter, almost into the room where I am lying in my narrow bed, fright raised in goose-pimples, when not dissolving into urine. (p. 33)

The fact that Mrs Golson has become a predatorial emu with a fearsome beak emphasizes the non-human image at the core of Eddie's psyche: it is elemental Nature itself, the natural world of the matrix, which invades and violates him. We are told that this is Eddie's recurring nightmare, that the *puer* has suffered this same dream, or variations on it, since early boyhood. This shows that Joanie's 'attack' is in no way an arbitrary experience but a part of his archetypal destiny, and that his experience of her is entirely dominated by psychic factors. The dream ends with the significant phrase, 'dissolving into urine', suggesting not only infantile terror and fright but also the process of putrefaction which is the inevitable consequence of this psychological deadlock.

Whenever faced with a crisis, E's immediate urge is to escape. He runs out on Marian Dibden because he cannot cope with marriage or heterosexual bonding. He flees from the Judge and Eadie because he cannot explain to them his sexual and personal dilemmas. And now, in the present crisis, he feels trapped and longs to escape. His first impulse is to flee from Joanie, since she appears to be the mistress of destruction. On the other hand, he reflects, Angelos is a handicap and a bore, and perhaps life would be better if he got rid of him and eloped with Joanie to Australia ('shall I be brave enough to ... commit myself to ... Joanie's steamy bosom, her gasps and blunders ...?', p. 98).[10] His evident confusion, his willingness to betray, his inability to decide on the enemy and adopt a course of action suggest that he is caught up in a psychological bind from which there is no external escape. His true enemy is himself, his own fatal bond to the matrix. E eventually flees with Angelos to another Mediterranean village, where they reside temporarily in a *pension*. Conveniently, the old, ailing Pluto/Hades suffers a heart attack and dies. White attempts a sentimental death-bed scene, hoping to inject into the narrative a saving sense of love, but the reader is too aware of Eddie as would-be-betrayer, as egotist and opportunist, to allow the final scene to convince. It is vain of White to expect more of us, since we have been asked throughout to discount the possibility of love ('"I am committed [to A] by fate and orgasm—never love"' p. 36). Angelos hardly breathes his last before E is bounding off into the night ('her gait long, loping, ungainly', p. 127), escaping to another part of the world and into another unlikely situation.

IV

E's phase as Eddie Twyborn, army officer and jackeroo, is not so much an ascension to masculinity as it is a mere re-exploration of his disintegrated state in outwardly male disguise. The opening sentences of Part Two exude the smells of decay, of shit, piss, 'the smell of sperm', 'the stench of death' (p. 133), making it clear that the putrefaction still dominates, that the ego continues to rot in the matrix. E's decomposition here takes the form of a reduction to the purely animal level of existence, to the merely physical, phallic attributes of maleness. And what surrounds and destroys him is the literal female womb and the voracious sexual appetites of women. E becomes all phallus, a kind of walking penis designed to entertain the female sex. Aboard the Australia-bound ship Margs Gilchrist is excited by his 'stiff', 'smooth' carriage, and 'looks ready to gobble [him] up' (p. 135). At the masked ball she 'thrusts a campaigning vulva as deep as possible into his crotch' (pp. 140–1), and Eddie is so terrified he is forced to lock himself in his cabin. Even as he sleeps 'Margie Gilchrist's exploratory vulva, or alternately the colonel's opulent crotch, was forced against [him]' (p. 141). There is no escaping arbitrary, aggressive sexual assaults, because life has reduced him to a mere sex object, an expendable source of animal eros. Wherever he goes in Australia he appears, as it were, as a male dog on heat, a prize spaniel which no one, male or female, can resist.

E is linked with the dog motif throughout the middle section, and at various points in the story other male figures, Angelos, Judge Twyborn, Don Prowse, are compared to dogs or are seen to have dog-like characteristics. Angelos is seen as 'an old Alsatian nosing the hem of [E's] skirt' (p. 29), and Eddie is compared to 'an enslaved dog ... licking the beringed hand casually offered for adulation' (p. 102). In mythology the Mother's animal aspect was often represented as a dog, or as a pack of hounds. It is of particular interest that the male votaries of the Goddess, the men who prostituted themselves in Her name, were called *kelabim*, 'dogs'.[11] The Goddess exploits the men as sexual instruments, as carriers of the radiant phallus, the object of fertilization and sensual pleasure. The men in *The Twyborn Affair* are reduced to dogs, and, like the victims of Circe who are turned into animals, fulfil merely an animal function in relation to their female associates.

The dog motif is particularly marked when Eddie makes his way home to Eadie Twyborn, a figure who is surrounded by terriers and strays, and who enjoys her role as mistress of 'a house of dogs' (p. 122).

And there was Eadie, crouched on her knees with a trowel in her hand, her beam broader in one of those skirts she had invariably worn, a miracle of Scottish weave and an intermingling of dogs' hair clotted with compost or manure. Oblivious as far as you could tell. As were the six or seven little red dogs, scratching, swivelling on their rumps, sniffing, one of them lifting a leg behind Eadie's back on a border of sweet alyssum. (p. 147)

Here we find Eadie as an instinctual creature, linked with earth and the animal world. Dogs and compost are brought together in this passage, an important conjunction in their symbolic relation to the mother–figure. Both are images of the male ego's decomposition, from human being to animal,[12] from living entity to decaying matter. And both forms of lower life serve the mother: the dogs provide her with animal warmth and affection ('"dogs were my best relationship"' she confesses at the end, p. 424), and compost enriches her earth, not only her Edgecliff soil, but the substance of her inner being. E's other decomposition, from male self to effeminate object, is also suggested in this reunion scene, as mother and son have their 'hands locked in sisterhood' (p. 149). The loss of masculinity serves the mother in that it provides her with the 'missing daughter', the experience of *heuresis* as she encounters the *puella*-aspect of her feminine nature.

As mother and son embrace, E feels weak and submissive. Eadie 'takes the initiative' and E is reduced to 'the passive object of her intentions' (p. 148). But even as he flinches at her power we are told, 'Wasn't this what he had come for? He closed his eyes and let it happen'. Eadie and E are overwhelmed by their mutual attraction, but they spare each other the indignity of going to bed. E realizes his incestuous desires in relation to Marcia Lushington, imagining himself returning to his mother's womb as he unites sexually with Eadie's estranged pal (pp. 222, 232, 234). The incestuous theme is perversely literal in this novel, as in all works since the collapse of White's symbol-making capacity. The return to the matrix is now enacted by sex with mother's pal, her acolyte (Basil and Manhood), or her daughter (Basil and Dorothy). The psyche can no longer present primary infantile drives in symbolic or cultural form. All imagination runs out of this central mythologem, so that now we are confronted with sexual melodrama and hollow equations: 'Eadie = Eddie. It was true ...' (p. 150). Disintegration is not merely a subject of this novel, but a condition of its aesthetic being, a disease which attacks the formal structure from the inside. As consciousness decomposes, so do the aesthetic forms, the symbols, the imaginative constructs.

V

Marcia Lushington of Bogong is experienced in the art of turning men into animals and playing the sex game to her advantage. Greg Lushington, the exploited partner in their 'open' marriage, is her deracinated pet or plaything, with about as much status in her life as Beppi the Maltese terrier; and Don Prowse is her 'stud bull', 'ram' (p. 289) and 'human animal' (p. 219). With Marcia, E feels he is 'no longer a lover, but some lean and ingratiating breed of hairless dog, licking her wrists, expecting an exchange of caresses'

(p. 291). E senses he is caught in Marcia's 'sticky trap' and that her desire is to 'imprison him in her womb' (p. 222). The devouring aspect of her nature is grotesquely highlighted in the graveyard at the back of the homestead, filled with the graves of her sons. These *pueri*, each bearing the name of her husband, are the products of her various lustful encounters, and none manages to live beyond two years of age. Adding yet another headstone to the collection seems to be one of her sports, and after E flees to Europe his own son is added to the yard. The mother is the murderer of male life, or rather, *puer* consciousness cannot break free of the deathly matrix.[13] As soon as the *puer* leaves the womb he is sacrificed to the earth, where he decomposes and returns his life to the soil. One of the headstones is inscribed with White's own birth date, 28 May 1912 (p. 230). It is a comic gesture, to be sure, yet also morbidly precise, expressing the author's identification with the buried, composting *puer*, the son who failed to break free.

Marcia views Eddie not exactly as a male lover but as a source of feminine sensuality and eros. '"You're different, Eddie. You have a quality I've always hoped for—and never found—in a man"' (p. 225). Again the composting *puer* answers to the mother's feminine instinct, providing her with an essential 'fineness' (p. 220) which she wants to add to her own being. The climactic point to their relationship is where they meet on the plains of Bogong and become giggling sisters for an afternoon, sharing secrets and simple joys 'like schoolgirls who have shed the boys during an interval at a dance' (p. 255). Marcia can get hard, animal sex from Prowse, her 'stud bull', but from E she hopes to gain that sisterhood and feminine solidarity that Eadie and Joanie also seek from him.

E's role as mother's daughter is strongly, even crudely announced in his relationship with Peggy Tyrrell, the toothless she-ancient of Bogong. When she sets her eyes on E Mrs Tyrrell licks her lips and says, '"I'll like 'avin' you around ...; you an' me 'ull get on like one thing"' (p. 185). '"It's the girls I miss out 'ere"' she explains. '"Never the boys"'. When E protests, '"I'm a boy"', Peggy replies, '"Bet yer mum would've been glad of a girl"' (p. 182). The crudeness and lack of subtlety here is indicative of the novel's qualities. It is not merely that Peg Tyrrell is crude: the fictional psyche itself lacks culture and refinement. Like Marcia, Peg is connected with death and devouring. Her favourite pastime is preparing corpses for interment, making the dead look beautiful before they are burnt or buried. '"It's the funerals I miss

out 'ere . . . They 'allus invited me ter do the layun out''' (p. 200).
The mother's supreme joy is to prey upon extinct life, to prettify
the face of death and construct an aesthetic ideal based on decay.

VI

The aesthetics of decay is the business of Eighty-Four Beckwith
Street, the whore-house directed by E in his role as Mrs Eadith
Trist, the 'inspired bawd' (p. 323). Part Three of the novel
concerns itself with the sordid life of the brothel, a place where
men come to suffer a kind of erotic disintegration at the hands of
aggressive whores. The favoured exercises at the brothel include
brutal sex, whips and chains, thrashings, 'acts of self-immolation'
(p. 329), and virtually any erotic activity guaranteed to produce
pain. As always in White, sexuality is conceived in terms of the
puer's sado-masochistic return to the matrix. Hence every paying
customer is 'lusting to be consumed' (p.332), and the whores,
personifications of the matrix, are anxious to oblige. '"I might
bite off the first cock I catch sight of"' (p. 325) says Elsie, and
Annabel cries, '"I need men—a constant supply"' (p. 312). Their
victims 'pass out', 'recoil' (p. 327), are reduced to wounded
animals (as E discovers through her concealed eye), and one, a
Brigadier Blenkinsop, dies astride a 'thrashing negress' (p. 361).
Part Three is excruciatingly literal, a bizarre display of animalistic
sexuality marking the collapse of the masculine principle and its
assimilation to the maternal maw.

E presides over these ritual bouts of sexuality like a priestess at
the head of an orgiastic cult. The prostitutes are 'vernal nuns'
(p. 324) or 'whore-nuns' (p. 328), the bawd herself a 'chaste
mistress', and the brothel a 'sexual institution'. In matriarchal
times, orgiastic rites were often supervised by male priests
(*kedeshim*) who dressed in women's clothing and who assumed
women's names.[14] In the early cults the priests were eunuchs,
their testes cut off in the initiation ceremony, but in later times
they took vows of celibacy. Their task, like E's, was to direct the
orgies but not to participate in them. The *kedeshim* were also
hairless, since hairlessness was associated with sexual abstin-
ence, and E's body, 'her legs, her arms, her jaw, were as smooth as
marble' thanks to the waxing techniques of 'Fatma the Arab from
Mansoura' (p. 397). The priests' sexuality was reserved for the
Mother Goddess, sacrificed to her image through castration or
celibacy, and not to be spent upon mere mortals. Many customers
and associates, including her patron Lord Gravenor, attempt to

get E into bed, but she rejects their advances. The frustrated Gravenor concludes that E is at once a cock-teaser and 'the patron saint of chastity' (p. 369). Like the *kedeshim*, E's sexuality is reserved for the mother (Mum Twyborn) and is not to be expended upon lesser figures.

The mythological parallel suggests that E has moved so far back into the mother–complex that his life is controlled by archaic mythic forces. Eadith Trist views her Chelsea career as a bold adventure, an expression of her individuality, but in reality it is non-individual and completely archetypal. E's regression has caused him to become identical with the very thing that consumes him: the destructive matrix. Instead of resisting disintegration he celebrates and institutionalizes it, setting up an orgiastic cult in order to 'seduce a whole society determined on its own downfall' (p. 321). White invites us to see E's career in the context of the general decline of the 1930s: 'In the age in which they were living it [being consumed] had become the equivalent of consummation' (p. 332). While some critics appear convinced by this historical argument, for me it is a mere sleight-of-hand, a convenient use of context to rationalize what amounts to a severe pathological disorder.[15] The facts show that, far from this being a moral essay on social decline, it is a work of committed decadence, a gleeful indulgence in psychological corruption.

Readers often express a sense of dissatisfaction with the last part of the novel. The prose tends to become watery, diffuse, the narrative structures contrived, the characters two-dimensional. Numerous figures cross the fictional stage, but we get to know none of them. Many of the whores remain completely anonymous, and are designated merely by the colour of their pubic hair. Gravenor remains elusive, remote, and E herself is distanced from us; we are never admitted into her inner world. It is not simply, as I have heard argued, that White is withholding interiority and keeping us at the surface, but that his fiction has lost interiority. What we see is all there is. Psychological regression has led the author into a literary impasse, where all we find is perverse, literally enacted myths, studied decadence, and surfaces. Leonie Kramer describes the last part accurately as 'empty virtuosity',[16] writing which uses technique and manners to cover a void. A fragment of Part Three tells us of a whore, Lydia, who had given up a musical career in Paris because she realized that all she possessed was '"virtuosity ... just that—nothing more than the desire to astonish—no heart or compulsion"' (p. 330). This might well sum up the state of White's art, no heart or force, just the desire to astonish through calculated indecency and polished surfaces. But even the elegant surfaces of E's temple cannot keep out the odour of decay, which is the true leitmotif of the novel. The high-class, newly renovated building smells of stale cigar smoke, dried semen and shit. It is an ideal metaphor for White's 'new', self-consciously renovated fiction, which has been erected upon the decomposing body of the *puer aeternus.*

Part of White's virtuosity consists in his supplying philosophical remarks to keep the illusion of depth alive, as has been noted earlier. These remarks are sprinkled liberally throughout the story, but are particularly evident in the last part, presumably because this is the part which most requires props and artificial support. White does not claim a great deal for his protagonist, but his skilful manipulations of the text do establish, often by negation as it were, that E is on a quest.

[Eadith Trist] could have cried ... for the actuality she had been grasping at all her life without ever coming to terms with it. (p. 324)

Yet whatever form she took, or whatever the illusion temporarily possessing her, the reality of love, which is the core of reality itself, had eluded her, and perhaps always would. (p. 336)

'I've never aspired to virtue. As for purity—truth—I've still to make up my mind what they amount to. But hope I may. Eventually.' (p. 381)

While appearing to be modest claims, or even statements of E's failure to achieve whatever abstract ideal is alluded to (core of reality, love, purity, truth), these passages leave the reader not so much with the sense of conceded failure as with the more basic sense of an existing journey of self-discovery. The asserted goal provides the reader with a welcome crutch, so that he is able to arrive at the positive conclusion that, however fragmented E's career and however disturbing his end, a search for meaning inspires his life and illuminates his suffering.[17] In fact, no such search exists; E's life is a series of evasions and escapes. The 'myths' in which he is involved are the result of regressions. The last thing he wants to do is discover himself: the reality would be too terrible and besides, he enjoys being lost, because then he can be found by the Mother and included in *her* individuation.

VII

The novel gains dramatic focus and direction at the end by the arrival of Eadie Twyborn on the London scene. As we first glimpse Eadie she is aged, morose, and dressed in black—almost as depressed a figure as the prematurely senile Joanie Golson whom E lifts from a Piccadilly gutter. Eadie is seen coming in and out of London churches, a prayer-book in her gloved hands, her face 'drained of human passion' (p. 420). She is like the weary Demeter, tired of searching, unable to find solace in conventional religion, anxious to discover new life and meaning. The day arrives when, seated on a wooden bench in a tram shelter, she strikes up a conversation with a woman beside her, whom she recognizes is E. '"Are you my son Eddie?"' she scribbles on the fly-leaf of the prayer-book. '"No"' writes E, '"but I am your daughter Eadith"' (p. 422). It is a memorable and humorous scene, not only because of E's candid admission and the humour of the setting, but because this is Eadie's triumph, her divine comedy as she discovers the essential ingredient of her whole-ness. '"I am so glad. I've always wanted a daughter"' (p. 423). Life flows back into Eadie's world, the women enjoy long, animated conversations, there is tenderness and talk of the future, and 'their harmony by now was a perfect one' (p. 423). It is an archetypal moment of celebration, reflected memorably in the Homeric *Hymn to Demeter:* 'They spent / the whole of that day / with hearts united, / and they warmed / each other's heart / with many gestures / of affection, / and her heart stopped / griev-ing'.[18] It is also significant that the *heuresis* occurs after the death of Judge Edward Twyborn, because in Greek myth the recovery of the daughter signifies 'the annulment of the male rape and incursion, the restoration after marriage of the matriarchal unity of mother and daughter'.[19] What takes place in the *mater* mystery is of no business to men, it is something which not only excludes but 'annuls' the male presence.

Eadie's immediate desire is to take E back with her to Australia, away from the violence and contingencies of Europe as it moves toward a second war. In this situation she reflects her pal Joanie Golson, who had similar plans for E at the start of the First World War. In many ways the mythic pattern is circular and repetitive, only Eadie is more successful in her handling of it. Although she does not manage a physical return to Australia with her daughter / *hetaira* she does achieve a powerful psychological vision of their shared life in New South Wales:

'As late as this perhaps we'd find we could live together. I can see us washing our hair, and sitting together in the garden to dry it . . .' Yes, it was the most seductive proposition: the two sitting in the steamy garden, surrounded by ragged grass, hibiscus trumpets, the bubbling and plopping of bulbuls, a drizzling of taps. (p. 425)

It is characteristic that the reunion should invoke an idyllic pastoral scene, because the earth is Demeter's realm, the world over which she rules, and recovery of Kore/Persephone brings joy to the earth and the sweetness of spring. The recovery of the daughter is an earth mystery and a fertility mystery, as is evident from the richness of the steamy grass and colourful flowers, the slightly drugged atmosphere of the garden, and the sensual image of the washing and drying of hair. The vision is surely a 'seductive proposition': E can now forgo his chastity and hairlessness and enjoy the sexuality, body and pastoral rituals of his mother and the maternal earth.

'But as from all such golden dreams, the awakening would surely devastate' (p. 425). Precisely. Not because 'all' golden dreams are illusory, but because this one is. The persistent dream in White's fiction, that of blissful unity with the mother–image, is an impossible situation. It is the fake paradise to which Theodora, Parker, Voss, and all White's *pueri* have aspired. Consciousness can never be at one with the source, because this very at-one-ment disintegrates it. The matrix is an acid-bath in which the ego dissolves and becomes strangely absorbed into its origins, the 'mother–world'. The mother prospers but the ego is annulled. Hence as Eddie Twyborn, in male attire but in woman's make-up, sets out on his last visit to Eadie before the two set sail for Australia, he is killed in the conflagration of a bombing raid. Although his death may appear arbitrary, a stroke of bad fortune as his personal life intersects with the century's events, it is completely inevitable from an inner perspective. The son is finally destroyed by the mother's embrace: the whole novel, indeed White's entire career, ends logically in this experience of disintegration.

As the dismembered, bleeding *puer* lies on the pavement outside his mother's hotel, Eadie is enjoying further dreams of pastoral harmony, drizzling taps, and playful bulbuls. She has married her child in death and it has made her content: 'this fragment of my self which I lost is now returned to where it belongs' (p. 432). For her, E has no reality or substance in himself, but is a mere fragment of her archetypal character. The lyrical ending has been enjoyed by many readers, but it has rarely been understood for what it is: the lyricism of the devouring mother, inspired to reverie by the son's blood-sacrifice, his 'crimson current' (p. 430), which now feeds back into her earth.

2   Poor Clare

> *He hesitated, then confided, 'You know she's a*
> *fake, don't you? The mask—the head—they were*
> *manufactured by the nuns. They'd be Poor*
> *Clares indeed without such a source of revenue.'*
> Franciscan priest (*Memoirs of Many in One*, p. 188)[20]

In *Memoirs of Many in One* (1986) the focus shifts from the shattered *puer* back to the mother. These are the memoirs of Alex Xenophon Demirjian Gray, and Patrick White is merely her editor and assistant. This playful literary device demonstrates and confirms what we have always suspected: the mother is the actual 'author' of the work and White is subordinate to her promptings and direction. 'Patrick' appears as a character in *Memoirs*, and he is a somewhat remote figure, decent enough, polite and obedient, but essentially insubstantial. He is significant only as an ancillary to the mother's creative process. He tidies up after Alex's death, sorts through her notes and letters, retraces her movements through Europe and Australia, and brings her imaginal life to literary realization. It is apparent that 'Patrick' does not understand what the mother is trying to do, or what she actually is. She is what remains of his own genius, a dissociated part of the self which now lies beyond his conscious control. In fact Patrick's distance and detachment is one of the mother's sources of despair. Patrick, she says, 'ought to know me better than his own heartbeat, but doesn't' (p. 89). She complains of the 'widening gap' between them (p. 90), and asserts that while Patrick recognizes the demands of art he has 'never exactly come good himself' (p. 124). He is a blind attendant to the creative process, one who dedicates his services and talents to something which lies beyond his understanding.

Alex Xenophon Demirjian Gray is an empty and impoverished figure. Not only does her editor fail to understand her, but she fails to understand herself. She is obsessed with the problem of her identity and is never certain of her real 'vocation'. She spends most of her time storming the gates of self-knowledge, for although she makes many attempts to discover 'something more positive than life' (p. 144), she is never given access to the inner world of the self. She remains on the external side of her own experience and imitates the Inner Way. Alex goes through all the motions, acts out the drama of individuation, adopts various masks and guises, but everything is phoney and contrived. Her life could be described as a psychopathic parody of individuation, in the sense that her acting out of the psychic drama leads her to criminality, vandalism, delusion and death. The desire to integrate her spiritual side leads her to seize a drunken derelict from Centennial Park (who she supposes is a mystic) and to lock him up in the 'priest's hole' in the attic. The desire for spontaneity and self-expression leads her to shoplifting, prowling and poaching, exhibitionism, and indiscriminate attacks on the public. And all the while she keeps telling herself (and White keeps telling us) that this psychopathic parody means something, that it is leading her to salvation. Her task is to play-act for all she is worth, to cajole herself and others into a sense of her higher status, and to bluff her way to enlightenment.

Memoirs of Many in One has been described as a 'parody-pastiche of the whole White oeuvre',[21] a deliberate attempt to send up his former preoccupations and interests. It is true that White delights in self-parody, not only for the sake of humour and playfulness, but also for the sake of violating his own career and 'mission', which has weighed heavily upon him. He is anxious in this work to let fly at his own literariness, as well as to abuse the business of literature: '"He's sick of writers ... He's sick of himself. Literature, as they call it, is a millstone round his neck"' (p. 177). *Memoirs* is an attempt to trivialize and abuse his work, to vent his rage upon his tragic fortune. There is a chilling awareness throughout of his own defeat, and so White indulges in a kind of wretched, anarchic fun, but it must be emphasized that Alex Gray is herself stuck in the parodic mode. Although the impulse to individuate is present, the means to accomplish it is not. Alex desperately imitates the patterns and postures of Elizabeth Hunter, Hero Pavloussi, Mary de Santis, but nothing works: every one of her imagined or actual excursions leads to disaster.

Finally, the mother archetype succumbs to the same degeneration that has long afflicted the *puer*. We can no longer point to the *puer*'s decay on the one hand, and the mother's health on the other. The entire psychic system—conscious and unconscious—has now degenerated. We have seen genius fall from the male ego to the maternal unconscious, but now even the unconscious cannot keep its dream of individuation alive. The autonomous archetype cannot go on indefinitely in a developmental vein. It is related biologically, if not consciously, to White's character, and gradually psychic disintegration must affect the whole system. The mother has managed a remarkable twenty-year career from *The Solid Mandala* to *Memoirs*, in which she rose Phoenix-like out of the ruins of the male psyche to achieve stability, self-possession and integration. The high point of her trajectory was discovered in *The Eye of the Storm*, but already in *A Fringe of Leaves* her achievements seemed less impressive; her wholeness had become partial, momentary, conditional. And by the time of *The Twyborn Affair* the mother's quest had begun to lose integrity, having degenerated to a farcical search for her 'lost self' in the form of her literal son–daughter. At the end of that novel she is less a plausible human character than a grotesque cartoon figure, greedily devouring its catch of human flesh and blood. Literalism, or the profane expression of psychic activity, is what reduces the mother's quest to farce, buffoonery and perversion. Literalism increases as psychic depth diminishes. As the mother contracts to a two-dimensional, cardboard persona, her behaviour becomes more bizarre and pathetic. She possesses inner urges that cannot be realized, and spiritual aspirations that cannot be fulfilled.

I

Alex Gray hides her poverty and insubstantiality behind a cloak of fantasy and high rhetoric: '"I can do anything I put my mind to"' (p. 43); '"I am superb"' (p. 45); '"I am Alexandra Xenophon Demirjian Gray of anywhere you like to name"' (p. 97). Throughout her career she suffers from delusions of grandeur and an inflated sense of self-worth. When the urge to individuate cannot enter and transform the inner person it remains on the surface and disturbs the superficial layers of the personality. Instead of a spiritual journey there is an ego-trip; instead of individuation there is eccentricity and individualism. The spirit of genius thus becomes a demonic force, puffing up the ego, spinning veils of illusion, creating all kinds of distortions and unrealities. It is this that gives the novel its high camp feeling. Like Alex's character, the aesthetic structure of the text is full of glittering surfaces, artifice and contrivance. It exists on the surface, not because White has decided to champion gay ideology, but because there is nothing on the inside. Many think that White has had his fill of depth and symbolism and, 'in the glow of the afterlife',[22] is shifting into a high camp mode as a way of 'celebrating'[23] life. But there is a desperation and a pathos in Alex's career which the frivolous 'drag-show' reading will not allow.

Alex believes herself to be genuinely inspired and so is willing to pit her own eccentric universe against that of the outside world, which she sees as drab and insane. Inevitably, she feels her position threatened and becomes paranoid. We read in the first paragraph: 'THEY will be watching, from inside the house, from the garden, the Park, or most disturbingly, from above'. She feels watched, judged, under attack. She suspects Hilda is 'spying on me through a peephole', that Hal is 'hiding something from me', and that others are involved in treachery. People seem to be wanting to snatch her memoirs, to destroy her secret world, and to deny her the 'creative' outlet she seeks in spontaneous violent enactments. It is to her advantage, of course, to see her psychopathic behaviour as 'creative' and to imagine that society is trying to steal creativity from her. Increasingly society becomes linked with repression, sadism, brutality, and is personified in the police (who often arrest her and carry her away) and in psychiatrists (who strive, she thinks, to make her insane like them). Ultimately, society becomes identical with the strait-jacket, and when fears of social consequences arise during one of her freakish episodes she has a vision of Professor Falkenberg 'holding out the seamless canvas jacket, its blind sleeves, its dangling tapes' (p. 101). '"Just you try to create, my girl,"' warns the psychiatric nurse, '"and you'll be back in this before tea's up"' (p. 172). This is the psychopath's view of the world: society is seen as a nightmare of repression and restriction, whereas 'to create', to express the personal self, is identical with a lunatic eccentricity which invariably invokes social reprimand. Life is a choice between two kinds of madness, one which has social support, and one which releases the self and personal desires.

Alex's overriding obsession is to find someone who will understand her, who will share her world and affirm its rightness. She longs to befriend the old derro in the Park, since he is an outsider like herself, and must also be superior to the society he rejects. The derro is dubbed 'the Mystic', since it is decided that 'his mind is on higher things' (p. 86). She contrives to lure the derelict to her house and lock him in the attic until the right moment when she will be ready to receive his special gift of knowledge. It is a ludicrous scheme, destined to lead to disaster. But like most of her eccentric plots, it contains an important unconscious intention. For her real need is to discover her own dereliction, and to realize that her own genius is itself derelict.

The force which drives her is not going to lead her to 'arcane knowledge' (p. 103), but merely to disease, despair and ruin. Hilda correctly observes of her adored figure: '"That's no mystic. He's a lousy old derro"' (p. 87). Even Patrick warns, '"He might not live up to your expectations of illumination"' (p. 93). But the mother is determined to make an idol of the wretched figure.

Although the derro refuses to play the role ('"What'uv yer brought me 'ere for? Waddayer expect a bloke ter do?"'), and although she is brought face to face with his wretchedness ('I am pervaded by the stench of cabbage, halitosis, and metho', p. 102), the mother still looks forward to the greater glory, to the transcendence beyond the decay. When it becomes painfully clear that he is no 'desert father, or prophet', Alex decides to instruct him in his neglected vocation:

'Listen,' I tell my deranged Mystic. 'You should know the difference between meat and flesh. You should know when your faith is being tried by your reactions to Our Lord bleeding on the Cross—and what the Holy Spirit expects of us believers.'
The Mystic only looks mystified, as though the metho is still stirring in his blood.
'You're the one,' I begin to scream, 'the one I expected guidance from— when now it seems I must guide *you* ...' (p. 112)

Alex orders the Mystic and his Dog out of the house: 'Burping, panting ... my pair of scrapped idols follow me down the path', but she does not scrap her delusions and fantasies, only the forms in which they were invested. The derro has *given* her the illumination she needed—the fact of her own wretchedness—but she has not known how to receive it. Her egotism has blocked the realization of her own dereliction.

II

Alex Gray shifts rapidly from one adopted persona to another. She appears variously as Diacono, Dolor, Magda, Eleanor Shadbolt, Cassiani the nun, Sister Benedict, Dolly Formosa, the Empress Alexandria of Byzantium, and at every change of costume we are meant to be dazzled by her complexity and range of character, but she does not really live any one of her remembered or invented lives. Next to Elizabeth Hunter, that supreme exponent of many-sidedness, Alex is an amateur and a fraud. Her roles are shallowly adopted and externally conceived. She is an inferior actress who hopes that sheer force of will will make up for lack of talent. She is capable only of caricature and burlesque, and imagines that it will all pass as a grand theatrical performance. And if any one of her roles fails to convince, she resorts to violence in order to impress her authority upon the world and to seize a power that would otherwise remain elusive.

The fantasy sequence in which Alex appears as Cassiani the nun clearly reflects her inauthenticity as a spiritual figure. Alex takes on the role of the servile nun of Ayia Ekaterni, the sweeper of mouse droppings and lover of Onouphrios the monk, because 'it was a kind of penance which might in time lead to salvation' (p. 35). Always there is an explicit, calculated 'meaning' behind her self-consciously spiritual endeavours. Her external grasp of the life of the spirit causes her to adopt spiritual clichés and empty religious trappings. The people on the island of Nisos rightly distrust her. They sense she is an 'impostor-nun' who will bring ruin to the island. It is apparent that 'the people' in this sequence personify her own guilt, her unconscious awareness of her own fraudulence. This accounts for her fierce hatred of society; she must at all times resist the voice that would oppose her delusive system. The people claim that she is 'mad' (p. 79), and then launch a bitter, xenophobic attack: '"You are a foreign devil. You have evil powers. No one in these parts has a blue eye"' (p. 80). The extremism of their attack corresponds perhaps to the extremism of her self-righteousness. The unconscious here resorts to extraordinary measures to break down her elaborately constructed facade. Alex merely exploits the situation to consolidate her position as alienated outsider. If the community sees her as an evil eye, she will make herself an object worthy of their contempt and blame:

Seized with a rage against the hopelessness and the hypocrisies of human-kind, I armed myself with my goat-hair *tagari* and started snatching the votive offerings from where they hung above the Saint's altar. I stuffed the metal tokens into the *tagari* and rushed from the church towards the mountain, now rapidly forming in the morning light. (p. 81)

This is no mere random act of violence; it is a significant act which epitomizes her own religious quest. For her entire career is a desecration of the sacred, a snatching at the tokens and emblems of religions. Unable to integrate the spirit inwardly, she seizes upon its external forms and imagines she has achieved spiritual richness. She has snatched bits from 'the Bible, the Talmud, the Jewish mystics, the Bhagavad Gita, various Zen masters, and dear old Father Jung' (p. 54), and thus has a jumble of tokens and images rattling in her *tagari*. But the tokens are worthless because unrelated to her inner life and lacking any context that would make them meaningful. In an alarmingly literal ending this scapegoat suddenly finds herself surrounded by a herd of goats, who befriend her and follow her down the mountain. On the one side stands Onouphrios and his Christian flock, on the other the devil Cassiani, flanked by 'the goat army' (p. 82). As we prepare ourselves for a battle between the sheep and the goats, Cassiani takes fright and runs off into the distance, her sack of tokens clanging awkwardly at her side. She flees not only from the judgement of the world but also from the realization of her spiritual emptiness.

Alex's major performance is as Dolly Formosa, the leading lady of the Arts-Council-funded 'Theatrical Tour of Outback Australia' (p. 125). Here Alex uses cunning and wile to bluff her way to a position of influence in the arts. She sees herself as a dispenser of culture to the improverished masses, a self-appointed ambassador of art and taste. As ever, there is a gulf between her conception of her role and the reality of her performance. Although she makes great claims for herself as artist and tragedienne, she actually presents third-rate burlesques of Shakespearean characters, and her Dolly Formosa monologues seem more like vulgar drag-show sketches than the avant-garde 'happenings' of her conscious intention. Alex's aim throughout is to startle the audience out of its complacency and to elevate it to her own level of supposed creativity. The theatre is her quarter of sanctioned and permissible insanity, and the audience are to become, if only for a sublime moment, her disciples in the art of madness. The fact that her one-actor show is called *Dolly Formosa and the Happy Few* suggests that the audience is to regard itself as a privileged band of witnesses to an esoteric spectacle. Of course the enterprise meets with disaster: on the opening night Alex fights on amidst boos, whistles and cat-calls. Voices from the back of the hall shout rudery, and 'at Peewee Plains there were eggs and tomatoes, quite a scandal' (p. 128). Alex refuses to be disturbed by the reaction; her egotism reads it as the audience's lack of readiness for her gift of vision. As she writes to Patrick: 'the audience is puzzled by much of what I do, which I take as a tribute to creativity' (p. 128).

However, the aim of her performance soon shifts from educating the audience to attacking and abusing it. A bad review from 'King Vampire Harry' of the *Sydney Morning Herald* marks the turning point. The aspiring actress had hoped to challenge the critic's 'professional bardolatry' with the 'truth' of her own self-revelations (p. 130). His negative response turns the actress sour and mean. On her final night she strides out to centre stage, strips off her costume, and aggressively parades her naked body before the audience. '"It's a shame,"' someone screams, '"the Government ought to protect decent people from such rot"'. Alex is unmoved: '"I have my convictions my belief in truth"'. Besides, she considers, the Happy Few who 'appreciate art', '"will understand as I shed my midnight robe, and my naked body conjures up the archetypes of birds, serpents, insects, many of them fiendish in their savage beauty ..."' (p. 137). Her attack on the public reaches a climax in a violent episode at the Sand Pit theatre, where Alex works as theatrical char and dogsbody. By this stage she becomes patently psychotic in her self-delusions ('"I am all. I am the Creator"'), and feels herself inspired to attack a public which continues to 'sit in judgment on the Pantocrator' (p. 166). During a performance at the Sand Pit, Alex pulls out an ex-army service revolver and opens fire upon the audience. Her prime targets are the rich ladies and over-fed gentlemen, the bourgeoisie who 'haven't suffered enough', but she also fires a shot at 'the Critic' who is seen rushing off to his 'Neptune's Cave'. The bullets are blanks, but they produce a heart attack, 'a crypto-corpse', injuries and terror. As the urban guerrilla exhausts her ammunition, officials seize the gun and rush her to the foyer, where Professor Falkenberg awaits her with the straitjacket: '"I hold out my arms for our embrace, and am soon snugly encased in the familiar canvas sleeves"' (p. 169). The old girl has had her fun, her 'creative' expression, and is returned again to the jacket and the asylum, which is the inevitable conclusion to her anguished display.

III

White urges us to sympathize with Alex Gray, to see her as a creative individual who is stifled by social convention and is forced to extreme measures in order to survive. In other words, he asks us to adopt Alex's delusive system as our own, to identify with her and look out upon the world through her crazed eyes. Predictably, most reviewers succumb to her inflated view of her own experience: 'Alex Gray is the most endearingly eccentric of all White's female characters. Whatever she tackles ... she plunges into it with the sort of recklessness and energy we can only admire ... The book is a celebration of the will to celebrate, to pummel out some necessary space for the wonderful and zany in a wretched and constricting world'.[24] Alex would be delighted with this assessment of her memoirs. We have mistaken her madness for genius, her violence for creativity, and see the world, along with terrorists, derros and revolutionaries, as an oppressive straitjacket inside which we have to 'pummel out' space for the psyche. In effect we have taken a pew next to her in the asylum, and become one of the 'Happy Few Who Know Better', hating the world, dreaming in our constriction of the pleasures of dereliction and abandonment.

The novel has involved us in a powerful conjuring trick: we are not merely invited to share a fictional world, but have been forced to adopt its values and beliefs. It is interesting to see how often and with what force we are drawn into Alex's psychopathic frame. In order for the novel to work, for the humour to be effective, for the confessional narrative to be enjoyed, the reader must develop a rapport with Alex and share her psychological view. It is part of Alex's literary scheme to make the reader see things her way, so that her pathology will be blurred by our empathetic connection. The audience will respond, she hopes, to her apparent honesty, intimacy and fleshy warmth. Many readers are convinced by her performance; or rather, their ground has been cleverly removed, and they cannot help but agree with her. White lacks the autonomy to achieve artistic detachment, or ironic presentation. He concedes to her self-dramatization and self-glorification. As Alex says herself, it is easy to make Patrick 'believe' in her (p. 23); 'I can get round Patrick' (p. 25). Just as the mother urged White to believe in previous novels that his devoured *pueri* were enlightened saints, so here she urges him to regard her own dereliction in inflated, religious terms.

At the end of *Memoirs* Patrick and Hilda undertake to follow the mother's movements through Greece, Italy and Egypt. For Patrick this excursion becomes a pilgrimage of faith and affirmation in the woman whose memoirs he is soon to edit. What was purely fantastic or invented in the mother's life now takes on substantial reality for him: he sees Cassiani the nun on a damp mountain track outside Ayia Ekaterni; he hears Alex's 'anarchic laughter' during a gun-fight in a public place. The world becomes alive with the mother's presence; she is a mythic figure who animates every scene with her hidden spirit. Her deification is made complete when Patrick and Hilda notice an uncanny resemblance between the remembered form of Alex on her death-bed and the masked, mummified body of Santa Chiara in a church in Assisi. Hilda recoils in fright, but Patrick stares in fascinated amazement, 're-living a personal relationship with a barely human figure in another setting, life slipping from the dark skull as we watched' (p. 189). He even imagines he sees a thread of blood trickling from the corner of Santa Chiara's mouth, just as they had observed blood pouring from Alex's mouth in the asylum. This sentimental, mawkish hallucination confirms for Patrick the saintly status of the woman in whose power he lies. One can almost hear the mother cackling in the background while Patrick has his private, sincere epiphany before a 'fake' mummy which had been 'manufactured by the nuns' to serve as a tourist attraction (p. 188). Just as the nuns would be 'Poor Clares indeed without such a source of revenue', so Alex Xenophon Demirjian Gray would be a poor, impoverished figure without her fabricated illusions of sainthood and higher status. But Patrick will ensure that her exalted image remains intact. What the mother wills, White enacts.

8 Conclusion: Problems of Unconscious Genius

The naive genius has to do everything through
Nature; he can do little through his freedom, and
will accomplish his idea only when Nature
works in him from inner necessity.

Schiller[1]

In this concluding chapter I would like to summarize the foregoing, as well as explore several theoretical issues which have been assumed or implied throughout the study. These include the role of the unconscious in the creative process; the power and autonomy of the archetypal complex; the idea of an inner 'genius' and the nature of its demands; and the problems that arise when psychic development is refused by the conscious personality. These kinds of issues are often felt to be 'too psychological' and remote from art. They are either left on the periphery of critical enquiry in the form of critical 'mysteries', or they are refused altogether and ignored. But in dealing with such a 'psychological' figure as White these issues become central to any real enquiry into the nature of his art and the functioning of his imagination.

The autonomy of the unconscious

'I don't believe artists know half the time what
they're creating. Oh yes, all the tralala, the
technique—that's another matter. But like
ordinary people who get out of bed, wash their
faces, comb their hair . . . they don't act, they're
instruments which are played on, or vessels
which are filled.'

Rhoda Courtney (*The Vivisector*, pp. 570–1)

White has often said that he experiences his art as a kind of alien will, a burden which is thrust upon him by an unknown source. Writing for White begins and ends in mystery. He does not consciously arrive at an idea or narrative line and proceed to write about it; rather is he seized by an impulse and driven to give it aesthetic form. Of course this is the Romantic notion of 'inspiration', of which Coleridge, Blake, Nietzsche and Schiller, among others, have spoken with such glowing and memorable descriptions.[2] To our secular minds the idea of the poet's Muse or *inspiratrice* seems archaic and superstitious. If I had been writing in an earlier time I would undoubtedly have chosen to speak of White's Muse, to argue that it was she who was responsible for his impressive output, that she whispered in his ear and coaxed him to literary creativity. Instead, I speak of 'archetypes' working in his unconscious, and of the psychic forces which direct and assail him from within. Some would argue that the idea of the autonomous archetype is just as mystical and bizarre as any classical notion of invisible creative beings. And perhaps they are right. The Jungian framework is simply a modern way of describing the irrational depths of human experience, a new way of mapping what remains essentially inexplicable. But in White's case the psychological approach to creativity is encouraged by the author himself, who makes use of the theory of the unconscious in numerous statements on the creative process:

My novels are largely works which rise up out of the unconscious; I draw very little on actual situations or people.[3]

The characters are not based on real people, they simply well up from the unconscious, and somehow a novel forms out of that.[4]

It is this invasive quality of his art which makes the creative act a tedious, even painful affair for White. The author feels as if he is being inundated by something beyond his immediate mental environment, that he is under attack from his unconscious. It is understandable, then, that White is frequently informing us how much he hates his artist's life and his subservience to imaginal forces.[5] White's situation is one where free will is at a minimum, and where his 'fate' approaches him in the form of the creative process, which compels him into its service.

White says that his novels 'usually begin with the characters; you have them floating about in your head and it may be years before they get together in a situation'.[6] These characters are the contents of his own unconscious, the separate figures (ego, *puer*, mother) which form the basis of his interior life and around which every novel is constructed. We have observed that a White novel is usually structured according to the life of the central character, and almost always ends with his or her death, or with some significant break in his or her career. White says that he is rarely certain how the protagonist's life will end once he has begun the novel.[7] 'I don't believe any of my novels has a 'plot'; they are just characters rubbing up against one another'.[8] There is no conscious pattern or plan as such, but an attitude of aesthetic receptivity to the personage, an allowing of the character to follow the course of his or her own destiny.

It is clear from this discussion that White's novels are not allegories, as several critics have suggested. Allegory presupposes that the author is in the supervisory or initiatory role, that he is using a character as a 'personification' of his own idea or point of view. White's characters are not animated concepts; they are powers, presences, figures of psychic life. Even where allegory is attempted—as in *Voss* or *Riders in the Chariot*—the characters themselves reject the imposed structures and follow their completely autonomous course in spite of the author's designs. It is always the will of the unconscious that is done, never that of the conscious mind.

Neither are White's works what his 'religious' critics would have them be: 'wisdom literature' (Veronica Brady), 'essays in mysticism' (Colin Roderick), 'twentieth-century theology' (Roger Sharr) or 'theosophical explorations' (Peter Beatson). None of these categories is appropriate because they too put White in the central position, viewing him as an instructor, as wise man or seer, instead of a writer who is grappling with something larger than himself, something he does not fully understand. During my own earlier phase as a 'religious' critic, White wrote to say that he was both annoyed and embarrassed at being referred to as 'a healer of our age'.[9] 'I am no intellectual or prophet. I simply put down what comes into my head ... If I am given occasional insights which may help others, that is fortunate, if also fortuitous.'[10] Too often this kind of remark is read as a self-effacing denial of greatness, or as a mark of truly religious humility, in which case the image of White as religious seer is reinstated and confirmed. Those who wish to set White up as a writer possessing unusual wisdom will find their conceptions shattered upon closer examination, as several academic projects have already shown.[11] White's achievement as a writer has virtually nothing to do with his 'mind', 'thought', or 'philosophy'. Interviewers are often astonished at the ordinariness of White's responses, and naively assume that the writer is shielding his genius from them. What they fail to grasp is that the visionary content is not born of his mind, but springs from deeper recesses from which White is himself peculiarly excluded. White is, in ways which we have still to explore, an unconscious genius.

Conventional literary criticism, as well as religious criticism, sees White as a 'mind' in control of his 'creation'. Leonie Kramer and William Walsh, for instance, see White offering ironic commentaries on the problems of modern life. *The Solid Mandala* becomes for Walsh 'White's Vision of Human Incompleteness',[12] just as *The Tree of Man* becomes for Kramer 'An Essay in Scepticism'.[13] White is misrepresented, not as a prophet this time, but as a modern intellectual; a writer with an earnest, humane vision; an erudite thinker; a professional, tidy writer, with the all-important ironic sensibility watching over his fictional creation. But this will not do. We cannot turn him into a George Eliot or a Henry James; there are too many incongruities, too much roughness. Like D. H. Lawrence, he is not essentially a detached intellectual but a passionate believer; he does not 'have ideas' but bears witness to inward realities. And like the author of *The Rainbow* he is never ironic in the face of immediate 'religious' experience: *The Tree of Man* is a sustained affirmation of the power and magnitude of archetypal forces. Unlike Lawrence, White does not have a credo, a plan, or a working model of the psyche. He is less definite than Lawrence claims to be. He gives the impression of a writer groping in the dark, occasionally reaching out for philosophical support, but often finding the wrong kind of support, the inappropriate frame for his archetypal vision.

White's novels are not commentaries on the human condition but *representations of the author's unconscious*. This of course is not to imply that the novels are entirely subjective. When White announces that 'All the characters in my books are myself'[14] this ought not suggest that we are dealing with a purely personal fiction. His novels are concerned with objective psychic reality as perceived and experienced by an individual writer. We respond to White's fiction because the forces at work in the author are also alive in us. The novels are about the interactions of archetypal persons, and as such they perform the function of mythology, revealing the life of the psychic underworld, showing us the pantheon of characters of which we are each composed. Throughout this work I have referred to 'White's mother–complex', but a more precise term would perhaps be 'White's experience of the mother–complex'. The complex itself is autonomous, a given mythic fact. All that truly belongs to White is the context within which that objective fact is encountered, or how the complex is handled. In the final analysis his signature upon the archetype[15] is his obsessive relation to the mother, his unwillingness to separate himself from her, and his refusal to co-operate with the internal developmental process. White's clinging to the unborn state is his peculiar pathology, his personal flaw. Thus in his work there is a mixture of neurosis and myth, a fusion of personal and archetypal contents.

Here I would like to reflect upon a couple of specific problems in order to throw more light on the role of the unconscious in White's fiction.

The work factor in the creative process

To say that the novels are autonomous products of the psyche is not to imply that they were written automatically, in a trance state or fit of inspiration. 'Autonomous' refers to the archetypal content, not to method, or to how the books were written. The unconscious insinuates itself throughout the course of the creative process, and the novelist does not have to write fast, get drunk, or perform mental tricks in order to encourage its presence. The unconscious is so strong in White's special case that his problem is how to defend himself against frequent inundation, rather than how to incite the unconscious into activity. The creation of White's fiction takes place in several phases. First there is the incubation period, which is largely subliminal, taking place below the threshold of consciousness. Then there is the gradual conception of the work; a few ideas and images become clear; perhaps there are a few notes. And then begins the execution of the work, which takes place in three stages: an initial draft, a second attempt (both in longhand), and a third typewritten manuscript containing revisions to the second draft.[16] White has said: 'My first draft of a novel is the work of intuition, and it is a chaos nobody but myself could resolve. Working it up after that—the oxywelding—is more a process of reason,[17] and elsewhere: 'When you first write the narrative it might be unconscious, but when you come to work it over you do it more consciously'.[18] White's art is a dialectical process between the primary impulses of the unconscious and the formative powers of the artist. An aesthetic awareness is brought to bear upon the given material in order to give it coherence and design. (I should point out that this aesthetic awareness is to be sharply differentiated from what I mean by consciousness. Consciousness is the function or activity which maintains the relation of psychic contents to the ego. Material from the psyche can be aesthetically shaped and ordered without it necessarily being related to the ego. This issue will be further explored in the following section.) The notion that aesthetic formalization and re-working destroys the pristine nature of the psychic material is a common misconception which is a legacy of Surrealism, Dadaism, and other popular movements which have attempted to enshrine the unconscious in literary and visual art. What cultists of the imagination fail to appreciate is that the unconscious itself seeks expression in the world of form, and that aesthetic attendance upon the material is complementary to the psychic process. As Graham Hough aptly suggests: 'It is a mistake to think that the formal elaboration of a work of art suppresses or smothers the unconscious; on the contrary, it is one of the very means by which the unconscious contents are enabled to appear'.[19] If the material remains in a crude shape—as a series of disconnected images and ramblings—then the psychic process itself could not be said to have reached fulfilment because it would be unappealing, and unassimilable by the cultural canon.

The crucial thing is that the substance of the work, the vision, is authentic. Throughout his various re-workings and versions White remains true to the archetypal content, even though his imposed interpretation may often obscure the psychic processes that he is delineating.

The use of historical models

At first glance it would appear that White's use of historical models contradicts the notion that his works are spontaneous products of the psyche. My own response to this problem is well expressed by Neumann.

> The fact that the poet uses extraneous material for the creative process ... does not disprove the inner associations presupposed by the archetypal interpretation, for the selection and modification of this material are decisive and typical of the psychic situation. Just as residues of the previous day are elaborated in dreams, so the existing literary and historical material is worked up by the 'editor' in the unconscious in order to assist the self-representation of the psyche.[20]

We are concerned with White's use of the figure of Leichhardt in *Voss*, and his employment of the known story of Eliza Fraser in

A Fringe of Leaves. In each case we have seen how the unconscious controlled the selection of material, and how it subordinated this material to its own ends. At the time of writing *Voss*, White's imagination was obsessed with the idea of ecstatic self-dissolution, of merging into the matrix, and his unconscious transformed the historical data according to this prevailing fantasy. So too at the time of writing *A Fringe of Leaves* the unconscious was primarily concerned with the interplay between civilized and primitive sides of the maternal character, and so the tale about Mrs Fraser's entry into the Aboriginal world and her return to white society provided an appealing model upon which the imagination could construct its symbolic tale. Neumann draws a parallel between the writer's use of historical matter and the dream's utilization of objective data from day-world experience. This is a constructive analogy, for in either case the primary, factual material is made secondary by its subordination to an imaginal process.

Thus even where White is at his most objective, telling stories of old Australia, the unconscious is silently at work, conditioning and directing the material at hand. As White himself phrases it, 'on a couple of occasions I have taken a historic character or moment as starting point'.[21] The historical material is taken by the imagination and reshaped according to its own needs and requirements.

Misreading the myth

The fact that White fails to grasp the meaning of his work is itself a testimony to the autonomy and authenticity of his vision. He creates the work at a formal level, but the content lives a life of its own, an archaic complex alive in the psychic depths. In novel after novel the same movement is established: the individual enters and is devoured by the mother–image, and the author misinterprets this as spiritual apotheosis and triumph. To mistake the *puer*/Mother myth for Christianity is to confuse the neurotic with the religious, and to overlook the destructive and retarding aspect of the incestuous drama. The son is consumed by the mother–world and he thinks he is returning into God; his individuality is snatched from him and he feels he is becoming at one with the cosmos. Basically, the ecstasy of dissolution (loss of ego and its limitations) is confused with the heightened feeling of religious integration and spiritual endeavour.

However, the distorted interpretation can itself be regarded as part of the archetypal syndrome. As the ego enters the matrix it is 'inflated' to super-human proportions, and this in turn leads to inflated readings of the experience. The son thinks he has reached the sublime, soared above the boundaries of good and evil, when he has in fact lost his humanity and regressed to a pre-egoic state. The mother archetype encourages this misreading. It is to her benefit that the son views her womb as the holy mandala, since this keeps him eternally bound to her service. The mother perpetuates her reign and increases her hold by making herself both erotically and spiritually attractive. The son must not only enjoy his incestuous experience, but must also regard it as a religious duty and spiritual responsibility. Each penetration of her womb is a new contact with the divine. If the son feels depleted, overcome by her savage maw, this is to be interpreted as the surrender of his will to God (as at the end of *Voss*). The entire enterprise is a mockery of Christianity, a high-camp, sado-masochistic ritual in religious dress.

The religious frame was not utilized until *The Tree of Man*, but throughout his early career White frequently applied inflated literary and cultural paradigms to his psychic experience. In *The Aunt's Story*, for instance, the Odysseus myth was used as a parallel to Theodora's psychic quest. There are numerous references to her 'odyssey', to Ithaca, the Gods, the blue waters of Greece, all of which create misleading expectations about the protagonist's inner journey. Homer's story is an heroic tale, about the descent of the individual into the underworld, the trials and sufferings encountered there, the divine guidance and intervention at crucial points, and the triumphant return of the individual to the human world. Theodora's story, on the other hand, is about disintegration and failure, a one-way descent into the maternal unconscious. She falls victim to the enchantment of the underworld, and, lacking divine guidance, mistakes this deathly abode for the goal of the spiritual journey. She is duped by the complex into seeing psychic disintegration as spiritual triumph.

Thereafter followed a series of misappropriated myths and symbols: *Hamlet* in *The Tree of Man*, Christian mysticism in *Voss*, Judaism and the Chariot of Redemption in *Riders in the Chariot*. With the support of these models White was able to convert defeat into triumph, and regression into spiritual enlightenment.

If the authorial commentary and design suggested that the spirit had triumphed, the narrative imagery made it clear that spirit had, in fact, been consumed by Nature. As the ego enters the matrix the narrative produces images of the destructive maw by which the ego is consumed: the 'jaws of roses', the overpowering force of Nature, the salivating mouths and gnashing teeth of women, the imprisoning houses of suburbia, the demonically destructive nature of inanimate objects, things, and matter. It was never recognized that these images were part of the central theme, and so they were forced to constitute a kind of shadow–myth, which was always projected outside the ego's world and carried by women, society, and external phenomena. The pathology of the myth was conveniently split off and invested in outside realities. Thus the ultimate cost of misreading was misogyny, hatred of society, and anti-materialism. The forces that overpowered and destroyed from within were thrust outside the 'spiritual' drama and carried by secondary fictional figures.

White's work is plagued with some dozens of 'teeth' mothers, each of whom is treated as an external enemy of the protagonist, as a diabolism of the outer world. The effect of this dissociation is that the matrix itself is never exposed as the demonic, gulping monster that it is, but appears innocent and mystical, while the 'mothers' carry the demonic element. The *puer* can go on imagining that the matrix is God, nirvana or mandala, while hating the scapegoat mothers. This serves the complex well, for it keeps eros within the incestuous frame, and other women (as well as the anima) are ruled out as potential rivals for the son's love.

It can be appreciated that the mother–complex is a formidable opponent to consciousness. It sets up values and preferences, tricks and illusions, and offers its own rewards; it is in every sense an insidious, self-perpetuating construct. White would have to exert tremendous discipline and be capable of genuine reflectiveness before the complex could be overcome. The problem is that the ego needed for self-observation is too busy shattering itself in the matrix. All energy is directed toward the complex, so that there is no self capable of standing apart from it. Jung argues that consciousness is built up and maintained by a 'process of differentiation'.[22] The ego must detach itself from the archetype in order to see where it is bound. White shows little desire to separate himself from the complex, to view his inner situation objectively or to gain control over it. Freud would say the 'separation anxiety' (the fear of aloneness) prevents the ego from detaching itself from the mother and inhibits the maturation of the personality. In Jungian terms the strength of the archetype overwhelms the ego's capacity for action and independence.

It must be admitted that White has not received much cultural or social support in the difficult task of inner exploration and self-analysis. Modern Western society knows very little about the inner world, and can offer precious little to the artist or man who finds himself caught up in it. White attempted to find solace by returning to the Church in the late 1940s and early 1950s, when he was struggling with his own inner experience of archetypal reality. But the Church has no knowledge of the unconscious and its mysteries, and has long since lost the ability to 'care for souls' in crisis. It cannot deal with an immediate experience of the numinous, and can only instruct the individual to have faith in the benevolent power of the One God. The Church does not believe in the many 'persons' of the psyche, and in its patriarchal-monotheistic stand simply represses the many faces—especially feminine archetypal faces—which assert themselves in the unconscious. If the Church were functioning adequately we would not require depth psychology, which, it is worth pointing out, is based largely upon feminine archetypes, maternal complexes and women's problems. As a man with a basically feminine unconscious, White found little nourishment in the Church and had to withdraw from it. Ironically, if the Church did anything at all, it was to exacerbate his misconceptions and play into the hands of the complex itself. The Church was telling him externally what the complex was saying inwardly: that a benevolent power works in the soul to lead the individual toward salvation. The complex borrowed the rhetoric of the Church to serve its own ends, and to lead White into psychological enslavement.

The literary establishment, also, could offer no support. It was naturally puzzled, confused, bewildered by his symbolic novels. At first it rejected them because they seemed un-Australian, elitist, mystical; later the establishment enshrined them because they attracted overseas interest and were being viewed as profound 'searchings' of the human psyche. European commentators adopted a eulogistic tone, as is evident in the opening line of Ingmar Björkstén's work: 'Purposefully and intrepidly Patrick White uses his pen to reveal ever deeper layers of human soul'.[23] But inflated acclaim is just as harmful as critical rejection. Criticism could not offer White any basis for understanding what he was doing and where he was going. If a critic was puzzled, he or she wrote to the author for the elusive clue, the hint, the lead, or interviewed him to ask for the 'influences' which could later be researched. It was felt that he was an intellectual who must have the answers. White's reticence and evasiveness were misread as modesty, or his refusal to be interviewed was misconstrued as arrogance, or as the quaint shyness of a 'recluse'. Priests and nuns interested in literature extolled his 'Christian' novels; Jungian critics celebrated his 'mandalas' and his 'vision of wholeness'.[24] Only in recent years have critics begun to suspect that the 'wholeness' is illusory, the 'unity' forced, or the 'Christianity' spurious.[25] But it is now too late for outside critical or intellectual correctives to have any influence on White's career.

The crucial time for intellectual assistance was during the 1960s, when White was actively searching for direction. He found Jung, Buddhism, Kabbalah, but of course all this was too vague and remote, too removed from his particular situation. He read Jung's mature work, *Psychology and Alchemy*, which concerns itself with mandalas and integration—not the kind of study that would help extricate him from a primary complex. Freud's work on incest and desire, Jung's early work on the *puer* and the mother–complex, might have been of use, but even here such writings might have been misapplied or abused. For intellectual knowledge of the problem is not enough; there has to be *emotional realization*, an inner, felt experience. Even psychotherapy would not necessarily have brought the desired change. There would have to be a thorough transformation within White himself. And this change, or revolt, had to come from the imagination itself, from within the fictional world.

The call for consciousness

> The unconscious united with awareness
> constitutes the poetic artist.
>
> Schiller[26]

In *The Solid Mandala* a new spirit and direction arises in White's work. White's undeveloped genius assumes personified form in the figure of Arthur Brown, who rejects the Christian frame and who urges the ego to *see* exactly what is taking place in the deep unconscious. '"All this Christ stuff . . . doesn't seem to work. But we have each other"' Arthur informs his twin (p. 200). Arthur's task is to destroy the ego's false intellectualism, and to bring it down to psychic reality. Arthur attempts to show Waldo the regressive bind or knot at the centre of his psyche, and to help him untie it. It would seem that a creative part of White's psyche is tired of the relentless bondage and infantilism, and longs to enter a new mode of existence. Moreover, if the deluded ego has its way, and its dream of dissolution is concretely realized, the entire psychic structure will be distroyed. There is a life-instinct in the psyche, a forward-striving impulse that urges growth and development, and which sometimes emerges in critical situations to attempt to alter a life which is headed for disaster. In dreams and fairytales, for instance, a 'helpful' figure sometimes emerges when the ego is lost, desolate, or at the brink of ruin. In Dante, being lost 'in a dark wood' is itself the precondition for salvation, which eventually manifests in the form of the anima—guide. Arthur Brown, however, is not just a magical figure come to help an ego which has lost its way. He is part of White's psyche, a living component of a threatened psychic structure. He is desperate to help Waldo, because unless he succeeds in educating the ego his own life will be lost. It is Arthur's plight which gives the novel a sense of urgency.

In urging Waldo to enter the matrix and to untie the knot, Arthur is calling for a new style of masculinity in White's fiction. In the past the masculine ego has either merged nihilistically with the matrix (Voss, Parker) or it has violently opposed and resisted it (Bonner, the huddlers). Neither response allows for a creative relationship between masculine and feminine, conscious and unconscious. What is needed is a masculinity which is capable of entering consciously into the maternal world, of seeing what lies there and of guarding against the dangers of annihilation. In reality, these dangers come from the ego itself, from its inertia, its infantile lethargy, its desire to be dissolved in the maternal embrace. The dragon to be slain by the hero before he wins the boon is simply himself, or his attachment to the source. Arthur, however, does not employ the harsh rhetoric of the hero myth: he does not ask Waldo to slay or kill the mother but simply to untie the knot. Untying is not a plundering or a subduing requiring the force of a Saint George. It is simply a loosening of the regressive bind, a freeing up of the attachment so that life can go on. Untying is a gentle act, something in keeping with White's own sensitive nature. And it does not imply any bruising or damage to the feminine unconscious, as do the classic heroic images of cutting, slaying or wounding. Many artistic men rightly refuse the crudely heroic models of masculinity, but where separation from the mother is required for development, the unconscious suggests more delicate ways of achieving the differentiation. White can hardly afford to damage or violate the maternal unconscious because it is the source of his creativity; he must liberate himself without machismo or heroics.

The task of untying the knot requires, first of all, that the ego should know and see the components of the entanglement. This is where Arthur struggles for expression, because the psychic contents are intangible and can only be known indirectly through symbol and image. The knot at the centre of the glass marble is an appropriate and carefully chosen symbol, but of course it means nothing to Waldo; it is dismissed as childish nonsense. Arthur's other symbols and preoccupations have a decidedly feminine-maternal character: Mrs Poulter, the plastic doll, the 'tragedy' of the cow and the still-born calf, the mother's ballroom dress, the poem celebrating the blood cycle of the feminine. Arthur keeps returning to these images again and again, attempting to make Waldo see, to cause him to reflect upon the urgent psychic realities. But although Waldo 'sees' these things he does not comprehend them in the way that Arthur intends. Hence the more insistent Arthur becomes in his revelation of symbolic realities, the more exhausted and irritated Waldo is in response.

This problem is by no means peculiar to Waldo, but is discovered in every White text and in every White character. Always and everywhere characters are confronted with crucial symbolic images which are never integrated in a meaningful way. Whether we refer to the image of the trochilus inside the crocodile's mouth, the dead man suspended upside down in a tree, or to the countless appearances of 'teeth' mothers, the symbolic products of the psyche are never consciously understood by the characters. They either regard these images as purely external and social, or they stare at them helplessly, with uncomprehending fascination. '"You do not know me"' says the terrible Mrs Jolley to Miss Hare, '"any more than you don't know nothing at all"' (*Riders in the Chariot*, p. 54). All the signs are present, all the material necessary for self-realization is on display, but the characters do not learn from their experience. As I have said elsewhere, the greatest tragedy of all in White's fiction is not that the ego is devoured, but that the imagination produces guiding and therapeutic imagery which is unacknowledged by the conscious personality.

The mirror is a classic symbol of consciousness and self-awareness. The mirror initiates introspection and allows for an experience of the self as 'other'. It is a recurring symbol in White; his characters are always seeing themselves reflected in mirrors, glass doors, polished surfaces. We could say that life keeps forcing them *into reflection*, but the symbolic meaning of this is ignored, and all too often the mirror becomes a mode of narcissism and aesthetic self-absorption. Waldo discovers his other self in the mirror as a schoolboy, and this self resembles Arthur, his *doppelgänger*, who simultaneously comes bounding out to meet him (p. 33). Waldo will allow aesthetic self-absorption in the mirror, but fails to see that reflection of this nature produces Arthur, whom he despises. Similarly, at the climax of the transvestite scene Waldo sees his mother–personality reflected in the mirror, but he enjoys this merely for its external form, for the high-camp glamour of the slatted fan and the festive satin dress, which is itself studded with tiny reflective beads. He is aesthetically involved in the mother–personality, attached to it, 'possessed' (p. 193) by it, but is not capable of reflecting upon it. Just prior to Waldo's fatal seizure Arthur holds up the satin mirrored dress 'so that Waldo might see his reflexion in it' (p. 212).[27] Arthur is calling for a conscious response to what is seen.

White's fiction has been governed by a kind of empty aestheticism, a delight in images for their own sake. Arthur is attempting to coax White into a new sense of artistic responsibility and moral awareness. It is not enough, ultimately, for an artist to blindly mine the imagination for its aesthetic resources and to refuse to become aware of what he is doing. Every activation of the unconscious requires, of necessity, a correlative act on the part of a responsive, moral consciousness.[28] Arthur Brown personifies the indwelling genius which has performed for White, has helped him establish a genuinely mythic literature in a new country, has been responsible for his rise to local and international acclaim. Now the genius asks for something in return. It asks to be understood and befriended. It asks to be allowed to grow up and to shrug off the burden of its puerility. By remaining stuck in the *puer*/Mother myth White retards his own genius, which is why Arthur emerges as a slightly 'retarded' figure. Arthur's handicap, however, is not physiological but metaphorical. He is the infantile shadow–brother who would become the bearer of the luminous mandala if the ego would attend his needs. He is the handicapped genius who must be 'kissed' into life.

It is difficult to say what kind of literature White would have written if he had co-operated with the developmental process. Perhaps it is foolish to speculate; but the keenness of Arthur's desire prompts us to speculation. Undoubtedly we would have seen a more positive literature, a literature where the human being is not devoured but transformed by his encounter with the inner world. We would have found a literature where the masculine holds its own against the feminine, thus bringing a truly androgynous vision into reality. White would have moved beyond the morbid stage of adolescent death–romanticism to a mature romanticism which offered hope to the individual and to consciousness. The negative, devouring uroboros would have been replaced by the mandala, a transformation which is already suggested in the ambiguous, fluid symbolism of Arthur's glass marble. The mandala would in turn abolish the destructive quest for eternity outside time and facilitate the discovery of eternity through time. Mystical endeavour would then not work in opposition to society, but would enrich and enliven it, connecting the social world with the living world of archetypal forces. This movement from nihilistic to transformative, Blakean mysticism was being offered by Arthur in his gift of the knotted mandala.

White was not equal to the demands of his genius. Arthur was urging him to consciousness, but White has always sought obliteration in the unconscious. We could say that the claims of his genius are defeated by the claims of the mother–complex. Waldo refuses to co-operate with Arthur's mandalic vision and in the end prefers dissolution in the matrix to Arthur's offer of new life. The images which Arthur places before him do not inspire him to awareness, but have the reverse effect of making him long for disintegration. As Arthur struggles to bring the mother–complex into view, Waldo's only desire is to surrender to it. He becomes more pathetic and self-destructive, enacting a fatal incest scene with Arthur in his mother's bed, and destroying his creative work in a ritual act of self-annihilation. As Arthur holds up the mirrored dress Waldo suffers a paroxysm and dies, preferring to wed the mother in death rather than separate from her in life. There is something final about this process of disintegration. Although every novel has portrayed a *puer* figure courting and finally achieving disintegration, this time it is not merely a literary anticipation of something longed for but an actual psychic event. There is a choice between consciousness and death, and Waldo chooses death. By so doing White's egoic self suffers an irreversible collapse, but it is a collapse of its own choosing.

With Waldo's death, Arthur's dream of wholeness is shattered. Arthur himself collapses into the unconscious and is overwhelmed by infantilism, darkness and despair. As a personification of archetypal genius, Arthur cannot die; he suffers a kind of psychological death and follows Waldo into the depths of the maternal world. He can no longer serve the masculine psyche so he becomes, as it were involuntarily, a creative force for the mother–personality. As the ruler of White's lower world, the Mother can exploit the fallen genius and make him serve *her* individuation. Mrs Poulter becomes a towering figure at the end, and moves rapidly along the road to self-realization. Unlike Waldo, who could not see beyond Arthur's infantile appearance and who denied him his divine role, Mrs Poulter is quick to recognize his spiritual significance: '"This man would be my saint ... if we could still believe in saints ... I believe in this man"' (p. 314). And where Waldo failed to recognize his own reflection in the glass, Mrs Poulter is able to see 'their two faces becoming one, at the centre of that glass eye' (p. 312). Mrs Poulter is full of joyful anticipation of the future, and boasts at the end, '"We've life to live yet"'. She is understandably optimistic, because the present windfall makes possible the successful careers of Elizabeth Hunter, Flora Manhood, Ellen Roxburgh, and numerous other female figures who embark on positive journeys of self-discovery. If individuation could not go on in the light of consciousness, it takes place in the unconscious, in spite of the ego–personality which rejects it.

The collapse of symbolization

With the disintegration of ego–consciousness into the matriarchal field, White's novels become simultaneously more mythic and less symbolic. The novels become more mythic to the extent that the Mother now takes the upper hand and carries out her archetypal quest throughout the works of the 1970s and 1980s. Yet the novels become poorer in symbolic content because the symbolization process has been aborted by the dissolution of consciousness. This point is crucial and must now be explored in greater depth.

In a sense symbolization and individuation go hand in hand, or are two ways of talking about the same thing. Symbolization is the process whereby the contents of the inner world acquire symbolic form, or become represented as archetypal images. The *puer*-type male, the subject of our present work, feels himself connected to an eternal mythic image, and his desire to unite with the mother is enacted upon a symbolic plane, through mystical ritual and through communion with Nature. He is freed from his personal fixation, his desire for the 'real' mother, and now participates in an archetypal mystery: son becomes *puer*, and mother Eternal Nature. In this way the blind, instinctual impulse is transformed and the psychic energy is allowed to flow into other channels. But when individuation is terminated by the ego's collapse into the unconscious, the symbolic drama comes to an end. The longing for the Mother is still apparent, but everything is now literalized. When this occurs the sacred ritual turns into an orgy of sex, worship becomes fornication, sanctity becomes sodomy.[29] The symbols of the Mother and the matrix no longer appear, or the psyche has lost its capacity to transmute biological impulses into symbolic patterns of experience.

Until *The Solid Mandala* White had managed to replace the personal fixation—so apparent in the early life of Elyot Standish —with symbolic ritual, to have his characters engage with symbols of the Mother. In Theodora's story this became a longing for the mythic world of Abyssinia and the lost Meroë; in Parker's a desire to merge with elemental Nature; in Voss's an obsession to unite with the mystical Goddess-figure. The *pueri* all longed for mystic anonymity, for the death–ecstasy of maternal containment. After Arthur's and Waldo's collapse, everything is acted out at a profane level. Duffield finds satisfaction only in fornication and orgasm ('O God he loved his Katherine Volkov gliding together through never smoother water', *The Vivisector*, p. 481), and Basil Hunter involves himself in constant incestuous activities with his sister Dorothy and his mother's acolytes. By the time of *The Twyborn Affair* the entire *puer*/Mother mythologem has contracted to a family romance between Eddie and Eadie.

The dissolution of consciousness leads to a dissolution of symbolic forms, for without consciousness the inner life cannot be represented at an abstract level, but can only express itself through bodily and biological processes. What properly belongs to the psyche falls into the lower world and becomes a burden of the flesh, for it can no longer be upheld in the subtle realm. White's career ends where it began, in the world of the personal mother–complex, where the archetypal image is still wholly subsumed by its human carrier. His career can be viewed as an experiment in symbolization, an experiment which failed because White refused to co-operate with the developmental process. There is a frustration of archetypal intent, and as a result of this White's cultural development is reversed and collapsed.

The surviving mythic theme—the mother's search for herself—

is burdened with literalisms of all kinds. Her quest is for the most part carried out at the external, physical level. Her desire to protect her animal nature becomes a literal concern for endangered animals (Alfreda Courtney). Her exploration of instinctual nature is carried out in orgiastic sexuality (Hero Pavloussi, Nance Lightfoot), and her longing to unite with her own feminine eros becomes a lesbian attraction for other women (Olivia Davenport, Eadie Twyborn). Descent into the psychic underworld becomes a trip to Van Diemen's Land (Ellen Roxburgh), or a repetitive journey down a stony, rutted road in a primitive setting (Joanie Golson). And the mother's desire to resume her sophisticated persona becomes a return journey to London or Athens (Mrs Roxburgh, Mrs Pavloussi). Everything takes place through external, literal phenomena. Somehow the mother too is without psyche, without access to the internal realm which can only be revealed in symbols and through symbolic exploration.

In *Memoirs of Many in One* this loss of interiority has become so acute that Alex Gray is reduced to a figure of buffoonery and farce. Literalism is not merely an obstacle in her course of self-discovery, but a disease which makes self-discovery impossible. Her life is a psychopathic parody of individuation, in the sense that her literal enactments of psychic impulses lead to criminality, madness and death. The impulse to individuate is present, but the means to accomplish it is not. We could say that the genius of individuation (Arthur) still inspires her, but that she lacks the substance and depth to realize its promptings. Thus, both son and mother suffer from the same disease, the same degeneration and shrunkenness which results when the symbolic dimension is lost.

The writing itself in the later phase becomes flat, non-evocative and two-dimensional. The prose in, say, *The Vivisector* or *The Twyborn Affair* lacks that quality of inwardness and luminosity which was evident in *The Aunt's Story* and other major works. In Theodora's world every event was also a psychic experience, it pointed beyond itself to other realms of significance, but in Eddie Twyborn's world events are presented merely as events, as external happenings.

This shift in literary style is not, as some have argued, the result of White's move from modernism to post-modernism.[30] Nor is it the result of White's decision to come out of the closet and champion gay ideology.[31] Explanations involving 'post-modernism' and 'gayness' may provide us with intellectual solutions, but ultimately they are facile and deceptive. Just as early criticism was blind to the rich vein of pathology in White's so-called 'religious' novels, so recent criticism ignores the pathological element in the 'gay' novels. Some critics believe that White has had his fill of religion and is now keen to celebrate the surface of life. These commentators find the blighted *Memoirs* 'a great comic novel',[32] or an entertaining send-up of his early preoccupations. Others believe that the humanist element in White has triumphed, and that he has left behind the esoteric world of Chariots and Mandalas. One critic argues that White is a modern Prospero, renouncing his magic in late career to affirm life in the ordinary world.[33] Still others maintain that he has no need of symbols—dubbed 'modernist trappings'—now that his repressed desires are exposed for all to see.[34] These readings ignore the pathological character of White's final phase. They misread involuntary processes for willed achievements, and impose optimistic explanations upon tragedy and disaster. The later fiction is non-symbolic because White is no longer capable of symbolic expression, and no amount of critical rationalization can disguise the fact of his artistic disintegration.

The absent father

> When the father is absent, we fall more readily
> into the arms of the mother. And indeed the
> father is missing; God is dead.
>
> James Hillman[35]

No writer of mythic or archetypal stature can be understood independently of his historical context. White's work is a mixture of personal and mythic contents, and at bottom the mythic element is conditioned not by personal experience but by the *Zeitgeist* or spirit of the time. It would take another book to discuss this aspect satisfactorily; all I can do here is to sketch in the broad outlines of the larger historical dimensions. It seems to me that White's vision has a bearing on two related though distinct areas of contemporary life: the psychic situation of Western culture in general, and the archetypal foundations of Australian culture in particular.

It hardly needs to be emphasized that we live in an age of dramatic change and cultural upheaval. The Judeo-Christian era, at least as we know it, is coming to an end. Nietzsche said that it died at the close of the last century, although Goethe and Schiller saw the end coming a good deal earlier. Ezra Pound, Yeats, D. H.

Lawrence have also given their own testimonials to the passing of an age, to the end of the dream of Reason and its triumph over the irrational. The patriarchal dominants of Western society are declining, and are rapidly being eclipsed by the long-suppressed contents of the deep unconscious. In symbolic terms, the Father is failing, losing his power, and the Mother Goddess is rising up as never before, claiming her rightful place with a colour of vengeance. We find the Mother's claims reflected in many aspects of contemporary life: in the new concern for Nature and ecology; in the revolution in sexuality and the new attitude toward the body and the instincts; in the liberation of women and the rediscovery of female power; in the concern for creativity and free expression; in the revival of occultism, magic and natural religion. The very fact that we look to the unconscious today, and distrust the traditional values of the super-ego and convention, is a turning toward the Mother and a loss of faith in the Old Father.

Much more could be said about this cultural transformation, but there are already a number of Jungian studies on the subject.[36] My specific aim here is to posit a broad cultural context in which White's psychological dilemmas can be placed and explored. He represents an age where the feminine is on the ascendant, where the old heroic ego is being defeated by the maternal unconscious. The feminist logo, the Venus sign with a clenched fist inside, is an apt expression of the force and anger with which the maternal archetype is asserting itself. The feminist movement is only one aspect of this psycho-cultural revolution, and an aspect which often confuses the situation by identifying the feminine with women and so reducing a massive archetypal phenomenon to a battle of the sexes. We should not confuse gender with archetype: masculine and feminine are principles, potentialities in every one of us. A liberation of the feminine affects the entire race, male and female alike.

Although the impact of the archetype on women may be essentially positive, in that their own archetypal foundations are invigorated and strengthened, on men the impact is more ambivalent. There is often an increase in sensitivity and creativity, an openness to the intuitive aspect of the psyche, but the archetype is so charged by its repression through centuries that the male ego can rarely cope with it. Everywhere today one witnesses the feminization of men, and modern jargon has it that such men are 'in touch with their animas'. This is a euphemism which disguises the fact that the so-called 'anima' (usually the mother) has actually swallowed and absorbed the masculine principle.

Many readers, for instance, see Eddie Twyborn as the New Man, the androgyne, representing a new, integrated mode of human sexuality. Nothing could be further from the truth, as my discussion of *The Twyborn Affair* demonstrates. It may be that, as we move inevitably toward androgyny, and toward a balance between masculine and feminine, the masculine will for a time be eclipsed by the feminine. This is perhaps an unavoidable crisis which will have to be endured. But let us not deceive ourselves into believing that the Eddie Twyborns and Boy Georges of this world are integrated and androgynous. It is apparent that we today hardly have any true models of androgyny, but when they do appear we will be able to differentiate between morbid possession by the feminine on the one hand, and the integration of the feminine with the masculine on the other.

To describe the modern, mother-bound male as suffering from a personal mother–complex is to miss the point of this universal and global problem. Most often such a complex is traced back and reduced to family problems, identity crises, and a domineering mother in early childhood. White's actual relationship with Ruth Withycombe White does not much concern me, although I am sure a Freudian critic could and probably will demonstrate that White's fiction is reducible to a boyhood neurosis. The point is that White's fiction reflects a universal situation and not merely a private disturbance. Hillman argues that the term 'mother–complex' is used and applied in a far too personal way. 'The neurosis [of *puer* and mother] is collective, affecting everyone with metaphysical affliction.' Although 'working out this affliction is individual', the neurosis itself is archetypal.[37] The same transpersonal perspective needs to be included in any consideration of the Absent Father of our time: 'The missing father is not your or my personal father. He is the absent father of our culture ... the dead God who offered a focus for spiritual things'.[38] Patrick White's is a Fatherless world, not because Victor (Dick) White failed to communicate successfully with his son, but because God is dead. The spiritual problems of the time are always potent forces in the life of an artist, no matter how nearly the personal family background approximates to the archetypal situation.

What is manifestly lacking in White's fictional world is the fathering spirit. There is nothing to oppose or counteract the tremendous absorptive power of the maternal unconscious. The father's task, archetypally, is to support the son in his quest and to help extricate him from the stifling bind to the maternal source. The father provides spirit and strength, either by reminding the son that he has descended into matter for a spiritual purpose, or by supplying him with tools of knowledge and reflection.[39] In the Christian story, God the Father takes on human form and endows the race of believers with the gift of spirit and the opportunity to live 'not by bread alone'. In various Hellenic myths the Father redeems the ego which is threatened with extinction: Daedalus shows Icarus how to fashion wings in order to escape the labyrinth and the devouring Minotaur; Athene, the masculine daughter of Zeus, lends Perseus the brazen shield and mirror of reflection, with which he is able to slay the Medusa and free the land from the petrifying aspect of the unconscious.

In psychological terms, support from the father could come in a number of ways: outwardly from tradition, ritual, work, philosophies and myths which provide direction, objectivity and self-knowledge; or inwardly from processes of *logos* and spirit, moments of clarity, ironic humour, insight that allow the ego to see through its delusions and entrapments. The father helps supply an objective, reasoned position against which one's introversion and self-absorbed obsessions can be examined and evaluated. The father himself can be destructive and tyrannical, as the myths of Saturn and Yahweh show, but to the mother-bound son he represents that sober glimpse of reality, law and discipline which is a much-needed antidote to pleasure-seeking and incestuous dissolution.

> *Lo, 'tis the Land of the grave of thy father!*
> Charles Harpur[40]

White's access to the archetypal father is impaired not only by the demise of the masculine in the Western world but also by the special conditions of Australian cultural psychology. On the Australian archetypal character and experience something has already been said.[41] I have attempted to show that in a young culture the Mother is the dominant archetype, and that ego–consciousness is generally held in thrall by and subordinate to the matriarchal world. In Australia matter triumphs over spirit, and Australians proudly, even aggressively, defend the claims of the body, the instincts, and material interests above those of the spirit. Australians are by and large caught up in an Oedipal cycle. We nurture and attend the maternal source, and distrust and 'knock' the Father. The Father in Australia is generally seen as a killjoy, as a negative *senex*, who stands between Australians and their world of idealized pleasure. The father–world of tradition, time, authority and spiritual discipline is refused. We debunk myths, denigrate religion, hit out at authorities, lop tall poppies, expose the folly in time-honoured traditions, and enjoy 'a good larf' at the Father's expense. We are a nation at war with the Father and the super-ego, which is often styled as British, stuffy and staid. In a sense it is our obligation and duty to rebel against the old British *senex*. We cannot live as if we are an extension of the British Isles; we must develop a unique, independent culture, and the first step in this task is refusing the Old World and killing off the Old Father.

America declared war on England and, as Americans are wont to do, enacted their fate at an external level. Their separation from the Old Father entered the realm of history and became an historical reality. Australians carry out a silent, internal war and harbour a world of suppressed violence, as is in keeping with our introverted character. The problem with internal war is that no one is sure when the fight is over. At least the Americans were able to slay the tyrannous *senex* and get on with the positive task of culture-building. Australians are never quite sure when they can stop hitting out at authority and *become* a new authority in their own right. This is a great danger: to be forever young and rebellious, a *puer aeternus* culture which never comes into its own. The secret of maturity lies in establishing a positive relationship with the father—not with the negative *senex*, necessarily, but with a new father, a viable father–world of spirit and wisdom. In a sense the *puer* must be allowed to grow up and become the new *senex*. The New Father grows slowly within and through the evolving culture, and, if he is authentic, will answer the needs and psychic requirements of the people. But if Australians persist in the knocking and debunking mode they will thwart this new development and miss the opportunity of growth.

As an expression of this fatherlessness Australian men find themselves insecure and anxious. There is no archetypal support for their masculinity and they feel existentially isolated. The enormity of the island continent, the towering dominance of Nature, and the actual distance from established civilization add to this sense of masculine insignificance. Hence in the 'Australian Tradition' mateship has been of central importance, the need of one male for another, the seeking of male companionship and support. The problem with this is that it often breeds a spurious masculinity, a masculinity intent on proving itself in displays of machismo and brute strength. Masculinity is often literalized but rarely internalized. On the outside a tough Aussie male, on the inside an insignificant *puer* longing to be mothered and drawn into the maternal matrix. Australian women often find themselves in the mothering role, for the *puer* can only know the feminine, and woman, as Mother. The wife is then burdened with the image of the negative mother, and the destroying matrix within the *puer* is experienced as an external enemy. There are numerous examples of this in Australian literature, especially in *The Fortunes of Richard Mahony*, where Mahony, restless *puer* and mystical wanderer, experiences his own wife as the *material-istic*, soul-destroying image of his own unconscious. In White the misogynist strain is rife, and woman is experienced as an enemy and threat to consciousness. There is a need for masculine rein-forcement, and this takes the form of homosexuality, Australia's most recent, genital version of mateship. Mates and gays both require masculine support; both are engaged in emotional flight from the feminine. For sensitive artists and others who are inwardly identified with the maternal matrix, the masculine side is least developed and so becomes the natural focus of erotic attention. In turning toward the aroused phallus the male sym-bolically attempts to arouse his own masculine spirit, to draw into himself the 'hot sperm seed of logos'[42] which is needed to combat the claims of the mother–complex. All too often, how-ever, as in the old-style mateship, this male mystery does not awaken the deeper levels of masculinity, but remains an empty ritual, a symptomatic enactment of the need for the fathering spirit.

In his late career White seems to have made the discovery that at the basis of his homosexuality is a desire to realize his love for his father, Victor White. The idea crops up time and again, in his later fiction and in the autobiography. 'Looking back', White writes of his brief affair with expatriate Australian artist Roy de Maistre, 'I was probably hoping unconsciously to consummate my love for a father with one who was everything Dick was not. My failure depressed me as much as my failure to communicate with my actual father'.[43] In similar vein, Eddie Twyborn realizes late in the day that his 'desire to devour the stuffy Judge—his man's smell! . . . more than half explains my relationship with Angelos' (*The Twyborn Affair*, p. 123). For me, White has realized a half-truth, for although he recognizes the need for the father and the fathering spirit he literalizes the desire in a way which obscures its symbolic basis. In late career, with the onset of psychological degeneration, every psychic impulse is given a sexual expression. The homosexual drive, so flaming with libidinal charge, is the archetypal desire of the *puer* to unite with the *senex*, that is, with his supreme masculine self. Just as Elyot Standish could not separate his desire to penetrate the matrix from the idea of returning to his mother's womb, so Eddie Twyborn fails to distinguish between his desire for the fathering spirit and the idea of toying with his father's genitals.

A memorable and poignant scene in *The Twyborn Affair* occurs when Eddie Twyborn, newly returned from Europe and his role as drag-queen Eudoxia Vatatzes, sits at dinner with his parents and embarrassedly reconstructs a childhood memory of *puer/senex* union.

'Do you remember—Father ... you took me with you when a court was sitting at—Bathurst I think it was. We shared an enormous iron bed with a honeycomb coverlet on it.'

'I don't remember,' the Judge said.

'I do.' Or thought you did. Oh yes, you *did*! 'I was so excited I lay awake all night listening to the noises in the pub yard. The moonlight, I remember, was as white as milk. It was hot. I pushed the bedspread off. It lay on the floor against the moonlight.' ...

Judge Twyborn was staring at his plate, at the soufflé he had massacred. ...

Eddie glanced at the father he had wanted to impress and comfort, who was looking as though he had a moron for a son, or worse, some kind of pervert: that honeycomb bedspread, the whole moonlit scene. (*The Twyborn Affair*, pp. 158–9)

This sensitive passage reveals both the son's literal longing, and the father's moral repulsion and conservatism. In a sense both parties are right: the son needs the *senex*, and yet the father is right to reject the son's erotic insinuations and fantasies. Eddie's desires are perverse because they cheapen the psyche's longing for symbolic connection with the *senex*. Impulses of the psyche are distorted when they are felt merely literally and physically. Nowhere is this more apparent than in Waldo's tragic relationship with Arthur, an essentially symbolic figure. Arthur attempts to give Waldo direction, meaning, insight—in fact, the fathering spirit—but Waldo thinks that Arthur merely wants to seduce him, to 'trap him ... in love-talk' (*The Solida Mandala*, p. 208). So Waldo 'gives in' to Arthur, goes to bed with him, but what is enacted there is not Arthur's transmission of the hot sperm seed of *logos* but merely Waldo's fantasy of incestuous union with the mother. There is a fundamental disjunction between ego and psyche which makes the psyche's impulses go unheard. White's tragic weakness is that he fails to respond imaginatively to the unconscious or to appreciate its symbolic language.

GLOSSARY OF PSYCHOLOGICAL TERMS

archetype The archetype is viewed as an inherent formative principle which is capable of releasing uniquely human patterns of imagery, thought, feeling, and behaviour. It is a content of the collective unconscious and is discovered in religions, myths, folk tales, visionary literature, and dreams. It is not used in the sense of any kind of recurring motif (Northrop Frye), but of a highly particularized psychic image. The present work confines itself mainly to the mother archetype, the structural foundation of White's art.

assimilation The absorption of one psychic content to another, usually the assimilation of the weaker element to the greater archetypal field.

castration Used in a symbolic sense to refer to the dismemberment of the ego by the mother archetype. I use the term whenever I am emphasizing the impotence and exhaustion which the ego is made to suffer in the incestuous state.

complex An emotionally charged unconscious entity composed of a number of associated ideas grouped around an archetypal image. It can interfere with the intentions of the will and possesses remarkable power and autonomy.

consciousness The relatedness of psychic contents to the ego and the function which maintains the relation of inner contents with the ego. It is not identical with intellect, mind or reason, but constitutes a kind of emotional knowing. *Conscious* derives from *con* or *cum*, meaning 'with' or 'together', and *scire*, 'to know' or 'to see'. Consciousness is 'knowing with' or 'seeing with' an 'other'. This is the function missing in White, because of the dissociation between ego and psyche.

ego Not merely the rational mind or intellect, but the conscious self and centre of one's field of awareness.

incest Used in a symbolic sense to refer to the urge of the ego to get back to the source, matrix and mother–image. It refers to the libido's natural tendency toward infantile situations, inertia and self-dissolution. It is closely related to Freud's death–instinct, when permanent incest is the goal of desire.

individuation The development of the individual as a being differentiated from the unconscious and its archetypes, and from society and its collective forms. After the collapse of the ego in Chapter Five, 'individuation' comes to mean the self-development of the archetype itself, its search for a wholeness which the conscious ego refused.

inflation The puffing up of the personality to god-like proportions. It often results when the ego identifies with an archetypal image.

matrix Latin, 'womb' or 'source'. It is used to denote the maternal aspect of the unconscious as the source and origin of life.

mother Used to denote an archetypal personality; rarely refers to a human, personal figure. The Mother is a mythic figure in the art and religion of virtually all races. She personifies the world of Nature, instinct, matter and the deep unconscious. White's *pueri* are all in search of this mythic figure and her realm of symbols.

mythologem (from C. Kerenyi) Denotes a living, evolving body of myth governed by a specific archetype.

participation mystique (from Lévy-Bruhl) Derived from anthropological research on the primitive mind and describes the state of at-one-ment between man and the external world. Adopted by Jung to refer to states of unconscious identity with any thing, object or person.

projection Signifies the transference of a subjective, unconscious process or content upon an object. Projections contaminate the outer world with psychic contents, and change the face of the world into an image of the subject's own unconscious. When this becomes extreme (as in Theodora Goodman's case) solipsism results.

puer aeternus Latin, 'eternal youth'. Refers to an ego held in a childlike, or childish, stage of development. This often results when the Mother archetype is strongly constellated, thus drawing the ego back into infantilism rather than allowing it to move forward into life.

unconscious A boundary-concept, which covers all those psychic contents or processes which are not controlled by the ego. The term is used both as a noun (in the sense of a psychic location or place) and as an adjective (as a condition or quality of a content).

uroboros Greek, 'tail-biting snake'. The symbol of the original unity of the universe, a unity before man and the advent of consciousness. Represented in almost all mythologies, and especially found in the alchemical sciences, where it is identified with the primordial dragon. It is the circle-as-beginning, to be contrasted to the mandala, which signifies the 'recovered' unity which includes humanity, time and creation. Identification with the uroboros automatically leads one out of time and space into an inchoate, eternal dream-state.

NOTES AND REFERENCES

page xii
1. Patrick White, *The Vivisector*, Penguin, Harmondsworth, 1973, p. 100.
2. James Hillman, 'The Great Mother, her Son, her Hero, and the Puer', in Patricia Berry (ed.), *Fathers and Mothers*, pp. 77–8.

Introduction

1. Patrick White, *The Solid Mandala*, Penguin, Harmondsworth, 1969, p. 145.
2. See Xavier Pons, *Out of Eden: Henry Lawson's Life and Works—A Psychoanalytic View*, Angus & Robertson, Sydney, 1984.
3. Patrick White, *Happy Valley*, Harrap, London, 1939, p. 28. A. D. Hope employs a similar image of Australian white society as a sore, or scab, in his poem 'Australia'.
4. The notion of Australia as a cursed landscape for its white inhabitants is evident in much Australian literature. It can be found, for instance, in early colonial poetry, in Henry Handel Richardson's 'Proem' to *Australia Felix*, in D. H. Lawrence's *Kangaroo*, and in Judith Wright's poetry.
5. Patrick White, *Memoirs of Many in One*, Jonathan Cape, London, 1986. Presumably, this is White's humorous quip in response to my own findings, put to him in personal correspondence and published in 'Patrick White: The Great Mother and Her Son', *The Journal of Analytical Psychology* 28, 2, 1983, pp. 165–83.
6. A. S. Byatt, 'The disreputable other half', *Times Literary Supplement*, 4 April 1986, p. 357.
7. A. P. Riemer, 'Visions of the Mandala in *The Tree of Man*', in G. A. Wilkes (ed.). *Ten Essays on Patrick White*, p. 116.
8. See the Conclusion, where the question of the autonomy of White's writing is explored in depth.
9. The term 'imaginal' is widely used in post-Jungian psychological discourse. It is employed here as an adjective in preference to terms

like 'imaginative' or 'imaginary', and occasionally as a noun synonymous with 'the contents of the psyche'.

10 These terms are borrowed from A. A. Phillips in his seminal essay,
'Patrick White and the Algebraic Symbol', *Meanjin* 24, 4, 1965,
pp. 455–61.

Chapter 1   The Incestuous Return

1 D. H. Lawrence, *Sons and Lovers*, Penguin, Harmondsworth, 1948,
p. 420.

2 Obviously, the psycho-dynamic model I am constructing here and
elsewhere relates to men, and in particular to the classic son/mother
pattern of relationship. The descent to the unconscious can be imaged
as a return to the womb for women, but often it is represented as an
incestuous embrace with the father, in which case we would speak
not of maternal but of paternal depths. Cf. E. Neumann, 'The
Separation of the World Parents', in *The Origins and History of
Consciousness*.

3 Matrix (Latin, 'womb') is used throughout this study as a term for the
womb-like structure of the deep unconscious. It also connotes Nature
insofar as it contains, surrounds and underlies human consciousness.
'Matrix' is used synonymously with 'source', 'archetypal source', and
'maternal source'.

4 This theme is explored in E. Neumann's essay 'Leonardo and the
Mother Archetype', in *Art and the Creative Unconscious*.

5 In my view the Freudian (reductive, literal, sexual) reading of the
incest urge encapsulates a mishandling of what is essentially a complex psycho-symbolic problem. It was on this crucial issue that Jung
based his divergence from the Freudian school in his pioneer work,
Symbols of Transformation.

6 Patrick White, *The Living and the Dead*, Penguin, Harmondsworth,
1967. All references are to this edition.

7 For background material on the way in which the son converts the
personal mother into a devouring creature of myth, see Jung,
'Psychological Aspects of the Mother Archetype', in *Four Archetypes*.

8 The 'Mother' is capitalized here in order to differentiate the archetype
from the personal figure. Whenever the word is capitalized, or
prefixed with Great, or Devouring, it should be apparent that a
mythic image is being evoked, not a human being.

9 The incestuous impulse is transformed between *The Aunt's Story*
(1948) and *The Solid Mandala* (1966), where it appears in a higher,
symbolic form, but it degenerates again into a literal, carnal desire in
the later novels.

10 Regarding the symbolism of the bay, cf. Jung, *Symbols*, pp. 271 ff.

[11] The matriarchal context of these and other symbols is discussed in E. Neumann, *The Great Mother*.

[12] The differentiation between uroboros and mandala is central to this study; the differences are discussed in Neumann, 'The Uroboros', *Origins*, pp. 5–28.

[13] Nihilistic source mysticism, which is the form of mystical experience discovered in White, is discussed at length (and contrasted with mature religious mysticism) in E. Neumann's essay, 'Mystical Man', in *Spring 1961* (Zurich; Dallas), pp. 9–49.

[14] Those critics who examine White's mystical aspect (Patricia Morley, Peter Beatson, Thelma Herring, among others) frequently overestimate his work and compare it to the mature mysticism of T. S. Eliot, Blake and Yeats. White's mysticism does not belong in this class, but should be placed in a context of adolescent mystical writing, such as that found in Herman Hesse, late Lawrence and Saint-Exupéry.

[15] The Latin term *puer aeternus* (the eternal boy) is employed in analytical depth psychology to designate the Mother's son, the man who remains eternally childlike (and childish) because of his incestuous fixation upon the mother, or, as in White's major works, upon *symbols* of the mother. See Marie-Louise von Franz, *Puer Aeternus*, pp. 2–3.

[16] Jung, *Symbols of Transformation*, p. 258.

[17] There is a significant parallel between Elyot's experience and White's own career. Before he became a full-time writer White had adopted the pose of a scholar and felt himself becoming 'that most sterile of beings, a London intellectual' ('The Prodigal Son', *Australian Letters* 1, 3 (1958), p. 38). However, this ought not be viewed as an attack on London intellectuals, but merely as a subjective remark about White's own artificially 'intellectual' stand at the time. That is to say, White's own intellect is sterile because it is used as a defence against the unconscious and is therefore disconnected from the sources of creativity.

[18] Marie-Louise von Franz points out that the *puer*'s negative experience of women usually results in homosexuality, where women are avoided altogether, or in Don Juanism, where the *puer* exchanges one woman for another in an endless search for the ideal woman. Cf. von Franz, *Puer Aeternus*, p. 2. White's homosexuality is implied in this work, but it is not actually announced until later in his career.

[19] The defensive, militant attitude of the *puer* who cannot cope with emotions is discussed in J. Hillman, 'Feeling and the Mother-Complex', in von Franz and Hillman, *Lectures in Jung's Typology*.

[20] This motif of the incestuous brother-sister pair runs throughout White's work, and achieves its literal realization in the coupling of Dorothy and Basil Hunter in their mother's bed in *The Eye of the Storm*.

Chapter 2   The Undying Mother

1   Patrick White, *The Aunt's Story*, Penguin, Harmondsworth, 1963. All future references are to this edition.

2   The father's maternal significance may seem somewhat peculiar, but it is by no means incomprehensible. In a major work on feminine psychology Gerhard Adler writes: 'A possible result of a faulty relationship to the mother is that the father is expected to provide the positive maternal side. This leads to an unconscious expectation that the man will be the exclusively good "maternal" father to whom the woman can play the loving and protected daughter' (*The Living Symbol*, p. 115 n).

3   J. G. Frazer's *Adonis, Attis, Osiris* (*The Golden Bough*, Part IV, vol. 1) is my basic reference with regard to the Attis-Adonis mythologem. This myth, I will argue, is part of the unconscious structure of the narrative.

4   J. J. Bachofen, quoted in Neumann, *Origins*, p. 45.

5   White is himself a chronic asthmatic, which reflects, one could argue, something of his own personal suffocation by the archetype. Freud and the post-Freudians have written extensively on the relation of asthma to the mother-complex.

6   Mrs Goodman is purely archetypal in this novel and is not, strictly speaking, a human character at all. Her archetypal status is her strength, but also her limitation, since she does not possess human depth or complexity, and does not undergo development. She is pure destruction; a diabolism of Nature.

7   By implication Abyssinia is the imaginal *locus* of the dark maternal archetype. Strangely enough, there is even an historical connection between Abyssinia (Ethiopia) and the matriarchal world. Studies have shown that Abyssinia was a strictly matriarchal world, and that its ancient capital, Meroë, was ruled over by a dynasty of queens. It is doubtful that White was aware of this archetypal connection; he chose a country which had a certain natural appeal as a mother-symbol.

8   Frazer, 'The Day of Blood in the Attis Ritual', *Adonis, Attis, Osiris*, op. cit.

9   Shakespeare, 'Venus and Adonis', lines 1019–20. *The Complete Signet Classic Shakespeare*, ed. Sylvan Barnett, p. 1690.

10   It has been suggested to me that 'Abyssinia' could relate phonetically to 'abyss-in-ya'. I do not think it is an intended pun, but there is a curious phonetic connection. Certainly Abyssinia is the abys-mal world which consumes her Australian Meroë.

11   Marie-Louise von Franz, *Puer Aeternus*, p. 1. The archetypal background of homosexuality is interestingly explored in John Sanford, *The Invisible Partners*, p. 97 f.

12   Patrick White, *Flaws in the Glass*, p. 154.

¹³ Majorie Barnard refers to Theodora as a saint and mystic in 'Theodora Again', *Southerly* 20, 1, 1959. Since her article there have been innumerable references to Theodora's saintliness, especially by Patricia Morley and Peter Beatson. John Beston ('Love and Sex in a Staid Spinster', *Quadrant* 15, 5, 1971) provides a Freudian challenge to the religious readings of the novel.

¹⁴ The South Asian cultures imagined the teeth on the face, but the American Indian culture and the Roman culture (for instance) preferred to put the teeth in the vagina. Cf. Robert Bly, 'I Came Out of the Mother Naked', *Sleepers Joining Hands*.

¹⁵ P. M. F. Janet, quoted in Neumann, *Origins*, p. 385.

¹⁶ Blake, *Europe* (10), and the *Four Zoas*. One can compare the return to the uroboros with several situations perceived as false by Blake, and the achievement of wholeness within the mandala with Blake's idea of the true spiritual goal. I thank Mr Michael Tolley of the University of Adelaide for this comparison.

¹⁷ We can even detect the voice of old Mrs Goodman in this dream-utterance, particularly in the give-away phrase 'more seductive than aspirin'. Mrs Goodman frequently recommended aspirin to ease away the pain of living: '"Ah, where would we be without aspirin!"' (p. 123).

¹⁸ Nor is it registered by White's consciousness. The author has simply written this passage straight out of his imagination, without any reflection.

¹⁹ Says J. F. Burrows: 'An ugly little ring, but part of the flesh: Theodora has at last come to terms with her mother' ('"Jardin Exotique": The Central Phase of *The Aunt's Story*', in Wilkes (ed.), *Ten Essays on Patrick White*, p. 106]. I think Burrows mistakes pathological assimilation by the mother for happy resolution. Many critics have tried to find signs of development and progress in Theodora's career. They tend to impose a positivist-humanist frame upon what is in fact a dark, anti-humanist narrative.

²⁰ Burrows: 'Thanks to the anguished searchings of Part Two ... Mrs Goodman is no longer a force in Part Three' ('"Jardin Exotique"', op. cit., p. 93].

²¹ This can be compared with the (temporary) dissolution of demonism after the Moraitis concerto.

²² Jung, *Two Essays on Analytical Psychology*, p. 141.

²³ James Hillman, 'The Great Mother, her Son, her Hero, and the Puer', in Berry (ed.), *Fathers and Mothers*, p. 82.

²⁴ In my essay, 'Patrick White: The Great Mother and Her Son' (*The Journal of Analytical Psychology* 28, 2, 1983], I adopted the view that the inflated presentation was White's personal distortion. It seems to me now to derive from the archetype itself.

²⁵ Frazer, 'Attis as a God of Vegetation', *Adonis, Attis, Osiris*, op. cit.

[26] Morley, Beatson, Burrows, Björkstén, and several others, celebrate the 'mandalic' rose and come to the conclusion that Theodora triumphs at the end. Thelma Herring asserts that 'though she defers to those who ... take her into custody, Theodora wins the game for her soul' ('Odyssey of a Spinster: A Study of *The Aunt's Story*', in Wilkes (ed.), *Ten Essays*, op. cit., p. 12).

Chapter 3   *In the Lap of the Land*

[1] James Hillman, 'The Great Mother, her Son, her Hero, and the Puer', in Berry (ed.), *Fathers and Mothers*, pp. 88–9.

[2] Patrick White, 'The Prodigal Son', *Australian Letters* 1, 3, 1958, p. 38.

[3] ibid.

[4] White, of course, was born in London, but spent his early childhood in New South Wales.

[5] White, 'The Prodigal Son', pp. 38–9.

[6] For material on the relation between *mater* and *materia* see Neumann, *The Great Mother*, p. 49 f, and Patricia Berry, 'What's the Matter With Mother?' in *Echo's Subtle Body*.

[7] White, *The Tree of Man*, Penguin, Harmondsworth, 1961. All references are to this edition.

[8] White, in Thelma Herring and G. Wilkes, 'A Conversation with Patrick White', *Southerly* 33, 2 (1973), p. 137. The incident is retold in *Flaws in the Glass*, p. 144.

[9] White, in an interview with Craig McGregor in *In the Making* (1969), p. 218.

[10] Cf. E. Neumann, 'The Lady of the Plants', *The Great Mother*, pp. 243–4.

[11] Quoted in Jung, *Symbols of Transformation*, p. 425.

[12] J. G. Frazer, 'The Myth and Ritual of Adonis', *Adonis, Attis, Osiris*.

[13] There is a close connection here with the Hanged Man in the Tarot, a figure suspended upside down in a tree. For an excellent discussion of this figure and his bondage to the Earth Mother, cf. Sallie Nichols, *Jung and Tarot*, Samuel Weiser, Maine, 1980, pp. 215 ff.

[14] Cf. Jung, *Mysterium Coniunctionis*, p. 457 f.

[15] E. Neumann, 'The Central Symbolism of the Feminine', *The Great Mother*, p. 47.

[16] Cf. E. Neumann, 'The Psychic Development of the Feminine', *Amor and Psyche*, p. 57 f.

[17] It is interesting that this union takes place at the head of a fiery staircase. Elyot's mother, Mrs Standish, was often imaged as a 'glowing' beauty—or as 'burning' or 'molten'—at the head of the staircase at Ebury street (*LD* p. 130). Later in the story she would also call to her son at the head of these same stairs (p. 13). Theodora Goodman consummated her symbolical union with her mother at the

head of the staircase in the burning Hôtel du Midi. In White's psyche there seems to be a recurring pattern (based on childhood experience?) in which the *puer*'s erotic libido is aroused by a marvellous image of the mother in this elevated position. It may be that the metaphorical 'fire' or libidinal energy generated in this moment graduated from the literary metaphors of *The Living and the Dead* to the more intensely 'fiery' scenarios of Theodora Goodman and Stan Parker's Madeleine. The *puer* is aflame with passion, but the incestuous fire is fierce and all-consuming.

18 The depreciation of Madeleine is carried a step further at the end of the story, where she reappears as suburban housewife Mrs Fisher, close associate of Mrs Forsdyke (née Thelma Parker).

19 I cannot understand how R. F. Brissenden can claim that White's 'presentation of Amy Parker ... is one of love and sympathy' (*Patrick White*, p. 27).

20 Examples of this reading can be found in Patricia Morley, *The Mystery of Unity*, and Peter Beatson, *The Eye in the Mandala*.

21 These vastly different styles of unitary experience are contrasted as 'infantile mysticism' and 'mandala mysticism' in E. Neumann's 'Mystical Man', *Spring 1961*.

22 White's own phrase from 'The Prodigal Son', already quoted at the beginning of this chapter.

23 John Hetherington, in his biographical sketch, 'Life at Castle Hill', in *Forty-two Faces*, p. 141.

24 Leonie Kramer, 'The Tree of Man: An Essay in Scepticism', in W. S. Ramson (ed.), *The Australian Experience*, p. 278.

25 See those critics cited in note 20 above, and also Roger Sharr, 'Old Women, Nuns and Idiots: Transcendentalism in *The Tree of Man*', *St Mark's Review* 86 (1976).

26 Cf. A. P. Riemer, 'Visions of the Mandala in *The Tree of Man*', in Wilkes (ed.), *Ten Essays on Patrick White*.

27 Ted Hughes in the *Listener*, quoted by John Barnes, 'A Note on Patrick White's Novels', *The Literary Criterion* VI, 3, p. 93.

28 A phrase borrowed from James Hillman, 'The Great Mother, her Son, her Hero, and the Puer', op. cit., p. 88.

29 See White's comments on the title in Herring and Wilkes, 'A Conversation with Patrick White', *Southerly* 33, 2 (1973), p. 136.

30 Joseph Conrad, *Heart of Darkness* (1902), Penguin, Harmondsworth, 1966, p. 8.

31 Both phrases are from Patrick White, *The Tree of Man*, p. 14.

32 Cf. Kirpal Singh, 'The Nostalgia of Permanence: Stan Parker in Patrick White's *The Tree of Man*', *ACLALS Bulletin* 4, 1976, and 'The Fiend of Motion: Theodora Goodman in Patrick White's *The Aunt's Story*', *Quadrant* 19, 1975.

33 On the puer as wanderer, see Jung, *Symbols of Transformation*,

p. 205, and also Marie-Louise von Franz, *Puer Aeternus*, p. 2 f, and James Hillman, 'Pothos: The Nostalgia of the Puer Eternus' in *Loose Ends: Primary Papers in Archetypal Psychology*, pp. 49–62.

34 The notion that Voss is a Nietzschean Superman is pervasive,and can be found represented in such works as R. F. Brissenden, 'Patrick White', *Meanjin* 18, 1959, and A. M. McCulloch, *A Tragic Vision: The Novels of Patrick White*. Manfred Mackenzie provides a useful critique of Nietzschean elements in *Voss* in 'Patrick White's Later Novels: A Generic Reading', *Southern Review* I, 1965.

35 All references are to the 1960 Penguin edition of *Voss*.

36 The general critical reading is that *Voss* is an essay in the power of the human will. Classic examples of this approach are the 'Notes' provided in the Longman edition (1965) of *Voss*, and G. A. Wilkes' essay 'A Reading of Patrick White's *Voss*' in *Ten Essays on Patrick White*.

37 Marie-Louise von Franz, *Puer Aeternus*, p. 221.

38 A term borrowed from Erich Neumann in his study "The Group and the Great Individual", *Origins*, p. 425.

39 White has said that *Voss* was first conceived during the early days of the Blitz, and that it was 'influenced by the arch-megalomaniac of the day', 'The Prodigal Son', *Australian Letters* 1, 3 (April 1958), p. 39.

40 Palfreyman describes his sister in terms which suggest the spirit of the earth: 'My sister is particularly fond of woodland and hedgerow flowers ... She will venture out in the roughest weather ... to see her flowers, and will often return with ... a string of scarlet bryony to wear round her neck' (p. 262). This same nature-spirit is a devouring figure, with a 'horrifying mouth' (p. 262). Once she 'flew in a rage, and threw [Palfreyman] out of an upper window'.

41 There is an obvious autobiographical element here. White himself attempted to sever the connection with his mother through a similar geographical flight: '[My mother and I] were too much alike. That is why we couldn't spend more than a couple of hours in each other's company without fighting, and why I chose to live in another hemisphere' (P. White, in a letter to D. J. Tacey, 12 January 1981).

42 There is a wealth of material on the differences between anima and mother, but see for instance E. Neumann, 'The Two Characters of the Feminine', in *The Great Mother*, and also *Amor and Psyche: The Psychic Development of the Feminine*.

43 James McAuley, 'The Gothic Splendours: Patrick White's *Voss*', in Wilkes (ed.), *Ten Essays on Patrick White*, p. 44. Despite McAuley's lapse, his essay remains for me the best study of the novel. For other references to Laura as anima, see Barry Argyle, *Patrick White*, Peter Beatson, *The Eye in the Mandala*, and Judith Wright, *Preoccupations in Australian Poetry*, Oxford University Press, Melbourne, 1965. The general confusion is an illustration of the psychological maxim that 'a little Jung is worse than none at all'.

44 For differentiations between the animus and Ghostly Lover, see especially Esther Harding, 'The Ghostly Lover', in *The Way of All Women*, Harper & Row, New York, 1946, and Emma Jung, *Animus and Anima*, Spring Publications, Dallas, 1974.

45 One advantage of the psychological reading of *Voss* is that one does not have to be bothered by the problem of ESP, 'occult phenomena', and telepathy, which has troubled so many reviewers and critics. Voss's contact with Laura is an inward, archetypal experience, and if Laura engages in similar psychic experiences in Sydney the connecting link is synchronicity, not telepathy. When we internalize Laura as an archetype there is no longer any need to talk about occultism and magic.

46 For material on the split between love and sex which results from the incest bond, see Robert Stein, 'The Incest Wound', *Spring 1973*, pp. 133–41, and his book *Incest and Human Love*.

47 Ancient images of Kali, the Devourer, often represented the goddess in blood-red garments, or showed her huge tongue to be spotted with blood. Cf. Neumann, *The Great Mother*, p. 152 f.

48 Cf. Laura's remark: '"How important it is to understand the three stages. Of God into man. Man. And man returning into God"' (p. 386).

49 Following Laura's cue leads to all manner of religious and mystical irrelevances, as displayed in Peter Beatson's essay, 'The Tree Stages: Mysticism in Patrick White's *Voss*', *Southerly* 30, 2 (1970).

50 Judd joined the party as a 'service to the Colony' (p. 136), which is why he must eventually abandon it, for Voss is not motivated by such patriotic concerns.

51 See E. O. James, *The Cult of the Mother Goddess*.

52 J. G. Frazer, 'The Myth and Ritual of Attis', *Adonis, Attis, Osiris*.

53 In like manner, Voss's blood is imaged as a ritualistic offering to a dry, thirsty earth: 'His blood ran out upon the dry earth, which drank it up immediately' (p. 394).

54 The Gorgon's capacity to turn men to stone, to *petrify* human consciousness, is strangely suggested in the corresponding Sydney scene: 'Mrs Bonner was petrified, both by the words that she did not understand, and by the medusa-head that uttered them' (p. 386).

55 White, 'The Prodigal Son', op. cit., p. 39. R. F. Brissenden sees Parker as 'a representative of common humanity' (*Patrick White*, p. 25), and G. A. Wilkes emphasizes the 'ordinariness of Stan and Amy, and the commonplaceness of their lives' ('Patrick White's *The Tree of Man*', in *Ten Essays*, p. 28).

56 R. F. Brissenden, 'Patrick White', *Meanjin* 18, 4, 1959, p. 412.

57 See for instance the eulogistic 'Introduction' by H. P. Heseltine to the Longman edition of *Voss* (1965), a text designed for use in secondary schools.

58 Heseltine claims that Voss is 'a hero [who] marches confidently into

the future', and that he 'leads his composite band into the interior not for the sake of material rewards but to help create a national legend' (ibid., pp. 389–90).

59 James McAuley, 'The Gothic Splendours', op. cit., p. 40.

60 Two important dissenters from the (un)critical celebration of White's Australianness are A. D. Hope (see his 1956 review of *The Tree of Man*, reprinted in *Native Companions*, Angus & Robertson, Sydney, 1974, p. 76) and John Barnes ('A Note on Patrick White's Novels', *The Literary Criterion* VI, 3, p. 93).

61 Judith Wright, 'The Upside Down Hut', *Australian Letters* 3, 4 (June 1961), p. 34. Reprinted in John Barnes (ed.), *The Writer in Australia*, p. 335.

62 I am indebted to David Malouf for this idea, and for conversations with him on this subject during September–October 1984.

Chapter 4   The Tree of Unborn Souls

1 D. H. Lawrence, *Studies in Classic American Literature*, Penguin, Harmondsworth, 1948, p. 31.

2 Colin Roderick, '*Riders in the Chariot*: An Exposition', *Southerly* 22, 2 (1962), p. 62.

3 All references are to the Penguin (1964) edition of *Riders in the Chariot*.

4 This important point is borrowed in part from E. Neumann's essay 'Mystical Man', *Spring 1961*.

5 Susan Moore ('The Quest for Wholeness in *Riders in the Chariot*', *Southerly* 35, 1, 1975) analyses Mrs Jolley as a purely external figure, and so misses the symbolic meaning of this figure's role in the novel.

6 I am using 'aboriginal' here in a general way, to refer to the natural, instinctual, archaic dimension in the psyche. Nothing occult is implied by this 'return' of the aboriginal spirit, simply an archetypal shift whereby Nature comes to triumph over Culture.

7 For crucial distinctions between father and mother archetypes, and the kinds of religion to which both give rise, see E. Neumann, *The Origins and History of Consciousness*, and Patricia Berry (ed.) *Fathers and Mothers*.

8 As Erich Neumann has shown, the habit of the earth-goddess of mourning her dead—i.e. victims whom she has herself destroyed—is a case of crocodile tears. Cf. *Origins*, p. 88 f.

9 C. G. Jung, *Symbols of Transformation*, p. 258.

10 Cf. Neumann: 'The son-lover ... experiences the destructive side of the Great Mother as something masculine. It is her murderous satellites who carry out the sacrifice of the son' (*Origins*, p. 179).

11 For an excellent account of the differences between Attis-Adonis and

Christ see John Sanford, *The Kingdom Within*, Lippincott, New York, 1970, p. 163 f; and Hugo Rahner, 'Earth Spirit and Divine Spirit in Patristic Theology', in Joseph Campbell (ed.), *Spirit and Nature*, Papers from the Eranos Yearbooks, Vol. 1, Princeton University Press, Princeton, 1954.

12 J. M. Robertson, *Pagan Christs*, Watts, London 1911, and Edward Carpenter, *Pagan and Christian Creeds*, Allen and Unwin, London, 1920.

13 J. G. Frazer, 'The Myth and Ritual of Attis', *Adonis, Attis, Osiris*, p. 267.

14 Frazer, 'The Day of Blood in the Attis Ritual', ibid., p. 268 f.

15 Robert Bly's interpretation of a section of the Book of Job, in 'I Came Out of the Mother Naked', *Sleepers Joining Hands*, p. 31.

16 Cf. A. P. Elkin, *The Australian Aborigines*, Angus & Robertson, Sydney, 1946; and Tony Swain, *Interpreting Aboriginal Religion*, The Australian Association for the Study of Religions, Adelaide, 1985.

17 The term *pueri* is used to include Miss Hare with Dubbo and Himmelfarb. In its original Latin usage the word denotes 'children' in the broadest sense, and is not limited to the masculine gender.

18 Compare this destruction of Xanadu with the 'devouring' of Stan Parker's world by the brick and fibro houses of suburbia. Society, matter, is portrayed in both works as the subduing matriarchal force.

19 White, 'The Prodigal Son', op. cit., p. 40.

20 R. F. Brissenden, *Patrick White*, p. 33.

21 I have in mind here essays and studies by Colin Roderick, Susan Moore, and Peter Beatson, among others.

22 S. Moore argues: 'the more one knows about medieval religious literature, particularly Jewish Mystical literature, the more sense one can make of the experiences of White's four living creatures . . .' ('The Quest for Wholeness', op. cit., p. 53). I would reverse this claim: the less one amplifies the super.mposed allegorical frame the better. A too intellectual approach to the novel ends up repeating and reinforcing White's own philosophical confusion.

23 White has Dubbo 'denying' Himmelfarb several times during the passion sequence, cf. pp. 408–10.

Chapter 5   The Tightening Knot

1 Patrick White, *The Solid Mandala*, Penguin, Harmondsworth, 1969. All future references are to this edition.

2 The complex is sometimes defined as an entanglement, or as a knotting together of undifferentiated psychic contents (cf. Cirlot, 'Knot', in *A Dictionary of Symbols*, Philosophical Library, New York, 1971, p. 172).

3 The pattern of descent-and-return is a widely used metaphor for individuation, with regard to the ego's initial descent into the unconscious, followed by its return to the upper world. Cf. John Alexander Allen, 'The Return', in *Hero's Way*, Prentice-Hall, Englewood Cliffs, N.J., 1971, p. 367 f.

4 Cf. Hillman, 'The Great Mother, her Son, her Hero, and the Puer', op. cit., pp. 77–8.

5 Cf. Neumann, 'The Uroboros', *Origins*, p. 11.

6 Many previous symbols—Theodora's black rose, Parker's circular vision, etc.—have been viewed as mandalas, either by White or his critics, but none has possessed genuine mandalic significance. Only Arthur's talisman possesses mandalic potential—and even this potential, as we shall see, is not actually realized.

7 It is fashionable in Australia (but not in America) for artists to distrust psychological analysis, believing that such analysis would dry up the well-springs of creativity. In a young, *puer*-culture it is to be expected that the bearers of imagination should regard the mind as intrusive and hostile, as a threat to imagination. The *puer* celebrates the mother (as unconscious) and denigrates the father (as mind, reason).

8 Arthur's life and creative burden can be interestingly illuminated by Romantic theory. Cf. M. H. Abrams, 'Unconscious Genius and Organic Growth', in *The Mirror and the Lamp*, W. W. Norton, New York, 1958.

9 Cf. Edward Edinger, *The Creation of Consciousness*, Inner City Books, Toronto, 1984, ch. 2.

10 Cf. Jolande Jacobi, 'The Helpful Shadow', *The Psychology of C. G. Jung*, Routledge & Kegan Paul, 1962, plate 3.

11 John Updike, *The Centaur* (1962), Penguin, Harmondsworth, 1966, p. 8.

12 '[A]t that moment [Arthur] felt Dad turn against him. It was some question of afflictions. Except in theory, the afflicted cannot love one another' (p. 230).

13 Jung, *Symbols of Transformation*, p. 293 n.

14 Neumann, *Origins*, p. 93.

15 Robert Graves, 'Athene's nature and deeds', *The Greek Myths*, vol. 1.

16 It must be pointed out that Arthur's retardation is more symbolic than actual. He is a shadow-figure, and is caught up in the unconscious, but he has the capacity to grow, to be transformed, like any archetypal figure.

17 Brian Kiernan, 'The Novels of Patrick White', in G. Dutton (ed.), *The Literature of Australia*, p. 476.

18 A. P. Riemer, 'Visions of the Mandala in *The Tree of Man*', in G. A. Wilkes (ed.), *Ten Essays on Patrick White*', p. 115.

[19] Thelma Herring, 'Self and Shadow: The Quest for Totality in *The Solid Mandala*', in Wilkes (ed.), *Ten Essays*, p. 82.

[20] Peter Beatson, 'The Skiapod and the Eye: Patrick White's *The Eye of the Storm*', *Southerly* 34, 3 (1974), p. 219.

Chapter 6   *The Mother in Search of Herself*

[1] Marie-Louise von Franz, '*Über religiöse Hintergründe des Puer-Aeternus-Problems*', in A. Guggenbühl-Craig (ed.), *The Archetype*, Basel, Karger, 1964, p. 149. English translation (by von Franz) in *Harvest* 12, 1966, p. 9.

[2] Patrick White, *The Vivisector*, Penguin, Harmondsworth, 1973, p. 165. All references are to this edition.

[3] Patrick White, *The Eye of the Storm*, Penguin, Harmondsworth, 1975, p. 263. All references are to this edition.

[4] Compare the change of tone here with that in Theodora's personality after the Moraïtis concerto, or the hotel fire. Once the ego is destroyed much of the demonism disappears, because the struggle is over.

[5] John Colmer, 'White's Progress', in *The Literary Half-Yearly*, 1978, pp. 178–81.

[6] A. P. Riemer, 'The Eye of the Needle: Patrick White's Recent Novels', *Southerly* 34, 3 (1974), p. 248.

[7] Colmer, op. cit., p. 178.

[8] See the Conclusion for a discussion of White's essentially passive role in the creative process.

[9] See the Conclusion.

[10] Cf. M. Esther Harding, 'The Moon Mother', *Woman's Mysteries*, p. 98 f.

[11] See R. F. Brissenden, '*The Vivisector*: Art and Science', in W. S. Ramson (ed.), *The Australian Experience*; and Thelma Herring, 'Patrick White's *The Vivisector*', *Southerly* 31, 1 (1971).

[12] A comparison can be made with *Voss*, where White identified the central character with the archetypal force that possessed him from within. The result there was a god-like inflation of the will; here it is an inflation of evil.

[13] Ingmar Björkstén, *Patrick White: A General Introduction*, p. 92.

[14] The grand epigraphs to the novel make clear White's spiritual designs, and his inflated conception of Duffield as 'the great Criminal, the great Accursed One—and the Supreme Knower'.

[15] The multiple attributes of this archetype in the novel are suggestive of archaic figurines where the goddess is represented with four, eight, or sixteen arms, signifying her many characteristics. Hecate was

represented with several faces and arms; Neumann, *The Great Mother*, p. 169 f.

[16] Cf. Jung, 'The Self', in *Aion*.

[17] Frazer writes of the 'sacred prostitutes' of Aphrodite, in *Adonis, Attis, Osiris*, p. 36 f.

[18] Cf. Walter Otto's memorable portrait of this goddess in 'Artemis', *The Homeric Gods*, p. 80.

[19] Esther Harding, 'The Virgin Goddess', *Woman's Mysteries*, p. 125.

[20] Paul Friedrich, 'Virginity', *The Meaning of Aphrodite*, Chicago University Press, Chicago, 1978, p. 86.

[21] This degeneration will be discussed more fully in the Conclusion.

[22] Compare this with Dubbo's image of Miss Hare as 'a curled possum in a dreamtime womb of transparent skin' (*RC*, p. 455). It is the same uroboric imagery here, only stripped of its poetry and mystery and revealed in a starkly pathological context.

[23] Frazer, *Adonis, Attis, Osiris*, p. 36.

[24] Cf. C. Kerenyi, 'Demeter', in Jung and Kerenyi, *Essays on a Science of Mythology*.

[25] See the story of the trochilus inside the crocodile, *The Aunt's Story* p. 23, and my discussion of it in chapter 2.

[26] Note that it is only de Santis and Manhood who experience the boon, since they are the ones who have worked toward psychic integration throughout the story.

[27] A. P. Riemer, 'The Eye of the Needle', op. cit., p. 262.

[28] P. Beatson, 'The Skiapod and the Eye: Patrick White's *The Eye of the Storm*', *Southerly* 34, 3 (1974), p. 219.

[29] Peter Wolfe, *Laden Choirs: The Fiction of Patrick White*, p. 197.

[30] White himself has acknowledged in his autobiography and elsewhere that history is used in *Voss* and *A Fringe of Leaves* merely as a starting point for his imagination. For a sensitive enquiry into the relation between fact and fiction in the present novel, see Jill Ward, 'Patrick White's *A Fringe of Leaves*: History and Fiction', *Australian Literary Studies* 8, 4, 1978, pp. 416 ff.

[31] Patrick White, *A Fringe of Leaves*, Penguin, Harmonsworth, 1979. All references are to this edition.

[32] There is a wealth of material available on Kore-Persephone, but a good introduction to her mythic pattern and phenomenology is C. Kerenyi, 'The Rape of Persephone', in *The Gods of the Greeks*.

[33] In her essay 'Neurosis and the Rape of Demeter/Persephone' Patricia Berry argues that the daughter's individuation is precisely in her conscious acceptance of the complexity and dynamic movement of her moral and psychological being; P. Berry, *Echo's Subtle Body*.

[34] The epigraph reads: 'A perfect Woman, nobly planned, / To warn, to

comfort, and command'. But who warns, who plans, who commands this self-created woman?

[35] Veronica Brady's claim that Ellen's 'making love with Garnet is, after all, more a surprise to her than anything else' is not only coy and inaccurate but a Christian cover-up of Ellen's explicit craving for adulterous sexuality. Cf. V. Brady, '*A Fringe of Leaves*: Civilization by the Skin of Our Own Teeth', *Southerly* 37, 2 (1977), p. 126.

[36] The term *nekyia* is from Homer's *Odyssey* and means 'descent to the Underworld'. It is used by Jung to describe a descent into psychic reality, as in his essay, 'Picasso', in *The Spirit in Man, Art, and Literature*, p. 139.

[37] Before Austin's death Ellen has a dream which highlights the psychological nature of the fatal attack (p. 140). The dream and Austin's psychological situation are discussed more fully in my essay, 'A Search for a New Ethic: White's *A Fringe of Leaves*', in C. Tiffin (ed.), *South Pacific Images*, pp. 186–95.

[38] The idea of a spiral sweep in the direction of the primitive is borrowed from Lawrence, who wrote of the necessity of making 'a great swerve in our onward-going life-course, to gather up again the savage mysteries', in 'Herman Melville's *Typee* and *Omoo*', *Studies in Classic American Literature*, Penguin, Harmondsworth, 1948, p. 146.

[39] As she recovers in bed Ellen is made to say: '"I am the one who has committed the crime. I think he could not believe in me. For that reason, he ran back"' (p. 309).

[40] Most critics of the novel make large claims for Ellen, and for the integration of her psychic being. Veronica Brady and John Colmer, for instance, see Ellen as the most 'integrated' of all of White's characters. Cf. V. Brady, '*A Fringe of Leaves*', op. cit., and J. Colmer, 'Duality in Patrick White', in R. Shepherd and K. Singh (eds), *Patrick White: A Critical Symposium*. Interestingly, White himself rejects the assertion that Ellen triumphs gloriously at the end but he does grant her a qualified or limited success: 'When Ellen puts on her corset and silk gown at the end she is resuming her guise as Mrs Roxburgh. Her decision to marry the English merchant *is* a regression, though not necessarily one which damns her' (Patrick White, in a letter to D. J. Tacey, 6 August 1978).

[41] Here I am extending White's own metaphor of the 'contradictory envelopes of flesh' of which his own character is composed; cf. *Flaws in the Glass*, p. 35.

Chapter 7   The Delight of Decadence

[1] 'E' is a form used by White, and a convenient way to refer to the character without having to use three names and multiple pronouns.

2   Cf. Dorothy Green, 'An Over-rated Invention?', in her collection of essays, *The Music of Love*, Penguin, Melbourne, 1984, pp. 47–63; also A. P. Riemer, 'Eddie and the Bogomils—Some Observations on *The Twyborn Affair*', *Southerly* 40, 1 (1980), pp. 12–29. Many student readers seem to arrive at the handy formula that White is exploring the androgynous ideal of a post-patriarchal, post-Christian society.

3   Eudoxia/Eddie writes in her/his journal, 'I would like to think myself morally justified in being true to what I am—if I knew what that is. I must discover' (p. 63). There are numerous similar philosophical posturings and trick remarks.

4   Compare Eddie and Joanie's situation with that of the broken, psychotic Arthur and the suddenly invigorated Mrs Poulter at the end of *The Solid Mandala*.

5   All references are to the Australian Penguin (Ringwood, 1981) edition of *The Twyborn Affair*.

6   For an excellent account of the mysteries of Eleusis see C. G. Jung and C. Kerenyi, *Essays on a Science of Mythology*.

7   E. Neumann, 'The Woman's Experience of Herself and the Eleusinian Mysteries', *The Great Mother*, pp. 307–8.

8   The motif of the pomegranate seems very much like an allusion to Kore-Persephone. It may well be that in this instance White has made deliberate use of the myth, but, if so, it is only because the given archetypal situation of the narrative has suggested this embellishment to him. The mythic content is primary, and, I would argue, a basically unconscious structure of the narrative.

9   Marcia's deceased child, referred to in Eadie's letter, is in fact E's son. Without realizing it Eadie is the grandmother of the mourned son whom she compares with her own 'lost' child. This is another example of the way in which the mythic pattern degenerates to a family soap-opera, a series of perverse literal associations.

10 The scheme to elope with Joanie is developed in several places (pp. 60, 80, 98), and seems to complement the mother's fantasy of rescuing the daughter from Hades. Angelo's seizure is partially provoked by his discovery of the counterplot: 'All this intrigue behind my back' (p. 109).

11 E. Neumann, *Origins of Consciousness*, p. 61.

12 It is interesting to note White's personal identification with the animal world, not only in his love for dogs, goats and pets in his life, but also in his fantasies of an after-life: 'I am a very low form of human being; in my next incarnation I shall probably turn up as a dog or a stone' (Craig McGregor, *In the Making*, p. 218).

13 Compare this with Arthur Brown's play of the still-born calf which cannot escape the mother's womb.

14 E. Neumann, *Origins*, p. 59.

[15] Dorothy Green nobly regards the novel as a didactic work which provides 'lessons' and which causes us to 'ask questions about' Western civilization and 'the consumer society' (*The Music of Love*, pp. 58 and 63).

[16] Leonie Kramer, 'Pseudoxia Endemica', *Quadrant* 34, 7, p. 67. Neil Jillett expresses the same sentiment in his excellent review of the novel, 'A Sexual Triptych', the *Age*, 29 September 1979.

[17] This is the comforting conclusion arrived at by virtually all the Australian reviewers (Kramer and Jillett excepted). John Colmer regards the work as a liberal-humanist 'quest' novel, finding its values 'compassionate', its direction 'positive', and seeing its 'androgynous' vision as 'a humanistic solution' to the problems raised throughout White's career (*Patrick White*, p. 84).

[18] Charles Boer (tr.), *The Homeric Hymns*, p. 129

[19] E. Neumann, *The Great Mother*, p. 308.

[20] *Memoirs of Many in One*, by Alex Xenophon Demirjian Gray, edited by Patrick White, Jonathan Cape, London, 1986. All references are to this edition.

[21] Kerryn Goldsworthy, 'A life Devoted to Narrative and Identity', *National Times*, 4 April 1986, p. 31.

[22] David Malouf, 'Patrick White: The Glow of the Afterlife', *Australian*, 5–6 April 1986, p. 48.

[23] Thomas Shapcott, 'A "Wicked" White Rips Us to Shreds', *Sydney Morning Herald*, 5 April 1986, p. 48.

[24] ibid.

Chapter 8   Conclusion: Problems of Unconscious Genius

[1] Friedrich Schiller, from '*Über naive und sentimentalische Dichtung*', quoted in Jung, *Psychological Types*, p. 131.

[2] See the statements of these and other writers in Brewster Ghiselin (ed.), *The Creative Process*, University of California Press, Berkeley, 1952.

[3] White, in an interview with Craig McGregor in *In the Making* (1969), p. 219.

[4] White, in an unpublished radio interview with Canadian Broadcasting Corporation, November 1973 (by courtesy of Professor Robert Wilson, University of Alberta, Edmonton, Canada).

[5] Cf. 'The Nobel Winner Who Hates Writing', the *Age* (Melbourne), 20 October 1973, p. 2.

[6] White, in McGregor, op. cit., p. 219.

[7] White, in the CBC radio interview, op. cit.

[8] ibid.

9   David J. Tacey, 'A Search for a New Ethic', in C. Tiffin (ed.) *South Pacific Images* (1978), p. 195.

10   White, in a letter to D. J. Tacey, 6 August 1978.

11   I am referring here to several undocumented cases where 'religious' studies of White's novels were undertaken at postgraduate level, and subsequently abandoned.

12   William Walsh, 'Patrick White's Vision of Human Incompleteness: *The Solid Mandala* and *The Vivisector*', in Walsh (ed.), *Readings in Commonwealth Literature*, Oxford University Press, London, 1973.

13   Leonie Kramer, '*The Tree of Man*: An Essay in Scepticism', in Ramson (ed.), *The Australian Experience*.

14   White, in McGregor, op. cit., p. 221.

15   These terms are borrowed from Leslie Fiedler, 'Archetype and Signature: A Study of the Relationship between Biography and Poetry', *Sewanee Review* I, 10 (1952).

16   These stages are outlined in the McGregor interview, ibid.

17   White, in the *Southerly* (1973) interview, op. cit., p. 139.

18   White, in McGregor, p. 219.

19   Graham Hough, 'Poetry and the Anima', *Spring 1973 (Dallas)*, p. 90.

20   Erich Neumann, *Origins and History of Consciousness*, p. 263.

21   White, in his National Book Council Awards Address, 1980, published as 'Patrick White Speaks on Factual Writing and Fiction', *Australian Literary Studies* 10, 1, 1981, p. 100.

22   Jung, *Psychological Types*, p. 448.

23   Ingmar Björkstén, *Patrick White*, p. 1.

24   Christian commentators include Veronica Brady, Roger Sharr, and Frederick Dillistone, and 'Jungians' (so-called) include Patricia Morley, A. P. Riemer, and I. Björkstén.

25   John Colmer, *Patrick White*: '*Riders in the Chariot*' and *Patrick White*. Leonie Kramer rightly sensed something amiss in White's religiosity, but concluded that White was offering ironic commentaries on religious problems.

26   Schiller, in a letter to Goethe, 27 March 1801; quoted in M. H. Abrams, *The Mirror and the Lamp: Romantic Theory and the Critical Tradition*, W. W. Norton, New York, 1958, p. 211.

27   There is an uncanny parallel between this statement, and a remark by Jolande Jacobi on the psycho-analyst's task: 'The analyst's job is to hold up a mirror to the patient so that he can see his rejected qualities [and] . . . accept them as part of himself' (*The Way of Individuation*, Harcourt, Brace & World, New York, 1967, p. 98). Arthur is in a sense White's (and Waldo's) psychoanalyst, trying to force the ego to recognize and accept unconscious contents.

28   This is my own psychological re-working of A. D. Hope's comments

on artistic responsibility in *The Cave and the Spring*, Sydney University Press, Sydney, 1974. Hope argues that the artist 'must carry out his side of the continual responsibility for maintaining the form and order of the world, the rising and setting of the stars ... They have to be kept going. They do not simply maintain themselves' (p. 14).

29 Cf. Jung: 'History has numerous examples of how easily the mystery can turn into a sexual orgy, just because it grew out of the opposite of the orgy' (*Symbols of Transformation*, p. 377).

30 This view is represented by Chris Wallace-Crabbe in 'Possible Selves', *Australian Book Review* 82 (July 1986), pp. 7–8.

31 See David Malouf, 'Patrick White: The Glow of Afterlife', *Weekend Australian Magazine*, 5–6 April 1986, p. 13; and David English, 'White's versatile nun', *Age*, 5 April 1986, p. 13.

32 Thomas Shapcott, 'A "Wicked" White Rips Us to Shreds', *Sydney Morning Herald*, 5 April 1986, p. 48.

33 Veronica Brady, '"A Single Bone-Clean Button": The Achievement of Patrick White', in C. D. Narasimhaiah (ed.), *An Introduction to Australian Literature*, John Wiley, Brisbane, 1982, p. 35.

34 David English, op. cit.

35 James Hillman, 'The Great Mother, Her Son ...', op. cit., p. 83.

36 These studies include Jung's own work, *Civilization in Transition*, as well as Edward Edinger's *The Creation of Consciousness*, Erich Neumann's *Depth Psychology and a New Ethic*, Edward C. Whitmont's *Return of the Goddess*.

37 James Hillman, 'The Great Mother ...', op. cit., p. 82.

38 ibid., p. 83.

39 For further material on the father archetype, see the essays by Augusto Vitale, Murray Stein, and Vera von der Heydt in Patricia Berry (ed.), *Fathers and Mothers*. See also Jung, 'The Significance of the Father in the Destiny of the Individual', *Freud and Psychoanalysis*.

40 Charles Harpur, 'The Dream by the Fountain' (1853), in John Barnes and Brian McFarlane (eds), *Cross-Country, A Book of Australian Verse*, Heinemann, Melbourne, 1984, p. 11, line 79.

41 See especially the final sections of chapters 3 and 4.

42 James Hillman, 'The Great Mother ...', op. cit., p. 83.

43 Patrick White, *Flaws in the Glass*, p. 60.

SELECT BIBLIOGRAPHY

Works by Patrick White (in chronological order)

Novels

Note: Penguin books have been cited in this study since these are the most readily available editions of White's novels. Listed below are first editions (in some instances Penguin and first edition paginations are identical).

Happy Valley. Harrap, London, 1939. Viking Press, New York, 1939.
The Living and the Dead. Routledge, London, 1941. Viking Press, New York, 1941. Macmillan, Toronto, 1941.
The Aunt's Story. Routledge & Kegan Paul, London, 1948. Viking Press, New York, 1948. Macmillan, Toronto, 1948.
The Tree of Man. Viking, New York, 1955. Macmillan, Toronto, 1955. Eyre & Spottiswoode, London, 1956.
Voss. Eyre & Spottiswoode, London, 1957. Viking, New York, 1957. Macmillan, Toronto, 1957.
Riders in the Chariot. Eyre & Spottiswoode, London, 1961. Viking, New York, 1961.
The Solid Mandala. Eyre & Spottiswoode, London, 1966. Viking, New York, 1966.
The Vivisector. Cape, London, 1970. Viking, New York, 1970.
The Eye of the Storm. Cape, London, 1973. Viking, New York, 1974.
A Fringe of Leaves. Cape, London, 1976. Viking, New York, 1977.
The Twyborn Affair. Cape, London, 1979. Viking, New York, 1979.
Memoirs of Many in One, by Alex Xenophon Demirjian Gray, edited by Patrick White. Cape, London, 1986. Viking, New York, 1987.

Poetry

Thirteen Poems. Unpublished, n.d. [1929 or 1930].
The Ploughman and Other Poems. Beacon Press, Sydney, 1935.

Plays

Four Plays. Eyre & Spottiswoode, London, 1965. Sun Books, Melbourne, 1967.

Big Toys. Currency Press, Sydney, 1978.
Signal Driver: A Morality Play for the Times. Currency Press, Sydney, 1983.
Netherwood. Currency Press, Sydney, 1983.

Short stories
'The Twitching Colonel', in *The London Mercury* 35, 1937, pp. 602–9.
The Burnt Ones. Eyre & Spottiswoode, London, 1964. Viking, New York, 1964.
The Cockatoos: Shorter Novels and Stories. Cape, London, 1974. Viking, New Yok, 1974.

Autobiography
Flaws in the Glass: A Self-Portrait. Cape, London, 1981.

Selected essays and speeches
'The Prodigal Son'. *Australian Letters* 1, 3 (1958) pp. 37–40. Reprinted in G. Dutton and M. Harris (eds), *The Vital Decade*, Sun Books, Melbourne, 1968, pp. 153–8.
'Patrick White Speaks on Factual Writing and Fiction'. *Australian Literary Studies* 10, May 1981, pp. 99–101.

Selected Criticism of Patrick White

Books
Argyle, Barry. *Patrick White*. Oliver and Boyd, Edinburgh, 1967.
Beatson, Peter. *The Eye in the Mandala. Patrick White: A Vision of Man and God*. Elek, London, 1976. Reed, Sydney, 1977.
Björkstén, Ingmar. *Patrick White: A General Introduction*. Translated by Stanley Gerson. University of Queensland Press, Brisbane, 1976.
Brissenden, R. F. *Patrick White*. Longman, for the British Council and the National Book League, London, 1966.
Colmer, John. *Patrick White: 'Riders in the Chariot'*. Edward Arnold, Melbourne, 1978.
——*Patrick White*. Methuen, London & New York, 1984.
Dyce, J. R. *Patrick White as Playwright*. University of Queensland Press, Brisbane, 1974.
Kiernan, Brian. *Patrick White*. Macmillan, London, 1980.
McCulloch, A. M. *A Tragic Vision: The Novels of Patrick White*. University of Queensland Press, Brisbane, 1983.
Morley, Patricia A. *The Mystery of Unity: Theme and Technique in the Novels of Patrick White*. McGill-Queen's University Press, Toronto, 1972. University of Queensland Press, Brisbane, 1972.
Shepherd, R., and Singh, K. (eds). *Patrick White: A Critical Symposium*. Centre for Research in the New Literatures in English, Flinders

University, Adelaide, 1978.

Walsh, William. *Patrick White's Fiction*. Allen & Unwin, Sydney, 1977.

Wilkes, G. A. *Ten Essays on Patrick White*. Angus & Robertson, Sydney, 1970.

Wolfe, Peter. *Laden Choirs: The Fiction of Patrick White*. University Press of Kentucky, Lexington, 1983.

Selected articles and interviews

Barnes, John. 'A Note on Patrick White's Novels'. In C. D. Narasim-haiah (ed.), *An Introduction to Australian Literature*. Jacaranda Press, Brisbane, 1965, pp. 93–101.

Brady, Veronica. 'The Novelist and the New World: Patrick White's *Voss*'. *Texas Studies in Literature and Language* 21, 2, 1979, pp. 169–85.

Brissenden. R. F. '*The Vivisector*: Art and Science', in W. S. Ramson (ed.), *The Australian Experience*. Australian National University Press, Canberra, 1974.

Herring, Thelma, and Wilkes, G. A. 'A Conversation with Patrick White'. *Southerly* 33, 2, 1973, pp. 132–43.

Hetherington, John. 'Patrick White: Life at Castle Hill', in *Forty-Two Faces*, Cheshire, Melbourne, 1962, pp. 140–5.

Kiernan, Brian. 'The Novels of Patrick White', in Geoffrey Dutton (ed.), *The Literature of Australia*. Penguin, Melbourne, 1976, pp. 461–84.

Kramer, Leonie. 'Patrick White's Götterdämmerung'. *Quadrant* 17, May/June 1973, pp. 8–19.

—— '*The Tree of Man*: An Essay in Scepticism'. In W. S. Ramson (ed.), *The Australian Experience*. Australian National University Press, Canberra, 1974, pp. 269–83.

—— 'Pseudoxia Endemica'. *Quadrant* 24, July 1980, pp. 66–7.

Lawson, Alan. 'Meaning and Experience: A Review-Essay on Some Recurrent Problems in Patrick White Criticism', *Texas Studies in Literature and Language* 21, 2, 1979, pp. 280–95.

Leitch, David. 'Patrick White: A Revealing Profile', *National Times*, 27 March–1 April 1978, p. 6.

McGregor, Craig. 'Patrick White', in *In the Making*. Nelson; Melbourne, 1969, pp. 218–22.

Mackenzie, Manfred. 'The Consciousness of "Twin Consciousness": Patrick White's *The Solid Mandala*', *Novel* 2, 1969, pp. 241–54.

—— 'Tradition and Patrick White's Individual Talent', *Texas Studies in Literature and Language* 21, 2, 1979. pp. 147–68.

Tacey, David J. 'A Seach for a New Ethic: White's *A Fringe of Leaves*', in C. Tiffin (ed.), *South Pacific Images*. South Pacific Association for Commonwealth Literature and Language Studies, Brisbane, 1978, pp. 186–95.

—— 'Patrick White: The Great Mother and Her Son', *The Journal of Analytical Psychology* 28, 2, 1983, pp. 165–83.

Selected Psychological and Mythological Studies

Adler, Gerhard. *The Living Symbol*. Pantheon, New York, 1961.

Baird, James. 'Jungian Psychology in Criticism: Theoretical Problems', in J. P. Strelka (ed.), *Literary Criticism and Psychology: Yearbook of Comparative Criticism*, vol. 7. Pennsylvania State University Press, University Park, 1976, pp. 3–30.

Berry, Patricia. 'What's the Matter with Mother?'; 'Neurosis and the Rape of Demeter/Persephone', in *Echo's Subtle Body: Contributions to an Archetypal Psychology*. Spring Publications, Dallas, 1982, pp. 1–34.

Bly, Robert. *Sleepers Joining Hands*. Harper & Row, New York, 1973.

Boer, Charles (translator), *The Homeric Hymns*. Spring Publications, Dallas, 1979.

Corbin, Henry. 'Mundus Imaginalis, or the Imaginary and the Imaginal', *Spring 1972*. Spring Publications, Zurich.

Edinger, Edward. *Melville's Moby-Dick: A Jungian Commentary*. New Directions Books, New York, 1975.

—— *The Creation of Consciousness*. Inner City Books, Toronto, 1984.

Frazer, J. G. *Adonis, Attis, Osiris (The Golden Bough*, part IV, vol. 1). Macmillan, London, 1976.

Freud, Sigmund. *The Ego and the Id*. Translated by Joan Riviere, edited by James Strachey. W. W. Norton, New York, 1961.

—— *On Creativity and the Unconscious*. Harper & Row, New York, 1958.

Gallant, Christine. *Blake and the Assimilation of Chaos*. Princeton University Press, Princeton, 1978.

Goldenberg, Naomi. *Changing of the Gods: Feminism and the End of Traditional Religions*. Beacon Press, Boston, 1979.

Graves, Robert. *The Greek Myths*, 2 vols. Penguin, Harmondsworth, 1955.

—— *The White Goddess*. Faber & Faber, London, 1961.

Harding, M. Esther. *Woman's Mysteries*. Harper & Row, New York, 1976.

Hillman, James. 'The Great Mother, her Son, her Hero, and the Puer', in Patricia Berry (ed.), *Fathers and Mothers*. Spring Publications, Zurich, 1973, pp. 75–127.

—— 'Pothos: The Nostalgia of the Puer Eternus', in *Loose Ends: Primary Papers in Archetypal Psychology*. Spring Publications, Dallas, 1975.

—— *Re-Visioning Psychology*. Harper & Row, New York, 1975.

—— 'Senex and Puer: An Aspect of the Historical and Psychological Present', in James Hillman (ed.), *Puer Papers*. Spring Publications, Dallas, 1979.

—— *Healing Fiction*. Station Hill Press, Barrytown, New York, 1983.

James, E. O. *The Cult of the Mother Goddess*. Thames & Hudson, London, 1959.

Jung, C. G. *The Collected Works* [hereafter cited as *CW*], 20 vols, edited by Sir Herbert Read, Michael Fordham, Gerhard Adler and William McGuire. Translated by R. F. C. Hull [except vol. 2]. Bollingen Series XX. Routledge & Kegan Paul, London; Princeton University Press, Princeton, 1953–84. Major references used in this study include:
—— *Freud and Psychoanalysis. CW*, vol. 4. 1961.
—— *Symbols of Transformation. CW*, vol. 5. 1956; 2nd edn 1967.
—— *Psychological Types. CW*, vol. 6. 1971.
—— *Two Essays on Analytical Psychology. CW*, vol. 7. 1953; 2nd edn 1966.
—— *The Structure and Dynamics of the Psyche. CW*, vol. 8. 1960; 2nd edn 1969.
—— *The Archetypes and the Collective Unconscious. CW*, vol. 9, part I. 1959; 2nd edn 1968.
—— *Aion. CW*, vol. 9, part II. 1959; 2nd edn 1968.
—— *Civilization in Transition. CW*, vol. 10. 1964; 2nd edn 1970.
—— *Psychology and Alchemy. CW*, vol. 12. 1953; 2nd edn 1968.
—— *Mysterium Coniunctionis: An Inquiry into the Separation and Synthesis of Psychic Opposites in Alchemy. CW*, vol. 14, 1963; 2nd edn 1970.
—— *The Spirit in Man, Art, and Literature. CW, vol. 15. 1966.*
—— *Four Archetypes.* Princeton University Press, Princeton, 1970.
—— and Kerenyi, C. *Essays on a Science of Mythology.* Princeton University Press, Princeton, 1969.
Kerenyi, C. *The Gods of the Greeks.* Thames & Hudson, London, 1951.
—— *Goddesses of Sun and Moon.* Spring Publications, Dallas, 1979.
Lederer, W. *The Fear of Women.* Grune & Stratton, New York, 1968.
Neumann, Erich. *The Origins and History of Consciousness.* Princeton University Press, Princeton, 1954.
—— *Amor and Psyche.* Princeton University Press, Princeton, 1956.
—— *Art and the Creative Unconscious.* Princeton University Press, Princeton, 1959.
—— 'Mystical Man'. *Spring 1961.* Spring Publications. New York.
—— *The Great Mother: An Analysis of the Archetype.* Princeton University Press, Princeton, 1963.
—— *Depth Psychology and a New Ethic.* Harper & Row, New York, 1973.
Otto, Walter F. *The Homeric Gods.* Thames & Hudson, London, 1955.
Sanford, John. *The Invisible Partners.* Paulist Press, New York, 1980.
Stein, Robert. *Incest and Human Love: the Betrayal of the Soul in Psychotherapy.* Penguin, Baltimore, 1974.
Ulanov, Ann Belford. *The Feminine in Jungian Psychology and Christian Theology.* Northwestern University Press, Evanston, 1971.
von Franz, Marie-Louise. *A Psychological Interpretation of 'The Golden Ass' of Apuleius.* Spring Publications, Zurich, 1970.

—— *An Introduction to the Interpretation of Fairytales*. Spring Publications, Dallas, 1978.

—— *Puer Aeternus: A Psychological Study of the Adult Struggle with the Paradise of Childhood*. Sigo Press, Santa Monica, 1981.

Index

Page references in italics indicate a figure shown in the text

abaissement du niveau mental, 33
Aboriginals, 80, 83–5, 106, 178–9; and
   the Dreaming, 114; and white invaders,
   xvi, 89
Adonis, 19, 23, 26, 45, 110, 242
amplification, in archetypal criticism, xx
androgyny, 185, 224, 230
anima: -bride, 78; as enclosed vessel, 56;
   in opposition to Mother, 56–7; popular
   misconception of, 72–3, 146, 229; as
   transformative feminine, 56, 73, 221
animus, 72, 73, 99, 101, 102;
   distinguished from 'Ghostly Lover', 73;
   infantile *puer-*, 74, 86, 98, 153
Aphrodite, 23, 78, 157, 164, 167
Apuleius, xxi
archetypal: depth criticism, xix–xxii;
   feminine, 12; power, 70; theory, xxi
Argyle, Barry, 73
asthma, 22, 58, 130, 242
Athene, and Perseus, 231
Attis, 19, 23, 45, 99, 189; and blood-
   sacrifice, 25, 110–11, 116; crucifixion
   of, 110; and Cybele, 55, 85, 105;
   festivals of, 25, 111; and self-castration,
   55, 85
Australia: archaic nature of, xvi, 89, 114;
   as 'country of the bones', 43, 81; and
   desert-mysticism, xvi, 82; as image of
   the unconscious, 87, 89, 174; legendary
   figures of, 67, 90; as mother-realm, 48,
   100, 175; nostalgia for, 42, 48, 69; as
   nullifying emptiness, 49; and the 'spirit
   of place', xvi, 89, 95, 97, 107; White as
   mythologist of, 119, 223

Australianness, xiv, 186; of White's
   fiction, xiv–xv, 89, 117–19; superficial
   level of, 88, 248
Australian ego: anarchic nature of, xvii,
   89; and animality, xiv; and British
   super-ego, xiv, 95, 118, 232; as
   colonizer and colonized, 95, 248;
   historical phases of, 89, 95; as Oedipal,
   231–2; puerile nature of, 90, 232
Australian experience: and descent into
   the unconscious, xiv–xv, 89–90, 95,
   107, 118; and Europe, 118; and the
   Father archetype, 231–3; and
   mateship, 232–3; and the Mother
   archetype, 90, 118–19, 231
Australian literature: images of the
   national character in, xiv, 117–18; and
   the 'unofficial' side of national
   character, xiv, 89, 118
Australian society: and destruction of
   spirit, 118–19, 231; materialism of, 49,
   119, 174, 231; at odds with Nature, xvi,
   95, 174; pagan character of, 118;
   precariousness of, xvi, 89, 112
authorial commentary, 87, 90, 173, 185;
   as Christian in outlook, xx–xxi, 50, 84,
   110, 113–15, 217; and White's 'reading'
   of his fiction, xx, 16, 44, 50, 64, 100,
   147–8, 196–7, 208, 216–20
authorial position: and belief in
   disintegration, 16, 44; and celebration
   of 'unborn' state, 92, 105; dissolution
   of, and replacement by archetype, 151,
   200, 208; and 'felt' burden of
   projections, 13, 14, 49, 93; identified

with *puer aeternus*, 2, 16, 92, 93, 109, 194; and lack of reflection, 82, 85, 125, 200, 218, 222–3; and refusal to recognize negative side of the *puer*, 16, 104, 105, 109; urged to change, 121–6

beatific vision, 8, 31, 61
Beatson, Peter, 73, 148, 173
Björkstén, Ingmar, 219
Blake, xxi, 33, 34, 38, 211, 224
Bodkin, Maud, xxi
Brennan, Christopher, 89
Brissenden, R. F., 118
Buddhism, 138, 220

Christianity, xx, 216, 219, 231; as aggrandizing framework, 50, 79, 84, 102, 110, 112; cannot accommodate negative side of Mother archetype, 61, 150, 219; as superimposed framework, xix, 50, 90, 91, 105–6, 113–15, 117, 119, 121, 216–20; disintegration of, 50, 121, 125, 148
Coleridge, 211
Colmer, John, xxiii
Conrad, Joseph, 69
consciousness: and aesthetic awareness, 215; the call for, 121–6, 137–44, 220–5
criticism, of White's fiction, 45–7, 66–7, 87–90, 117, 119, 158, 173, 181, 191, 219–20; and avoidance of pathology, 34, 151, 228, 243; conventional, xix, 213; follows authorial commentary, xix, 87, 119, 249; humanist, 151, 213, 228, 255; and inflated readings, 42, 45–7, 66, 84, 146–7, 151, 185, 207; and misuse of Jung, 66, 72–3, 146, 220, 244, 246; and national identity, 88; and the need to follow imaginal structure, xix–xx, 90; religious, 64, 148, 212, 220, 243

Daedalus, and Icarus, 231
Dante, 73, 221
Davies, Robertson, xvii
de Maistre, Roy, 233
death-romanticism, 224; in *Voss*, xvi, 71, 79, 80
decadence, 196–7
decay: of male ego, 147, 184–6, 190–2, 195–7; of mother-figure, 201–8, 227
Demeter, 68, 122, 169, 175, 198–9; and Eleusinian mysteries, 187–8
development: lack of, 15, 124; rejected, 92, 140–1, 148, 214, 226; retarded,

9, 131
developmental process, 10, 73; and White's fiction, 223–4
doppelgänger, 128, 138, 142, 223
Dyce, J. R., xxiii

Earth Mother, 5, 7, 72; in *The Aunt's Story*, 26, 43, 45; in *The Tree of Man*, 51–7, 59–67
Edinger, Edward, xxi
ego: collapse of, 144–8, 166, 189, 224; dependent upon maternal realm, 9, 61, 130; emerging, 4, 127; loss of, 11, 28; and mythology, 9; re-education of, 121, 221; rejection of Mother, 3; resistance to the unconscious, 2, 81–2, 86, 95–6, 123, 127, 139; weakness of, 22, 35, 86, 129, 131, 141
Eliot, George, 213
Eliot, T. S., 241
emotional realization, 220

fantasy, 33, 40, 75; involuntary, 33–9
fairytale, xx, xxi, 123, 173, 221
father/Father: Absent, 4, 9, 98, 198; in Western culture, 228–31; archetype, as *logos*, 98, 231; and daughter, 18–19; in myth, 9, 231; spirit of, 49; and tradition, 231–2; weakness of, 21, 107; in *The Aunt's Story*, 18–19, 20, 36–9; in *Riders*, 95–8; in *Twyborn*, 233–4; *see also* Australian experience
feminization of men, 229–30
feminism, xxi, 176, 226
Frazer, J. G., 111, 167
Freud, xviii, xxi, 1, 242, 218, 220, 237
Freudian psychology, 38, 58, 230, 240, 243
Frye, Northrop, xxii–xxiii
Furphy, 117

genius: attempts to liberate the ego personality, xviii, 122, 124, 131, 137; nature of, 122, 132, 223; remains unrealized, 125, 132, 138, 223; taken over by the Mother, 160, 163, 200–1, 202, 225; unconscious, 122, 124, 146, 213, 220, 250
Goddess, 10, 11, 49, 52, 62, 85, 135; as beckoning enchantress, 69, 73, 76, 80, 84, 101, 211; and Circe, 73, 193; and Diana, 134; and Gorgon, 85, 94, 231; and Kali, 78; seductive-devouring, 11, 69, 76; as Aboriginal woman, 84–5; in *Voss*, 69–70, 75–81; *see also* specific mythic figures; Earth Mother; Great

Mother; Mother

Goldenberg, Naomi, xxi

Great Earth Mother, *see* Earth Mother

Great Goddess, *see* Goddess

Great Mother, 5, 8, 20, 49, 56, 78, 141, 146; and defeat of spirit, xxi, 50, 110; *magna mater*, 49, 67, 78, 91, 143; in *Riders in the Chariot*, 91, 97–117, 120; *see also* Mother

Hades, 175, 188, 189, 191

Harpur, Charles, 231

Hecate, 157–8

Herbert, Xavier, *Capricornia*, xiv

hero: anti-, 67, 88, 90; and modern era, 229; presentation of, 87–8, 113, 247; traditional tasks of, xv, 90, 129, 221

Herring, Thelma, 146

hetaira, 187, 198

heuresis, 187–9, 193, 198

Hillman, James, xii, xxi, xxii, 44, 48, 228, 230; *Re-Visioning Psychology, Puer Papers, Healing Fiction*, xxi

Hippolytus, 134

historical models, 174–5, 215–16, 252

Homer, 198, 217

homosexuality: and fear of matrix, 123, 133; and high camp, 184–5, 189, 202, 217, 223; and need for masculine spirit, 233–5; and the *puer*, 27, 233, 241, 242

Hough, Graham, 215

Hymn to Demeter, 198

images, *see* key mythological images

imagination: and artistic responsibility, 223; autonomy of, 3, 19, 82, 117, 120, 125; demands a response, 126, 137, 223; guiding and therapeutic, 131, 222; language of, 1, 2, 122, 125, 138, 222

imprisonment, xiii–xvii, 97; as chosen state, xvii; matriarchal, 18, 55, 67; the way out of, 121

incest: metaphor of, 1, 5, 27, 41, 83, 116; as permanent state, 149; problem of, 2; never resolved, 3, 123; reappearance of, in late career, 3, 149; taboo, 5, 10; *see also* Jungian terminology

incestuous: brother/sister pair, 72, 166, 226, 241; fantasies, 2, 72, 149, 155, 193; libido, 18, 122; transferred to father/daughter relationship, 18–19; regression, 13, 83, 142–3; *see also* matrix

individuation: crisis of, 121; misuse of paradigm of, xix; possibility of, 124, 137, 140; in reverse, 42, 150, 163, 225

infantilism, 55, 90, 124, 145, 149, 167, 221, 224

Isis, 105, 111

John Barley-Corn, 19

journey motif, 1, 32, 69, 72, 83, 89, 124, 139, 150, 217, 225

Judaism, xx, 91, 102, 217

Jung, C. G., xxi, 1, 73, 205, 246; quoted, 9, 44, 109, 218; supposed 'influence' of, on White, xvii–xix, 220; *Psychology and Alchemy*, xx, 138, 220

Jungian: criticism, *see* archetypal depth criticism; psychology, xxi, 73, 211, 218–19, 229

Jungian terminology: anima, explained, 56, 73; animus, explained, 73; complex, concept, 7, 121, 143, 230, 249; consciousness, defined, 215; imaginal, defined, 239–40; incest (symbolical), defined, 1, 240; mandala, defined, xx, 5–6, 163; matrix, defined, 1, 240; Mother (archetype), defined, 1–4, 240; projection, concept, 10; *puer aeternus* (the eternal youth), defined, 9, 109, 241; *pueri*, defined, 249; symbol, explained, xx; uroboros (primal circle), defined, 5–6; *see also* Glossary of Psychological Terms

Kabbalah, xvi, 220

kedeshim (transvestite priests), 195–6

kelabim (male prostitutes), 192

key mythological images (in chronological order): union with the earth at Ard's Bay, 4–7, 15–16; the trochilus inside the crocodile, 22–3, 170; dead man suspended upside down in a tree, 55–6; the lily, 69–70, 78–9, 85, 90; the tree of unborn souls, 91, 97, 107, *108*, 109; the knot, 121–3, 131, 137–8, 144, 221–2

Kiernan, 145

Kramer, Leonie, 66, 196, 213

Lawrence, D. H., 1, 91, 213; *The Rainbow*, 213

Lawson, Henry, xiv, 89, 175

literal: aspects of the fiction, 117; . confused with mythic level, 2, 31; incestuous pattern, 1, 193; blocks way into psyche, 13, 15

literalism, 2, 75; in later fiction, 166, 188, 193–6, 202, 226–7, 234

McAuley, James, 73, 88, 246
Malouf, David, 89
mandala: confused with uroboros, xviii–
  xix, 29, 45–7, 65–6, 146–7, 217; loss
  of, 144, 163; possible creation of, 123–
  4, 137, 146, 223–4; *see also* Jungian
  terminology
masculinity: the call for a new style of,
  121–2, 221; decline of, in Western
  culture, 229–30; ineffectual, 174, 178,
  185, 195; in Australian society, 232–3
materialism: and female characters, 53,
  67, 77; and psychic projection, 49,
  65–6, 116; triumph of, 67, 116
matrix: devouring, 34–5, 40, 49, 57, 116,
  133, 190; identification with, 44, 69,
  196; paradoxical nature of, 35, 70, 83–
  4; return to, 5, 15, 39, 49, *54*, 59, 81,
  111; sublimely beautiful, 70, 79;
  toothed, 32, 40
matter: aggressive aspect of, xvi, 49, 116,
  218; and the later novels, 150; and
  magna mater, 49, 67, 244; *materia*, 150
matriarchal: character of fiction, xvii;
  force, 69; gods and deities, 45;
  possession, 185
Medea, 169–70
misogyny, 133, 140, 218, 233
mother/Mother: archetype, 3, 7, 32, 42,
  97, 122, 144, *see also* Jungian
  terminology; death of personal, 3, 15,
  18, 32, 100, 171–3; demonic aspect of,
  13, 16, 30, 80, 94, 101; disappearance of,
  upon complete regression, 28, 42, 43,
  151, 251; devouring, 2, 4, 11, 20, 57, 72,
  84, 170, 190, 194; as dragon, 22, 31;
  dual character of, 3–4, 14, 18, 57, 78,
  97, 101, 103–4; and fantasy of
  matricide, 30–1; Goddess, *see*
  Goddess; marriage with, 41, 60, *68*; as
  murderess, 38, 40, 116, 194; Nature, *see*
  Nature; negative, 3, 8, 18, 28, 58, 61;
  never achieves mythic representation,
  19–20, 66; projected upon female
  figures, 7, 11, 16–17, 20, 40, *54*, 58, 61,
  77, 93–4, 133–4, 233, *see also*
  misogyny; personal, 2, 13, 97, 226; as
  personification of matrix, 2, 10, *see also*
  matrix; positive, 4–7, 11, 101;
  mythologization of, xix, 4, 7, 18–19,
  78, 226, *see also* Earth Mother;
  resistance to, 2, 13; and suffocation, 22,
  30–1, 58; and teeth, 32, 38, 50, 65, 116,
  see also Teeth Mother; as whore, 13; as
  witch, 19, 39, 94; *see also* Great

Mother; women
mother/child relationship, 57–9; *see also*
  puer aeternus
mother-complex: and author, 13, 213–14;
  autonomy and strength of, 16, 29, 36,
  44, 57, 136, 214, 218; crisis of, 122, 224;
  and the 'illusion of enlightenment',
  44–5, 47, 50, 79, 124, 217; and the
  inflated reading of White's fiction, 44–
  5, 50, 79, 84, 110, 216–17, 219; and
  metaphysical ideas, 44, 64, 218; need
  for awareness of, 121–6, *see also*
  authorial position; stages of, xxiii, 122;
  symbolized by the knot, 121–4, 220–2;
  triumph of, 150, 196; as universal
  problem, 230; *see also* Jungian
  terminology
mother-figure (in later phase of White's
  fiction): and archetype of the Self, 163,
  171–2; degeneration of, *see* decay;
  eclipses White's ego personality, 151,
  159, 173, 183; feeds upon decaying
  puer, 147, 167, 185–6, 194; female
  acolytes and servants of, 160–70, 173,
  186; growth and development of, 145–
  7, 149, 183, 202; male servants of,
  152–8, 166–8, 176–81, 193–4; and
  movement toward wholeness, 150,
  154–7, 159–68, 171–83; and
  psychopathic parody of, 201–4, 227;
  and search for lost daughter, *see*
  heuresis; self-realization of, 160–1,
  172–3, 225; utilizes aborted
  individuation process, 148, 150, 159–
  60, 225; White as servant of, 151, 156,
  208–9; and as 'editor' of, 200
mother-image, 8, 32, 100; transferred
  upon sister, 15, 72
mother-symbols, 226, 242; cave, 7;
  circular bay, 5; earth, water, 5; moon,
  52, 70; rose, 40–1; rounded stones, 5,
  15; trees, 5, 55, 67; uroboros, *see*
  uroboros
mysticism, 66, 91, 98, 151, 217, 241;
  nihilistic source, 5–6, 87–8, 226
myth(s): of the Great Mother, 49, 67, 73,
  91, 216–17; and narrative structure,
  90–1, 94, 119; and realism, 94, 128;
  stages of, 124–5, 225; White's fiction
  as, 213–14, 228; and neurosis, 214,
  230
mythologem: Attis-Adonis, 110, 242;
  pagan, 119; *puer*/Mother, 147; gives
  way to Mother/daughter pattern, 189;
  contracts to a family romance, 226

narcissism, xvi, 46, 223
Nature: cycle of, 20, 23, 112; Great Round of, 5, 93, 114; *mater natura*, 19, 119; maternal character of, 4–5, 65; sacrifice of earth-spirit, 19, 23, 26, 110, 113; symbolic union with, 3–7, 43–7, 51–2, 65–7; *see also* Earth Mother
nekyia, 178, 182, 217, 253
Neumann, Erich, 134, 187, 215–16
Nietzsche, 69, 211, 228

Odysseus, 90, 217
Oedipus(-al), 8, 19, 130, 231

Persephone, Kore-, 175–6, 180–2, 187–9, 199, 254
paradise: demonic, *24*, 41, 65; search for childhood, 9, 23, 33–4, 77, 81, 92, 172, 190, 199; the Second, 33–4, 172
pagan: character of fiction, xxi, 91, 105–6; ritual, 76, 85, 102
projection: 'bounces back', 30; mechanism of, 3–4, 10, 13, 20–2, 40, 58–9, 93, 124, 134, 218; *see also* authorial position
psychic inflation, xv, 44, 158, 217
psychosis, 44, 46
puer/puer aeternus: as artist, 50, 105–9; as boy-god, 19, 110, 112, 153; defensive, militant attitude of, 11–12, 241; destroyed by Mother, 50, 65, 77, 101, 109–13, 116, 194, 199; father as, 19, 96; as human sacrifice, 72, 110, 172, 194, 200; insufficient awareness of, 61, 66, 70, 85, 103, 150; Jung on, 9, 109, 220; misrepresented as Christ-figure, 50, 91, 110, 216; self-destructive character of, *see* self-disintegration; sense of betrayal, 72, 99–100; serves the Mother, 19, 79, 98–104, 142; as wanderer, 69, 245; *see also* authorial position; Jungian terminology
pueri, 81–4, 91, 115, 120, 194, 249

reflection: crucial moment of, 30, 96; lack of, in characters, 23, 36, 56, 85, 94, 222–3; the need for, 121–6, 143, 220–2; *see also* authorial position
regression, xix, 1, 13, 40, 65, 196; attractiveness of, 92
religio, 125, 139
Richardson, Henry Handel, *The Fortunes of Richard Mahony*, xiv, 233
Riemer, A. P., xvii–xviii, 146, 173

Schiller, 210, 211, 220, 228
self-castration, 32, 85, 104, 195
self-disintegration, xv–xvi, xix, 226; erotic delight in, 11, 27–8, 35, 43, 59, 124; in *The Living and the Dead*, 4, 7, 16–17; in *The Aunt's Story*, 18, 26–32, 40–7, 217; in *The Tree of Man*, 53–5, 64–7; in *Voss*, 69–72, 79–85, 216; in *Riders*, 92–6; in *The Solid Mandala*, 123–4, 129–33, 142–4, 224; in *The Twyborn Affair*, 184–6, 190–6, 199
senex (father), 232–4
sexuality: incestuous, 28, 61, 63, 155, 166, 226; and sado-masochism, 28, 158, 195, 217; in *The Tree of Man*, 51–3, 59–61, 62–3; in *Voss*, 75; in *Riders*, 99, 104; in *The Solid Mandala*, 133, 142; in *The Vivisector*, 155–8; in *The Eye of the Storm*, 163, 166–8; in *A Fringe of Leaves*, 177, 180; in *The Twyborn Affair*, 184–8, 191–6, 199
Shakespeare, 'Venus and Adonis', 26; *Hamlet*, 217
Sirens, 37, 73, 76, 79, 90
society: as insane, 46, 203; invested with psychic projections, xvi, 49, 66, 116, 203, 218; and the later novels, 151; rejection of, 26, 58, 88
solipsism, 46
source, *see* matrix
super-ego, xiv, xvii, 229
symbolism: artificial patterns of, xx, 92, 119, 120; and allegory, 119–20, 212; collapse of, 166, 188, 193, 225–8; disintegrates into sex, 226–7, 234; natural, xx, *see also* mother-symbols; and quality of prose, 227; and transformation of libido, 19, 27, 225–6

Teeth Mother, 32, 33, 92, 93, 103, 150, 218; as therapeutic image, 94
Theseus, xvii, 133
Tiresias, and Athene, 135
transvestism, 135–6, 143, 149, 184–5, 189, 195–9, 223

Übermensch, 69
unborn soul, 91–2, 96, 107–9, 114, 134, 147, 214
unconscious: collective, 73, 229; disintegrative effect of, 16, 34, 65, 86–7, 96; dissolution into, 7, 55, 65, 76; perceived through external phenomena, 12, 34, *see also* projection;

seizes control, 33, 70, 150, 211; as source of creativity, xviii, 126, 129, 140, 200, 210–16, 222; and Muse, 211; structure of the narrative, 2, 91, 213

unconscious, relation to conscious: in creative process, xix, 125–6, 132, 211–15; split between, in Australian culture, xvi–xvii, 89, 95; in White's fiction, xvi, 2, 23, 36, 56, 86–7, 90–1, 95–6, 121–6; in White's psyche, xvii, 82, 106, 149–51, 162–3, 216–25, 235

Updike, John, 129

uroboric image, 6, 47, 92, 146; cannot enter reality, 8, 39, 44

uroboros, xviii, 5–6, 16, 29, 39, 114; and glass marble, 123, 146; and nautilus shell, 36, 37; oceanic oneness of, xix, 7, 45–6; paradoxical nature of, 40; and rose, 40–1, 46–7; subversive quality of, 5–6, 46, 224; triumph of, 147, 163

vagina dentata, 32

von Franz, Marie-Louise, xxi, 27, 71, 149

Walsh, William, 213

White, Ruth Withycombe, 230

White, Victor (Dick), 230, 233

Wolfe, Peter, 174

works (in chronological order): *Happy Valley*, xvi, xxiii; *The Living and the Dead*, xix, 1–17; *The Aunt's Story*, xx, 3, 18–47, 50, 70, 122, 170, 217, 227; *The Tree of Man*, 3, 49–67, 130, 213, 217; *Voss*, xvi, 3, 50, 69–90, 212, 215–16, 217; *Riders in the Chariot*, xx–xxi, 50, 91–120, 122, 212, 217, 222; *The Solid Mandala*, xiii, xviii, 50, 121–48, 166, 184, 213, 220–6, 234–5; *The Vivisector*, 149, 152–9, 186, 226; *The Eye of the Storm*, 149, 156, 159–74; *A Fringe of Leaves*, 156, 174–83, 215–16; *The Twyborn Affair*, 149, 184–200, 226, 230, 233–4; *Flaws in the Glass*, xxiii, 27, 127, 233; *Memoirs of Many in One*, edited by Patrick White, xvii, 200–9, 228

women: in opposition to Mother archetype, 51–3, 60–1, 74–5, 218; psychic experience of, 73, 240; *puer's* experience of, 11, 27, 49–50, 54, 133–5, 233; as scapegoats, xii, 62–4, 218, *see also* misogyny; as temporary bearers of positive image, 11, 52–3, 59–61, 75

Wright, Judith, 73, 89

Zeitgeist, 125, 228